A SWORD *for* CHRIST

The execution of Charles I, 30 January 1649.

A SWORD for CHRIST

The REPUBLICAN ERA in GREAT BRITAIN and IRELAND

JONATHAN COBB

BIRLINN

For Burgy

First published in 2021 by Birlinn Ltd
West Newington House
10 Newington Road
Edinburgh
EH9 1QS

www.birlinn.co.uk

ISBN: 978 1 78027 692 2

British Library Cataloguing in Publication Data
A catalogue record for this book is available from the British Library

Papers used by Birlinn are from well-managed forests
and other responsible sources

Typeset by Initial Typesetting Services, Edinburgh
Printed and bound by Clays Ltd, Elcograf S.p.A.

Contents

Introduction

> It is certain that not a drop of rain falls without the
> express command of God.
>
> John Calvin, Institutes

As a young pupil, it would have been interesting to learn why the
United Kingdom of Great Britain and Northern Ireland had a Royal
Navy and a Royal Air Force, but an apparently non-royal army. It was
just the 'Army'. Did this reflect some subtle class distinction given
military meaning or was it perhaps a temporary designation while it
waited for the return of royal patronage? Yet the years went by and
nothing in the army's title changed. It was only later that the penny
dropped with the knowledge that this title, rather than the result of
oversight, was in fact the consequence of a part of history in which
a professional body of military men became intimately involved in
a type of British state that was experienced neither before nor since.

The period between the defeat of the royalist army at Naseby
and the Restoration of the monarchy with Charles II encompassed
a series of experiments in the governance of the British Isles and
Ireland as the victors of the civil wars groped for a settlement that
would ensure peace in the former realm. This quest was both religious and political in character, for the wars had been as much about
rival interpretations of Protestantism as a challenge to monarchical

authority in the early modern state. An interval which witnessed the emergence of the army as the primary arbiter of government coincided with an extraordinary catharsis of religious belief and the consummation of the passions ignited by the Reformation. It was also a time in which the quasi-military political culture to which the civil wars gave rise brought a new and harsher edge to acts of British colonisation that some argue marked the true beginnings of the British Empire. Indeed, that span of a mere fifteen years is arguably one of the most dynamic periods of modern British history. The discredit to which Charles I had brought the institution of monarchy, and the fierce intensity that characterised the later stages of the civil wars pointed to a fundamental change in the future governance of the British Isles and Ireland. The time had seemed ripe for a new order resting on a bedrock of the 'godly' and sanctioned by an Almighty who had already delivered providential military victories for the future makers of the Republic.

The dynamic of the republican era can seem chaotic. In an effort to marshal some sense of order from the frequently shifting kaleidoscope, a number of accounts are coloured by attempts to precisely define the 'revolutionary' demographic that populated this extraordinary epoch. This is particularly true of narratives that err towards a determinist view of history, often based on the perceived clash of class and economic interests. Yet classifications such as the 'natural classes of government' and the 'emerging middle class' are rarely if ever found in sources of the period. Contemporary chroniclers, like the royalist Edward Hyde, refer more enigmatically to persons of 'quality' and 'degree'. Further subdivisions into Presbyterians, Independents and Commonwealthsmen are more helpful in understanding the motivations of the protagonists of the period, and were terms used by contemporaries. But the strands of religious and political thought that they are assumed to define distinctly often blurred and frequently merged. Across them all fell the shadow of the sword.

The stage-set of the period was populated by a cast of colourful characters who frequently belie the drab hues in which it was subsequently painted by some historians. There were poets and social reformers as well as princes, soldiers and religious fanatics. These individuals, often with a great deal of moral and physical courage, redefined what it meant to be devout, made proposals for the further evolution of the state and articulated a philosophy of the community of citizens that is of continued relevance to modern institutions. But in their common attachment to the idea of a citizenry under God, they were far less revolutionary than radical. Political debate was most frequently articulated and settled by reference to Scripture. It was also an era in which the spread of literacy saw the emergence of a distinctive female voice in a society where the primacy of men over women was held to be axiomatic. The contemporary diaries, letters and poems of the likes of the Puritan Lucy Hutchinson, the royalist Ann, Lady Fanshawe, the 'matchless Orinda' and the uncrowned Queen Henrietta Maria reveal an acute sensibility about the tenor of the times and the motivations of the protagonists. Unlike the memoirs of some of the male participants that were written up long after the events they described, a number of the women capture the vigour and immediacy of the events as they were unfolding.

Central to an understanding of this dynamic period is the professional fighting force brought into being as the New Model Army in 1645. It was fundamental to the success of the parliamentary cause in the civil wars and provided a bulwark and arsenal to the new regime. But the ethos and needs of the soldiers (particularly as regards to arrears of pay and indemnification for their acts of 'rebellion') increasingly came into conflict with those of the civil state. The spiritual orientation of troops, which was so important to both their morale and sense of identity, contributed to the friction in the nations' religious arrangements as the civil authorities tried to square the circle between public conformity, and personal belief and conscience. Although the direct intervention of the army in politics in 1647 and again in late 1648 led ineluctably to the execution of the king, the temperament and conservatism of its commander, Sir Thomas Fairfax, ensured that the architecture of the new state was largely left in the hands of the civilians. The further deployment of the army after the defeat of the royalists in the second civil war was as much driven by the civil establishment's desire to keep it at arm's length as to any incipient imperial design. Yet despite the decisive military victories that ushered the Republic into being, the subsequent interventions of the army in politics, and the rule of the major-generals, merely confirmed the unsuitability of soldiers to be the principal source of governance in an overwhelmingly civil state.

Above these developments loomed the presence of one man: Oliver Cromwell. From relative provincial obscurity he emerged as one of the ablest of the commanders of the parliamentary forces during the civil wars, a reputation that was cemented during the early years of the Republic and which ensured his authority over the political and constitutional developments that followed. His ascendancy in the new regime owed everything to his prowess as a soldier and military tactician, and his reputation is in no way diminished by the occasional ineptitude of his opponents. Yet, Cromwell was an inadequate politician whose religious zeal arguably clouded his practical judgement in matters of statecraft. His ambivalence towards many of the aspects of the regime that he had helped to create, and the division of his loyalties between the army and the civil state of the Republic, ultimately proved to be fatal to its survival. Despite his powerful personality, martial reputation and strongly expressed faith in God, he could be indecisive and his public utterances clouded by imprecision. Cromwell is perhaps best understood as a pious layman turned professional soldier who found himself in charge of a counter-revolution against the refined absolutism of the early Stuart state, a role for which he was intellectually unprepared and temperamentally unsuited.

That the Republic gave way to the Restoration of Charles II owes less to the shortcomings of Cromwell's successor, his eldest son Richard, than to the father's failure to embed the state that emerged from the civil wars. It also owed much to the enduring appeal of monarchy, which seems highly paradoxical in view of the signal failure of the early Stuarts to consolidate the Elizabethan regime that they inherited, and the political and religious crises which they provoked. The resultant civil wars were fought, in part, over radical and unacceptable concepts of constitutional authority, ecclesiastical hierarchy and royal governance promoted by Charles I and his court. It says much for the tenacity and guile of his son that the Restoration happened with what in hindsight seems so little ado. By contrast to the many resources enjoyed by the Republic, the future Charles II played a weak hand with considerable adroitness. Physically brave and morally adaptable he kept the monarchical claims of his dynasty alive and the early Republic on its toes. By holding out the prospect of a restoration light on revenge (at least in England) with limited restitution of his father's state, he ensured a return of the British Isles and Ireland to a Stuart monarchy, an event which for many years had seemed highly improbable.

The condition of both Ireland and Scotland during this period is also critical to an understanding of it. After its defeat at the battle of Worcester in 1651, most general accounts see Scotland retreating into mist. Its role in the advent of the Republic is rich in paradox. Scotland had given rise to the Stuart monarchy of the British Isles and Ireland, while also being at the epicentre of later resistance to it. In contrast to the forces arranged against the regime of Charles I in England, the agenda of those who opposed the king in Scotland was overwhelmingly religious. It is not possible to conceive of a parliamentary victory in the first civil war without the military support provided by the Scots. But by turning on the new regime they had inadvertently done so much to install, the Scots irretrievably lost the opportunity to preserve an independent state. Barricaded behind a wall of religious certitude that clouded reasoned judgement, the controlling Scottish elite fatally overestimated its ability to dominate events. In the military campaigns that ended in defeats at the battles of Preston, Dunbar and Worcester, Scotland serially gambled with the future of its distinctive polity and lost.

In contrast, by the time the fighting ended on mainland British soil in 1648, Ireland had achieved something very near to self-rule and had come close to neutralising the political hold of the

Anglo-Scottish colonists. Its history during the republican period is chiefly recalled for the sackings of Drogheda and Wexford, and for a rare bloody nose the Irish gave to the soldiers of the New Model Army in Munster. The actions of Cromwell, and the regime which gave his ten-month military campaign sanction, have been described as deplorable but somehow anomalous. Yet the record showed the ruthless intent that lay behind the civilians' blueprint for a land considered ripe only for exploitation by the victors, manifested in the acceleration of the ethnic cleansing that became official republican policy in the years immediately following the conclusion of Cromwell's campaign.

Earlier narratives of the Stuart and republican epoch tended to concentrate on the protagonists grouped towards the apex of society, whether at the local or national level. Certainly, the period cannot be understood without a grasp of the religious, cultural and political sensibilities of the elites whose power rested on economic dominance, the ownership of land, religious orientation and complex webs of patronage. In an effort to rebalance the traditional understanding of the period, more attention has been focused on activity at the base of society, and the rapid advance of literacy during the period has furnished rich sources of evidence in the pamphlets and diaries of the time. The Levellers were certainly of their time rather than ahead of it, and much of their activity can be understood as that of a protest movement against the injustices thrown up by the wars. They called for social improvement and political representation for those citizens (and there were many) who had suffered so grievously from the fighting and who had been poorly served by the institutions that were supposed to protect them. As a protest movement, the Levellers also gave an organised voice to women, and it is perhaps this that gives their activities such significance. But they have arguably generated a level of political interest somewhat out of proportion to their contemporary impact, a possible consequence of their appropriation as exemplars by the modern-day British Left. Their programme certainly amplified the political dimension of the civil wars, and their demands that rulers be accountable provided a rudimentary blueprint for the democracy that was later to emerge on the mainland British Isles. Yet their brief span of activities caused too much friction at a time when the elites on the winning side were struggling to deliver a settlement. Crucially, their threat to the good order and discipline of the New Model Army, which was anyway preoccupied with more material matters such as pay and re-employment after disbandment, ensured that they were ruthlessly suppressed.

In contrast to the Levellers, in recent years more attention has attached to the role and impact of the independent religious congregations and 'sects', to the millenarianism of groups such as the Fifth Monarchists and the emergence of the religious dissenters whose cultural and spiritual character continues to be felt today. The religious context of the period was much more pertinent to the daily lives of people of all classes than the additional political imperatives identified by the Levellers. People were more interested in the quality of their parish priest than abstract constitutional principles. Faith also informed the distinctive cultural character of the period. There was a 'determinist' narrative in seventeenth-century Britain, but it was a religious one founded on the belief that society was divided between the damned and the saved, that nothing one did on Earth could alter one's fate in the afterlife and that God's providence was the ultimate arbiter in human affairs.

Faith dominated allegiance, and one of the overarching themes of the period is the attempt to reconcile the energy released by the Reformation with the loyalty demanded of the citizenry if the political state were to be a settled one. It was also religious belief and practice that undermined the stamina of the republican political state and poisoned relations between the constituent nations of the British Isles and Ireland. While Cromwell himself exhibited a high degree of toleration of the strands of Protestantism that discomfited many of his contemporaries, the regime of the 'godly' coincided with a period of aggressive cultural suppression and draconian economic reallocation in Ireland, as well as a period of fierce intervention in Scotland that took on many of the characteristics of martial law.

Ireland is often referred to as Great Britain's first colony, but the concept of benign stewardship was wholly lacking in what was in essence a conquest that aimed to complete the earlier medieval invasions. The period bequeathed a legacy of cultural bitterness that still adds grit to the relations of the United Kingdom and Ireland today.

1

'To fight against the King'

Naseby

> The Lord of hosts is with us, the God of Jacob is our refuge.
>
> Psalm 46

Shortly after first light on the morning of 14 June 1645 a small group of mounted officers and dragoons rode along a ridge about three-quarters of a mile to the north of an English Midlands hamlet called Naseby. A thick early morning mist had not yet cleared and in the limited visibility the soldiers' faces displayed anxious impatience. In the still air they could hear the faint but unmistakable rumbling of thousands of hooves and feet drumming the ground with their movement. The most senior in the group was Sir Thomas Fairfax, a thirty-three-year-old Yorkshire gentleman who had been appointed to overall command of parliament's largest force in the field. This had recently been reorganised as a professional fighting unit that became known to posterity as the New Model Army; the day ahead was to be the first real test of its worth. To the south of the little group, a force of about 14,000 men had been on the march towards them for over three hours, having been galvanised by regimental chaplains with prayers and psalms. Sir Thomas's reconnaissance party was looking for the main body of the royalist army, the pickets of which his scouts had discovered the day before.

In fact, he was better informed about the relative positions of the two groups of forces than were his opponents; the night before, a council-of-war had taken place between the king and his senior officers and advisers at Market Harborough, at which there was some debate about how they should respond to the likely positions and intentions of the parliamentary army in their vicinity. Charles had already asked for reinforcement from the West Country but the royalist commander there, the argumentative and bibulous Lord Goring, had demurred. The king's army numbered some 9,000 men, over half of which were cavalry under the command of his talented and opinionated nephew, Prince Rupert. Suspecting they might be outnumbered, the royalists faced an unpalatable choice: they could either withdraw northward and risk attack and defeat whilst on the move, or they could force an engagement against a potentially superior force in the hope of outmanoeuvring their opponents.

However, morale in the royalist lines was good. In one of the biggest royalist successes of the war so far, the town of Leicester had recently been invested and captured. Leicester had a thriving commercial economy based on the finishing of primary goods and it had provided a good weight of resource to the parliamentary side. In the aftermath of the siege, Charles's victorious soldiers had enthusiastically plundered the traumatised civilian population on the losing side. Furthermore, their triumph was seen to have induced a sense of alarm amongst the more excitable in the parliamentary opposition in London, and Fairfax had been ordered to break off his own siege of the royalist capital at Oxford to engage with the threat. Yet the royalist commanders considered the formation that they were to face as unproven, and there had already been much scoffing about the 'New Noddle' army.

Indeed, a certain *de haut en bas* attitude towards the opposition had been one of the undisguised prejudices of the royalist side throughout the war. Deprecating the perceived pretensions of those rebels who lacked 'quality' the royalist balladeer John Taylor (who was himself from a modest background) wrote:

A preacher's work is not to geld a sow
Unseemly 'tis that a judge should milk a cow
A cobbler to a pulpit should not mount
Nor can an ass cast up a true account.[1]

The belief that they were defending the social order and the erroneous sense that the king's army contained a preponderance of proper gentlemen gave its senior ranks a high degree of self-esteem, which was not always matched by military aptitude. They felt entitled to victory. Thus emboldened and in perhaps the most momentous military decision of the civil wars, the order was given by the king to give battle.

By eight o'clock in the morning the bulk of the royal army had taken up position on a small ridge to the north of the one on which Fairfax had earlier cantered. Today, a view of this position shows it barely distinguished by a small wood and clusters of farm buildings. On the king's right flank stood cavalry under the command of Prince Rupert, while the centre of the line comprised infantry under Sir Jacob Astley, a large number of which were Welsh levies. The left flank of the royalist line consisted of another, but less dense, formation of cavalry recruited from the north country and commanded by Sir Marmaduke Langdale, an enormous man for his times, who stood over six feet tall. About 700 yards to their south, the larger mass of the New Model Army was laboriously drawing-up into battle formation. Fairfax had originally intended that his force should occupy the highest ground to the north of Naseby but had been dissuaded by his subordinate, and commander of the horse, Oliver Cromwell, who argued that such a commanding position would deter the enemy and thus deny the opportunity for a decisive encounter. Instead, the New Model Army drew up on slightly lower ground, in lines that extended for nearly a mile, although they still overlooked the royal formation further to their north.

By ten o'clock, the cavalry on the king's right could barely contain their impatience. Men were starting to dismount to relieve themselves. The horses were padding the rough turf and to Prince Rupert's subordinates the crab-like movements of their opponents seemed an opportunity, although they belied a larger force that they could not see in the folds of ground to the south-east. The order was given for the cavalry to advance. They did so, gathering speed as they started to gallop downhill across the pot-holed and fallow ground towards the cavalry that faced them on the New Model's left wing. There was some irritating but largely ineffective flanking fire from dragoons that Cromwell had ordered to occupy hedgerows on the western side of the field of battle. Slowed by the uphill slope, the sweating mounts nonetheless crashed into the opposing formation of cavalry under the command of Cromwell's future son-in-law, the lawyer Henry Ireton.

It was a powerful and determined assault and within half-an-hour, it looked as if the king's army was about to bring off an improbable victory. In the slashing melee, Prince Rupert's cavalry had the momentum; the New Model wing broke off and Ireton himself was briefly made a prisoner. Meanwhile, the royalist centre had advanced and was beginning to successfully engage the opposing infantry under the command of Philip Skippon, an experienced soldier who had cut his teeth in the war on the Continent between the Dutch and the Spanish. After an initial exchange of fire from cumbersome matchlock muskets that were as much a menace to friend as to foe, the perspiring hordes in their heavy wool, stiff leather and iron-clad uniforms came together in a vicious press of pikes, swords and firearms swung as lethal clubs. Skippon was shot and wounded, but retained his power of command. The smell of sweat, dung and smoke rose above the ringing tumult of oaths, yells and the heavy breathing of adrenaline-fuelled exertion as the numerically inferior army of the king pressed its advantage.

Having broken Ireton's cavalry, the royalist troopers then found themselves faced by those packed formations of New Model infantry which until now had been unobserved in the folds of ground behind Fairfax's front line. Deterred by the dense mass of bristling and deadly pikes, Prince Rupert's horsemen succumbed to the indiscipline they had shown at Marston Moor the previous year (a battle, the largest of the civil war to date, in which the royalists had been thoroughly worsted by a superior and better-led force). Instead of turning to support the royalist infantry on their now exposed flank, they galloped on in pursuit of the fleeing enemy cavalry that they could still see. Soon they were amongst the New Model Army's rear echelon, whose baggage train provided another tempting distraction. With his elite cavalry out of command and over the horizon, the king was forced to watch as the army of Fairfax seized the initiative in a stunning counterattack led by Cromwell from the army's right wing.

Taking full advantage of the downhill slope, Cromwell's cavalry unit, his experienced 'Ironsides', gathered momentum before charging into the weaker body of cavalry commanded by the doughty Langdale. Having shot and cut their way through, they shortly began to invest the infantry in the royalist centre and completed an encirclement as Ireton's residual troops pressed from the other flank. By the time that Prince Rupert's exhausted trumpeters had recalled his exuberant troops to the main point of action, it was nearly over. The king, perhaps recalling the heroism of his royal predecessor at Bosworth, made to charge with his Life Guard to rally his surrounded troops but was roughly reined-in by a member of his entourage. The surviving members of his cavalry escaped, leaving the exhausted foot soldiers to fend for themselves. The last sight of the fight that Charles had was of his infantry crying for quarter in the middle of a blood-soaked Northamptonshire landscape.

By now though a battle-lust gripped the New Model soldiers who had come so close to death and defeat in the mid-morning, and with inhibitions released a vicious rampage ensued as they attacked the royalist baggage train gathered behind the lines to the rear. There were many women present among the wagons: wives, lovers, other camp followers and spectators. Amidst a terrible din of screaming, many were murdered or brutally mutilated by having their cheeks slashed and their noses cut. Shrieks in native Welsh were mistaken for the cries of the hated 'popish' Irish as the heavily armed soldiers scythed about them. As well as over 4,000 prisoners, a large quantity of cannon, powder, provisions and other valuables were captured, including the king's gilded carriage. Inside was discovered a heap of his correspondence which his enemies wasted no time in publishing. Propaganda in the form of pamphlets was rapidly becoming one of the defining features of the era and *The Kings Cabinet Opened* glossed the apparent depths of the king's perfidy against his subjects whilst adding another layer of angry righteousness to the cause of his opponents.

For the relieved and delighted commanders of the New Model Army, the battle was both a vindication of its existence and, they hoped, a turning point. In the twelve months before the battle, the royalist forces had faced ever mounting odds, yet had shown a surprising resilience. After the heavy defeat at Marston Moor, Charles's forces had sprung back with the king himself leading his troops to victory and his opponent, the Earl of Essex, to total embarrassment at the battle of Lostwithiel in Cornwall in late August 1644. A royalist army also survived a mauling by a force twice its size at the second battle of Newbury in the autumn of the same year. Whilst parliament had the support of the most economically dominant towns and regions of the realm, and had almost complete control of the nation's coastline, the king could still count on resources in the Midlands, Lancashire, Wales and the West Country, and a large army in Ireland. He also held the port of Bristol and the strategically important town of Chester.

Thus by the end of the year, serious dissensions were breaking out in the parliamentary ranks about the conduct of the war and the inability of their side to land the decisive blow. With victory seemingly out of reach, those who favoured a negotiated settlement were far more persuasive; even those militants who had been at the genesis of the dispute with the king had come around to this point of view. These included Sir Arthur Hesilrige, a survivor of a group of five MPs whose attempted arrest by the king in person had provided some useful kindling for the conflagration of war in England.

Yet safely installed behind his fortifications at Oxford, the king's responses to peace terms, discussed over a period of desultory negotiation at Uxbridge, offered little hope of a settlement. Meanwhile, against a background of increasing rates of desertion and instances of mutiny at places such as Leatherhead and Henley, the parliamentary high command came under mounting criticism for its apparent lack of zeal in closing out the struggle against the royalists in the field.

On the parliamentary side, the strategic direction of the war was in the hands of the Committee of Both Kingdoms. This was an Anglo-Scottish body composed of seven noblemen, fourteen English MPs and four representatives from north of the border. It had been formed in the wake of the Solemn League and Covenant, the formal compact made between Charles's opponents in the two realms in the autumn of 1643. A number of its members also held commands in the field, which meant that the Committee found it difficult to provide a consistent level of dispassionate oversight and co-ordination of the campaign against the king. Operationally, the conduct of parliament's military initiatives were in the hands of the commanders on the ground, the most senior of whom was Robert Devereux, the Earl of Essex. A somewhat prickly old Etonian of stout appearance and an alumnus of Oxford University, Essex was the heir to his treasonable father, who had been executed for rebellion against Elizabeth I. It was perhaps this legacy and his keen awareness of his rank that informed the earl's understanding of his political responsibilities during the civil war in England that broke out in the summer of 1642. Whatever his limitations as a commander however, he enjoyed immense prestige. In the opinion of the chronicler and royal counsellor Edward Hyde, by no means an unbiased judge, Essex had been so central to the opposition to the king 'that they owed not more to the power and reputation of parliament than to his sole name and credit: the being able to raise an army, and conducting it to fight against the King, was purely due to him, and the effect of his power'.[2]

Nonetheless, Essex became strongly associated with that cadre in the parliamentary ranks that wanted to come to terms with the monarch, and his undistinguished record in the field was further highlighted by the reversals received by his army in the West Country in the autumn of 1644. His apparent want of energy and enthusiasm in a conflict that was turning by degrees bitter and vicious, was critically noted. His fellow nobleman and commander of parliamentary forces from London to the Wash, Edward Montagu, the Earl of Manchester, came in for similar disapprobation. Hyde noted, perhaps by way of contrast to Essex, that Manchester was of a gentle and generous nature, and had clear reverence for the person of the king. For critics however, the war effort against the royalists was led by men whose hearts were not really in it.

In contrast to its later period, the military operations of the first years of the civil wars were conducted in an atmosphere of relative diffidence by the protagonists. One reason was the complementary social rank and assumptions of the leading members of each side. The names of commoners such as Pym and Hampden have come down in history and lore as prime movers in the clash between absolute and representative rule, between king and Commons and between autocracy and the Common Law. In fact, it was the noble grandees (particularly those of a strong religious conviction), fulfilling what they regarded as their ancient role as restraints on the monarch, who were the vanguard of the initial resistance to Charles I in both England and Scotland. This is unsurprising given their prestige, wealth and powers of patronage both at court and in the composition of the representative assemblies of each country. The Scottish nobility had been the first signatories of the Covenant (which bound its adherents to defend what was asserted as the 'true' Protestant faith) in 1638. In England, it was the Earl of Essex, together with the Earls of Northumberland, Pembroke, Holland and Viscount Saye and Sele, who were appointed to lead parliament's Committee of Safety formed in the summer of 1642 when a peaceful accommodation with His Majesty was still earnestly desired.[3] Amongst the elites there was little desire to remove the king, still less the institution of monarchy or the hierarchical nature of a polity based on social rank. In *Behemoth*, his history of the Long Parliament which lasted from 1640 until 1660, the philosopher Thomas Hobbes pithily described the stand-off: 'there was no blood shed: they shot at one another nothing but paper'.[4] But then the king raised his standard at Nottingham, thereby formally declaring war on all his subjects.

Yet the prosecution of a successful modern war of manoeuvre using firearms and artillery was hampered by the quasi-medieval methods of raising and sustaining an army in the field. The private and mercenary armies of the feudal period had given way to a system of militia, whereby localities that roughly corresponded to modern county boundaries took responsibility for the raising of forces in times of national danger. Controlled by civilians, these were complemented by levies raised from the larger towns, of which the most important by far was London. The urban and county militias were often referred to as 'trained bands', a somewhat misleading title given they were mostly composed of unenthusiastic amateurs who preferred to make a living rather than make history. It was the ultimate control of these militias that formed one of the biggest bones of contention between the king and parliament, and which frustrated attempts at reconciliation between them.

However, the poor potential of the militia was rapidly revealed by the exigencies of civil war. It proved hard for each side to deploy locally raised troops in a national campaign for a sustained period, although in this regard parliament was to gain a decisive advantage with the support of Scottish troops, who seemed more inclined to fight further from their homes. Desertions were rife as the soldiery drifted back to their localities, driven by the demands of family, the seasons and other commitments. A parliamentary committee ruefully acknowledged that, 'We know they are men of trade and employment and cannot well be absent from their occasions.' By far the biggest source of discontent and desertion, however, was pay, the lack or delay of which was a factor that has been much underrated as a dynamic of individual motivation and collective success during the period. It was thus the somewhat ephemeral nature of the opposing armies that gave the earlier years of the first civil war their episodic quality.

While Scotland had proved to be a fertile source for the recruitment of soldiers and officers to the protagonists in the Thirty Years
War, the military culture of England was far less well developed.
Apart from some bloody, and largely unsuccessful, Elizabethan
excursions against the Irish, English land forces were of much
reduced significance after the dynastic struggles of the fifteenth
century and Henry VIII's campaign against the Scots. The martial
ambitions of the British state had been constrained by regal caution,
the limitations of finance and the natural barrier conferred by its
island status. A number of individual Englishmen, such as Skippon,
had served with distinction abroad, but if the rheumy eyes of chair-
bound warriors had been cast back in the early years of the 1640s,
they would have as likely fallen on the naval exploits of Sir Francis
Drake as on the land campaigns of Henry V, Edward IV or the Black
Prince. In contrast to the gigantic military struggles on the continent of Europe during the post-Reformation period, the clashes on
British soil seem puny. By the time the opposing forces of the first
civil war had lined up for their first major engagement in England
at Edgehill in late October 1642, the rest of Europe had been consumed by warfare for nearly a quarter of a century. Almost three
times as many troops were deployed by King Gustavus Adolphus at
his great victory over the Imperial armies at Breitenfeld in 1631 as
the total of both sides sent into action at Edgehill, and the number
of fatal casualties sustained by both sides on the Saxon plain dwarfed
those killed, maimed or made prisoner under the faint autumn sun
in Warwickshire.

The lack of a professional martial ethic showed in other ways too.
While contemporary accounts are full of the ferocity of the fighting,
many also describe the amateurishness and unpreparedness on both
sides that has beguiled future generations. Amongst the forces assembled by parliament were the 'old decayed serving men and tapsters',
roundly derided following their poor showing in battle at Edgehill.
There are the tales of occasional chivalry and courtesy: defeated
royalist garrisons being allowed to march out under regimental colours and with their side arms, and the gentlemanly correspondence

between the parliamentary commander Sir William Waller and his friend and royalist opponent, Sir Ralph Hopton. Even the pre-war paintings of the aristocracy by Van Dyck manage to make the wearing of military uniform look vaguely camp.

Yet it was not just the elite at the national level that contained too many *faux* soldiers. Far away from the National Gallery where these Van Dycks hang is St Chad's Church, the site of which is mentioned in the Domesday Book. It sits in the little village of Farndon in southwest Cheshire. At the time of the civil wars the surrounding area had a royalist disposition and the church was damaged in the fighting. Today, in the Barnston Chapel can be seen some stained-glass windows which portray royalist troops, who were at the sharp end, in all their finery too. There is Sir William Mainwaring with his long hair, floppy feathered hat, wide silk sash hung from his shoulder and leather boots with their fashionable open brim below the knee. He carries a short staff, perhaps to give emphasis to his rank. Elsewhere is a daintily clad drummer and a glass image of William Barnston with similarly flamboyant headwear, a somewhat complacent smile and a neat goatee beard. He has a sash around his midriff and carries an ornate halberd that looks as if it has a ceremonial rather than military function. All have the wide, white, turn-down ruff or collar which was such a common feature of civilian and military dress during the period, and all are armed with swords. None look even remotely menacing.

By the winter of 1644 the bloody and frequently amateurish encounters had produced a stalemate which had sapped the will of many of the protagonists on the parliamentary side, and an atmosphere of desperation became almost tangible. The lack of decisive success caused a spiritual loss of confidence amongst the MPs. Were they perhaps being punished by God for the sins of presumption and covetousness in taking on the king? As the war had lengthened, so the consequences of defeat seemed greater and the senior commanders, the Earls of Essex and Manchester, were inclined to cut parliament's losses. On the other hand, the increased ferocity of the fighting and the apparent intransigence shown by otherwise weakened royalists made others more determined than ever to win; there was no point in going backwards.

One of the most outspoken exponents of this position was the cavalry commander and MP for Cambridge. Now aged forty-five, Oliver Cromwell had been an early opponent of the personal rule, but not amongst the first rank of the parliamentary leaders. His background was relatively modest – indeed, he had suffered a severe diminution of his circumstances and social status in his thirties, and was only financially rescued by the death of his wife's uncle. As an MP, he lacked a deep source of well-connected patrons and had already fallen out with the powerful Montagu family even before he joined the Eastern Association (then the largest of the military units deployed against the king), commanded by its scion, the Earl of Manchester. But he was a man with a profound belief in God's providence and the hand of the Almighty in human affairs, and although this was hardly an exceptional bias for the times in which he lived, the Huntingdon squire was particularly energised by it. He lived in an age when individual religious witness was rapidly becoming a mark of social distinction – faith in God was itself a divine and very personal gift from the Almighty, without which it was impossible to achieve salvation. Those that had it were of the Elect, which can perhaps explain the ecstasy with which many like Cromwell articulated their beliefs. In Cromwell's case, God's grace provided rich compensation for the lack of grandeur in his earthly background and for the other challenges, both spiritual and material, that he had faced as a younger man. Despite, or perhaps even because of that, he was no snob and had a powerful if sometimes domineering charisma. This contributed to his manifest ability to both inspire and motivate those under his command, and he had found tactical success in the field as a cavalryman where others had struggled.

Cromwell's experiences in battle in command of his 'Ironsides' fostered his conviction that neither social background nor denominational faith were impediments to successful endeavour, and he had little sympathy with those who insisted on obedience to their own religious manners. To him, 'Presbyterians, Independents, all have the same spirit of faith and prayer; the same presence and answer; they agree here, know no names of difference: pity it should be otherwise anywhere.'[5]

The fact that he was the only son brought up in a household of sisters in an era when the lower status of women was an article of faith, was surely significant to the future development of his personality. Although immensely sure of his mind once made up, his fervent outbursts and strongly expressed opinions had an intimidating quality. His disposition to periods of brooding melancholy did not invite intimacy from any save his closest family and friends. Many of his publicly recorded statements are noted for their prolixity and frequent ambiguity; but they also reveal passionate intensity rather than great intellectual subtlety. He had a more instinctive understanding of the absolute than the relative. But his growing military reputation as a skilful and (above all) successful tactician meant that his views on the conduct of the fighting were highly influential. He now came forward as the leading sceptic of the direction of the war by publicly criticising his nominal superior, the Earl of Manchester.

The debilitated state of the forces of each side required radical action if one or the other was to prevail, and matters came to a head as 1644 drew to a close. Cromwell (who, as Hyde noted 'had not yet arrived at the faculty of speaking with decency and temper') launched a withering critique of his own side and accused the earl of a dereliction of duty that even hinted at cowardice.[6] His assault was highly uncomfortable to many, but, in the current conditions, was persuasive enough. In December 1644, Zouch Tate, an MP for Northamptonshire, proposed in the House of Commons what was later to be known as the 'Self-Denying Ordinance'. The measure required *inter alia* serving officers who were also members of either House of parliament to surrender their commissions. The ordinance did not preclude the reappointment of MPs whose martial ability was in no doubt, but it did lead to the replacement of the Earls of Manchester and Essex, whose command had been tainted by their perceived attitude and lack of decisive success. Some others, like Sir

William Waller, took the opportunity to stand down from armed service voluntarily, exhausted and perhaps disillusioned by the turn the war was taking. The abnegation of the Self-Denying Ordinance gave the MPs both an opportunity to wash away the sin of their rebellion and a clean sheet for the military.

But it was also controversial. Some perceived that the ordinance would mean that the new force would be far less under the control of parliament than the existing army, composed mainly of the local militias and led (with varying degrees of competence) by local Presbyterian notables and other godly men of property. There was debate as to whether the soldiers should sign up to the prevailing religious agenda of the king's opponents. It was agreed that officers and soldiers should take the Covenant which bound the English to their Scottish allies, but not that they should give the MPs a blank cheque by affirming a religious settlement that was still in the process of being decided. Further, the ordinance also had the effect of formalising the breach between the Commons and that large section of the House of Lords associated with the peace party.[7]

The peers made heavy work of passing a measure deemed to be of urgent military necessity. In a rhetorical swipe at Cromwell, the Earl of Manchester made a lengthy and cross speech in which he deprecated the aspersions that had been cast upon the integrity of the army's aristocratic commanders. With a full measure of hauteur and injured pride, Manchester moaned, 'I shall not plead my abilities to serve you, I shall only justifie my integrity in your service, which if any shall contradict, if they be such as have either known me, or seen my Actions . . . I doubt not but that they will (there) find such results as will give them occasion to ask me pardon for the injury they have done me.'[8]

Resentful that their traditional patronage over appointments had been usurped, their lordships also raised objections to fifty-one of the commissions planned by the new body's commander.[9] For the parliamentary cause, the man chosen to lead this new formation would be a pivotal decision. Among their own ranks, it had already been established that there was a dearth of the requisite qualities. In terms of his military record, the MP from Cambridge seemed an obvious choice. But Cromwell had already made his mark in other ways and had some influential enemies. He seemed altogether too self-righteously outspoken and argumentative, and he had quarrelled with his commanding officer and social superior. His religious views and apparent toleration of religious Nonconformity amongst his soldiers were also deeply suspect to many of his fellow MPs, while an earlier contretemps with parliament's Scottish allies over their unbending attachment to their own version of the Protestant faith had caused friction in the Anglo-Scottish League. His whole personality and outlook seemed to make him an obvious risk if the new body was to cohere as an effective unit while remaining congenial to its political masters.

Instead, parliament turned to Sir Thomas Fairfax. Born in January 1612 and educated at Cambridge University, he was the elder son of Lord Ferdinando Fairfax, an influential north country nobleman who after service to the king against the Scots joined the parliamentary side and led its operations in Yorkshire. Fairfax and his father commanded formations at Marston Moor, a battle in which Sir Thomas's younger brother Charles was killed, and in which he himself was badly wounded in the face. Somewhat taciturn and with a swarthy complexion complemented by a mane of jet hair, 'Black Tom' combined a dutiful disposition with a serious mind that was streaked by ambition. He showed a reverence for learning and was as ardent a bibliophile as he was determined a soldier. No zealot, his Protestant religious temperament was piously if unexceptionally expressed, unlike that of his wife Lady Anne, who was a staunch Presbyterian. Although his health gave him problems throughout his life, he was physically brave; his determination to be in the thick of the action had led to a series of injuries displayed on a body composed of livid scar tissue. But, as with Cromwell, there had been growing recognition of him as a skilful and resolute soldier who commanded the confidence and loyalty of his men.

Fairfax's record, religious disposition and the influence of his family amongst the large group of Yorkshire MPs who had served under his father in the field, meant that he was well placed to assume a position of senior command. He had also attracted the attention of those MPs on the Committee of Both Kingdoms, such as Oliver St John and Henry Vane, who were amongst the most critical of the war effort under the Earl of Essex. Under the terms of the Self-Denying Ordinance, it helped that Fairfax was not himself an MP, although he was not lacking in political ruthlessness where matters of honour were at stake – his appointment to command of the New Model Army was preceded by the execution of Sir John Hotham, a fellow member of the Yorkshire gentry whom the Fairfax family had pursued for dereliction of duty and alleged treachery in the parliamentary cause at Hull. A skilled soldier who shared the social assumptions of his political masters, 'Black Tom' seemed to be an eminently sensible choice to lead the New Model Army.

To lend a degree of urgency and impetus to the formation of the new force before the royal forces could rally again, the MPs obtained an advance payment of £80,000 from the city authorities of London.[10] The more ruthless intent behind the formation of the New Model Army was also shown in the commission given to Fairfax: for the first time, there was no reference to a requirement to protect the (sacred) person of the king. There was an ironic convention of rebellion against a sitting monarch such that it was the action of wicked advisers and councillors, rather than the sovereign himself, which gave rise to discontent. Indeed, so powerful was the hex associated with harming the actual person of His Majesty, that in those encounters in the civil wars where Charles was personally present, parliamentary troops had been seen to waver. Implicitly, the time for squeamishness had passed.

Organisationally, the regimental system of the New Model Army followed that of the various associations and militias that had formed the base of parliament's forces in the regions; at its core was the Eastern Association that provided over half the land army available to the king's opponents and which had been commanded by the Earl of Manchester. Plans were made for a smaller establishment of some 22,000 troops and agitation occurred amongst the cadre of surplus officers that were unable to find a position in the new force; some, like Colonel John Dalbier, a soldier of fortune who had served under Essex, were later to change sides to the service of the royalists. Recruitment of soldiers proved a more difficult task, particularly for the line infantry, and there were instances of disobedience amongst impressed men; recruits from Kent had to be escorted up the Thames under armed guard to their newly reorganised units. Critically, all soldiers were required for national service and to be deployed wherever directed, although this was understood to be on the mainland of the British Isles. The ad hoc sartorial arrangements were replaced by a uniform of red wool, Venetian scarlet being the cheapest pigment that could be bought in quantity. Better protection was given through the wider distribution amongst the troops of thick leather jerkins and metalled protection of head, neck, breast and thigh. The distinctive helmet with its face visor and jutting neck-guard worn by the cavalry recalled those of the Roman legions, and became an emblem of the wars and of the later Republic.

Some overdue attention was also given to training and skills, and *The Souldiers Catechism* was issued as a pocket-sized source of qualification and instruction. Different disciplines were refined to concentrate the hitherto disorderly battle drills of musketeers and dragoons. The pike-armed formation that so resembled the *phalanx* of the ancient world was perfected as a devastating obstacle to charging cavalry. Scales of pay were standardised across the whole army to remove the incentive for soldiers to enlist in areas where pay and conditions were superior. Initially, daily pay scales were set at 2 shillings for a cavalryman, 18 pennies for a dragoon and 8 pennies for a foot-soldier. In aggregate, the monthly cost of the New Model Army was estimated to be some £45,000. At rates that were barely competitive with those that could be commanded in civilian employment, particularly for the infantry, the issue of remuneration was to remain one of great practical and political significance, and was ultimately to curdle the relationship between the military and its civilian masters. But for the time being, England had its first professional national army.[11]

Effective and efficient armies do not however, arise from detailed plans on paper or the verbal commands of officers alone. Some individual units, such as the cavalry 'Ironsides' so admired by Prince Rupert, already had a strong *esprit de corps* based on fighting ability. Bonds of admiration and loyalty between officers and men had also been forged in other units ably commanded by experienced men like Philip Skippon, who was appointed sergeant-major general of the New Model Army, with responsibility for the infantry. But the royalist armies had some able and admired commanders too, and the relative skill and determination of the field officers of the New Model Army are only two factors in their ultimate victory. Some looking for a unifying ethos have alighted on the social composition of the new force. In Cromwell's 'plain russet-coated captain that knows what he fights for and loves what he knows' has been perceived the military echelon of an emergent, aspiring, literate and skilled class, located somewhere between the lower levels of the proprietor class and the proletariat.[12]

Yet the royal armies were equally variegated as to social composition, albeit with an added Celtic twist. Certainly, the intention of Fairfax was that commission and promotion in the New Model Army would depend on ability and seniority rather than social rank; indeed, he turned down the recommendation of his own father, who attempted to win a command for an inexperienced protégé. But a positive bias in favour of those who lacked social distinction could not be inferred. Cromwell's attitude was equally pragmatic: 'It may be it provokes some spirits to see such plain men made captains of horse. It had been well that men of honour and birth had entered into these employments, but why do they not appear? Who would have hindered them? But since it was necessary the work must go on, better plain men than none.'[13]

Of greater significance was the religious radicalism of large sections of the officer corps at the New Model Army's inception, which had also been a particular feature of the Eastern Association. Men such as Nathaniel Rich, Thomas Rainsborough, Thomas Harrison, John Pickering, Daniel Axtell, William Packer and the psalm-singing troops they led were to give the new formation a distinctive character that was unique in the post-medieval history of British men-at-arms.[14] The New Model Army brought national organisational shape and recognition to a group of men whose motivation in taking up arms against the regime was highly influenced by their religious outlook and piety, and the ways in which they sought to give expression to it. Arguably, religious zeal generated a professional ethos and produced a powerful *esprit de corps* so that in time, and with each success, the New Model Army came to understand itself as doing the Almighty's work. In an early encounter of the new formation near Taunton, a Captain of Horse called out 'O fellow souldier, let us remember of God, and not fight in malice, but do his work, and leave the success to Him, and you shall see, through God's mercy, we will stand close to you.'[15] Therein were the sentiments of a powerful and tight-knit cadre of men which truly believed that their profession enjoyed divine sanction.

Unlike the Thirty Years War, which may be understood as a dynastic struggle which drew additional motive from religious differences and an emerging national awareness, the sources of the armed conflict in the British Isles and Ireland were primarily religious: in the melting pot of passions released by the progress of Church reformation in the sixteenth and seventeenth centuries coalesced profound differences of opinion about the relationship between the state and the individual, and where each stood in relation to the Almighty. For a significant portion of the wealthier and more educated elements of society who had influence as well as conviction, the process of Church reformation never seemed to go far enough, and episodes of backsliding only increased their resolve to see change. At the very least they were determined to promote a life appropriate to the truly devout amongst their families, servants, employees and immediate communities. This demand for greater 'purity' gave this cohort its name, although its usage has come to be understood as pejorative.

Where his father had trod on these shifting sands with a degree of circumspection, Charles I had taken a more robust approach to the religious context of his rule. These were not simply matters of scriptural interpretation, Church organisation and the correct forms of worship in a Protestant *ecclesia*. In one of his first acts as the new king in 1625, Charles passed an Act of Revocation in Scotland that recalled, in return for modest compensation, all Church land and dues that had been disbursed amongst the laity since the time of James V. The progress of Church reformation in the British Isles and Ireland had been accompanied by a fundamental economic and political shift as resources previously owned by the Roman Catholic Church were transferred into the hands of the laity by a process of expropriation, patronage and other forms of redistribution. Existing elites amongst the nobility enjoyed further enrichment while the proprietor class gained commensurately in wealth, authority and political influence (particularly at the local level) at the expense of the former hierarchy. Any attempts to reverse or even modify this settlement risked more than religious disruption.

Charles I was a profoundly religious man too, and one who had a deep and abiding conscience; he was easily able to convince himself of his good intentions. In William Laud, his Archbishop of Canterbury, the king had found a kindred spirit whose approach to religious practice was appropriately solemn while favouring a more elevated aesthetic in matters of devotion. Laud's attempts to achieve a uniformity of Protestant worship across the British Isles and Ireland overlay, nourished and swelled the other discontents that eventually erupted in war. In particular, they allowed the doubters and his opponents to portray his initiatives as a plan to move the realms in the direction of the great anti-Christ, Rome. Although the threat from Roman Catholic Spain held a strong place in popular imagination, Catholics by this time represented no more than a small fraction of the population of the mainland British Isles. At the time Charles acceded to his throne, their political, if not social, authority was minimal at the local level and more vestigial still at the national one. But later, it was easier to mobilise popular anxiety and rage through the vernacular of 'popish' plots, Marian martyrs, Irish armies and the threat to the island's security than by reference to the more esoteric elements of Anglican worship and theology.

The great irony of Laud's approach was that it was partly informed by his desire to head off the regrettable drift to Rome that had been observed in a number of high profile and aristocratic conversions at court. Charles too was a devout Protestant and his faith was perhaps the only point of friction in the close and loving relationship that he established with his French Catholic consort, Henrietta Maria. But her religious persuasion only fanned the flames of dissent, and the Roman Catholic rebellion that broke out in Ireland in 1641 turned suspicion into angry apprehension. The impact of the religious policies of Charles I and his archbishop, and the reaction they provoked, long outlived the execution of both. Perhaps the most powerful social dynamic of the Reformation was the way in which it leveraged the growing literacy amongst the populations of Europe and promoted a culture of popular accessibility to religion through the reading of Scripture that had arguably been lost by the more hierarchical Roman Catholic tradition. Its very success created the vibrancy that spawned the multifarious strands of Protestant faith, whose adherents increasingly came to claim them as authentic.

Laud's reforms seemed to challenge this accessibility: a new and inflexible service order and altar rails, the wider use of clerical vestments, a more elaborate liturgy and an intolerance of any who questioned the new dispensation, all suggested an authoritarian and exclusive Church. They also challenged the more intellectual approach to devotion of the Puritans. Above all, the revival of attempts to reassert the authority of an elite ecclesiastical hierarchy at the expense of the laity ran counter to the conception of a religious state based on an English variant of the presbytery of Calvin's Geneva held by a large proportion of the elites. Some voted with their feet: over the period of Charles's personal rule when parliament was in abeyance, many joined co-religionists by emigrating to the Netherlands. Of greater significance, some 20,000 sailed to the north-east of America, there to found a commonwealth in which they re-established what they regarded as the authentic version of the Church back home, which had been so disarranged by the autocratic Laud and his acolytes. This demographic movement easily dwarfed that of the earlier Stuart period which settled in Virginia, and which included the famed but tiny community of separatists established by the Pilgrim Fathers.[16] The Massachusetts Bay Company gave this association of the pious a commercial dimension too, and attracted financial backing from grandees in the mother country, like Robert Rich, the Earl of Warwick, who shared their religious outlook.

For the ordinary man and woman back home in England, Laud's initiatives disrupted the rhythms of their religious life. Above all, they seemed to constrain the choices by which the individual could come closer to the Almighty and disturbed the heterogeneous but generally well-tempered environment that the Protestant polity had become. Increasingly, matters such as infant baptism began to take on political significance and became socially disruptive within families and communities. Preaching too came under threat from the insistence that ministers of the Church stick to their own localities and Laud's script. Yet preaching, as revealed in the diaries of the artisan Nehemiah Wallington, was an ideal medium by which the unchurched, the curious, the pious and the otherwise busy could gain religious inspiration and even entertainment. There was a particularly strong culture of itinerant preaching in the major urban areas such as London and England's second largest city, Norwich. Outside the Communion of the established Church, a flourishing garden of different manners of celebration of the Protestant path to God's grace had taken root. This 'independence' of religious disposition, reinforced through the medium of preaching by regimental chaplains such as Hugh Peter, became a defining characteristic of the New Model Army. But in the furnace of war, attitudes and views based on religious preference and difference began to harden; the liberty implicit in man's relation to his Maker which had been so hopefully identified by Luther a century before curdled and then hardened into distrust, bigotry and violence.

2

'There is no probability but of my ruin'

Selkirk

God preserve our Kingdom from these sad troubles much longer!

Letter from the Corporation of Bath
to the New Model Army

No flames of civil dissension are more dangerous than those that make religious pretensions the grounds of factions.

Eikon Basilike

In Scotland the evolution of the Protestant state had taken on an added dimension with the close association of the Kirk with a growing and protective sense of Scottish national identity, most markedly amongst the Anglo-Scots ethnic mix of the Lowlands. The union of the two Crowns with the coronation of James VI as the first of that name in England and the diminution of Edinburgh as a political centre of gravity in favour of London had aroused a sense that the distinctive Scottish state would be subordinated to its neighbour. Furthermore, the Kirk remembered the time under James's mother when it had played a leading and decisive role in national affairs. Regarded as bleakly oppressive by its opponents, the Calvinist philosophy of an Elect which was predestined to enter the Kingdom of Heaven held a particular appeal in the southern part of Scotland, from which its adherents were to prove unwavering. The polity inspired by Calvin and Knox gave the pastors, doctors and elders of the Kirk significant sway in the life and politics of the country north of the River Tweed. Meanwhile, the Gaelic-speaking, frequently quarrelsome and nominally Catholic ethnic mix of the Highlands added to the Kirk's sense of identity as a leader in a less than truly godly state.

The Presbyterian model of Church government that it adopted was also averse to hierarchy without being truly democratic. Together with the Puritans of England, the Kirk shared a profound distrust of episcopacy, a feature of the established Church south of the border that came to be seen as increasingly alien as Charles I instigated his idea of a religious settlement for all his realms. The succession of his father James to the throne of England had given hope to the Kirk that its Presbyterian model with its austere liturgy, preference for extempore devotion, tough moral discipline imposed by Church courts and strong emphasis on repentance would become the standard for the two realms. Had not James himself disparaged the established Church of his southern estate with its 'evil said masse in English', and its, to him, unfamiliar Book of Common Prayer?[1] But the Stuarts' admiration of the obedience that was such a feature of religious life in Scotland did not dispose them to obedience to the strictures of the Kirk itself. What is more, the episcopacy of England was better attuned to their conceptions of social hierarchy below the level of the throne, while the elevated ritual to be found in England's historic cathedrals and the comparative beauty of her set prayers, songs and residual iconography had an aesthetic that was far more in keeping with a monarchy that was God-anointed.

The catalyst for the civil wars in the British Isles and Ireland had been Charles's attempts to impose, without trial or even much consultation, a Scottish Prayer Book. As a curtain raiser for what was to follow, the introduction of the book, with the full majesty of Scottish bishops in attendance, occasioned a riot in the precincts of St Giles' Cathedral. Within a year the rumpus had given birth to a national Covenant that seemed to unite Lords, Commons and Kirk. Superficially a document that professed fealty to a king who had been misled by wicked counsellors, the Covenant became the means of distributing the subversive notion that this loyalty was dependent on the monarch being willing to defend the true Protestant religion. For the regime's opponents in England, the speed and decisiveness of the Scottish disobedience proved to be a wake-up call. The abject performance of Charles's armies in the so-called Bishops' Wars that followed increased the sense of dismay and disenchantment, and finally led to uproar when the bill for the fiasco landed in the lap of a recalled English parliament.

Amidst the blizzard of political pamphlets and all the passions ignited by Ship Money, prerogative courts, forced loans and *habeas corpus*, it is perhaps forgotten that the first shots of the civil wars were fired between Protestant Covenanters and Episcopalians upon the banks of the River Dee by Aberdeen. For the Scots, the quarrel with the monarch was a religious rather than a political one, and in their relations with the parliamentary opposition in England they perceived an opportunity to defend their religious state at home while extending it south of the border as the price for their military support. In the discussions that preceded the formal conclusion of alliance between the parties in 1643, a conference of Scottish and English divines in London debated 'the reformation in Church ceremonies and discipline so much longed for'. The Westminster Assembly eventually produced an outcome that was accepted by the Kirk, but the voice of the independent congregations outside the proposed Presbyterian Church was clearly heard then and later from the likes of Philip Nye, an Oxford-trained theologian who had returned from exile in Holland, and Thomas Goodwin, a Puritan divine. Their tract, *An Apologeticall Narration*, denounced separatism but argued passionately for organisational freedom around a central Protestant canon.

Over time, the passionate arguments for toleration of different Protestant congregational arrangements were to remove any chance that the military alliance with the Scots could be hardened by religious allegiance. But in the meantime, the military resources available to Charles's opponents in England were transformed by the addition of the sizeable and experienced Scottish army. In January 1644, 21,000 troops crossed the border in a blinding snowstorm and rapidly established dominance over the north of England. Unlike the forces operated by either side south of the Tweed, the troops assembled by the Scots contained a high proportion of men who had seen action on the Continent during the course of the Thirty Years War. A large number of officers had had to be released from their service contracts to the Swedes in order to return to the army of the Covenant. It was an Anglo-Scottish army under the command of Alexander Leslie, the Earl of Leven (who had held commissions in the Protestant armies of both Holland and Sweden), which combined to defeat the royal army at the largest encounter of the civil wars, the battle of Marston Moor.

The Solemn League and Covenant not only bound its signatories to protect the Kirk and to assimilate all the reformed Churches of the British Isles into one, it committed them to the extirpation of 'popery' and to ensure the (long-delayed) reformation of the Church in Ireland. In the strain of war, a further religious imprimatur was thus given to an intensification of the process of cultural suppression and economic expropriation of the majority Roman Catholic population that had been pursued by the Stuart regime. The main physical manifestation of this policy had been the encouragement given to the plantation of swathes of the island by cohorts of the godly, of both English and Scottish descent, particularly in Ulster and Munster. The outbreak of the Irish rebellion in 1641 was a result of the dislocation caused by this demographic incursion, and the deliberate exclusion of the majority Roman Catholic population from public life. As in Scotland, the rebellion generated its own rubric of national solidarity, this time in the Confederate Oath of Association brought to life at Kilkenny in 1642. Like the Covenant too, the early leaders of the Irish confederates were careful to stress their allegiance to the Crown.

But the religious dimension of the rebellion was cemented by a synod of the Irish clergy which blessed it as a just war. The Catholic clergy was, by western European standards, unusually closely integrated with all elements of native Irish society and held a position of powerful cultural authority. Ireland's position on the geographic margins of Europe, its low level of literacy and the social cohesiveness fostered by the Church meant that Ireland had been particularly impervious to the march of the Reformation. The Roman Catholic Church had as powerful a sense of its ancient mission to spread authentic Christianity as did the Kirk. What had started as a political rebellion as the Irish Catholic elites attempted to wrest back their old position of eminence rapidly degenerated into ethnic strife as native former proprietors repossessed their land. The savagery of some of the encounters fuelled a lurid propaganda on both sides and pamphleteers swiftly rendered the horrors in graphic detail. Charles was appalled by the rising but parliament did not trust the king to deal with either recalcitrant Calvinists in Scotland or rebellious priests in Ireland, and fears that he might use the growing political crisis in England to raise an army in Ireland to suppress his opponents back home fuelled the advance to an English civil war. In reaction to the revolt, parliament passed the so-called Adventurers' Act, which raised loans to crush the rebellion, redeemable in the land of the vanquished. Endorsed but not enforced by Charles, the Act later became the legal justification for conquest and cultural subjugation.

Unlike the arguably decisive military impact of the Scots, that of the Irish was mostly latent. As the wars progressed on the mainland British Isles, Ireland enjoyed a period of rule analogous to self-government. James Butler, Marquis of Ormonde, the leader of the royal army charged with suppressing the original rebellion, reached an uneasy ceasefire with the confederates, who were themselves divided on the issue of their loyalty to the Crown. The violence was mostly confined to an Irish dimension, although the struggle between the 'planters' and the native Irish saw a Covenanter army land in Ireland in support of their kin in Ulster, while Alasdair MacColla crossed the Irish Sea with his 'kerns' to lend an exotic patina (and useful military experience) to the Highland campaign of James Graham, Marquis of Montrose. However, the arrival of an Irish Catholic host in Scotland did not immediately disturb the deployment of the main body of the Scottish army under the terms of the Solemn League.

Although Montrose had been in the vanguard of the Scottish nobles who originally took the Covenant, he later developed an almost romantic attachment to the Stuart dynasty, a loyalty that was all of a piece with his sense of being an heroic figure cast from the mould of an earlier chivalric age. Born in 1612 he was, like Cromwell, an only son raised in a family of women, and he inherited his title when he was fourteen. His likeness on display at the Scottish National Portrait Gallery shows a lively and somewhat sensual countenance encompassed by unruly blond locks atop a neck unfeasibly lengthened by his body armour and wide linen collar. He was educated at the ancient University of St Andrews, developed a love for poetry and was a keen sportsman, not least in the emerging game of golf. Criticised by some commentators for his affectations, he was less motivated by abstract political thought than by an innate belief in the charismatic power conferred by educated aristocratic breeding.[2] But while he might have had a streak of vanity, what is not in doubt is that he was also a highly talented and bloodthirsty leader of irregular troops.

At the battle of Tippermuir, on 1 September 1644, in one of the most astonishing feats of this or indeed any war, his numerically inferior and poorly armed gathering of Highlanders saw off a force of Covenanters twice its size by energetically flinging pebbles and stones at them. But in reality his guerrilla campaign was mostly directed at his fellow magnate the Marquis of Argyll, and there is little evidence that the royalist high command, which had enough troubles of its own, took his military value particularly seriously. Motivated as much by the prospect of plunder and the settling of old scores as by the royal cause, the Highlanders preferred a marauding military style which made them difficult to manage and impervious to discipline.

Perhaps Montrose's real achievement was in keeping his small force in the field for so long. After sacking Aberdeen and winning some brutal encounters with clan Campbell, which were but pin-prick victories against the wider forces of the Solemn League, Montrose and his depleted army were finally run to ground in September 1645 in the borderland near Selkirk.

Here they encountered an overwhelming force under the command of David Leslie, who had performed with some distinction on the left wing of the army of the Solemn League at Marston Moor. The encounter at Philiphaugh was not a battle, but rather a massacre. The Irish mercenaries were butchered to a man and, urged on by their ministers, who were half crazed by bigoted hatred, the victorious soldiers murdered the women and children of the accompanying baggage train and conducted a thorough hunt for any papist survivors. Although smaller in scale and geographical scope, the later stages of the civil wars easily matched the character of the Thirty Years War on the Continent in terms of their barbarity. Between 1642 and 1651, the cost in human lives on the mainland of the British Isles as a proportion of the population is estimated to have exceeded that of the Great War of 1914–18.

Quite apart from the instances of fighting, the general instability was profoundly detrimental to the wider civilian population. The character of local governance had much changed as the old ruling elites and 'persons of quality' had been superseded by County Committees which were populated by men whose narrow focus was on winning the war. The administration of justice had become a lot rougher. The strain caused by poor harvests and surging prices, the levies used to finance the war, the disfiguration of the landscape by fortifications, the predatory actions of both sets of opposing forces as they marched about the country and the increasing use made of 'free quarter' to sustain the soldiery, provoked strong antipathy in local communities. There were desperate pleas to ease the burdens of war. From Bath came a petition from the mayor, aldermen and citizens 'in fear and trouble, beseech(ing) you to give advices . . . touching our city's distress at the present time . . . that in such ways get favour from the Commander to spare further levies as we hear the troops are coming onward for our City and our houses are emptied of all useful furniture, and much broken and disfigured; our poore suffer from want of victuals, and rich we have none.'[3]

One manifestation of this dismay was the Clubmen movement which emerged in the closing stages of the first civil war. A spontaneous coalition of anxious and frightened citizenry, it was symptomatic of an overwhelming desire for peace and protection amongst people of all ranks who felt abandoned by the forces of law and order. The movement was particularly prevalent in the west of England and in the south-west, where the balance of military fortune often shifted and where the disruption was consequentially greater. In some areas, large bands of Clubmen impeded the conduct of military operations and had to be dealt with accordingly. These local 'home-guards' of civilians determined to preserve their livelihoods and to keep the opposing combatants away, were a sign of a profound desire for peace that was later to morph into a more radical social agenda.

Amongst the elite who had been at the genesis of the parliamentary revolt against the personal rule of the monarch, the mutation of the war into an existential struggle for survival that embraced all classes was a profound shock. The breakdown of the rhythms of local government overseen by the proprietor classes struck at the bedrock of a social order based on deference to rank and wealth. More insidiously, the passions ignited by the religious dimension of the war threatened a complete breakdown of the national state as conceived by that elite. If men and women were free to act according to their religious consciences, there was no guarantee of loyalty to the sources of civil authority. Without a secure state headed by a monarch, property would not be protected. Laud's attempt at achieving uniformity had been fatally undermined by its symbiosis with a capricious and seemingly unaccountable royal regime, itself tainted by a strong whiff of Catholicism. The archbishop had been arraigned and beheaded, and the Puritans brought within the fold of rebellion, but the Protestant sects and independent congregations were seen as an increasing threat to the homogeneity of faith that seemed essential to the restoration of stability of the state.

Of particular concern was their influence in the New Model Army where the divine, Robert Baillie, thought that the soldiers had been 'seduced to Independency, and very many of them have added either Anabaptism or Antinomianism or both'.[4] Baillie was one of the Scottish representatives at the Westminster Assembly, but his alarm was not narrowly partisan; the insights of the English Presbyterian chaplain to the army, Richard Baxter, showed as well the degree of Protestant Nonconformity amongst the troops. Baxter was a Puritan divine from Worcestershire whose memoirs, although written with the benefit of hindsight, provide an important narrative of the nature of the religious disputes of the period. Although (as he later claimed) he initially regretted his decision to decline an invitation to minister to the troops under Cromwell (instead he was attached to Colonel Whalley's regiment), Baxter came to see the general as something of an incubus for heterodoxy and subversion. After Naseby, 'When I came to the Army among Cromwell's soldiers I found a new face of things which I never dreamt of: I have heard the plotting . . . which intimated their intention to subvert both church and state.'

Nonetheless, the minister set to work 'gently arguing with the more tractable . . . and many honest men of weak judgement and little acquaintance with such matters'. Most men, he discovered, were 'ready to hear the truth', but 'A few proved self-conceited hot-headed sectaries [who] had got into the highest places and were Cromwell's chief favourites . . . and were the Soul of the Army.' He perceived too a strong antipathy towards the Scots and their promotion of 'Priestbyters' and noticed the contempt that they had towards other soldiers in the army 'that were not of their mind and way'.[5]

Roman Catholicism corresponded to the external threat; the sects seemed to contain the germ of a new enemy within the lower levels and the base of the social pyramid. The alliance formed with Scotland under the Solemn League has been interpreted as one with the practical priority of securing troops while closing the north to the royalists.

But the Presbyterian solution to Church governance, which these allies represented, held a strong appeal by offering a model by which social discipline could be brought to the civil state, with the influence of the traditional elites restored. Later, Hobbes's blueprint of civil society in *Leviathan* was perhaps as notable for the way it articulated many of the inner certainties and prejudices at the upper levels of society as for its abstract political thought.

It is difficult to find a better representative of these assumptions than Denzil Holles, the MP for Dorchester. Born at the turn of the century, he was the third son of the first Earl of Clare and was a precocious and much favoured child. His happy upbringing included a boyhood acquaintance with his future sovereign, and his family moved amongst the highest echelons of the elite. This background imbued him with a remarkable level of confidence and a keen awareness of opportunities for dramatic self-expression. Educated at Christ's College, Cambridge, he was first elected in 1624 and both inside and outside the House of Commons he became a leading member of the opposition to Charles's personal rule. In a famous scene in March 1629 he and Sir John Eliot held the Speaker of the House in his chair while a list of grievances was read out before the dissolution, an act of defiance for which the pair were arrested. Enjoying the prestige that went with political imprisonment during this period, he was loudly in the vanguard of the attack on William Laud and his promotion of episcopacy, although his attitude to the person of the king was couched by deference. His Protestantism had an international dimension too, and he was vocal in his support of the 'Winter Queen', Charles's younger sister who, with her husband the King of Bohemia, had been ousted in the struggle that became the Thirty Years War. Charles was not so impressed by this *faux* chivalry that he did not attempt to round up Holles again, together with four others of his most vexatious opponents in the Commons, in early 1642.

Benefiting hugely from this *coup de théâtre*, the irrepressible MP was emboldened in his disobedience and he became one of the main choreographers of the final steps of the dance that fatally led to war. But, in common with so many of the well-bred rebels, Holles's mental geography did not truly embrace a resort to arms. Once the conflict was actually joined and experienced by him at first hand at Edgehill, whatever martial ardour he possessed rapidly waned and he became a leading member of the influential group that sought an end to the fighting by political settlement with the king. Eclipsed by the growing atmosphere of resolve among the more militant, he nevertheless strongly opposed the Self-Denying Ordinance. For him and others, the measure turned the army into an unguided instrument of war and risked the transformation of a political and religious struggle controlled by the traditional elites into a more obvious military insurrection with its own brand of spiritual dynamism.

After their successful military intervention southwards, the Scots too had begun to have second thoughts. Given the significance they attached to the Solemn League and Covenant, and in view of their military contribution, the Scots were seriously underrepresented on the Committee of Both Kingdoms.[6] It did not help that the four commissioners that spoke for them in London were relative unknowns, save for Archibald Johnston, Lord Wariston. He was born in the first decade of the century, the son of a well-to-do Lothian family, and had a depth of religious fervour which in its earlier manifestations may have seemed deranged even to his godly contemporaries. Given to intense prayer and introspection, his *Diaries* reveal a man in almost continuous, and anguished, communication with his Maker. Having lost a much-loved wife in the prime of her youth, the spiritually tortured lowlander felt that the Almighty owed him favour, and he came to regard his growing influence (if not wealth) as just reward for keeping faith with God through his tribulations.[7] He had a powerful conviction too that the Kirk was the vanguard for the Almighty's work on Earth. Wariston had had a hand in the drafting of the Covenant, had travelled south with the Scottish army and had taken an active part in the Westminster Assembly, which had set the religious objectives of the alliance. Intensely devotional and apt to consider practical matters as manifestations of divine will, he and the other commissioners were insufficiently equipped to contribute to the military strategy of the war, and the long line of communication back to Edinburgh did not help.

Back in Scotland, the evolution of the struggle and its social consequences were also disturbing the equilibrium of the elites. The nobly born there had as elevated a sense of their leadership role as their peers further south. But in a much smaller and more clannish population, political disagreements in Scotland took on an added piquancy, seasoned with fierce personal rivalry. The ascendancy of Archibald Campbell, Marquis of Argyll, and the growing influence of the more militant sections of the Kirk amongst the laity, was resented not only by Montrose but also by other members of the aristocracy who preferred the reinstatement of a well-ordered and deferential hierarchy under a Stuart king surrounded by his nobles. Campbell's star has rather been cast in shade by that of his great antagonist, James Graham, and the verdict of posterity on their characters and motives has perhaps been distorted by their striking dissimilarity of looks.

Whereas Graham is invariably portrayed looking vigorous and attractive, likenesses of Campbell (who was five years older) take on the appearance of an angry buzzard. In the famous painting by David Scougall, the Marquis of Argyll appears in somewhat sour-looking middle age, his hair severely corralled by a black skullcap. Beside the pronounced squint in his left eye rests an enormous beak of a nose which runs down to a mouth contorted by cynicism. However, the cast of his vision did not prove to be a handicap; in 1623 as a young man he won second prize in an archery competition at St Andrews (although it is not recorded whether this was for accuracy or effort). Certainly, he had an acute perception of the interest of his clan and was ruthless in its advancement – his reputation for deviousness attracted much resentment amongst his fellow magnates. Yet of the two men it was Argyll who was to display a better command of politics; both were patriots, albeit on different sides of the same coin. But whereas Argyll maintained a consistent intellectual loyalty to the ideal of a Covenanter state, Montrose was far more intuitive and he acted as a magnet for the discontents.[8] A great deal of *Schadenfreude* was generated by his serial embarrassment of his rival in his Highland campaign, not least by the tales of Argyll's concern for his own personal safety at the expense of his troops. A strong advocate of the alliance with the English rebels, Campbell's prestige suffered.

In the field, tensions between the Scottish and English commands had risen well before the formation of the New Model Army. The Covenanter army had not been deployed as an act of philanthropy and the precedence attached to the payment of the soldiery of each nation rapidly became a bone of contention. It did not help that the advance of the Scots southwards soon took on the appearance of an occupation and many angry missives were despatched to London, not the least of which came from the Fairfax family. Sir Thomas was particularly vexed that his own loyal Yorkshiremen should suffer arrears to the benefit of their allies. The growing influence of the independent congregations was also causing friction, and matters came to something of an emblematic head in the quarrel between the recently promoted Cromwell and a Scottish counterpart. Taking up the cause of a regimental officer cashiered by the Scots for his Nonconformist religious views (he was accused of being an Anabaptist) and for his refusal to take the Covenant, Cromwell seemed to be angrily reacting as much to overweening Scottish presumption as defending a soldier's liberty of conscience.

But it was the affront caused by Cromwell's religious sensibilities that was taken the most seriously. As Hyde pithily noted in *The History of the Rebellion*:

> Their sacred vow and covenant was mentioned with less reverence and respect, and the Independents, which comprehended many sects in religion, spake publicly against it . . . So that the Scots [commissioners] plainly perceived that, though they had gone as far towards the destruction of the Church of England as they desired, they should never be able to establish their Presbyterian government; without which they should lose all their credit in their own country and all their interest in England.[9]

Despite the decisive collaboration at Marston Moor, relations did not much improve in the atmosphere of victory as the Scots decided to linger in the north. To MPs like Holles and magnates like Argyll however, the Solemn League offered the prospect of a more deeply unified and settled Presbyterian realm. With the tacit support of the Earl of Essex and the Scottish commissioners, Holles tried unsuccessfully to have Cromwell impeached for endangering the alliance. But in 1645 the religious agenda of the Scots seemed of less relevance than the military imperative of winning the war, and the formation of the New Model Army was a distinctly English affair. In a further sign of the rupture to come, Fairfax did not commission a single Scottish officer in his new command. The complete victory of the New Model Army at Naseby increased the sense of Scottish unease, as they perceived that an army in whose formation they had played no part could just as easily be turned against them as against the king. Now distracted by the intensification of the civil war at home, the scope of the Scottish army's operations south of the border began to abate. In time their relative inactivity enticed Charles, who would come to see that redemption from his English enemies might be delivered by the original Stuart state.

The character and disposition of the monarch in whose name so much blood had been spilt was arguably decisive in the shaping of events at this critical moment in British royal history. He had been born at Dunfermline in Scotland in November 1600, the youngest of three surviving children. His spindly frame (Charles was diagnosed with rickets) and retarded rate of growth did not augur well for his survival in an era when infant mortality was commonplace. He also had a pronounced stutter in his speech which was of intense irritation to his father, whose own articulations were impaired by a tongue too large for its mouth and which caused him to drool most unregally when he became agitated. But survive Charles did, notwithstanding the strictures of the monarch, who ordered that the young prince's legs be encased in painful iron callipers to straighten them. Remote from his parents, his early upbringing was entrusted to the care of courtiers whose attitude was conditioned by the knowledge that he was the 'spare' to the much more exalted 'heir', his elder brother Henry. His introspective personality was allied to a good brain however, and he certainly was not lacking in physical bravery. He enjoyed the absorption of reading and took his studies seriously, not least those of relevance to his religious faith.[10] Yet Charles also seems to have been a somewhat withdrawn boy – all his life he could not bear to hear voices raised in his company and he developed a forbidding *froideur* to keep those of whom he was unsure at a distance. He grew up without that depth of love that he was to find much later in life in the person of Henrietta Maria, his uncrowned consort.

In 1612, Prince Henry died of typhoid and Charles, whose self-esteem had been corroded by the somewhat bullying and dismissive attitude of a brother whose approval he craved, was now (after his father) the cynosure of the dynasty. His parents started to take a greater interest in his progress and Charles was more deeply assimilated into a court ritual that was in turn both formal and licentious. His plainly bisexual father had a penchant for good-looking male favourites, of whom the most influential was George Villiers, later created Duke of Buckingham. The reserved adolescent prince was initially reluctant to extend his own favour to the louche courtier, but once it was given (to the delight of the king, who referred to both the favourite and the heir as 'his babies') Charles's loyalty was deep, unswerving and uncritical. However, when allied to the stubbornness born of his earlier alienation, this attractive feature of his personality was seriously to impede his statecraft when he became the sovereign in his turn.

In the increasingly complex world of the government of post-medieval society in western Europe, this facility was attracting serious intellectual attention. In his *Political Testament*, the King of France's first minister, Cardinal Richelieu, brought his wide experience to bear in setting out for his master (Louis XIII) the most practical and effective maxims of government. Nothing, from the ordering of the clergy and state diplomacy to the judicious use of favours and the treatment of courtiers, appeared to escape his attention. His advice seemed tailor-made to the assessment of those men upon whose advice the Stuarts came to depend, with varying degrees of success: 'There is no plague more capable of ruining a state than the host of flatterers, slanderers and people preoccupied with forming cabals and intrigues at court. They are so industrious at spreading their venom in various insidious ways that it is difficult to avoid it unless one takes the greatest of care.'[11]

But it was Richelieu's pithy thoughts on the intrinsic purpose of near absolute royal government that were perhaps the most arresting:

> The public interest ought to be the sole objective of the prince and his councillors, or, at least, both are obliged to have it foremost in mind, and preferred to all private gain. It is impossible to overestimate the good which a prince and those serving him in government can do if they religiously follow this principle, and one can hardly imagine the evils which befall a state if private interest is preferred to the public good and actually gains the ascendancy.[12]

James I was also developing his own theory of monarchy, the more mystical elements of which held a strong appeal to his heir. In his *Basilikon Doron* the Stuart monarch commended the importance of hierarchy while deprecating popularity and described the character of a true sovereign as a sort of stern but loving paterfamilias who took pains for his subjects and objections from none.[13] But the most important and sacramental feature of the state was the assertion that the sovereign was God's representative on Earth. Here, James sought to intertwine his Calvinist education with conceptions of an ecclesiastical hierarchy appropriate to such an absolute ruler. In time, this rubric was absorbed by the son with a level of devotion such as if his father had produced holy writ. In the mind of Charles, the conviction was further embellished by a high aesthetic sense by which his own personal rule became a cultural phenomenon. But it might have been better had he read the *Political Testament*.

This was the king who, after Naseby, commenced an odyssey around the southern half of his realms, a journey which was to end in his capture, imprisonment and ultimate death. Although a poor judge of military and political odds, Charles was both morally as well as physically courageous. He was not averse to sharing the dangers of his troops and instinctively understood the importance of the monarch being seen to be resolute and active. It is perhaps for this reason that royalist morale did not fall in proportion to its military resources. In the field, however, whatever grip his depleted and far-flung forces had was being steadily chiselled away. In Somerset, Lord Goring managed briefly to rise above the bickering of his divided command but was outmanoeuvred by Fairfax and suffered defeat at the battle of Langport. Maintaining tight discipline in the ambush set by the royalists, the New Model troops led by Cromwell swiftly outflanked their opponents and started a rout that Goring hoped to forestall by setting fire to the village. The harshness and futility of this incidence of scorched earth enraged local Clubmen, who later set about the fleeing troops.

Langport was a further victory for the New Model Army and, not for the first time, Cromwell was heard exulting the result as the work of God. Over 2,000 prisoners were taken. At Bristol, the increasingly frustrated Prince Rupert surrendered to Fairfax after a brief siege, but not before pleading by letter to his uncle to come to terms. Charles's reply was highly illustrative of both his inflexibility and his steely inner resolve: 'I must say there is no probability but of my ruin. Yet as a Christian I must tell you that God will not suffer rebels and traitors to prosper nor this cause to be overthrown.'[14] Seeing his obligation to the Almighty, his dynasty and his friends in that order, Charles was completely certain of the correctness of his position, futile as it seemed to be.

His continued resistance seemed to raise the spirits if not the means to give them military edge. Arriving in a besieged Chester in September 1645, the same month as Montrose was defeated at Philiphaugh, Charles was just in time to witness another defeat from the town's battlements. Having got the king's party to relative safety behind the city's walls, the gallant and ubiquitous Sir Marmaduke Langdale then led a savage day-long cavalry fight against a superior force under the parliamentary commander Sydenham Poyntz, in an attempt to break the chokehold around this strategically important site. To avoid entrapment, the disconsolate royal retinue then headed for Wales, leaving the town in the hands of the recently ennobled Lord John Byron, the ancestor of the eponymous romantic poet. Against appalling odds and subjected to incessant shelling, the slowly starving garrison of soldiers and townsfolk managed to hold out for a further four months. Unlike the forbearance shown by Fairfax towards his adversaries at Bristol, which encouraged their surrender, the siege of Chester was commanded by the inflexibly aggressive Sir William Brereton. Elsewhere remembered for the undisguised lack of admiration of the 'slovenly' living conditions and habits of the Scots revealed in his travel journal from 1636, Brereton refused to countenance a surrender that would have preserved for his opponents both their lives and the deserved honours of war.[15] Believing that there was little prospect of quarter, Byron's garrison fought on in the vain hope that their king would eventually prevail.

Elsewhere, the grinding nature of operations continued. At the third attempt in as many years, troops under the direction of Cromwell finally managed to storm Basing House in Hampshire in the autumn of 1645. The siege of strongly fortified and often stately homes was a feature of the civil wars and provided microcosms of the fighting that have seized the imagination. Basing was no exception, being the complex redoubt of John Paulet, Marquis of Winchester, and one of the most senior English Roman Catholics in the royal service. Basing had been a favourite retreat of the queen and her court, and in October was host to an extraordinary assortment of soldiers, Jesuit priests, refugees, thespians and other celebrities behind the pockmarked walls. Among the latter were Wenceslas Hollar, the celebrated Bohemian engraver, and Inigo Jones, the renowned practitioner of the classical style in architecture who had designed the Queen's House at Greenwich (for Charles's mother) and the sumptuous banqueting house at Whitehall in London.[16]

Now in his seventy-third year, Jones had been brought to Basing and was happy to lend some badly needed tone to the grim situation of siege, as well as advice on how the architecture of the defences could be shored up. Together with the dramatist and poet Ben Jonson, with whom he had had an uneasy collaboration, Jones had presided over the production of the masques that came to define the court style of the Stuart regime. These lavish and expensive pageants with their arresting costumes and lavish stage sets were perhaps an inadvertent, if not-so-subtle, contribution by Jones to the Baroque movement, the preferred aesthetic of the Catholic Counter-Reformation. They certainly attracted a great deal of angry attention from opponents of the queen and her Catholic manners, and came to symbolise the gulf between a seemingly wasteful and idolatrous regime and the godly. The fact that Jones was himself one of the Puritans, albeit one whose commercial self-interest trumped religious introspection, was seemingly overlooked.

The antagonism of religious and cultural differences in the period is better seen to advantage in the career of William Prynne, the Puritan polemicist. He is remembered in the textbooks for the cruelty of his judicial treatment for criticising Laud and the episcopacy, and for the act of *lèse-majesté* contained in his voluminous tome *Histriomastix*. But Prynne had not just been exercised by the subversive ritual that he perceived in the masques. His whole agenda can be viewed as severely Calvinistic with a heavy dose of misogyny. Of fierce and often angrily expressed principle, he was a talented and prolific wordsmith. But the ideas and prejudices which he did so much to energise curdled into a militant joylessness that contaminated future perceptions of the age, and which gradually became intolerable even to his contemporaries. The influence of the Puritan zealots ensured a form of cultural immolation as the war progressed. Theatres were closed or demolished, and public holidays and celebrations based on the old Christian calendar forbidden. Repentance (communally expressed by public fast days), rather than celebration, became the order of the day. Parliament commanded all church organs destroyed and ecclesiastical music was anathematised.

There was much denunciation of the 'superstition' of humans and of the alleged profanity of inanimate objects, and the conditions of war ensured that the fanaticism of the militantly righteous contaminated attempts to adopt a more rational and secular narrative of rebellion and the search for a settlement.

Rather, any progress towards enlightenment was obscured by a heavy atmosphere of intolerance, the creepy sadism of the witch-hunts conducted by Matthew Hopkins and the summary execution of prisoners (especially Roman Catholics) who professed the wrong faith. The iconoclasm was not confined to artefacts that lent themselves to a Catholic interpretation. The little chapel constructed at the command of Henrietta Maria to house her Capuchin monks and host her devotions might have seemed like fair game in the circumstances of seventeenth-century warfare, but the non-denominational masterpieces by Rubens inside were also ripped to shreds as well as many other precious items. Nothing that could be construed as remotely sacramental or as an aesthetic aid to contemplation was to be permitted. The military were more than willing to be co-opted in the rage of iconoclasm. Early in the war, the wooden choir and beautiful stained-glass windows of Ely Cathedral had been enthusiastically smashed to pieces by troops under the direct control of Cromwell.

The long night of civil war continued, testament to royalist tenacity but also the thoroughness of the New Model Army. Fairfax distinguished his resolute campaign in the south-west by showing good sense in his conciliation of local Clubmen, and paying sums sufficiently enticing for royalist soldiers to give their parole. Others were happy to surrender upon the promise that they would keep their property. The last major engagement took place on 21 March 1646 at Stow-on-the-Wold in Gloucestershire, where Sir Jacob Astley and his Welsh recruits surrendered after a brief struggle. Charles, thinking he now had more to gain from a more politically active approach than waiting for the well-known dissensions in the parliamentary ranks to crystallise in his favour, left his capital at Oxford in disguise. In the early hours of a May morning his small party passed the Minster church and entered the Saracen's Head in the Nottinghamshire village of Southwell. Resting amongst the snoring innkeeper and his family, the scarcely recognisable king composed himself for inevitable captivity. His destination was the besieged town of Newark-on-Trent, on the front line of the Scottish army in England.

3

'We are here by the King's madness'
Newcastle

We believed that the War was only to save the Parliament and Kingdom from Papists and Delinquents and to remove the Dividers, that the King might again return to his Parliament.

Richard Baxter, *Reliquiae Baxterianae*

Newark in the spring of 1646 was a royalist town under assault. Commanded by Lord John Belasyse, it contained a mint for the hard-up royal cause to which wealthier citizens were encouraged to give precious and other metal objects to be turned into coins. As at Chester, the garrison had been holding out for a lengthy period when Charles appeared amongst the ranks of the besieging Scottish troops. Their senior commanders could not have been completely surprised by their royal windfall as overtures towards an agreement between Charles and the rebels of the Covenant had already taken place, facilitated by a representative of the French government. These moves had, however, been baulked by the king's strict adherence to his Anglican faith and by his acute understanding that the spiritual equality of his otherwise kingly status with that of his Elect subjects would make him no king at all. Now in their hands, the Scottish commanders wasted no time in ensuring that Charles was kept well away from their English allies; Lord John was ordered by his sovereign to surrender and then the Earl of Leven's troops struck camp and headed north to Newcastle, with the king given little deference aboard the Scottish train of march.

Sequestering Charles in modest accommodation and isolating him from his advisers, the Scots kept up a rhetorical assault on their royal prisoner for over six months. Various divines and members of the nobility came to entreat with him to accept both Covenant and a Presbyterian settlement; the aging, ill and heavily bearded theologian Alexander Henderson, who had played such a significant part in drawing up the Covenant and at the Westminster Assembly, exhausted himself as he tried, weeping on his knees, to persuade the Stuart monarch. Appeals were made to the king to accept the Covenant and to honour the reforming instincts of his royal predecessors. But, in an affront to his dignity, he was continually exhorted to repent. Charles remained implacable, although his letters to his consort betray the heavy emotional strain that he was under, and the importance he attached to her approval and understanding of the line he took with his captors.

The part played by Henrietta Maria in the religious politics of the period has been somewhat cast into shade by the role of her husband. Denounced by contemporaries as a Roman Catholic provocateur, focus has attached to her public pilgrimages to the Martyrs' shrine at Tyburn, her patronage of the controversial masques and her company of Sir Jeffrey Hudson, the celebrated dwarf who provided diversion in the tedious intervals of court life. Her success in spurring the conversion of those members of the court whose Protestantism was only skin-deep was a source of profound aggravation in the growing opposition to the regime. Criticism of her was also motivated by a good deal of misogyny: in a highly patriarchal society, it offended many that she seemed to exercise an entirely inappropriate sway over her husband, and certainly the tone of many of their letters suggests that she was capable of tough love as well as plain speaking. Her political importance and personal faith (which contributed to the anti-Catholic hysteria of the period) were important enough for parliament to impeach her in 1643, and her credibility and that of the king was further undermined in the eyes of their opponents by the correspondence contained in the pamphlet *The Kings Cabinet Opened*, which revealed the attempts by Charles to raise Roman Catholic troops to serve his interests.

Born in the winter of 1609, she was the fourth child of Henri IV (*Le Grand*) of France and his second wife, Marie de Medici, a gene pool which might later have conferred exalted success in circumstances other than those in which she found herself as a vivacious fifteen-year-old. In 1625 she was subjected to the matrimonial lottery that was such a feature of early modern statecraft at the highest levels, and was bundled off to Britain to marry a man nine years her senior who had just succeeded as king. The early years were not a success; her adolescent high spiritedness and frank demeanour challenged the far more reserved nature of Charles, while her covey of French attendants and her religious faith prevented a fuller cultural assimilation – she never really mastered the English language. Of greater symbolism was her spirited refusal to be anointed by a Protestant bishop, so she was never officially crowned as queen. But she developed an abiding loyalty to her equally diminutive husband, which was reciprocated in turn so that they came to enjoy one of the most uxorious and loving relationships in British monarchical history.

The centrality of her position in very visible and elaborate court ritual, and her insensitivity to the Protestant susceptibilities of her host country, are suggestive of a frivolous personality. But while she lacked the guile of a father who was unknown to her (Henri was assassinated before her first birthday), Henrietta Maria had powerful instincts and an intelligent will. Combining an evidently high sexual drive with devotional intensity, she went on to bear the king nine children. Her second, the future Charles II, whose appearance she likened to that of a swarthy monkey, was born in the summer of 1630. The progress of the civil wars saw her offspring scattered around the kingdom: at best left in the care of friendly gentlefolk, wandering as fugitives or made virtual prisoner by their parliamentary foes. It is difficult to determine, but easy to imagine, the strain caused to both Charles and Henrietta Maria by the intense disruption to their family life, but apparent royal resilience may have been aided by their own experiences as children whose parents knew little of their offspring or, as in the case of the king's own father, barely seemed to care.

Nonetheless, when the fighting started Henrietta Maria was energetic in trying to raise assistance for the royalist cause abroad. Returning from a trip to raise money and support from Holland by pawning royal jewels, she was attacked by a parliamentary naval squadron off Bridlington and very nearly killed. She was later cloistered in the king's war-torn capital at Oxford. In the drab and cramped conditions of the colleges people began to get on each other's nerves. The dwarf Sir Jeffrey was challenged to a duel, to which his antagonist brought a water squirt; the knight repaid this patronising insult by shooting him dead. Outside, the religious intensity of the struggle soon became a matter of personal safety to Henrietta Maria herself. The king was particularly downcast by the opprobrium directed against his consort which 'doth afflict me, that she should be compelled by my own subjects and those pretending to be Protestants to withdraw for her safety . . . [Her] merits would have served her for a protection among savage Indians. The fault is that she is my wife.'[1]

In a sign of diminished royal confidence, she was persuaded to leave Oxford and, heavily pregnant with her ninth child, she bade farewell to her husband at Abingdon in July 1644. It was the last time she was to see him.

Abroad again in France, Henrietta Maria was as politically active as her diminished status and gender permitted. Her efforts though sometimes lacked adroitness. Attempting to directly importune her nephew, the child-king Louis XIV, for his support she was rebuffed by an indignant French government for her interference in his minority. But the correspondence with her husband over the course of 1645 and during his incarceration by the Scots reveals a steely pragmatism in the face of Charles's determination to do nothing that would compromise his conscience. An almost mystical attachment to his Anglican faith was at the core of Charles's moral being. This was no exercise in mulish credulity; as a divinely anointed sovereign, the Church and its arrangement were central to the authority, prestige and patronage of a Christian monarch. From Oxford he had written 'the nature of Presbyterian government is to steal or force the crown from the king's head. For their chief maxim is . . . that all kings must submit to Christ's kingdom, of which they are the sole governors, the King having but a single and no negative voice in their assemblies, so that yielding to the Scots in this particular, I should both go against my conscience and ruin my crown.'[2]

The king's religious scruples also got in the way of organising support in Ireland. James Butler, the Marquis of Ormonde, had been holding up the royalist cause there since the outbreak of the rebellion. Aged thirty-six, he had previously been appointed lord lieutenant in 1644 and came from a line of 'Old English' aristocrats on whom the British state had traditionally relied to keep Ireland in a state of peace. A general of firm Protestant convictions, whose wisdom and resolution were later noted by Hyde, he loyally executed the king's strategy of buying time from the Catholic rebels in order to facilitate the transfer of an army back to the mainland of the British Isles. But, as the Confederacy was itself divided, these tactics lacked ambition and they inadvertently allowed an opportunity for the growing military ascendancy of Owen Roe O'Neill, kinsman of Sir Phelim O'Neill, leader of the 1641 Irish rebellion in Ulster and whose loyalty to the Crown was negligible. Yet Charles further complicated his strategy by using the Catholic Earl of Glamorgan to conduct secret negotiations with the Confederacy behind Ormonde's back. It would seem that the earl exceeded his brief; while Charles was happy to give a vague promise of religious toleration, he would not countenance any diminution of the position or property of the established Church in Ireland. Embarrassed by the discovery of his intrigues, the king was forced to repudiate his emissary.

Owen Roe O'Neill used the hiatus to pursue his military campaign against the Scottish Covenanter troops in Ulster, scoring a notable victory against them in June 1646, a month after the king had surrendered to the Scots at Newark. In one of the largest military engagements of the war in Ireland, the opposing forces engaged in a vicious fight at Benburb, a small settlement close to Armagh. Urged on by their priests and chieftains, the victorious Irish troops exacted a brutal revenge on the floundering Scottish troops for the blood their compatriots had shed at Philiphaugh nearly a year before. With Ormonde's own force uselessly adrift on a sea of prevarication and the royalist-inclined elements among the confederates spurned, Henrietta Maria scolded her husband: 'I am astonished that the Irish do not give themselves to some foreign king; you will force them to it at the last, seeing themselves offered in sacrifice.'[3] In the end, the impasse was broken by the papal nuncio to the confederates who denounced the accommodation with Ormonde and threatened any who adhered to it with excommunication. To Cardinal Rinuccini, the preservation of Charles's throne was of less importance than the defence of the Roman Catholic Church and the authority of its clergy.

As the year wore on with her trying to keep up the king's morale, Henrietta Maria's letters took on a tone of increasing exasperation with his evident lack of willingness to compromise on the religious question and his equivocation on the issue of control of the militia. She wrote again: 'Do you think that when I see you so resolute in the affair of the Bishops and so little in which concerns yourself and your posterity that I am not in great despair . . .?'[4] She instinctively understood that an accommodation with the Scots on anything other than their terms was unlikely to be achieved – after all, their fierce attachment to their model of Presbyterianism was the trigger for war in the first place. But Charles parried her arguments with a logic of his own 'unless religion be preserved, the Militia will not be much useful to the Crown . . . and certainly if the Pulpits teach not obedience (which never will be if Presbyterian government be absolutely established) the King will have but small comfort of the Militia'.[5]

Ensconced amongst those whom he hoped would change his fortunes, the king felt closer to events, and his awareness of the dissensions amongst his English and Scottish foes gave him, as he saw it, an opportunity to exploit. His letters show that he genuinely believed that the Scots would come to heel in the end, understanding that any established Church of whatever stripe needed the protection of the Crown against the forces of anarchy.

Much criticism has attached to Charles's sustained stubbornness over the course of his years in captivity and his failure to accept the variety of terms that were presented to him. The fairness of this critique rests on a reading of his personality but also upon the assumption that the terms offered to him were deliverable by their sponsors. Charles perceived both a lack of unity of purpose in the coalition assembled against him and that the entreaties of his captors reflected alarm that the English were deviating from their own religious agenda. For the Scots, the compromises required by the Kirk to maintain a harmony with their southern co-religionists were proving to be a strain. After much contentious debate, the Westminster Assembly had agreed a new *Directory for Public Worship* for the two realms to replace the Book of Common Prayer, although certain modifications were made to the Scottish version.

But there was a distinct whiff of repressive dogmatism. In a growing sign of intrusion into family life, the *Directory* dispensed with some of the ritual around infant baptism; now neither the traditional sign of the cross nor godparents were authorised. Life imprisonment was later ordained for any who publicly rejected infant baptism while death was prescribed for blasphemy which denied the Trinity. The Kirk was satisfied by the grim discipline but was far less happy with the English approach to Church governance. In particular they doubted the ordinance which made ecclesiastical courts subservient to parliament and the proposals for greater lay authority in the presbytery. The Kirk was also implacably opposed to even the most modest proposals for limited toleration of Protestant congregations outside the presbytery. But the attempted alignment of English religious practices with those north of the border further disrupted the old established Protestant Church south of it. Quite apart from the theological dislocations, during the course of the fighting over two dozen ordained clergy were killed, while scores more either fled or were turned out of their benefices. The growing intolerance was to add a large body of Anglicans to those independent congregations who were also unhappy with the determined advance of Presbyterian absolutism.

Thus the disruption of war hardened the opposition to the attempted reformation of religious manners by the Kirk and its allies. If Laud had stirred things up, the Presbyterians were hardly calming them down; indeed, they seemed to be continuing the assault. In response to the new *Directory*, numerous pamphlets had appeared on the vexatious issue of baptism. Just as serious, the dogmatism was a challenge to the freer spirits of the army. In his despatch to parliament after the victory at Naseby, and again after the capture of Bristol, Cromwell had publicly championed the right of his soldiers to enjoy their own religious consciences undisturbed. Moreover, he asserted that this was what they were fighting for. These notions were far too radical to those of Presbyterian persuasion in the House of Commons, which declined to publish what appeared to have the makings of a manifesto. With the Independents both literally and metaphorically on the march, the Presbyterian divine Thomas Edwards published *Gangraena*. Using a suitably graphic title to style the infection he perceived in society, he castigated the army as a hotbed of sectaries and subversives. He went on to deliver a broadside against those 'mechaniks taking upon themselves to preach and baptize, as Smiths, Taylors, Shoemakers, Pedlars, Weavers etc. There are also some women preachers in our times.'[6] To Edwards, the involvement of females in anything other than a passive role would have been the final straw, and deserving of special condemnatory emphasis.

But the sects had access to presses too and attracted support from observers inclined to toleration of heterodoxy. William Walwyn deprecated Edwards' condemnation as an 'extream fury' that was neither motivated by theological rigour nor by a search for truth. Instead, he accused the Puritan of pique. The sects, he argued 'spoile you not only of your gaine, but of your glory and domination, things dearer to you than your life: of your glory, in denying your ministry to be successive from the Apostles: of your domination, by denying unto you any more authority to judge of doctrines or discipline than any other sort of Christian men.'[7]

A middle-aged member of London's large commercial class, Walwyn was one of the more attractive characters of the period in that he had a depth of Christian social conscience that marked him out among his peers. The grandson of a Bishop of Hereford, he had made his fortune as a merchant-adventurer. In his tract *The Power of Love* printed in 1643 he had referred to the poor as 'imprisoned Christians' and had asked how the wealthy could be godly yet show such indifference to the lack of means or even sustenance in others. He was particularly critical of the doctrine of the Elect, believing rather that 'all men might be saved and come to the knowledge of the truth'. As an authentically Christian spirit who was dismayed by the physical and moral oppression he perceived in society, he was to become a leading philosopher of the anti-war sentiment that had been seen in the phenomenon of local Clubmen and which later coalesced in the Leveller movement.

Charles's reluctance to accede to the proposals presented to him was not illogical in view of the divergences in the coalition assembled against him. Suspicious of the peace moves mediated by the French, parliament had already ordered the public burning of terms submitted by the Scottish commissioners when it was further aggravated by the sleight of hand that had spirited away the monarch to the north country.

Charles may have felt that he had given a significant sign of his willingness to end the civil war in Scotland by ordering Montrose to disband his forces, but despite the arguments of Argyll and the earnest sermons and rebukes of the divines, he would neither take the Covenant nor would he sanction Presbyterianism. Growing impatient and fearful that separate peace negotiations were undermining the whole basis of the Solemn League, Argyll persuaded his colleagues to accept the terms that were drawn up by the English. But the latter had by now been emboldened by the surrender of the king's capital at Oxford in June and the collapse of organised royalist resistance. Accordingly, parliament packed off the Earl of Pembroke to present what became known as the Newcastle Propositions. These were far less a basis for enduring peace than non-negotiable terms for unconditional surrender presented by a victor who was not inclined to be magnanimous.

The practical and political restraints on the king augured a new constitutional configuration: all major offices of state and the judges were to be nominated by parliament and control of the militia was to pass from the king for twenty years. The first change was to be permanent while the second allowed parliament to resume control of the militia during periods of national danger. At a stroke, the king was relieved of the means to a government appointed by him and of the instruments to give ultimate effect to his laws and policies. Parliament was to immediately assert these new arrangements by taking responsibility for the crushing of the rebels in Ireland. The religious terms were familiar enough but arguably pointless given Charles's known scruples. The king was to sign the Covenant, episcopacy was to be abolished in England as in Scotland, and religion was to be reformed across the whole of the British Isles and Ireland along Presbyterian lines. A strong current of vindictiveness ran throughout: a large number of named royalists were exempted from pardon while 'delinquency' would be punished by expropriation of no less than two-thirds of the offender's property. Harsh measures were to be enforced against Roman Catholics, with the children of any 'recusants' to be compulsorily educated in the Protestant faith. In a further act of aggrandisement and ideological supremacy, everyone throughout the polity was to take the oath of the Covenant. A desire for wider civic reconciliation was entirely absent as the authors focused solely on the aims of those constituencies which had directed the fight against the king.

As an added but unspoken incentive to the sovereign, his foes now had three of his children in their custody. The Pembroke mission was cordially received by Charles but when it was pointed out that the terms were final, he rebuked the earl's presumption. Maintaining a dignified equanimity, the king did not however spurn the propositions on the spot but agreed to give them his full consideration. In the longueurs, his wife maintained her watch from her modest court at Saint Germain-en-Laye. On easier terms now with Cardinal Mazarin, her letters also showed her trying hard to ensure that she was joined by her elder son. Even by the colourful standards of his ancestors, the adolescence of the Prince of Wales was unusual. Now aged fifteen, he already physically towered over his parents. His face more closely resembled that of his grandfather Henri IV with its rich and deep pigmentation, prominent nose, full lips and heavily lidded eyes which partially obscured a look of amused intelligence. In temperament too he seemed more influenced by his French blood-line; unlike his grave and somewhat humourless father he was affable and more easily amused. He later came to perfect the Stuarts' apparent talent for dissembling, although his sunnier disposition seemed to make his intrigues and backtracking less threatening.

Aged twelve, he had been present with his father at Edgehill and later held titular command of the royalist forces in the south-west. As Fairfax closed in, he managed to escape from the perimeter held by Hopton at Falmouth in early 1646 and sailed to the Scilly Isles. He was pursued by a parliamentary naval squadron which was fortuitously scattered by a storm, allowing the young prince to escape with his retinue to Jersey.[8] In the atmosphere of danger and excitement, the young Charles seemed to relish all the attention and came quickly to realise that he was to fulfil a special role if his dynasty were to be preserved. The importance of keeping royal feet on British soil possibly accounts for his sojourn in the islands off the coast, but also showed the reluctance of his advisers to expose a seemingly impressionable youth to the Catholic machinations of the French establishment amongst which his mother had taken residence. It was, however, more important to Henrietta Maria that the head of the family try not to escape overseas if an acceptable compromise with his Scottish captors could be secured.

Charles I spent the summer and autumn of 1646 mulling over the Newcastle Propositions and prevaricating when pressed. Robert Baillie lamented that 'We are here by the King's madness, in a terrible plunge.'[9] As Charles was unmoved by the ambiguous charm of the wily Argyll and the earnest prayers and rebukes of the divines, the nobles backed the Duke of Hamilton to see if he could persuade the sovereign to accept terms. A youthful yet ranking aristocrat who had briefly been third in line to the throne following the death of the first royal infant in 1629, Hamilton had been indulged with positions and titles. But he proved an inadequate representative of the Stuart interest in the moves that preceded the Bishops' Wars of 1639 and 1640, and in the later struggle. The king's disappointment in him was such that by the time he turned up at the Oxford court after the English war had been in progress for well over a year, he was locked up. His reputation sullied by suspicion of treachery, he was released from St Michael's Mount by the forces under Fairfax and once again found himself before a sceptical king.

In time Charles was prepared to cede temporary control of the militia, but with his conscience piqued by the memory of his earlier sacrifice of the loyal Earl of Strafford, whom he had sent to the scaffold in 1641 after he was condemned to death by parliament, he would not countenance further retribution against his friends and supporters. However, he was at the last able to persuade himself to accept a trial run of a Presbyterian settlement for three years. His concession was an anticlimax which failed even to win over those within the Scottish negotiating team who were sympathetic of his predicament. One observed, 'It has ever been the King's fault, to grant his peoples desyres be bitts, and soe late, that he ever lost his thanks.'[10] The royalist Hyde was reluctantly to come to the same conclusion.

To his wife, none of these concessions made much sense – the king was abandoning the one instrument by which he could enforce his authority while she was sure that the three-year trial period would be used against him at its termination. Far better to accept the religious agenda in full and retain his Protestant beliefs – in her view, his personal faith was hardly the key issue. Had not her father Henri

Le Grand abjured his own religion entirely to secure the French Crown? Spurning his conscience in as loving a way as her frustration permitted she could not, however, conceal her bitterness towards those whom she regarded as their true enemies, writing that 'As long as Parliament lasts, you are not King; and as for me I shall not again set my foot in England.'[11]

But eventually Charles wore out his captors and in an astonishing ceding of the initiative, the Scots gave up. With their soldiers use-lessly left hanging around in the muddy fields about Hadrian's Wall and the fragile hospitality of their north country hosts exhausted, they succumbed to the royal obduracy. In a heated debate, the idea of bringing an un-Covenanted monarch north of the Tweed was flatly rejected and rather than impose a settlement on him at the point of a sword, they decided to go home.[12] Robert Baillie well expressed the feeling of anxious disappointment amongst the Covenanters and wrote 'The King, all his lyfe, has loved trinketting naturally and is thought to be much in that action now, with all parties, for the imminent hazard of all. Our greatest fear is that the malignant[s] . . . have drawn him to the Independents for the undoeing of Scotland and the Presbyterian party here.'[13]

There was anxiety too that their continuing association with the king might provoke a military reaction from their fractious English allies, which they were ill-prepared to parry.

For in truth, Scottish resources had been ground down by the war and financial considerations played a major part in their decision. With their treasury empty, there followed a lengthy haggle with London. The bill for what they could justifiably claim was decisive support was invoiced at well over £1 million. The Scots had ensured a preponderance of military might and had thrown a *cordon sanitaire* from the Solway Firth to the Wash that the royalists had been unable to penetrate. Their strategic impact had at the very least prevented any chance of Charles winning the war. They had been motivated from the first by a desire to protect and then evangelise the polity of John Knox; but now in further consideration of the apparently luke-warm coincidence of interest with their English allies of convenience, of the militant divisions evident at home and the obduracy of the king, they decided to cut their losses.

The Scots finally agreed a figure of £400,000, to be paid in instalments, an amount which their royal prisoner considered derisory. Charles was to draw a number of conclusions from this *démarche*. He correctly inferred that his opponents believed the monarchy remained absolutely central to any settlement and to the re-establishment of peace and good order. He was thus determined to exact a high price for the legitimacy that he would give to any religious and political arrangement he was inclined to favour. But in the rapidly shifting political conditions he overestimated his personal significance and seemed to think that principled obduracy was more becoming of a sovereign than adroit manoeuvre. In his dogged belief that he was indispensable, his natural predilection for secrecy and dissembling fatally undermined residual confidence in the royal institution and hastened his own end.

The withdrawal of the Scottish army of the Solemn League proved in retrospect to be the high watermark of political influence for that loose, but largest, grouping in the English parliament whose agenda had been dominated by their Presbyterian disposition and coloured by their growing anxiety at the religious orientation of the New Model Army. In the wake of that army's victories, the so-called Independents achieved greater authority. These were MPs who had argued for a more vigorous prosecution of the war and who were distinguished too by their religious orientation which favoured congregational independence. Their numbers in the House of Commons had been augmented after Naseby by the decision to hold elections for those seats left vacant by death, absenteeism and the exclusion of active royalists. The legitimacy of this move had arguably been made easier by the decision of the king to adjourn his own 'mongrel parliament' at Oxford in the spring of 1645. The election of new members took place in an environment where the rhythms of the traditional elites and the familiar patterns of patronage had been disrupted by the war. It brought to parliament men in their late thirties or early forties, of whom a number were sons of knights or senior officials. Many were of humbler rank than their predecessors, and did not necessarily share the predominant religious outlook and prejudices of the House of Commons which they joined. Furthermore, some, like the new member for Aylesbury, Thomas Scot, were also inclined to a more adventurous constitutional reform than were the Presbyterians.

Among the cohort was the newly reinstated MP for Berkshire, Henry Marten. Born in 1602, the son of a wealthy magistrate with lands in Berkshire and Oxfordshire, a painting of him shows a dark and somewhat insolent-looking man seemingly on the verge of uttering an expletive. Denounced by Charles as an 'ugly rascal and whoremaster', Marten was a lawyer whose nominal Protestantism did not get in the way of a fairly colourful private life, and he spent his periods outside parliament being pursued by his creditors. He was not a man who was easily impressed by consensus among his peers. No religious hypocrite, he advocated toleration on the grounds that Christ had not minded 'tares amongst the corn'. In the same vein he had been contemptuous of the motives of the divines at the Westminster Assembly who would 'fain take Christ out of his throne that themselves might sit in it'.[14] Beside a biting manner that passed for wit, he did however have a compassionate side, which saw him speak up on behalf of defeated royalist opponents and later champion the plight of prisoners of war. His republican political views were more decided still and he had opined to Hyde that 'I do not think one man wise enough to govern us all.'[15] For views 'abhorred by the whole nation', he was briefly locked up in the Tower of London by order of the House in 1643, and on his release took part in the fighting by energetic command of the Berkshire trained bands. Restored to his seat in the House of Commons in January 1646, Marten was joined in sympathy by his fellow lawyer Edmund Ludlow (the son of Sir Henry Ludlow), who sat for one of the two prestigious county constituencies of Wiltshire. Like his father, who had been in the van of the opposition to the king's personal rule, Ludlow was an articulate exponent of a more radical political agenda. He was also a Baptist (which put him out of sympathy with his Presbyterian colleagues) and a firm believer in the separation of Church and State.

Also elected during this period was the Member for Cardiff, Algernon Sydney, the great-nephew of the Elizabethan soldier-poet Sir Philip Sidney. Although described by a contemporary as having a 'rough and boisterous temper' he also possessed a powerful intellect, and his later *Discourses* on the subjects of liberty and government is considered one of the seminal works of the age.[16] Having fought at Marston Moor aged twenty-two and been wounded, he declined the offer of a commission at the inception of the New Model Army on account of a sore leg and took no further military part. Cast from a similarly aristocratic mould was Thomas Chaloner, who, like Sydney, was resolute for the prosecution of the war and who also became a convinced republican. To this growing but loose coalition of freer spirits were added the soldiers Thomas Harrison and Thomas Rainsborough. Harrison was the son of a butcher who had become mayor of Newcastle-under-Lyme. His religious views had a millenarian and apocalyptic flavour, an aspect of his piety that was widely shared and accentuated by the seemingly epochal nature of the wars. Something of an extrovert, which added charisma to his religious views, he had been one of the more able officers to make the transfer from the Earl of Manchester's Eastern Association to the New Model Army. In company with Ludlow and Marten, he was part of the growing band of the more radically inclined that was altering the demographic of the House of Commons. Rainsborough was the offspring of an admiral in the fleet built up by Charles I before the civil wars. The son joined the parliamentary navy and held various commands before achieving the rank of colonel in the New Model Army. The happy versatility implied by his military career was, however, overshadowed by his overbearingly zealous temperament. The unfortunate impression he gave to subordinates was reinforced by a somewhat incoherent manner: he was later to be on the receiving end of mutinies by both his soldiers and his naval ratings.

The military cadre in parliament was augmented too by a number of personalities who were more closely associated with Cromwell, like the legally trained and deeply pious Charles Fleetwood, another son of a knight who was appointed as a regimental commander in 1644. Another was Henry Ireton, who was born into a Nottinghamshire family of Nonconformist minor gentry. Following his cool perform-ance in the Naseby campaign, he was elected MP for Appleby in Yorkshire in October 1645, when in his mid-thirties. Behind the elfin and friendly face of his portrait lay a character that was intensely religious, and the diarist Lucy Hutchinson noted him as 'having had an education in the strictest way of Godliness and being a very grave and solid person'.[17] He was also determinedly ambitious; in the distinctly unromantic setting of the siege of Oxford, Ireton had wooed Cromwell's daughter Bridget and then married her. His mili-tary duties as Commissary General restricted the impact he was able to make in the House of Commons. Yet outside, Ireton's character (which combined Puritan sensibility with legal training and mili-tary experience) was to produce one of the most influential political thinkers in the New Model Army. The contemporary propagandist and turncoat royalist Marchamont Nedham called him the 'penman general of the Army'.[18]

The growing weight of the Independents in the House of Commons was the inverse of the declining impact of the House of Lords, whose numbers now sitting in regular attendance at Westminster scarcely reached two dozen. Although this small cadre remained politically active and influential, the prestige and authority of the class as a whole had waned. The Self-Denying Ordinance and the formation of the New Model Army had signified that the nobil-ity were no longer trusted well enough to lead. The duration of the civil wars meant that it was also harder to remain agnostic as to the conflicts' purposes: the suffering and cost meant that a return to the *status quo ante* with the apex of the old elite restored was increasingly doubted. With the victories of the New Model Army, the descent of the English nobility from its position just below the pinnacle of the state became palpable. If nothing else, Naseby, Langport and Chester had reinforced the assumption behind the Self-Denying Ordinance that rich blue blood was not a prerequisite of military success. As the chaplain Richard Baxter later observed, the army was 'partly the envy and partly the scorn of the nobility'. Even peers of the royalist side had already seen the writing on the wall – at Oxford loyalists such as the Earls of Sussex and of Arundel had entreated the king to come to terms to salvage his realm and the old order.

In mirror image, others on the parliamentary side such as the Earls of Bedford and Holland had come to doubt their earlier opposition to the king for similar reasons. In an echo from the trough into which this class had descended, the Earl of Essex died in September 1646. Huffily disdainful of the creeping democratisation and religious indiscipline he observed in the New Model Army and in the conduct of the war, he had been the leading aristocratic patron of the Presbyterian interest and the peace party in both Houses. Parliament voted the extraordinary sum of £5,000 to observe the obsequies and his funeral was a magnificent state occasion at Westminster Abbey. After his unsuccessful attempt to improve the aesthetic of siege conditions at Basing House, Inigo Jones was on better form for his new clients and designed an elaborate catafalque for the event. An effigy of the earl was erected upon it, resplendent in parliamentary robes atop his soldier's uniform. After weeks of awed and respectful inspection by members of the London public, the figure was pulled to pieces by an apparently crazed rustic from Dorset who objected to the idolatry. It was an apt symbol of the zeitgeist.

This was far from the only attack on the elites in that year. Richard Overton was a young intellectual who had received a poor man's degree from Cambridge University. He was a skilled wordsmith as well as theologian *manqué* and had already produced a number of pamphlets under the pseudonym 'Martin Marpriest', a sly and ironic reference to the Puritan Marprelate tracts of the previous century. Overton challenged the perceived tyranny of the Presbyterian agenda and seemed to question the whole doctrine of predestination. To the consternation of Richard Baxter, his pamphlets were much appreciated by the soldiers of the army where 'being dispersed in their quarters, they had such books to read when they had none to contradict them'.[19] Temporarily secure in his anonymity, Overton would have enjoyed too the angrily unfocused denunciations of William Prynne, who was ever alert to any deviation from the true Puritan path. In the summer of 1646 however, he took up the cause of John Lilburne.

'Freeborn John', the younger son of a distinguished Durham gentleman, was one of the more extraordinary figures of the extra-parliamentary political agitation during this period. Before the onset of the civil wars he had become (like Prynne) something of an exemplar for all opponents of arbitrary rule by his defiance of the Star Chamber, the principal institution of royal absolutism. He seemed to have a martyr complex and continued to noisily proselytise his disobedience despite successive and severe physical punishments and internments in gaol. He enlisted in the parliamentary army, was captured by the royalists and defied the attempt to try him for treason. It might have all ended there but he was released in a prisoner exchange and the Earl of Essex was sufficiently impressed to offer him £300 for his stout-heartedness in the parliamentary cause. But Lilburne was neither a man to accept favours nor one to submit easily to authority. Spurning the earl's magnanimity he took a commission in the forces of the Earl of Manchester and fell to quarrelling with his superiors. There, his antics attracted the attention of Cromwell, who adopted him as an exemplar of the principled but otherwise unpaid soldiery.

Yet Lilburne's mind seemed to have been on an even higher calling. He refused to take the Covenant on the grounds that it denied freedom of conscience, and resigned from the army to pursue a pamphlet campaign against the Presbyterians. In any other time or context, Lilburne's noisy, persistent and single-minded refusal to conform to legitimate authority might have marked him out as a vexatious bore, but his opinions about the abuses of power and his apparent sincerity attracted more thoughtful dissenters, including Overton. Not content with an abstract quarrel about Church governance, Lilburne decided to widen the range of targets for his indignation by publicly denouncing in print the alleged judicial tyranny of the House of Lords, a theme that was to continue to colour the agenda of radicals. A diminished band of their lordships politely but firmly summoned him to appear before them, but Lilburne refused to recognise them, objecting to their role as both judge and jury, and denied their authority to try him as a free-born man.

Notwithstanding this, the peers decided there was no alternative but to incarcerate him, whereupon Overton supported him with a tract of his own, *An Alarum to the House of Lords*. Having broken cover, the author was gaoled in his turn but this did not seem to inhibit his output, and pamphlets such as *A Defiance Against All Arbitrary Usurpations* continued to pour forth. The truculence of the men was more than matched by the heroism of their wives. In addition to running their households on intermittent and insufficient funds, both Mary Overton and Elizabeth Lilburne sustained the radical impetus, organising the printing of their husbands' views, and were beaten up, ridiculed and imprisoned for their loyalty. In early 1647 Mary Overton, by now heavily pregnant, was dragged off to Bridewell where she miscarried. She was held without trial for over six months.

4

'Against all arbitrary power, violence and oppression'

Holdenby House

'Twixt kings and subjects there's this mighty odds,
Subjects are taught by men; kings by gods.

Robert Herrick, Hesperides

While Lilburne and Overton were languishing at Newgate and in the Tower, and their wives suffering every indignity, their sovereign was enjoying the apparent change in his fortunes. The Scots' withdrawal from England was not a happy parting and, in a sign of mistrust, New Model units under Philip Skippon rapidly moved into the areas vacated by their erstwhile comrades-in-arms. The Earls of Denbigh and Pembroke returned to Newcastle to take the king into the care of parliament at the end of January 1647, and his progress south was a far grander affair than that accorded him northwards by the Scots eight months earlier. Large crowds gathered en route out of curiosity, but there was cheering too; the snowdrops were starting to burst through and peace seemed to be at hand. Sir Thomas Fairfax met him at Nottingham, where Charles had raised his standard five years before. It was the second time the men had met, the first being when the Yorkshire knight had tried unsuccessfully to petition the monarch at one of the largest popular gatherings that preceded the war in England on Heworth Moor. Now, the lord general greeted his royal opponent with a degree of well-judged deference but there was no further elucidation of the Newcastle Propositions, which remained the only peace terms on the table.

The king was taken to Holdenby House in Northamptonshire, a truly enormous construction of the Elizabethan age. Bought by James I, it was later mostly pulled down and today the only remains of the original property commissioned by Sir Christopher Hatton are two magnificent ornamental arches in the adjacent grounds. The king was quartered with several more degrees of civility than he had experienced on Tyneside; he was allowed access to his Anglican chaplains and the local Puritan notables were most cordial in their welcome. His movements too were relatively unsupervised, notwithstanding that it was well known that he had tried to escape by sea from his Scottish captors at the end of the previous December. He continued to hunt, and some semblance of court ceremony was maintained. But to all intents and purposes, Charles was now shorn of his practical power if not his mystique, and parliament had other more pressing issues.

The one matter which nearly all members could agree upon was the heavy and continued financial burden of war. The Assessment was a tax earmarked solely for the military – a neat irony given the king's hypothecated levy of Ship Money had stirred up so much trouble for his regime. Furthermore, the overall burden of taxation had risen almost sevenfold from the early 1630s at a time when prices had also been rising fast, exacerbated by a succession of poor harvests during the years of armed struggle. The prerogative taxes which had been used by the king had been replaced by parliament with excise duties which were much more closely correlated with overall economic activity. The customs duties also made a contribution and in this respect parliament's holding of the capital, a major European entrepôt, was critical, as was its control over most of the major ports. London was also important as a centre of finance rivalling that of Amsterdam and the king's opponents were heavily reliant on the loans that were syndicated and advanced by the city. But trade had been seriously disrupted, despite the best efforts of the navy, and commerce in and around British waters was plagued by piracy and the interdiction of privateers authorised by other Continental powers. With the disruption of tax collection outside the capital, London came to understand that it was bearing a disproportionate burden of the cost of the war. The many tradespeople who had made a living from the activities of the court and royal regime before it decamped to Oxford were particularly suffering from a reduction in their circumstances.

To bridge the gap between income and military expenditure, those 'delinquents' opposed to the parliamentary regime, and wealthy institutions that were now deemed redundant, were targeted for their cash. After a lengthy voyage through both Houses, the ordinance abolishing episcopacy in England, Wales and Ireland had at last been brought to harbour in the autumn of 1646, the final impetus for enactment being the need to find the money to pay the Scots, for which the land of the established Church was now earmarked. Yet there was simply not enough to go around. At the conclusion of the fighting, the arrears outstanding to the troops south of the border were approaching the sum negotiated to pay off those north of it. Some units had not been remunerated for nearly a year, and rank seemed to give no precedence in the queue – Fairfax's father, Ferdinando, who had played such a pivotal role for parliament in the north country, was owed over £11,000. The now mostly idle troops settled down to garrison duties as they awaited payment and further orders, and thus they continued to burden towns and local communities – the vouchers issued by parliament throughout the war in exchange for services and supplies were now valued scarcely higher than the worthless scrip issued by the royalists. Even more oppressively, households and whole communities were subjected to the demands for 'free quarter' from troops unable to pay their way as they waited for remuneration. Popular petitions started to appear calling for disbandment. Under the circumstances, the need to reduce substantially the military establishment was logical and was a mostly consensual view amongst MPs.

In the past, the politicians would have been able to rely on a high rate of desertion – even after Naseby thousands of parliamentary troops had drifted back home, a recurrent practice for which the New Model Army had been formed precisely to counter. But in the early spring of 1647, such expectations were to be confounded by a determination to be paid by the soldiers who had risked their lives over successive years. There was also a pressing need to raise a well-motivated force to deal with the flaring of the crisis in Ireland. The defeat of the Scottish army in Ulster had brought O'Neill's forces to the gates of Dublin. Ormonde held out but in view of the condition to which his royal master had fallen he now wisely passed the Irish parcel back to parliament in London. This was the responsibility of a subcommittee of the Committee of Both Kingdoms, now the de facto government with the king in its hands. Meeting at Derby House, it was the focal point for co-ordinating political action by the Presbyterian grouping in parliament and included the MPs Sir William Waller and Sir Philip Stapleton, who had commanded the bodyguard of the Earl of Essex. The leaders on the floor of the House of Commons included Denzil Holles, the recently elected Edward Massey, who had been appointed to command parliament's forces in the West Country in 1644 and Sir John Clotworthy, a religious zealot from Ulster who had led the ferocious assault on Henrietta Maria's undefended chapel. Their collaboration took on greater urgency with the departure of the practical bulwark of their agenda, the Scottish army.

Yet the MPs seemed unable or unwilling to make the mental transition from being rebels against the regime to masters of it. Rather than prepare for peace by carefully managing the army's expectations, mobilising a force sufficient for Ireland and planning for a general military drawdown having met the obligation to settle arrears, the Presbyterian faction instead approached the continued existence of the New Model Army as a constitutional and religious threat that they were determined, at the very least, to neutralise. Incautiously, they invigorated their campaign by trying to subvert Fairfax, the one man whose loyalty on the basis of probability and past behaviour could reasonably have been assumed. Observing that military office no longer seemed to be any bar to becoming an MP, 'Black Tom' offered himself for election but was mysteriously thwarted. His reputation with his parliamentary colleagues had suffered a diminution the previous year when he had urged the disbandment of Edward Massey's forces. With no desire to needlessly prolong the suffering of war, Fairfax had been alarmed by the indiscipline shown by Massey's troops in the West Country at the very moment of victory and as Fairfax had been trying to defuse the agitation of the Clubmen movement. Specifically, Fairfax was angered by Massey's apparent breach of the terms that had ensured the surrender of the royalists at Worcester.

But Massey had exercised a command deemed to be independent of the New Model Army, and his allies in parliament were not inclined to abrogate it. His honour and that of the wider army at stake, Fairfax addressed the unexpected ambiguity in his authority by ordering disbandment anyway; it was a rare false move by this reliably thoughtful soldier. His opponents were affronted by this display of soldierly initiative and later tried to have him removed from his command by proposing he be replaced by Richard Graves, another officer of more obvious Presbyterian outlook who had been commissioned into the New Model Army at its inception. It was a preposterous motion given Fairfax's prestige and Graves's level of seniority. It was, nevertheless, only narrowly defeated by 159 votes to 147 when debated in the Commons in February 1647.

At this crucial juncture, which thereafter saw the basis of trust between the New Model Army and parliament break down irretrievably, both Fairfax and Cromwell succumbed to illness. The latter was incapacitated for a number of weeks by an 'impostume of the head', and Fairfax by a poorly healed shoulder injury which was complicated by a recurrence of the painful gout and gastric ailments he had suffered from early adulthood. The House of Commons had already passed a motion for disbandment without arrears for all units not earmarked for service in Ireland when petitions started to come in from units demanding back pay, provision for war widows and indemnification for actions carried out during the fighting. There was also widespread reluctance to volunteer for service in Ireland on the vague terms provided and the perception grew that parliament was trying to divide the army by getting a portion of it out of the way by sending it overseas.

Frightened now by the stirrings of a full-scale mutiny, Holles led the Commons to pass a 'Declaration of Dislike' which attributed treasonable intent on the part of the petitioners and branded them as enemies of the people. The Presbyterians also took advantage of the debilitation of both Fairfax and Cromwell with the proposed appointment of Philip Skippon as army commander, with Massey taking Cromwell's job as Lieutenant General of Horse. The Declaration and the blatant attempts to divide the loyalties of the soldiers were avoidable and unnecessary provocations, and Fairfax rallied himself sufficiently to call a gathering of over 200 officers at Saffron Walden who presented a united front when the commissioners despatched by parliament tried to suborn them individually with offers of promotion and pay. They declared their allegiance by refusing to serve in Ireland unless commanded by Fairfax and Cromwell.

After a series of rowdy debates, the House of Commons passed another motion for disbandment, but this time sweetened it with an offer of £70,000 in payment of arrears, a small fraction of the amount owed. The high command seemed disinclined to press such a poor offer on their men but the hotter heads in the Commons now had the bit between their teeth. A force of over 2,000 men under the command of Colonel Michael Jones had been successfully despatched to Ireland and the MPs now saw no reason to stand by the earlier offer; on 25 May the Commons ordered general demobilisation. Apart from the troops standing by to follow Jones, all other units were to be disbanded individually beginning in the first week of June without payment before they did so. For good measure, the Self-Denying Ordinance was dusted off and New Model officers who were also MPs were presented with a choice: they could retain their commissions or their seats, but not both.

The rupture in the parliamentary ranks meant custody of the
king was critical to each side – he was, in the words of Fairfax, the
'Golden Ball cast between the two parties'.[1] The subsequent seizure
of Charles at Holdenby has often been presented as an unauthorised
coup by junior officers, the success of which the senior New Model
commanders were then minded to exploit. Cornet Joyce, a former
tailor, was a well-regarded subaltern and one of the 'agitators', a small
cadre that had emerged from the soldiery to articulate the justifiable
administrative and legal demands of their comrades-in-arms. Joyce
arrived at the Elizabethan monstrosity in the company of a large
body of 500 soldiers, having secured the arsenal at Oxford before-
hand. He had also prepared a report to be despatched to Cromwell,
Fleetwood and Sir Arthur Hesilrige, all of them MPs, on successful
completion of the mission. The operation thus appeared to have been
carefully planned but reflected some doubt as to whether the small
garrison in charge of the king would resist, or if the sovereign himself
would decline to accompany Joyce. The commander of the troops
at Holdenby had a rank and authority that far exceeded that of the
cornet, but the overwhelming display of force nullified his verbal
bluster. It was, however, the king who showed the most sangfroid
and self-possession. Having kept the new arrivals waiting all night,
the following morning Charles went out to meet them. Standing in
front of the heavily armed and vizored cavalrymen on their powerful
mounts, he was not intimidated but calmly asked by what authority
the junior officer acted. Joyce was momentarily flummoxed by his
desire to get a move on and his obvious reluctance to reveal the source
of his (unwritten) orders. Struggling to get his by now bored and
frisky horse under control, he answered by gesturing to the soldiers
behind him. 'It is as fair a commission and as well written as I have
seen a commission written in my life,' was the king's ironic response
and then he commanded that the troopers respect his sacred royal
person before climbing purposefully into his carriage.[2]

He was escorted to Childerley Hall, a short distance to the
north-west of Cambridge and was met by Fairfax (who kissed the
outstretched royal hand) and Cromwell, the first time the latter

had come face to face with the king. With the main body of the army drawn up at Newmarket, Charles in their possession and the Scottish army out of the way, there seemed little point in waiting for further initiatives from the antagonistic politicians. Cromwell's son-in-law, Ireton, now emerged as an influential political figure within the military, drawing up a *Solemn Engagement of the Army* which formally brought together all the issues for which the 'agitators' had been demanding satisfaction and accompanied it with an oath of solidarity. A General Council of the Army was created which was composed of the senior officers plus two junior officers and two other ranks from each regiment. Its president was James Berry, a New Model officer of humble origin from Shropshire who had served with distinction. In an attempt to identify those most responsible for the crisis in the relations between parliament and the army, articles calling for suspension were drawn up against eleven MPs who were judged to have shown the most hostility towards the New Model Army: Holles, Stapleton and Clotworthy were all identified, as were stalwarts of the parliamentary cause John Glyn and Walter Long, who had acted as a whip for the Presbyterian vote in the Commons. Both Massey and Waller appeared on the list too, their past military contribution nullified by their connivance with the civilians.

Ireton also had the ambition and intellectual sensibility to conclude that something else besides the *Solemn Engagement of the Army* was required to articulate the reasons why the English soldiers had fought over five weary years. The amount of blood and turmoil demanded it. The political consciousness of the troops had been stirred by the paper war, which had been fought just as vigorously as that by the armies in the field. It was an age where there was the greatest of respect for the written word and not just for the Bible; one of the first acts of Fairfax following the surrender of Oxford had been to place a strong guard on the Bodleian Library to prevent damage or looting. The conflict arguably witnessed the birth of a national press with the royalist *Mercurius Aulicus* competing against *Mercurius Britannicus* to provide news and highly coloured, frequently entertaining and ribald propaganda. The issuance of pamphlets rocketed over the period and the Thomason Collection in the British Library contains over 20,000 items. These generated a heightened level of religious and political debate, and complemented unauthorised preaching which had come back into its own following its attempted suppression by both Laud and, in their turn, the Presbyterians.

The political and religious temper of the army was undergoing change, although in aggregate it was still far from revolutionary. The abatement of the fighting had seen a subtle alteration in the composition of the middle and lower ranks of the officer corps. Those with responsibilities elsewhere and the means to wait for their outstanding pay had slowly started to hand in their commissions. Presbyterian orientation and obedience to the widespread civic desire for disbandment may also have played a part. In many cases, they were succeeded by their seconds-in-command. This left a more concentrated cadre of men which saw the army as a way of life and a bringer of status, among them John Okey, the colonel who had commanded the dragoons at Naseby, William Goffe who was later to achieve success in Scotland and Thomas Pride, a former drayman and brewer who later gave his name to one of the seminal political events of the period, the notorious Pride's Purge. The way of the soldier also continued to attract those men of more radical religious persuasion such as Nathaniel Rich and Richard Overton's brother, Robert.

These men and the professional soldiers like them were, in Ireton's view, more deserving of recognition than just an up-to-date pay packet. The lord general was minded to be supportive and so was brought forth *A Declaration from Sir Thomas Fairfax and the Army*. As a fundamental it stated a right 'To assert and vindicate the just power, and Rights of this Kingdom in Parliament for those common ends premised against all arbitrary power, violence and oppression and against all particular parties or interests whatsoever.'

The document also contained some thoughtful proposals for an updating of the constitutional architecture: a maximum duration was to be set for biennial parliamentary terms and the sizes of the constituencies were to be in better proportion to their contribution to national taxation. There was a far more conciliatory tone than in the Newcastle Propositions: religious Nonconformists of Protestant persuasion were not to suffer disabilities, royalists were to be treated with a degree of leniency and an Act of Oblivion was proposed to end 'the distinction of parties'. More pertinently still was the assertion that the New Model Army was not just a tribe of hired mercenaries but the armed wing of the godly fight for liberty. Although authorised by parliament, the *Declaration* hinted at the army as a free agent. To Ireton, the officer corps was to be central to any settlement, not just an adjunct to it.

However, to a large grouping of the political class at Westminster, the rebellion against parliament's authority by an army contaminated by sects was plain. Furthermore, the constitutional challenge of the attempted impeachment of eleven leading members recalled the worst provocations of the king's despotism. With Fairfax refusing to disband, the New Model Army was seen as a profound threat to the state, and the Presbyterian grouping moved to shore up its position in London. The Committee of Safety was revived and actions were taken to secure control of the London-trained bands under the command of Waller and Massey. This was not a negligible force and, when fully deployed, nearly matched in size that of the New Model Army. The capital's authorities were of a reliably Presbyterian persuasion and propaganda was disseminated which attempted to discredit Fairfax's soldiers. In the febrile atmosphere, some officers were roughed up. In Yorkshire however, their attempts to split the forces under the command of their collaborator Sydenham Poyntz from their colleagues in the New Model Army failed. The 'agitators' amongst the units there declared solidarity with the troops in the south and Poyntz was arrested by soldiers stationed at Pontefract. Fairfax moved swiftly to replace him with a reliable and energetic young officer, John Lambert and the kidnappers of the former commander were given £30.

The stage was set for a showdown, as became clear to the king, shortly to be quartered in some style at Hampton Court. There, his interlocutors were not the wearisomely high-minded and long-winded divines of the Kirk but the seemingly pragmatic Cromwell and Ireton assisted by Sir John Berkeley, a royalist who was nonetheless trusted as an intermediary. No longer dealing with zealots, Charles seemed to strike a modest rapport with his captors reinforced by the earlier decision to reunite him with his younger children, upon whom he had not set eyes for a number of years. The affecting scene where they were all brought together had drawn discreet sniffles from even the battle-hardened officers in attendance. It soon became clear that the agenda of the soldiers was far from doctrinaire and that, in Cromwell's words, 'No man could enjoy their lives and estates quietly without the King had his rights.'[3]

There was some distance in the perception between the two sides as to what those rights actually should be, although Charles surely recognised that the afflatus of the earlier period of his personal rule had gone for good. He was presented with 'Heads of Proposals' which built more detail onto the earlier *Declaration*. These were drafted by Ireton and Lambert with much input from both the Earl of Northumberland and Viscount Saye and Sele, the leading peers of Independent inclination in the House of Lords, as well as from several members of the Commons, including Oliver St John and Henry Vane. The monarch and his family were to be restored to their former dignity. Parliament was to become a permanent feature of the constitutional landscape, its sittings limited to a maximum of 240 days in a year. The present assembly was to set a date for its own termination. The Privy Council was to be replaced by a new body, the Council of State which would be explicitly accountable to parliament. Royalists were prevented from holding office for five years and parliament was to have control of the appointment of government officials and the officers of both army and navy for ten.

The religious clauses were a model for toleration contemplating not just the freedom of Protestant conscience but the liberty to practise it as well. The literary flame of the Anglican settlement, the Book of Common Prayer, was reauthorised but its use not made mandatory. No one was to be penalised for failing to attend church nor for participating in other acts of Protestant worship. In a sign of a formal break with the agenda of the Scots and their Kirk, no one was to be obliged to take the Covenant. Episcopacy, so dear to the heart of the king, was to be retained as a feature of Church government but its role was to be largely symbolic, which should have pleased the Presbyterians. The reform of the law and of tithes was also contemplated.

Ireton's document was indeed magnanimous, for in the circumstances of a complete parliamentary victory it was balanced, fair-minded and attempted to draw the heat from the religious dogmatism that had poisoned the debates of the state for so long. It demonstrated a recognition by the army command that although the New Model Army had been the instrument which had won the war and had the king in its custody, it needed to show a constructive commitment to peace and constitutional legality. With its focus on reform of the institutions of state, there was, tellingly, no linkage with arrears. The king's advisers could scarcely believe it: 'never was a Crown so near lost so cheaply recovered', as Sir John Berkeley exclaimed. Charles displayed less enthusiasm, believing that the army needed him more than he them and with some exasperation Ireton had to explain to his sovereign that the Heads of Proposals were likely the only credible bridge between king, army, the Lords and a significant section of the Commons. It was the moment when Charles could and should have legitimised the proposals, based on the favourable odds for their acceptance. But instead of seizing the strategic initiative, he prevaricated. It was an extraordinary blunder which even his closest advisers immediately recognised.

With the king naïvely convinced that he was indispensable and well enough informed to play off the army and the factions in parliament against each other, the simmering pot of London that had been briskly stirred by the Presbyterians finally boiled over. Cromwell had already observed of the capital, 'There want not, in all places men who have so much malice against the Army as besots them . . . Never were the spirits of men more embittered than now.'[4] The fourth week of July

1647 was marked by widespread disorder. The city had become an unhappy congregation of all those whose lives had been disrupted by the war and many were offended by a Puritan social regime that intruded upon their daily rhythms, and increasingly also their leisure. The dislocation of everyday working life was bad enough, but the shutting of theatres and other places for pastimes and enjoyment, and the replacement of feast days with fast days, meant there was little pleasure to be had even in idle hours. Some rationalised the armed conflict, and all the disruption, as a sign of a millennium, and the coming of the rule of the saints, but for many the war regime had become a joyless and increasingly unnecessary imposition.

London was also beginning to fill with demobilised soldiers, particularly royalists who had nothing to lose from whipping up trouble. Others took it upon themselves to preach sectarian views from any available space that could be used as a pulpit. The large knots of the maimed and of war widows were standing rebukes to the authorities who seemed unwilling to address energetically the need for peace. In an atmosphere of seething resentment, crowds of apprentices and disbanded soldiers went on the rampage, and at the Skinners' Hall another *Solemn Engagement* was laid out for signature, this time calling for a restoration of the king. Some with known connections to the New Model Army were attacked. The rioting spread and the House of Commons was invaded. Amidst the melee MPs were jostled and excrement thrown, and, in an act that was now on its way to becoming a parliamentary tradition, the Speaker was once again squashed into his chair as the protestors demanded a resolution to invite the monarch back to London. Fearful for their safety, a small group of peers that included the Earl of Manchester and fifty-seven MPs fled Westminster to seek the protection of the army. A convalescent Fairfax, now unambiguously in command of all land forces available to parliament in England and Wales, perceived his opportunity to intervene before the London militia could present a serious military challenge. Soon a large plume of dust was observable in the summer haze outside the city limits: the mass of the New Model was on the move towards the capital.

Anxious to avoid a further outbreak of civil war, a paler and pained lord general marched 15,000 troops onto Hounslow Heath. At his invitation, the smart ranks of soldiers were reviewed by the speakers of both Houses of Parliament and by over one hundred members. Over the next few days the regiments marched or rode into London; discipline was good and the wearing of sprigs of greenery and flowers by the troops dissipated the earlier sense of menace among the citizens. Others were less sanguine: having so roundly denounced in print the heresy he perceived in the New Model Army, the author of *Gangraena* thought it prudent to leave town. Crucially, there was no resistance from the local militia, such was the display of overwhelming force. On 7 August an enormous parade was conducted in Hyde Park and a more relaxed atmosphere prevailed. Amidst the lines of troops the individual standards of the units waved in the slight breeze and onlookers drew up more closely to look at the pikes, armour, muskets and field artillery that had been dragged into place.

Fairfax moved to the city and installed himself as the new Constable of the Tower. He ordered a copy of Magna Carta to be presented and, laying his hand upon it, he melodramatically declared the ancient document was that for which the army had fought. The incident perhaps showed the true limit of Fairfax's political imagination and in his little performance there was no reference to the Heads of Proposals. Shorn of the eleven most troublesome Presbyterian members who had fled, parliament showed its delight at the bloodless occupation and Fairfax's apparently restrained ambition. Seen now as the bringer of peace, he was feted in the House of Commons where a special bench was prepared for him to watch proceedings. With the members in a mood of thrilled obeisance, Fairfax moved to consolidate his present advantage: the London authorities were purged of their most antagonistic elements, the mayor arrested for treason, and steps taken to split up and neutralise the trained bands. Much more impressively, work began almost immediately to demolish the fortifications that surrounded the city and they were swiftly razed under the expert directions of New Model engineers. The royalist pamphleteers had a field day at the pricking of London's pride:

Is this the end of all the toil
And labour of the Town
And did our true works rise so high
Thus low to tumble down?[5]

Shortly afterwards came the encouraging news that Colonel Michael
Jones's small vanguard in Ireland had inflicted a severe defeat on
a numerically superior confederate army at the battle of Dungan's
Hill. The New Model Army looked as if it was the elite military force
of the age.

Fairfax was at the zenith of his power and authority but he was
neither a Caesar nor a Solon. His temperament and intellectual outlook were informed by a powerful awareness of soldierly duty and a
reverence for an established order. His sense of political possibility
was shaped by his serious reading of books about the past rather
than the pamphlets of the moment and his preferences were perhaps
closer to those of his great antagonist, Denzil Holles, than he would
care to admit. He recognised that the New Model Army, although
a powerful agent of a divided parliament, lacked the legitimacy to
impose a settlement on its own account. He probably sensed as well
that Ireton's proposal for religious toleration would perhaps be a step
too far in the current environment; he was alert to the sensibilities
of those many officers and men who, like him, were of Presbyterian
orientation in their religious faith. Having expended so much of
his physical energy in fighting the war he now preferred the role of
éminence grise in the quest for a settlement, and saw his personal
priority as keeping the army together in a state of tight discipline
while its outstanding material grievances and arrears were addressed,
and demobilisation planned and executed. The task of advocating
the army's ideas with the king remained in the hands of his senior field commander and his Commissary General, both of whom
provided a link to the politicians by virtue of their membership of
the Commons. But Ireton was also heavily engaged in planning a
more robust regime for the funding of the army and there followed
a period of drift.

Charles continued to show the keen awareness of division amongst his adversaries that he had displayed at Newcastle but he was temperamentally and intellectually unsuited to the task of negotiating in good faith. Rather than energetically identifying areas of common ground with adversaries who, like the Scots, seemed to lack the full confidence of knowing what to do with him, he chose to dissemble. At Hampton Court his prevarications and evasions showed a dread of further failure – in fearing to make a firm choice that he might come to regret, he effectively made none at all. Now he fell back on his Anglican faith, which remained unshakeable, and derived moral strength from his mystical attachment to the authority that had been vested in him by the Almighty. His morale was strengthened too by his more congenial surroundings, the occasional games of bowls and tennis, and regular contact with his younger children at Syon House. As he had been at Holdenby House, he was accorded many of the trappings if not the power of monarchy.

He was further indulged by those who came to treat with him. Ireton probably better understood the king's capacity for duplicity and had a more intelligent grasp of the strands that pointed, however haphazardly, towards a settlement, but he was very much the junior to his more exalted father-in-law who, on the circumstantial evidence, entertained an obscure affinity for the army's royal captive. As a younger man, Cromwell had claimed a moment of searing personal revelation and his unswerving belief in God's providence was cemented by his experience of the war and the vindication of the New Model Army. In Charles he found a man with a similar access to faith. It is not too much to imagine that he identified a kindred spirit; they were of nearly the same age. Neither was given to much levity and each approached life with a degree of seriousness and reverence for God that seemed diminished in others. Both were heavily and emotionally orientated towards family life; their respective spouses had each borne nine children and both sets of parents had experienced the death of offspring in both infancy and childhood. The king and the general were also noted for being able to attract deep loyalty and devotion from their tight inner circles of friends and confidantes. Each had endured a degree of personal trauma in their younger years. Cromwell seemed impressed that the king's poised and dignified manner continued to shine through adversity; the sovereign was clearly of some intangible and higher authority. In short, Charles Stuart was of the Elect but had been led astray.

That he was still distracted was thrown into relief by a new flirtation with the Scots. Their army had returned home to a country afflicted by plague, and in a state of political disgruntlement only partly mollified by the payment of the first tranche of arrears agreed in London. The sense of disappointment in the religious establishment was profound, although there were clear divergences on the best way to proceed. The Kirk held to an absolutist agenda which was utterly uncompromising. Argyll remained wedded to the terms of the Solemn League as the only plausible basis for the continued union of the two realms in which Scottish interests could be secured. Others, now gathered round the Duke of Hamilton and his younger brother William, the Earl of Lanark, were more inclined to take the king's earlier preference for a trial run of Presbyterianism at face value. At least this offered the chance to salvage something from the war, which, for the Scots, had been going on for nearly a decade. Accordingly, the Scottish commissioners presented themselves at Hampton Court to prepare the ground.

The king was further distracted by the appearance of the Marquis of Ormonde who had handed over Dublin to the units under Colonel Jones. Charles bore him no ill will for the regrettable lack of success to which he, the king, had contributed and calmly accepted Ormonde's attempted precis of the highly confusing strands of allegiances in Ireland. The Marquis was informed of the new possibilities offered by the Scots and was encouraged to see what he could do to re-energise the royalist cause. The House of Commons was sufficiently alarmed by the wavering loyalty of their nominal ally that they resubmitted the Newcastle Propositions to the king, and just to be on the safe side authorised an increment to the New Model Army's establishment to take it over 26,000 troops. Meanwhile, Cromwell and others continued their increasingly weary representations at

Hampton Court, attracting the sympathy of Berkeley, who admitted that 'in all my conferences with him [Cromwell], I found no man, in appearance, so zealous for a speedy blow as he; sometimes wishing that the King was more frank, and would not tie himself so strictly to narrow maxims'.[6] Charles continued to split hairs and prevaricate all the same, although he allowed it to be understood that he was presently minded to prefer the Proposals over the Propositions. But no one seemed to be terribly sure.

In the atmosphere of stasis, the impetus for constitutional and social change was more energetically articulated outside parliament, and the so-called Leveller movement increased its purchase. The term itself was pejorative; Cromwell characterised them as men whose aims were at 'levelling and parity' within society and not in a good way.[7] The objections to their agenda were as much religious as political, as their championing of the exercise of the natural rights of freeborn men (few including Lilburne thought of women as equally capable) seemed to deny the doctrine of predestination and the impulse of God's grace in men's actions. The first Leveller petition had been published in March 1647. It identified the House of Commons as the 'supreme authority' in the land and denied the peers jurisdiction over the lower House. All oaths that compromised the exercise of Nonconformist views were to be repealed and anyone should be permitted to preach peaceably. The law should be reformed and conducted in English and tithes were to be voluntary.

Whilst the Leveller plea for toleration resonated with many of the Independents, the novelty of the suggestion that the Commons was the source of constitutional authority rather than a sanction of it was contrary to the views and experience of the larger group of MPs. This, and the effrontery of the proposals in respect of the Lords, ensured that the petition was passed to the public hangman for burning by the narrow vote of ninety-four to eighty-six. Yet the pamphlets and manifestos produced by radical printers such as William Larner continued to pour forth. Both Overton and Lilburne were still prisoners, although the latter seemed to enjoy an occasional parole which he used to appear in town dressed as an officer, notwithstanding he had resigned his commission some two years before. Where Lilburne preferred a full-frontal assault on each and every locus of authority of which he disapproved, Overton sharpened his attacks by the use of humour and irony. In July he arranged a more serious publication, *An Appeal from the Degenerate Representative body, the Commons at Westminster, to the Free People in General.*[8]

Praising the 'right worthy patriots of the Army' for entering into 'a Solemn Engagement against the oppressing party at Westminster', Overton listed the many fundamental injustices presently suffered by the common man and which were to form the basis of the Leveller programme for social amelioration and reform. He started his analysis by an appeal to what was surely taken as a universal truth: 'Now as no man may abuse, beat torment or afflict himselfe, so by nature no man may give that power to another seeing he may not doe it himself.'

His principal insight was the increasing use of arbitrary power, whether by the agents of the king or parliament, and the corrosive effect that the wars had had on the administration of justice and on legal practices that were anyway overdue for reform. In particular he demanded that 'all other vexatious and unnecessary courts be abolished' and that 'Neither the high court of Parliament, nor any other inferior court or magistrate whatsoever may commit any free man of England to prison upon any pretended contempts as is frequent in these days, but only for transgressions and breach of the knowne Lawes of the Land . . .'

The close proximity of the soldiers to the printing presses and discontents of London meant that there was more time for these insights to be brought to bear on the otherwise idle troops. But of all the influences on the minds of the soldiery, this was the one Richard Baxter feared the most as 'Yet a more dangerous party than all these amongst them who took the direct Jesuitical way.'[9] Among their propagandists, John Wildman proved to be a persuasive and intelligent advocate. Wildman was the son of a Norfolk trader who, like Overton, had received a poor man's degree from Cambridge.

He served briefly in Fairfax's unit before returning to civilian life to take up a role as a full-time political activist and his contacts in the army ensured he received an audience. There he formed a collaboration with Edward Sexby, an articulate private soldier in Fairfax's Life Guard who had been one of the earlier 'agitators' but who now argued for a more ambitious agenda than, to him, the narrow and prosaic issue of army pay. Wildman found himself appointed to a committee of the General Council of the Army that considered the Heads of Proposals and quickly came to the conclusion that the slow pace of progress at Hampton Court was a sign that the king had suborned the senior officers to the royalist agenda. Cromwell himself had pleaded with Lilburne to desist from his attacks while negotiations were in progress, but the sense that the wheels of change were grinding far too slowly was palpable.

Even 'Freeborn John' understood that he dare not take on Fairfax directly, such was his prestige, but he lambasted those other officers, without naming them, who had 'most unjustly stolen the power from your honest General [Fairfax] and your too flexible adjutators'. He found a more appreciative audience in Thomas Rainsborough, who spotted an opportunity to further his own ambitions. In September, he and the acknowledged republican Henry Marten sponsored a motion in the Commons to break off all negotiations with the monarch, which was nonetheless comfortably seen off by Cromwell and the parliamentary authors of the Heads of Proposals. But impatience continued to build and in October, Fairfax was presented at his headquarters in Putney with a document entitled *The Case of the Army Truly Stated*. It was less of a manifesto than an insubordinate accusation that the high command was not doing enough about getting on with the requirements of the rank-and-file soldiery that had been identified in the *Solemn Engagement*. Amongst the complaints were proposals to appropriate the dean and chapter lands of the ancient cathedrals in an (insufficient) attempt to pay arrears and ongoing commitments. The wealth of the city, which was imagined to be uselessly tied up in bonds and other instruments of financial obligation, was also targeted.

Just as controversial were the radical ideas that parliament be purged and that all 'freeborn' males aged at least twenty-one should have the vote, unless they were 'delinquent' (royalist). At this point, the maintenance of good order would have dictated that the soldiers who were pressing the document on their colleagues be disciplined. However, it was noted that the paper had been signed by the 'agitators' of a mere five out of thirty-two regiments, although to the lord general's chagrin that included his own Life Guard.[10] The General Council of the Army was there to debate issues pertinent to military welfare and Fairfax also judged that both his subordinates, Cromwell and Ireton, needed a sharper incentive to justify their presently stalled strategy in open forum. In a sign that he himself did not yet take the threat posed by the Levellers too seriously, he ordered a clearing of the air.

5

'For the common good of man'

Putney

A poor plain countryman by the spirit which he hath received is better able to judge of truth and error touching the things of God than the greatest philosopher.

William Dell

We are not a mere mercenary Army, hired to serve any arbitrary power of a state but called forth and conjured by the several Declarations of Parliament for the defence of our own and the people's just rights and liberties.

A Declaration from Sir Thomas Fairfax and the Army

In the late autumn of 1647 Putney was a mid-sized community of about a thousand people. Consisting of a long street running south to north which ended at the bank of the Thames, it was surrounded by meadows and farmland. A proportion of the population were engaged as watermen (there was as yet no bridge linking it to the north side of the river) and Putney was becoming popular as a place within easy reach of the capital that was freer of the crush, the smells and the health hazards of the metropolis downriver. Fairfax had sited his headquarters there, symbolically between the king at Hampton

Court and the politicians at Westminster. In late October the church of St Mary's, which still stands at the head of the high street with the Thames below it, was chosen as the place best suited to host a gathering of the General Council of the Army. It met on the 28th with the representatives of the regiments (two junior officers and two soldiers per unit) crammed in cheek-by-jowl with unit commanders, other senior officers and the headquarters staff of the New Model Army.

They were joined by a number of the civilian activists accredited to the army, including John Wildman and Max Petty. Thomas Rainsborough also appeared although he was supposed to be on secondment to the navy, where the zeal and loyalty of the seafarers were now in some doubt. Yet he was determined to attend in order to show up his bete noire, Ireton. There had been accusations in *The Case of the Army Truly Stated* that the high command had reneged on its earlier commitments and that nothing 'had been done effectually'. Fairfax therefore directed that a proper minute of proceedings be taken, a job given to William Clarke, who was secretary to the General Council and proficient in the newfangled skill of shorthand. Other scribes were kept at bay. Clarke's extant record, which covered the first four days of discussions, provides one of the most vivid accounts of the extra-parliamentary debate about the constitution during this period. More powerfully, it sheds light on the motivations of the principal protagonists and the profound religious intensity that imbued the army's consideration of political questions.

The original formation of the General Council of the Army was the natural expression of the understanding that as the New Model Army was taking part in God's mission, then all ranks should have a voice. It is doubtful that the majority of the participants at Putney, least of all Fairfax, would have understood the gathering as primarily a political event with clear objectives that would be democratically decided. Yet the participation of civilians at a military conference was extraordinary enough and confirmed the soldiers' sense of themselves as the armed wing of the godly nation, not a caste apart. The record shows that remarkable latitude was given to each speaker, irrespective of background, rank or reputation. There were heated words and a wide range of views but the overall impression was of an army that was determined to stick together in a union of the devout, notwithstanding the differences of opinion. A simple soldier, identified as 'Buff Coat', brought this home with quiet dignity in front of his peers and superiors by observing 'we have here met on purpose, according to my engagement, that whatsoever may be thought to be necessary for our satisfaction, for the right understanding one of another, might be done that we might go on together'.[1]

Most of those present were to say 'amen' to that, but the debate had begun with an extraordinary verbal assault by one of its most junior participants. Expressing strong dissatisfaction with the snail-like progress at Hampton Court, Edward Sexby declared to Cromwell and Ireton that their 'credits and reputation hath been much blasted' by their efforts with Charles. He strongly doubted their captive's sincerity, observing, 'We have laboured to please the King, and I think, except we go to cut all our throats, we shall not please him.'[2] There was a hard debate about the extent to which the commanders had reneged on the *Solemn Engagement* of the summer and it was directed that this imputation be examined by a committee. However, it was also clear that the main target of this accusation was Ireton. The temperature of proceedings in the church was further raised by events outside. On the second day of the gathering, an inflammatory pamphlet appeared on the streets. Entitled *A Call to all the Souldiers of the Armie, by the Free People of England, Justifying the Proceedings of the Five Regiments*, it was authored by Wildman and its contents could easily be interpreted as an incitement to mutiny. Sexby's denunciation was magnified by the accusation that Cromwell and Ireton were double-dealing: 'This is certaine, in the House of Commons, both he and his father Cromwell, doe so earnestly and palpably carry on the King's designe, that your best friends there are amazed thereat'.[3]

More serious was the exhortation that the soldiers 'create NEW OFFICERS'. With reputations and discipline under threat, Colonel William Goffe nonetheless proposed that the assembly seek the guidance of the Almighty. This was welcomed and the house of Mr Chamberlain, a local Puritan, was made available for a prayer meeting that went on for over seven hours. With his unshakeable belief in divine revelation and the workings of God's providence, Cromwell had strongly endorsed the recourse to the Almighty and Ireton was happy to concede that 'Every one hath a spirit within him.' But over successive days it became apparent that God had some pretty vehement views on the matters in hand and the commanders perhaps came to regret their invitation that their soldiers become prophets. Now the main point of contention was a new Leveller document entitled *An Agreement of the People.* Unlike its immediate predecessor, *The Case of the Army Truly Stated*, which was an army document with civilian input, the *Agreement* was more clearly of the streets and likely penned by William Walwyn, who had joined with Overton in the petitions for the release of John Lilburne the preceding year. It was he who had attacked the intemperance of Edwards' *Gangraena*.

Whereas the *Case* was essentially a list of grievances, the *Agreement* was a better drafted and more markedly constitutional document. It proposed a polity based on the exercise of natural rights that had been immanent since time immemorial until, the authors contended, they had been usurped by the Normans. The realm was effectively to become a republic. The current parliament would wind itself up within twelve months, be replaced by one elected biennially by eligible males and would have supreme legislative and executive authority. It would not, however, have the right to interfere with religious conscience nor impress men for service in the military, an aspiration that seemed to undermine the whole basis of the armed forces. Although imprecise and even contradictory in parts, the *Agreement* introduced the novel concept that members of parliament were deputies as much as representatives. The size of constituencies was to be determined not by reference to contribution to taxation but by size of population, which implied full manhood suffrage. But the question of who exactly would get a vote turned out to be the nub of the debate recorded by Clarke.

For a man who was supposed to be somewhat intense and

introspective, under the goading of Rainsborough and Wildman, Ireton discovered in himself at Putney the power of articulate (if somewhat long-winded) oratory. Neither the metaphysical obscurities of his father-in-law nor the witty put-down were Ireton's style, but he delivered a determined rebuttal of the Leveller proposals. In his view, the vote should be exercised only by those with a 'permanent fixed interest in this kingdom', and that appeals based on so-called natural rights implied anarchy, for 'If you will resort only to the law of nature, by the law of nature you have no more right to this land or any thing else than I have.' The Leveller state would 'destroy all kind of property or whatsoever a man has by human constitution' and he could not consent to it.[4] But to Rainsborough, Ireton's legalistic examination of the purpose of a soldier's 'engagement' and his pious high-mindedness just sounded like condescending bombast. After another of Ireton's lengthy interventions he exclaimed:

> I think that the poorest he that is in England has a life to live as the greatest he; and therefore, truly, sir, I think it's clear that every man that is to live under a government ought first by his own consent to put himself under that government; and I do think that the poorest man in England is not at all bound in a strict sense to that government that he has not had a voice to put himself under.

Calming his inner firebrand, Rainsborough went on to argue that the individual was given reason precisely that all may order society more equitably. After all, in his view there was nothing in Scripture that proscribed even the lowliest man from choosing his ruler: 'I do not find anything in the Law of God, that a lord shall choose twenty burgesses, and a gentleman but two, or a poor man shall choose none: I find no such thing in the Law of Nature, nor in the Law of Nations.'[5]

This was altogether too much for even some of the civilian Levellers present who, like Max Petty, thought that dependants such as servants, apprentices who lived with their masters and paupers should be excluded from the franchise. Certainly, there was to be no female voice in the political state of the godly, and if Rainsborough (who had relatives in Massachusetts) had heard of Annie Hutchinson's spirited rebellion against the Puritan patriarchy of New England, he wasn't letting on. The debate continued, although in some exasperation Colonel Hardress Waller, a cousin of the blacklisted Sir William Waller, wondered out loud what all the abstractions had to do with the army. There was surely a more urgent practical need, to address the burden of the war on the people and the temporising of parliament, which he thought should be purged. Cromwell favoured further prayer, which prompted some eye-rolling by Wildman who, having less faith that God would give unambiguous guidance to the assembled soldiery, muttered 'Wee cannot find anythinge in the worde of God what is fitt to bee done in civil matters.'[6]

In consideration of the property-less troops who had actually done the fighting however, perhaps the most poignant remarks on the subject were those of Sexby, who fairly observed that if these men could not have a vote, then they were mercenaries after all. But in the face of Ireton's conviction and Cromwell's temporising, it seemed a wan hope. Rainsborough, sensing that he had lost the argument in this assembly, demanded a general rendezvous of the whole army to settle the dispute.

With everyone else somewhat distracted and bored by the abstruse debate between Ireton and the Levellers, over the following days the gathering went on to consider the issue of what to do about the king, a subject of dissatisfaction that seemed far easier to articulate and grasp. Now men came forward to say that the Almighty (whose cosmic attention seemed to be wholly absorbed by the debates) had given them special insight on the nation's ills. Among them, Captain Francis Allen claimed that He had told him that He particularly disapproved of the monarch's power of veto or 'negative voice'. For Cromwell's prayer meetings had not only become entangled in esoteric matters like the franchise, they had also more clearly confirmed the growing sense of disenchantment amongst the officer corps with the sovereign and, taking the Book of Samuel as his authority, Captain Bishop won approving nods with his identification of Charles as 'that man of blood'. Fairfax knew, however, that in spite of Leveller efforts at infiltration, the overall political temper amongst the rank and file soldiers was acquiescent at this stage. Indeed, there was growing evidence of sympathy for the king; ordering the regiment of Colonel Robert Lilburne (brother of 'Freeborn John'), to Newcastle, it instead held an unauthorised gathering at which a number of soldiers declared their allegiance to the person of the sovereign. Pay was still the primary source of discontent and the lord general prevailed upon the parliament for another six weeks of salaries and for the Assessment to be raised from £60,000 to £100,000 a month.

On 6 November, Fairfax, who had been unwell and absent from the debates up to this point, took the chair from Cromwell. Saying very little, within two days he had heard enough. Prayers for the intercession of the Almighty were one thing, but a free-for-all discussion on the king and, by extension, the constitution was something else entirely. What is more, he suspected (like Waller) that the abstract political arguments had little resonance with the troops in the field, who were motivated by other more practical concerns. Cromwell, Ireton and Rainsborough had gone on for long enough and the discipline of the New Model Army was at stake; it was time to bring matters to a halt. The 'agitators' were ordered back to their regiments. He further directed all available units to muster at three separate rendezvous at which firm orders would be given in the company of officers and men together.

In the midst of these arrangements, Charles bolted from Hampton Court. His flight was interpreted as yet another example of his bad faith, but in this instance he seemed to have been genuinely motivated by concerns for his safety. There is some evidence that Cromwell, impatient at the slow progress of negotiations, attempted to focus the king's mind with alarming reports about his well-being. In the last week of October, Lanark had arrived at the palace in the company of fifty horseman and urged Charles to ride north with the Scots. He demurred but shortly afterwards withdrew his parole, a clear indication that he was minded to escape the charged atmosphere of

London. Oddly, he was not removed to a place of greater security than the large and rambling palace, and he absconded with minimal effort on the night of 11 November, leaving a complacent note saying that he looked forward to resuming his role as father-of-the-nation once all the discontents had been calmed. Knowing that if he left the shores of his realm he would be finished, he chose to remain in the care of the army and headed for the Isle of Wight, whose governor, Colonel Robert Hammond, was a kinsman of Cromwell.

Hammond was no walk-on extra and had been a senior member of the army team that had negotiated with Charles at Hampton Court. He was known to be in favour of a personal settlement with the king but had recently become disenchanted with the direction of events and doubted the sincerity of both sides. He was also hostile to the extra-parliamentary agitation in London and had asked Fairfax for reassignment from regimental command to the vacant governorship. He was in regular correspondence with Cromwell and the latter had appeared on the island to reconnoitre it earlier in the autumn. Hammond had probably hoped for, but did not expect, a quiet life and took in Charles with a show of reluctance. He called the senior members of the island community together, both royalist and otherwise, and asked them not to use the sovereign's presence to stir up trouble. The king and his still substantial personal retinue was accommodated 'with all demonstration of respect and duty' at Carisbrooke Castle, a grim-looking yet tolerably comfortable medieval fortress close to the inland town of Newport.[7]

At his headquarters, Fairfax and a committee that included Cromwell had prepared a remonstrance which aimed to reassert discipline and solidarity behind the chain of command. Promising to 'live and die with the army', Fairfax undertook to continue to press for the troops' material welfare and the care of widows. The lord general also committed to use his authority to press for a timely dissolution of parliament, notwithstanding that the current one had expressed its strong opposition to both this proposal and the *Agreement of the People*. He also backed the idea of fixed term assemblies thereafter but the nature of the electoral franchise was left deliberately vague. However, Fairfax also made clear that if he was not supported by the body of the army, he would resign his commission. In the middle of the month the first of the rendezvous was held at Ware in Hertfordshire.

The commander rode up with an impressive retinue, but before he could utter a word, Rainsborough barged his way through and insisted on a reading of the *Agreement of the People*. Worse was to follow as two former officers, Colonel Eyre and Major Scott, were observed inciting the ranks of the troops. They were swiftly put under guard but now two other bodies of soldiers arrived, unauthorised, wearing Leveller ribbons on their hats and brandishing copies of the *Agreement*. In silent fury, Fairfax noted that one of the regiments, which appeared to be officerless save for one captain, was none other than Robert Lilburne's, which was supposed to be on its way to Northumberland. The other was the officer-MP Thomas Harrison's battalion. Cromwell, perhaps angry with himself for indulging the Levellers at Putney and embarrassed for his commander-in-chief, drew his sword and together with a number of other senior officers swiftly fell upon this display of disobedience, tearing away the ribbons and throwing the pamphlets on the ground. Nearly a dozen supposed ringleaders were identified, arrested and swiftly condemned. There was then some anguished debate, after which several of the men were released, but an implacable Fairfax was determined that an example had to be made. In the fading November light, three men were selected to draw lots and in a grim ritual the loser, Richard Arnold, was shot to death by the two others at the head of his regiment. It was a salutary warning and an effective one; the awed troops rallied behind their chief and his remonstrance, and left the field shouting support for 'The King and Sir Thomas.'

The other rendezvous at Kingston and Ruislip Heath passed off without incident. Later, Rainsborough sincerely repented his insubordination and was packed off to the fleet, where he should have been all along. In due course, other officers were also pardoned once they admitted the error of their association with the Levellers.

Good order and discipline had been restored, although amongst the officers deep animosity towards the king remained. Fairfax's nipping of the Leveller bud also received endorsement from the Nonconformist religious communities of the capital, which in the same month produced *A Declaration by Congregational Societies in and about London* authored by the leading Independent and Baptist ministers. Often overlooked, it was a powerful expression of religious Nonconformism at the intersection with political radicalism and it confronted the Levellers head on. It firmly asserted, 'It cannot but be very prejudicial to human society and the promotion of the good of commonwealth, cities, armies or families to admit of a parity, or all to be equal in power'. To give emphasis, it went on to aver that 'The ranging of men into several and subordinate ranks and degrees is a thing necessary for the common good of man.' The *Declaration* was a powerful message of social conservatism that provided a strong clue about the later direction of political events.[8]

As at Hampton Court so at Carisbrooke, Charles was permitted to negotiate with anyone of whose credentials he approved and the Scottish commissioners were soon ensconced. Not that he was finished with his 'juggling', in Cromwell's exasperated phrase. Peace feelers were maintained with parliament on the basis of his acceptance of a trial run for Presbyterianism, the handing over of control of the militia and free pardon for the rebels. His overtures, which had the merit of consistency with the position that he had taken at Newcastle twelve months earlier, were however ignored while the two Houses dusted off the Propositions. Under the circumstances, the Scottish mission was highly persuasive. With much grumbling and some outright opposition from the Assembly of the Kirk, the Committee of the Estates in Edinburgh had sent Lanark and the Lord Chancellor of Scotland, the Earl of Loudon, to treat with the king. Loudon was a kinsman of the Marquis of Argyll and was there to ensure that Lanark did not drift from his instructions. They were joined by John Maitland, the Earl of Lauderdale, an enormous man of passionate Covenanter principle who had the unnerving habit of delivering his forceful opinions in a spray of spittle.

Notwithstanding this, the proposals once developed were far more emollient than before. The terms were heavily influenced by the agenda of the Hamiltonian group of the Scottish nobility, who were determined to re-establish their former political eminence, which had been eroded by the Kirk and its lay supporters. Charles was asked to work for a more effective union between his two realms, grandees from north of the border were to have a greater presence in his council and he was to spend more time north of the Tweed. In an important concession to the commercial classes and in recognition of the imperatives of economic as well as political union, Scottish merchants were to enjoy the same trade benefits in England as at home. Presbyterianism would get a trial run for three years. The king would not be required to take the Covenant, but he was contracted do all in his power to stamp out error, heresy and 'scandalous doctrines'. The list of these deviants was a lengthy one and bore the heavy hand of the Assembly: Baptists, Arminians, Brownists, Seekers, Antinomians, Anti-Trinitarians, Familists and other 'independents' and 'separatists' were all to be ruthlessly suppressed. It did not seem to occur to the divines of the Kirk that the sheer number of alternative belief systems thus listed reduced their own to that of another sect with all the blind authoritarianism of a cult. However, the most momentous part of what became known as the 'Engagement' was the promise of an army to enforce its terms.

Seemingly on the point of abandonment by their erstwhile allies and otherwise determined to reassert control over the whole process of negotiation with the king, some in the Presbyterian grouping at Westminster realised that a few degrees of latitude towards the Independents was now inevitable. Parliament drew up the Four Bills, which were presented at Carisbrooke on Christmas Eve. Drafted by the diminished body of the House of Lords they were passed to the Commons and in a sign of continuing divergence and exasperation amongst its members, they were approved by a slender majority of nine votes. The Bills and accompanying annexes hardened the constitutional terms contained in the Newcastle Propositions and were a much more explicit test of the king's good faith. Charles was now invited to give his royal assent to a list of measures that had hitherto been ordinances and to formally acknowledge that the parliament had been right to rise against him. Lest he or his successors be tempted to compel the nation in future, command of the armed forces was effectively to pass from the sovereign for good. Further, parliament would be able to adjourn whenever and to wherever it saw fit, from which could be inferred the right to self-perpetuation. The formation of a 'royalist' party was forestalled by the cancellation of all peerages, royal appointments and proclamations since 1642; future appointment to the House of Lords and the holding of office by former royalists would be subject to parliamentary approval. Named luminaries such as Prince Rupert were to be punished, although the leniency implied in the proposed execution of no more than seven senior royalists would hardly have commended itself to the king, who was still deeply troubled by his complicity in the decapitation of the lieutenant of his personal rule, the Earl of Strafford.

To Charles, the religious terms were as uncompromising as before, notwithstanding that in the fourteenth annexe to the Bills was a sign of recognition that a Presbyterian state would have to make some accommodation with Nonconformists. An implicit distinction was made between liberty of conscience and the toleration that had been envisaged by Ireton and his colleagues in the drafting of the Heads of Proposals. There was to be neither gainsaying of the decisions of the Westminster Assembly nor any unpicking of the new *Directory for Public Worship*. The regime was expressly designed to avoid anything contrary to those points of faith, 'for the ignorance whereof men are to be kept from the Sacraments of the Lord's Supper'. The belief that no error should be strewn upon the path between man and his Maker was sincerely held and toleration was thought synonymous with impiety.

But in the determination to extirpate any threat of heresy, the exercise of liberty of conscience was to be severely constrained. The outward practice of Nonconformist views was only permitted in so far as they were conducted without disturbance to the 'peace of the kingdom', which provided a public order rationale for any future suppression. Tithes could only be enjoyed by conformist ministers and Sunday observance was to be compulsory. The 'indulgence' did not extend to the 'printing, publishing or preaching of any thing contrary to the principles of the Christian religion' as officially defined by the new Articles of the Church of England. To those ends, episcopacy and the Book of Common Prayer were outlawed as per the ordinance of 1646. The arrears of the soldiery were to be met by the forced sale of the property of the Anglican hierarchy, a proposal which had already been shown to be deficient. Anglicanism was effectively treated in ways similar to that of the 'popish religion'.

It was too much for Charles, who correctly judged that he was to be reduced to a mere figurehead in a religious polity which negated the whole basis of his God-given sovereignty and of his Anglican faith. At last he made a decision: Westminster was rejected in favour of Edinburgh, and Scottish soldiers would be raised to suppress the English rebels. Suspecting that they were about to be double crossed, there were angry words between the parliamentary commissioners and the monarch. Hammond was sent to the king's chambers to find the accord and attempted to search Charles's person. Appalled by this affront to the royal dignity, the king shoved the officer away. In angry surprise, Hammond pushed the sovereign back. It was a symbolic moment with both men and the horrified attendants probably realising that a Rubicon had been crossed.

In a mood of bitterness, the English commissioners returned to London, leaving orders that Charles was to be kept in closer confinement. Berkeley and other personal advisers and intermediaries were dismissed. The capital to which the delegation returned had just experienced another bout of disorders and rioting. To the simmering anger caused by an increase to the Assessment which some were openly refusing to pay was added the fury at the attempt to suppress Christmas celebrations and the hanging of decorations in the streets. Similar disturbances were recorded in Canterbury and Ipswich. From the notables of twenty counties came a petition to parliament against the continued usage of free quarter by the army. It baulked at the support expected of the civilian population by 'a degenerated, mutinous, seditious and rebellious soldiery, long since voted by you to disband'. Like the plague of Egyptian locusts, the army, 'their horses, wives and trulls have totally consumed all the money in our purses, the corn in our barns . . . and exposed us . . . to the merciless jaws of penury'.[9] Antagonism towards the military had also been enhanced by the effect of the Indemnity Ordinances, which effectively reduced the chance of redress for those civilians at the receiving end of military misbehaviour or exploitation. In a clear sign of unhappiness with the regime propounded at the Westminster Assembly, there arrived further numerous reports of parishes where tithes were being withheld from ministers who used the new *Directory* rather than the Book of Common Prayer.

Meanwhile, the Levellers kept up their agitation and Lilburne, who had enjoyed a brief period of parole, was thrown back into the Tower for continuing to criticise the peers and the supposed dealings between the senior officers of the army and Charles. He was joined by Wildman. On 3 January 1648, and warmly encouraged by Cromwell, who appeared to be regretting his earlier indulgence of the monarch, the Commons passed the Vote of No Address, which formally broke off negotiations with the king, effectively ensuring that a settlement would be reached without him. The majority in favour was far larger than that which had approved the Four Bills, and reflected a harder attitude towards the sovereign amongst the members of the Commons that was greater than the other differences between them. The peers though were more difficult to persuade with several, including Northumberland, Warwick, Pembroke and Manchester, dissenting. Under Fairfax's leadership, the General Council endorsed the Vote on the understanding that it was aimed at Charles personally rather than the monarchy in general; at the invitation of the Commons he sent soldiers into the precincts of Westminster, which concentrated the minds of their lordships. Through Lauderdale, the Scottish commissioners (somewhat disingenuously) also objected, although their voice lacked official weight as the Committee of Both Kingdoms was dissolved on the same day as the Vote.

At the same time, Fairfax moved to further consolidate the chain of command; the General Council of the Army was adjourned with decisions to be taken henceforth by the Council of Officers alone. Notwithstanding uncertainty about the reliability of the Scots (the terms of the Engagement did not become public until the last week of February), he also ordered disbandment to proceed now that Ireton had brought some measure of order to the arrangements for pay. However, in a clear sign of partiality to the core of the New Model Army, the troops earmarked for demobilisation were those units whose loyalty had been compromised by the subversion of the MPs and the machinations of Levellers the previous year. Included amongst the latter was Fairfax's own Life Guard. In general however, the process went smoothly and over the first three months of the year, the land forces were substantially reduced.

One place where it did not go calmly was in Wales, where the mostly Celtic population was also loyally royalist and where there was a correspondingly strong aversion to the cost of maintaining an intrusive standing army. Here, instructions to the parliamentary forces to disband were rebuffed and as usual, refusal was motivated by arrears. By the time a more competent officer had arrived with money to grease the wheels of demobilisation, the mutiny (exploited by royalists) had become a full-scale insurrection across most of south Wales with over 12,000 rebels and untrained local levies in the field. Officers who had previously fought with distinction in the parliamentary cause now turned on their erstwhile comrades. Sporting the motto 'We long to see our King' the renegades also produced a manifesto demanding a personal treaty with the monarch and that the Protestant religion 'as it now stands established' be restored.

Giving his subordinate his first independent command, Fairfax ordered Cromwell to destroy the turncoats, a commission which had a further incentive in that its holder had recently been awarded extensive estates around Swansea and in South Monmouthshire by parliament. It was not to be the only time in Cromwell's career when military action happily coincided with economic self-interest. Yet he was also appalled that the rebels should so plainly turn themselves against the manifest will of God and excoriated 'their iniquity, double because they have sinned against so much light and against so many evidences of divine presence going along with and prospering a righteous cause'.[10] His former comrades in arms were committing apostasy. Cromwell set about the task with great zeal and resolution, and although helped by the destruction of a royalist force in Glamorgan by a subordinate, he was soon heavily engaged in a series of sieges, the most strategically important of which was Pembroke Castle. The soldiers of God cut little ice with the locals and the New Model force was soon plagued by a form of guerrilla war by opponents 'who being put out of all hope of mercy, are resolved to endure the utmost extremity'.

The bitter campaign in Wales was but one aspect of what became a second civil war – its contaminated pod dispersed even more malignant seeds than the first. The confusion bred particularly vicious fighting and an absence of mercy towards many of the defeated. In part, this reflected the exasperation of a populace that was desperately trying to recover the rhythms of peace, remove the physical reminders of war and return to more normal lives. There had been attempts at reconciliation between former antagonists at the local level. But these had been overshadowed by the work of the parliamentary Sequestration Committee that had been established in the Goldsmiths Hall and which had charge of the land and property seized from the royalists and other 'delinquents', and the enforcement of fines for their recovery. In the wake of the king's obstinacy and in a determination to remove royalists from the wider political process, parliament had also issued an ordinance in October 1647 which expelled all who had opposed it from local office and magistracy. Faced with more passive forms of disobedience such as the reading of the banned Book of Common Prayer, the MPs also ordered a drive to conformity. For many royalists, there seemed nothing more to lose.

One victim of the intensification of the po-faced purges was the poet and minister Robert Herrick. Contemporary engravings of him suggest a man who enjoyed life without taking it too seriously and certainly he seemed devoid of the sort of ambitions that motivated better known poets of the cavalier genre such as Sir John Suckling. Born before the death of Shakespeare, the chubbily contented bard was an acquaintance of Jonson and came to the ministry late in life. His great piece *Hesperides* was a work of joyful sensibility in which his epicurean tastes were never far from the surface. But his devotion to 'maypoles, hock carts, wassails, wakes' and blooms of flowers and earthly love put him out of sympathy with the local authorities, as did his obvious royalist sympathies. To all intents and purposes, he seemed harmless enough but in the atmosphere of heightened intolerance he was driven from his parish on Dartmoor. Denied the traditional 'one-fifth' that was granted ex-ministers, he ended up as a virtual destitute in London, sustained by the occasional charity of his hard-up friends. It was not an uncommon fate, and one that made the process of national reconciliation so difficult and drawn out.

For Fairfax, however, it was the military problem that was the most acute because so much of the disorder took place in areas where the demobilisation of parliament's forces was most advanced. In ultimately prevailing, the lord general showed his prowess as a strategist as well as an efficient fighter of battles. Some of the biggest challenges came from areas such as Norfolk, Suffolk, Kent and Essex, which had previously been solidly behind the struggle against the Stuart regime. With the support of ministers from their pulpits, more petitions came into London demanding a reduction in the burden of taxation, a treaty with the sovereign, disbandment of the army and a return to legality. There were also more markedly pro-royalist demonstrations: the Mayor of Norwich ordered a public feast and the lighting of bonfires as a mark of loyalty to the king. Hardress Waller was despatched to the south-west to deal with a royalist rising by native-speaking Cornishmen.

The most serious threat in England came from Kent, where the indefatigable Henrietta Maria at last perceived her opportunity in the disenchantment of the populace. She now persuaded the aged but good-natured Earl of Norwich to leave his exile and return to the king's service. This he did, perhaps motivated by the desire to make amends for the lacklustre performance of his son, Lord Goring, when the chips had been down nearly three years before. In the third week of May, he raised a substantial but untrained force at Maidstone which was joined by large numbers of restless and otherwise indolent former royalist soldiers and officers from London. Royalists also quickly gained control of major towns along the Medway. Fairfax got together a scratch force of 6,000 men and was preparing to march when news was received that a part of the navy had mutinied in the Downs, an anchorage off the coast of Kent.

In the National Maritime Museum at Greenwich is a magnificent painting by Sir Peter Lely. It shows Peter Pett and the stern of the *Sovereign of the Seas*, one of the largest warships of the seventeenth century which he, as a master shipwright, had designed and built at the Woolwich yards. The prolific contemporary diarist John Evelyn described the ship in an entry for 1641 as a 'monstrous vessel' and the 'richest that ever spread cloth before the wind'.[11] The painting puts representations of the much later HMS *Victory* in the shade, and certainly the awed expression on Pett's face suggests that he realised he had produced a war-winner. The strategic intention behind the vessel and others of an expanding Royal Navy had been one of the causes of the conflict as the king had attempted to finance his ambition with a prerogative tax, Ship Money, which had previously been levied from coastal inhabitants for their security. The king's insistence that threats to national security were a matter for his exclusive judgement and his attempt to turn Ship Money into a national tax that might be diverted into purposes other than those for which it was intended was central to the political dispute between sovereign and parliament. Charles was not the first monarch to perceive that the realm's security and commerce depended on a well-provided navy and his intentions may have commanded wider political support had not the means of achieving it become conflated with opposition to his personal rule.

The civil wars saw the largest proportion of the fleet fall under the control of parliament, which was thereafter administered by the Earl of Warwick as Lord High Admiral. In 1643 he was additionally appointed to head the parliamentary commission overseeing the colonies ('plantations'); in company with other Puritan members of both Houses such as Oliver St John and Viscount Saye and Sele, he had extensive commercial interests in both the Caribbean and in New England, and seemed to be the natural choice for such a role. Warwick was not entirely motivated by narrow economic self-interest – he supported the community which broke away from Massachusetts to form a new plantation on what is now Rhode Island so that they could follow their own less dogmatic brand of Protestant faith. It was generally agreed that Warwick and his fellow commissioners did a good job managing naval affairs and expanding the size of the fleet. With potential aggressors in Europe distracted by the Thirty Years War, their main strategic duty was to keep the Irish Sea under firm control to forestall any chance of Charles getting military support from that quarter. This was done with great gusto and ferocity by Vice Admiral Richard Swanley, who pursued the sizeable squadron employed by the Irish Confederacy.

Equally important was the task of keeping England's commercial routes open, particularly as parliament was heavily reliant on customs revenue to finance its war effort. The conflict in Europe and a legacy of piracy had led to a free-for-all on the high seas, and depredations by corsairs and legally sanctioned privateers put pressure on trade and in particular the commercial interests of London. Privateers operated by the Confederacy out of Dunkirk and Ostend menaced the English Channel. Other European powers were not slow to take advantage of the conflict in the British Isles and Ireland. Spain had already seized the colony of Providence Island in the western Caribbean and there were a number of serious clashes between English and European merchantmen and naval vessels throughout the wars. Important British commercial interests in the Baltic and Mediterranean were also degraded. The growing fleet held its own but Warwick was forced to stand aside as a consequence of the Self-Denying Ordinance and in 1648 the naval arithmetic was fundamentally changed by the ending of the Thirty Years War in a series of treaties concluded that summer and autumn. At last, there was a chance that Henrietta Maria would realise her ambition of engineering a major European intervention by either the Dutch or the French in her husband's realm.

An effective contribution by the fleet to the parliamentary war effort did however mask a growing antagonism between the navy and the New Model Army, not solely characterised by the timeless disdain of the sailor for the landlubber. The navy had fulfilled its duties without the fundamental need for reform in the face of failure, which had seen the formation of the army. Its war fighting credentials had been gradually honed and despite the absence of the religious intensity which underpinned the morale of the land forces, the sailors took great professional pride in their mastery of all the conditions that God threw at them on the water. As well as tension caused by the issue of pay that also prevailed on land, the navy became caught up in the dispute between the New Model Army and parliament in 1647 when it was suspected of having facilitated the defection of the eleven members whose hostility to Fairfax and his army had provoked the crisis. The appointment of the choleric and suspicious Rainsborough to the fleet was a spectacularly ill-judged attempt to ensure the loyalty of the sailors and his tardiness in confirming the commissions of a number of well-regarded officers was interpreted as a direct attempt to subordinate the navy to the army.

The resultant mutiny also saw the vital coastal forts at Deal, Walmer and Sandwich fall into rebel hands, and Dover was besieged. Rainsborough was lucky to escape with his life and he returned in high dudgeon to dwellings in Yorkshire where he was later killed by royalists sent to arrest him in the growing cycle of viciousness. His passing created a martyr for the Levellers and his funeral in London was turned into a large political demonstration. But while his radicalism had created a stir among the agitators of the army, it had been firmly rebuffed by the navy. In some desperation, Warwick was recalled and although his reassurances were enough to retain the loyalty of Portsmouth, he was unsuccessful with the mutineers of the Downs, who sailed off to join the Prince of Wales and thereby create the nucleus of a royalist invasion force from the Continent.

6

'To struggle with inevitable fate'

Preston

They turn the Council of War into a Council of State and there debate and resolve all public affairs as if they were another Parliament.

Anonymous, *Animadversions upon the Armies Remonstrance*

It is inconceivable that subjects should imagine such extraordinary ideas against the King.

Cardinal Mazarin

Back on land and in atrocious summer weather that did for yet another harvest, Fairfax brought his small army by a series of forced marches to Maidstone. A fierce battle through the town was fought against opposition stiffened by experienced royalist officers but eventually 'Black Tom' prevailed. Once again, quarter was offered by Fairfax to those who would disperse peacefully, and most of Norwich's largely amateur force did so then and over the following days. The earl himself bravely led the remaining half of his original force on to London, where the parochialism of the Kentish rebels finally overwhelmed their residual loyalty to the king. Faced by London militia under the command of Philip Skippon, many refused to march past their county boundary and Norwich was left to lead a tiny remnant of about 500 diehards around the capital. In a brave feat that astonished the citizens of east London, his force swam with their horses across the Thames near the Isle of Dogs to join with the royalists in Essex. There, at Colchester, was later to develop one of the bitterest sieges of the civil wars.

Further to the south-west, another royalist phoenix arose in Surrey in surely one of the most futile episodes of the entire civil war period. Henry Rich, Earl of Holland, was the younger brother of the Earl of Warwick. Lacking the brains of his sibling and being of diminished integrity, Holland's role in the conflict with the king was marked by serial defections. Although briefly a favourite of Henrietta Maria, he badly bungled his royal commission during the Bishops' Wars with Scotland and repaid the confidence placed in him by siding with the growing agitation against the king. He was a member of the parliamentary Committee of Safety convened before the outbreak of hostilities but later came to regret his opposition and found his way to the exiled court at Oxford, where he was ostracised. Holland was piqued by his treatment and returned to London, where he superfluously denounced English Catholic support of the royal cause but was prevented from resuming his seat in parliament. He nevertheless remained active behind the scenes as a member of the peace party and retained a stubborn belief in his influence as a high-ranking courtier. Finally, he unambiguously raised a standard for the imprisoned king on 4 July 1648 at Kingston-upon-Thames and was joined by the Duke of Buckingham and his younger brother Francis Villiers. Lacking military competence, they were reliant on the turncoat Colonel Dalbier, who had failed to find a commission in the New Model Army after his service with the Earl of Essex.

Despite several futile and largely farcical attempts to escape from his quarters at Carisbrooke involving wigs and contortions through window bars, the king was in no position to lend authority or practical help to these resurrections of the Stuart cause; indeed Charles had already disowned the Welsh uprising. Holland was able to muster fewer than 500 supporters. In an extraordinary rodomontade that saw the royalists ranging between Reigate Castle (which they attempted to capture) and Peterborough, the group was doggedly pursued by New Model soldiers. Holland was captured and sent to the Tower in disgrace, his perfidy adding to the sense amongst the troops that the parliamentary cause was riddled with treachery. Lord Francis Villiers was killed and his body mutilated after an engagement on Surbiton Heath: he was surprised while on a diversion to see a local mistress, although other accounts had him fighting bravely in a rearguard action as the royalists' diminished band moved north. Whatever the circumstances, Villiers, whom Hyde called a 'rare beauty', was accorded the wistful admiration that the British reserve for hopeless but bravely borne causes. The Puritan poet Andrew Marvell composed an ode to the modern Leander in which fascination with the noble's good looks and doomed crusade overbore consideration of his military prowess – 'Yet what couldst thou have done? tis always late. To struggle with inevitable fate.' In a war in which the operation of God's providence was so clearly one-sided, it seemed an apt reflection on the royalist campaigns.

On the same day that Holland was rallying his followers in Surrey, the Duke of Hamilton was completing the muster of his invasion force in the Scottish Borders near the village of Moffat in Annandale. It had taken fully six months for the 'Engagers' to assemble an army barely one-third of the number that had been authorised by the Estates in Edinburgh, in furtherance of the agreement with the king at Carisbrooke. Once again, the fatal purism of the Kirk compromised the pursuit of unified Scottish interests, although the ministers were not the only ones to perceive the risks of taking on their former English allies and the New Model Army. The divines were unpersuaded by the offer of a trial run for Church government by Presbyters – had not Charles himself at Newcastle said that he would do all in his power to ensure that the three-year period would be no dress rehearsal? More importantly, his refusal to take the Covenant undermined their whole conception of a state of the godly and was a denial of that which many Scots of all degrees held sacred.

But neither could the divines conceive of reaching an accommodation with the English and their schismatic army, and they gave short
shrift to commissioners sent north to reach a mutual understanding.
The Assembly denounced the Engagement, condemned Hamilton as
a traitor and censured their own parliament. In consequence a majority of ministers preached against it from their pulpits, which proved
to be such a powerful deterrent against successful recruitment that
a quota system had to be adopted in many areas. But in the longer
term the split between the Engagers and their opponents thoroughly
undermined the Covenant as the basis for a settled Scottish state.

As in England, a second civil war erupted north of the border
and in Ayrshire a large force of Covenanters that were unwilling to
serve faced up to a smaller Engager unit that was compelled to retire
after a bloody skirmish. In spite of his aristocratic agenda, Hamilton
was unable to command the undivided support of his fellow nobles;
neither the Earl of Leven nor David Leslie would agree to add their
badly needed military experience to the enterprise. Nonetheless,
with the backing of a majority in the parliament, Hamilton pressed
on with his arrangements. There was better news from south of
the border, where the royalists were able to take advantage of the
diminution of parliamentary forces under Fairfax's demobilisation
plan. Forces under the command of the irrepressible Sir Marmaduke
Langdale took control of Berwick. Carlisle was also brought under
the royalist banner, which at least gave options about the route into
the north country, thus preserving the tactical initiative. Further
south and in an extraordinary coup, royalists were soon to take possession of Pontefract Castle, which was generally considered as one
of the most impregnable fortresses in England. Hamilton was also
promised a seasoned force of Ulster Scots under Robert Monro, the
successful and ruthless commander of the Scottish Covenanter army
fighting against the confederates in Ireland.

The man sent back north by Fairfax to deal with the burgeoning
Scottish threat was John Lambert. Not yet thirty, with long blond hair
and a debonair manner, Lambert was an intelligent and ambitious
officer from Yorkshire who shared a number of local connections

with the Fairfax family. He was the younger son of Josias Lambert, who made a profitable living from the wool trade until impoverished by the slump in prices in the 1630s. He died during his son's early teenage years. John Lambert later married Frances Lister, an equally ambitious lady whose family came from the West Riding and who were influential in the politics of Yorkshire and the strategically important port of Hull. He had fought under Ferdinando Fairfax in the Northern Association and had already served with some bravery at both Nantwich and Marston Moor, when he was badly wounded in 1645. After a convalescence, Lambert returned to the army as a colonel of foot in the New Model Army and once again fought at Fairfax's side in the campaign in the south-west of England and later at the siege of Oxford.

Lambert was tough-minded and very much a soldiers' soldier, an attribute that commended him to the uncomplicated and phlegmatic lord general, and at the conclusion of the hostilities in 1646 he was prominent in the moves to ensure that parliament met its obligations to the troops. As he was legally trained, he was also involved in the process to impeach those members of the Commons most at odds with the New Model Army, and helped Ireton to draft the Heads of Proposals. On religious matters, Lambert was not known for doctrinaire opinions and his close personal affinity with Fairfax was highly important to the development of his later career. 'Black Tom's' father had recently died and amongst the titles passed on was the custody of Pontefract Castle, now in royalist hands. With his landed interests directly threatened by the Scots' line of march, the lord general's appointment of his fellow Yorkshireman was a mark of high trust and confidence. Having gilded his growing reputation by restoring order and discipline after Poyntz's abortive *putsch* at the head of the residual Northern Association, Lambert now commanded forces depleted by demobilisation. Nevertheless, he approached the threat posed by the Scots with energy and resourcefulness.

The subsequent Preston campaign, as the Scottish Engager invasion became known, was a tactical triumph for the English with longer-term strategic consequences. Taking in hand his small but highly motivated force, Lambert was able to keep the royalist troops assembled at Carlisle and Berwick at bay, but once Hamilton crossed the border, the overwhelming size of the invading army compelled him to retire. Astutely, he concentrated his units at Appleby to cover both sides of the Pennines should the invaders choose to take either route and provided a force of scouts to maintain contact with the Scots once Hamilton decided to march south via Lancashire, the better able to join with the insurgents in Wales. There was no welcome now from the inhabitants of a power nominally joined to them by the Solemn League. In appalling weather conditions which played havoc with the supply and sustenance of both armies, Hamilton's relatively untrained force trudged into England in torrential rain, frequently dispersing raiding parties to seek food for the soldiers and fodder for their hungry horses. The duke was personally brave but completely unsuited to the task of directing operations in a decisive manner. He was not helped by the quarrelsome relationships among his senior commanders, who rendered contradictory advice about the army's dispositions. The most battle-hardened of his troops were still arriving in dribs and drabs from Ulster which meant that he had his most experienced soldiers to the rear rather than in the vanguard.

Much more seriously, as he passed south of Lancaster and across the Forest of Bowland towards Preston, he allowed his whole force to become dangerously spread out. Displaying the usual impatience of cavalrymen when forced to advance with the footslogging infantry, the senior commander of his horse, John Middleton, persuaded Hamilton to let him press on south, the better able to seek rations for the whole army. With the line of march now dangerously attenuated, the Scots were practically oblivious of the new threat developing on their eastern flank for, in mid August, Cromwell arrived with badly needed reinforcements. For the second time, he had been given independent command and he used it ruthlessly, driving his troops, who were weary from their recent exertions in Wales, to league up with Lambert hundreds of miles to the north-east. Cromwell arrived by a circuitous route and was forced to march via Leicester to pick up badly needed coats and boots from a community of artisans that had hardly recovered from their trauma three years before. But after the savage fighting and campaigning in Wales, the uniforms of his soldiers were so threadbare and worn that they resembled an army of scarecrows. Eventually, the two groups joined up at Knaresborough where, seizing the opportunity to split Hamilton's much larger force into smaller chunks that allowed him to hold the tactical advantage, Cromwell now conducted one of the more daring manoeuvres in British military history.

Advancing swiftly south-west down the Ribble Valley, Cromwell paused briefly at Stonyhurst Hall, the home of a local Roman Catholic. Today it is a Jesuit boarding school and in its refectory, under the gaze of the portraits of the college's seven recipients of the Victoria Cross, stands the vast oak table on which Cromwell allegedly spent the night before his *coup de main*. On the morning of 17 August 1648 he marched onto the high ground to the north of the River Ribble hoping to cut Hamilton's army in two, thereby sealing off the line of withdrawal for much of his force. For once, the duke had held to good advice from Sir Marmaduke Langdale, who was leading a screening force to the east of the main body precisely to deter the thrust that Cromwell was now endeavouring to make. But the New Model scouts were better organised and, having bloodily dispersed the royalist flank guard in a surprise attack, Cromwell advanced on the main body of the Scottish army as it converged on Preston. The duke himself narrowly avoided capture in a skirmish from which his outnumbered command group bravely extricated itself, but he now faced a highly mobile force without the benefit of his own cavalry, the bulk of which was far to the south near the town of Wigan. There followed a desperate attempt by the badly mauled Scots to regroup and Hamilton conducted a night withdrawal southwards to reunite with Middleton. Redeploying in darkness while still in contact with the enemy is a most risky manoeuvre even for commanders with far more skill than Hamilton, and the move was a disaster; both men had the same idea which they failed properly to co-ordinate and each set of troops unknowingly passed each other going in the opposite direction as the cavalry retraced their move back north.

For Cromwell, the immediate problem was to prevent the Scottish army from withdrawing towards their homeland and joining with the seasoned troops of Monro, but when he discovered that his adversaries seemed to be heading further into England, he set off in hot pursuit. At this point the discipline, skill and morale of the aggressively led New Model soldiers proved decisive. Both sides had taken heavy casualties and the surviving soldiers were exhausted, but it was the will of the Scots that broke first. Middleton's force was scattered while the infantry were harried back towards Wigan and thence to Warrington, where thousands were taken prisoner under the leaden skies. Many were attacked by furious local inhabitants who had been brought to the end of their tethers by the continued disruption and depredations of the war. Their senior commanders galloped off to the south-east, still arguing like cockerels about who bore responsibility for the debacle. Hamilton eventually surrendered and was unceremoniously hauled off to London to join the growing band of royalist notables now lodged in the Tower as neighbours to the incarcerated Levellers.

As the Scots were being pulled apart on the Lancashire heath, further to the south the siege of Colchester was reaching its bloody denouement. There was to be no offer of 'quarter' now, and Fairfax conducted a ruthless campaign to starve the garrison into submission with escapees either killed on the spot or sent back stripped of their clothes, as were a group of women who had attempted flight. Contemporary broadsheets described a vicious struggle with the use of poisoned bullets by the defenders and the determination of the besieging troops to cut off the town's water supply. Eventually the garrison was forced into submission. The blue-blooded amongst the prisoners, namely the Earl of Norwich and Lord Capel, were interred; no such luck awaited those who had given their parole after earlier royalist defeats. Summarily condemned as 'soldiers of fortune', Sir Charles Lucas and Sir George Lisle were both shot amongst the shattered buildings of the town, but not before the former had defiantly justified his action as his duty to his sovereign, whose commission he held. But whereas Fairfax's attitude to victory was grimly pragmatic, if judicially questionable, Cromwell professed to see the hand of the Almighty in his great victory in Lancashire.

The divines in Scotland came to the same conclusion and the news of Hamilton's defeat was greeted with prim-lipped satisfaction. In the south-west of the country, locus of the fiercest opposition to the Engagement, a popular rebellion broke out supported by members of the nobility. Argyll lent some of his clan Campbell soldiers to the enterprise. The military element of the so-called 'Whiggamore' rising was crushed with some ease outside Stirling by the hardbitten soldiers of Monro's army who had survived the rout of their colleagues at Preston. But the wider royalist defeat had taken the political wind from the sails of the Engagers and Argyll regained his earlier dominance with the tacit approval of the Kirk. His most urgent priority was to forestall an invasion by the victorious English troops; certainly Cromwell interpreted his commission as one to extirpate the Scottish military threat on whichever side of the border it manifested itself, and Argyll's entreaties that he stay south of the Tweed fell on deaf ears. Against negligible opposition, the New Model soldiers occupied Edinburgh and its environs in the first week of October. For all his moral antipathy towards the evangelising intolerance of the Scottish Presbyterians, Cromwell's practical concerns ensured that there was a limited meeting of minds when he eventually came face to face with Argyll and Wariston. His military mission was satisfied by the agreement of the Scots to disband the larger part of their army, an order that was received with a great deal of indignation by those troops who had remained undefeated. He also indicated approval for a thorough weeding out of those 'disaffected elements' which had had any hand in the process of 'Engagement'.

With his northern flank secured, Cromwell headed southwards to deal with Pontefract, leaving Lambert in Edinburgh with a force thought to be of sufficient size to ensure the Scots' good behaviour. The political consequences of the Preston campaign were to be far reaching. The perfidy of erstwhile Protestant allies thoroughly discredited the Presbyterians as a political force and reframed the rebellion as one in which English national interests would henceforth take precedence as a matter of policy. It made it far easier to conceive of Charles Stuart as a traitor in his own right, not one misled by 'evil counsellors'. In Scotland, it led to an extended purge of the political elite, the military cadre and those elements within the Kirk deemed insufficiently zealous, such that many were ejected from their ministry. Given the relative size of its population, the clear-out resembled a form of cultural revolution, later enshrined in the notorious Act of Classes, and led to a hollowing of the nation's leadership. For Cromwell, the denouement showed that he had some skill as a politician and made his military victory more complete. Although his correspondence at the time cast his triumphs firmly at the feet of his Maker and betray little sense of a personal agenda, Cromwell could have been forgiven a moment of self-exaltation. It was a victory for him alone, without patrons other than God.

The second civil war had a deep effect on the sensibilities of those who had to do the fighting. For many senior royalists the defeat meant facing up to penurious exile or uneasy accommodation with the regime of the victors. For an unlucky multitude of captured royalist and Engager soldiers, there was only the prospect of servitude in the tropical heat of the plantations in the Caribbean. A few, like George Monck, had been nimbly able to transfer their allegiance from the losing to the winning side and prosper accordingly. The fighting had been the manifestation of a much deeper groundswell of unrest which was rooted in anger at the social and economic consequences of the first civil war, a strong current of royalist loyalty and antipathy towards the military class in general. For the New Model Army, the renewal of the struggle had come as a profound spiritual shock, particularly to the more pious and godly of the officer corps. The insurrections cast doubt on the sanction that they believed God had given to their complete victory in 1646 and the initial reaction of the army was instinctive – a prayer meeting was called at Windsor which lasted for over three days. The abiding themes were of repentance and seeking God's guidance for the completion of what everyone had hitherto assumed to be His will.

In achieving a victory at both the first and second time of asking, the attitude of the soldiers hardened such that 'they thought God's providence would cast the trust of religion and the kingdom upon them as conquerors'.[1] Its piety affronted, the political conscience of the New Model Army took further shape, the meshing of some of those strands of radicalism that had been detected at Putney. The king, who there had been likened to a biblical nemesis, was now specifically identified as the author of the nation's ills and the officer corps pledged to hold him to account. There was scarcely less antagonism towards the parliament which had tried to split the army in 1647, too many of whose members had seemed to be in league with the treacherous Scots, and who were disdainful and hostile to the spiritual orientation of the men who had actually done the fighting on their behalf. As the soldiers had been on their knees at Windsor, another blast had come from the divines of the Presbyterian ministry which in a *vindiciae veritatis* lamented the breaking of the Covenant and condemned the sectaries and their disruptive impact on the soldiery. As in the previous year, the army strongly sensed that it was being sold short by a hostile establishment.

The fearful mood of the political class was different. Contrary to the understanding of the Council of Officers, the Vote of No Address was honoured more in the breach than in the observance. In a sign of reorientation at Westminster, a group of MPs who had been in favour of a resolute prosecution of the war and whose numbers included Oliver St John, Viscount Saye and Sele and Bulstrode Whitelocke now tried to engage directly with the king in an effort to detach him from the Scots. This grouping had formerly provided the civilian impetus to the Heads of Proposals. It was far less preoccupied than the army with the idea of Charles's personal guilt and concluded that abiding peace would remain elusive so long as the king remained unreconciled to his military defeat in 1646. In this there was some common ground with the Presbyterian party whose numbers were augmented, to the consternation of the New Model Army, by the return to their seats of the ten surviving MPs (grouped around Holles) whom the army had previously censured. The priority of the Independents was severely to restrict the king's constitutional powers while providing some latitude on a religious settlement; for the Presbyterian group it was precisely the other way around. A majority retained the belief that the role of parliament was to sanction legitimate rule, not to provide it. On this point, there had been enough consensus for the Commons to vote in April by 165 votes to 99 'not to alter the fundamental government of the kingdom'.

Behind these manoeuvres was a desperation for peace and minds concentrated by the approach of London towards an economic breaking point. The unrest in those eastern areas formerly at one with the parliamentary cause and the increase in the Assessment meant further, and now intolerable, strain was placed on the financial resources of the capital. The appetite and ability of Londoners to bankroll a war that seemed without end had been thoroughly dulled by the renewed struggle and disruption. An additional burden was the defection of a material proportion of the fleet to the service of the royalists and the king's son and his advisers had wasted little time in deploying his naval windfall for predatory attacks on commercial shipping in the Thames, the Medway and in the Channel. Westminster was assailed with desperate demands for a settlement with the king. There was now a coincident conviction amongst the political elite that a civil solution by way of a personal treaty should be found before a martial one became unavoidable or anarchy overwhelmed the state. In the words of the Independent MP Nathaniel Fiennes, everyone wanted 'a safe well-grounded peace'. Accordingly, the MPs formally repealed the Vote of No Address before Fairfax had even prevailed at Colchester and while Cromwell was following up his victory at Preston.

Once more, Charles was denied his request to be heard in London but official talks were resumed in the third week of September 1648, this time in the town hall of Newport on the Isle of Wight. The stage management of the event was such that the king could have been forgiven for thinking that he was negotiating from a position as victor. He was accorded all the deference due a more exalted monarch and installed beneath a great canopy of state supported by a team of advisers much larger than that which he had enjoyed in his years of captivity. Opposite him was the fifteen-strong parliamentary delegation, arrayed in a position of apparent supplication. The group contained six members who had served on the Committee of Both Kingdoms and included half a dozen peers, among them the Earl of Nothumberland, the Earl of Salisbury and Viscount Saye and Sele. In unconscious emulation of Christ's trials in the desert, forty days were set as the time limit on negotiation.

The Newport process ultimately proved to be a triumph of hope over experience. Neither side seemed to have learnt much from prior attempts at a settlement but the difference this time was that Charles was faced by a more unified cohort of the various groups that had provided the intellectual ballast of the revolt against him. Control of the militia and the principle of ministerial accountability to parliament were conceded by the monarch but once again the stumbling block proved to be the proposed religious settlement. The king, knowing that those who adhered to the Covenant had been much weakened, may also have persuaded himself to hold out against the Presbyterian element by the presence amongst his adversaries of the Independents marshalled by Henry Vane.

In his mid-thirties, Vane combined a high intelligence with administrative zeal and he was one of the leaders of that group in the Commons which had argued for a more vigorous prosecution of the war. His portrait is distinguished by his heavily hooded eyes with their sceptical and somewhat condescending stare. He had been educated at Westminster School and Oxford, and seemed to have had a searing religious experience in his early teens. His decided views were a challenge to his more worldly and conventional father, although both eventually shared in the opposition to the personal rule of Charles I. In common with a number of evangelicals, the younger Vane's progressive sense of religious enlightenment drew him to the plantations in north-east America, although he was hardly a frontiersman, and his comfortable progress was eased by patronage back home – his father was a commissioner for the colonies, after all. Yet he impressed his peers enough to be elected governor of Massachusetts, and was known as both a constitutionalist and a man of sincere faith who believed in the liberty of conscience of others. He had served too on the Committee of Both Kingdoms and had shown great practical application. Now at Newport, he had few illusions about the good faith of the monarch and was out of sympathy with the agenda of Holles, but in common with the others he was motivated by the desire for peace.

Knowing that the issue of the proposed power of the Presbytery was a weak spot, the king nevertheless squandered an opportunity to place the onus of delivering a successful religious agreement on his opponents. Instead he kept his previous position; he was only prepared to concede a trial run for Presbyterianism while retaining the body of the episcopacy to take over once the experiment had been concluded. In desperation, the theatrical Holles went down on his knees to implore his sovereign to concede the bishops and save the talks from intercession by the army. But the king, feeling that he had got the better of the theological arguments, was obdurate. In any case, Charles was by now negotiating with negligible sincerity and his correspondence showed he was determined to renege on his word even at the point of giving it.[2] Appalled by the thought that he was being asked to sanction his metamorphosis from absolute sovereign to constitutional eunuch in a theocratic state he became desperate to flee, naïvely believing his concessions would facilitate his escape. Nonetheless, the talks dragged on beyond the date originally set for their termination. Despite his hopes to the contrary, the king was secure as a prisoner and now the priority was to get him to sign into law those concessions he had given verbally lest he go back on his manifestly untrustworthy word. Focused on the closure of a settlement being negotiated over a hundred miles away but which seemed to be tantalisingly within its grasp, parliament's attention drifted away from the growing radicalism in the army.

Once again, the spark for the gunpowder of unrest amongst the soldiers of the New Model Army was arrears. For the crucial three months of September through November while the civilians argued on the Isle of Wight, the military went without pay. Fairfax had sited his command centre at St Albans and within easy reach of those like Edmund Ludlow who were not part of the Newport negotiating team and had their own radical agenda to propagate at army headquarters. The zealous Ludlow tried to persuade Fairfax that the New Model Army's godly interests were vulnerable in the current negotiations and urged the army to bring the Newport process to a halt. The lord general was unmoved by these importunities but Ireton was strongly minded to exploit the leverage conferred by the soldiers' recent victories. His Puritan sensibilities had been outraged by the perfidy of the royalists and the king's manifest determination to resist the will of God. He was likely also spurred by indignation that his parliamentary collaborators in the drafting of the Heads of Proposals were now prepared to treat directly with the discredited monarch without due consideration of the military. Likewise meeting the phlegmatic resistance of Fairfax, he offered his resignation. The lord general refused it, suspecting that his subordinate was becoming overwrought in his determination to provide an abstract rationale for the army's actions and needing Ireton to focus on his practical military duties instead.

But each passing month reminded Fairfax that the civilians were again reneging on the practical aspects of their contract with the New Model Army. As during the longueurs of the peace process the previous year, the interval that succeeded the conclusion of the fighting in the summer of 1648 provided a vacuum that the Levellers attempted to fill. The visceral intensity of the second civil war was more suited to the re-emergence of Lilburne, who had been coincidently released from gaol at the repeal of the Vote of No Address. In spite of his denunciations of the army 'grandees' over the course of the previous twelve months, the radical had all the self-confidence to immediately use his new liberty to pay Cromwell a visit in the north. He was, however, disappointed by the general's apparent lack of political imagination in his moment of victory. Nevertheless, the Levellers had learnt the lesson of their rebuff the previous year and returned with an agenda in which the challenges to constitutional authority were toned down and proposals for social amelioration amplified. A

news-sheet entitled *The Moderate* began to appear as an alternative to
the propaganda broadsheets of the war years. Critically, the former
ambiguity of their attitude towards the military was softened by the
identification of the soldiers as saviours of the nation and seekers of
religious liberty.

On 11 September a Leveller petition to the 'Commons of England
in Parliament Assembled' was delivered. Representing 'well-affected'
persons from the city of London and its immediate environs,
the document attracted 40,000 signatures, itself a colossal feat of
organisation. Of the twenty-seven proposals, eight were reserved for
constitutional matters and there was no mention of the franchise,
the source of so much friction at Putney. King and lords were to be
retained but neither was to have a 'negative voice' in respect of the
determinations of the 'supreme' Commons. Some judicial matters
were identified for reform. Trial by jury by citizens rather than aristocrats was held sacrosanct, and punishment ought to fit the crime.
Specifically, imprisonment for debt was challenged. There were, too,
a number of economic and financial recommendations, including
an attack on the hated Excise; instead, individual subsidies ('the old
and only just way of England') should be favoured over indiscriminate national taxes. There were calls that trade and merchandising
should be freed from monopoly and tithes abolished in favour of a
fairer way of paying the clergy. Refuting the widespread imputation
that the Levellers aimed at common ownership, property was held
to be inviolate. On the vexed issue of religious toleration, the document called for complete freedom of worship but reserved a right of
'un-compulsive' leadership in spiritual matters to parliament.

The Leveller document was animated by the spirit of equality before
the law rather than social revolution. It was a powerful statement
against the war regime and the exemplary measures (tax; military service under compulsion; the suspension of justice) that had been used
to sustain it. The Commons was preoccupied with the agenda for
Newport and not minded to have it usurped by extra-parliamentary
agitation whose sole locus seemed to be London. It rejected the petition, provoking widespread rioting in the capital. The funeral of the

recently assassinated Rainsborough was also exploited with a large display of public protest. Outside the capital, the Leveller agenda did achieve some wider resonance in the New Model Army and soon supportive petitions came from a number of regiments, many now under the direct command of Cromwell in the north.

At Windsor, Ireton worked on his own proposals. Over the course of the autumn these were developed and debated in the Council of Officers and emerged as the *Remonstrance of the Army*. Although early drafts were written in the sententious style of the commissary-general (the royalist periodical *Mercurius Pragmaticus* teased him as 'one that was bred up to long indentures'), the final document was in fact the work of a number of hands including those of Hugh Peter, who supplied suitable biblical references.[3] In tone and content, it was an intensely religious document and emphasised that the army had fought to remove the 'snares and chains' from 'conscientious and zealous men', and to 'give freedom and enlargement to the Gospel'. Here was the hand of Cromwell exercised through that of his son-in-law. The Presbyterian agenda of rigid conformity was rejected. Whereas the Heads of Proposals had been conceived as a basis for governance and peace, the *Remonstrance* was more fundamental, arguing that the relationship between the ruler and the ruled should take the form of a civic covenant. It aimed at the removal of the current sovereign, to be replaced by an elected king subject to a written constitution. The current parliament, which had been sitting since 1640, was to be dissolved.

The *Remonstrance* was also unmistakably an army document – Leveller input was solicited by the radically inclined Ireton and Harrison, but the agendas of each group of soldiers and civilians were only ever linked rather than joined. The authority and acquiescence of the lord general was critical and the narrative that suggests he was merely an observer of the developments over the autumn of 1648 is unconvincing. Fairfax's forceful entry into the political arena was dictated by circumstance rather than ideological conviction and he determinedly restrained the impulses of his more radical colleagues in the Council of Officers. While the Newport process dragged on, the army remained unpaid and Fairfax was tired of the continual opprobrium aimed at the troops. Throughout the period, he was consistently and sternly critical of the system of free quarter which, although authorised by the MPs, compromised 'the honour of Parliament, the good of the People and the reputation of the Army'.[4] It was not the fault of the soldiers that the politicians seemed to be making so little progress.

He was also acutely aware that his public assurances about the material welfare of the troops, which had won the day at Ware, were being eroded by the apparent irresponsibility of the politicians to the detriment of his authority. In the north, Cromwell alike was angered by the attitude of the politicians and piqued by the imputation of some MPs that his arrangements with the Scots had been far too lenient. He condemned the talks in the south as 'a ruining hypocritical agreement', reflecting the more militant mood of his troops. Yet his letters to Hammond reveal that he was hesitant about the political direction of the army and minded to let God's providence show the path ahead. His secretary, Richard Spavin, captured the feeling of exasperation, writing 'I verily think God will break that great idol of the Parliament and that old job-trot form of government of King, Lords and Commons.'[5]

By contrast, Fairfax was further forward in wishing to break the impasse. Unlike Ireton, he was far less exercised about the need for physical retribution against the king. However, Charles's duplicity could no longer be disputed and he accepted that the monarch would have to be formally called to account. The problem was how to concentrate the minds in parliament while acting within the bounds of constitutional legality. Fairfax had already publicly subscribed the proposal that the parliament should be wound up, but that this should be achieved by self-dissolution. Ireton was more militant and favoured annulment, with the army effectively acting as the agent of change. Determined to observe what he considered the proprieties, Fairfax authorised a direct appeal from the New Model Army to the king to come to an agreement on terms that would have been entirely familiar to him. Charles, gratified by the apparent weakening of the commissioners and by the prospect of a return to London to argue his case, spurned Fairfax's initiative. The Council of Officers' only logical move was to send the *Remonstrance* to parliament, which went with a covering letter in the hand of the lord general himself.

The last ten days of November 1648 proved to be a pivotal period and a remarkable pamphlet appeared on the streets, declaring that the civilians' patience with the army's petitioning and political interference was at an end. The *Animadversions upon the Armies Remonstrance* was a closely argued and full-fronted assault on the presumptions of the Council of Officers, with Ireton singled out for special censure.[6] Written by the Presbyterian MP Clement Walker, who was a close associate of William Prynne, the document ridiculed the amateurism and contradictions of the soldiers' interventions: by taking charge of the king, the army had nonetheless allowed him access to the 'most malignant of his party' (thus prolonging the war), while Ireton seemed not to know whether he had been for or against the Vote of No Address. Fairfax was scolded too for presenting a Leveller document although he had previously disowned the movement at Ware. How could the army object to a personal treaty with the monarch when the most senior commanders had previously insisted that his dignity and rights be preserved? Furthermore, the officers' attempts to forge a settlement on their own authority had directly contravened specific ordinances of parliament, such as the one abolishing episcopacy. They were subverting the Newport process (the only chance of peace) as 'being inconsistent with their independent interests' and their demand that the king be brought to justice was contrary to all law. Most seriously, their disobedience of the MPs' instruction to keep the New Model Army away from London and refusal to fully disband was a clear threat to peace, and if parliament were to be dissolved there would be nothing to protect the citizenry from a military dictatorship.

In such an atmosphere of tense recrimination and military unrest, the process at Newport was further extended by the MPs and the *Remonstrance* was laid aside without consideration. Instead, the members debated a new militia ordinance to bring the military establishment more formally under civilian control, implicitly disbanding the New Model in the process. As Lucy Hutchinson noted in her memoir, the army was to be 'the peace offering of this un-Godly reconciliation'.[7] A prayer meeting was called at Windsor officiated by Hugh Peter, but Fairfax was now beyond waiting for the intercession of the Almighty. Ireton's intense lobbying and the anxious agitation of mid-ranking officers like Waller, Rich, Hewson and Pride now appeared prescient; the politicians at Newport seemed determined to 're-inthrone' the king and abandon their obligations to the army. His honour and that of his officers thoroughly insulted, Fairfax decided to act, in the first instance by securing Charles. Colonel Ewer was despatched to the Isle of Wight but in the excitement seemed to bungle his orders – Hammond was indignant at the termination of his commission without what he considered to be proper parliamentary authority and headed to Windsor to seek clarification, where he was firmly enlightened. In the interim, the king was conveyed without ceremony across the Solent to the forbidding and desolate sea-fortress of Hurst Castle.

Cromwell was commanded to return to London to ensure that there was no perception of division amongst the senior officers. With the army on the move from Windsor and threatening the *coup d'état* that many like Holles had feared for so long, the Commons belatedly debated the *Remonstrance* and rejected the army by a majority of 125 to 58 votes.[8] The Speaker's offer to sweeten the rebuff with overdue pay was ignored as the New Model Army proceeded to occupy London, which it did on 2 December without resistance. Among its acts was to secure bullion and gold plate held at the guild and livery halls as security for payment of arrears, and soldiers were forcibly billeted on any who demurred. Egged on by the irrepressibly dogmatic Prynne (who had recently been returned as the member for Cornwall, and who now demanded Fairfax be cashiered and his troops condemned as rebels), the MPs separately voted to continue to pursue a personal treaty with the discredited king. The die was cast, but Fairfax had already placed his hand on the hilt of his sword.

7

'In the name of the people of England'
Westminster Hall

This is not a law of yesterday, Sir, but a law of old.

John Bradshaw

For the people and truly I desire their Liberty And Freedom
as much as any body whomsoever. But I must tell you that
their Liberty and Freedom consists of having of Government
those laws by which their life and their goods may be most
their own. It is not for having *share* in Government, Sir; that
is nothing pertaining to them. A Subject and a Sovereign are
clear different things.

Charles I

Though the change of a government were believed not to
be lawful, yet it may be lawfully obeyed.

Francis Rous MP

The purging of parliament under the direction of Colonel Thomas
Pride in December 1648 was a disastrous episode in the relationship between the army and the civilian politicians who had led the

rebellion against the king. In hindsight the New Model Army's actions in the previous year now appeared as a full dress rehearsal complete with a public political statement, the proscription of named MPs and the occupation of the capital. The difference was that whereas in 1647 the New Model Army could plausibly claim to be intervening at the behest of parliament, this time there was no such invitation. It was an act of despotism which, in its scale, not even Charles I had attempted.

At the time, the soldiers' action was all of a piece with the circumstances of a nation still in a state of civil war. The Scots had merely been quelled and had offered no more than their parole under the direction of a clique around Argyll. Considered to be still in full rebellion, Ireland seemed close to secession and in an ominous development, the Dutch had signed a naval agreement with the Confederacy which amplified the maritime threat posed by the fleet under the sway of the king's son. Civil unrest continued to present a threat to public order, particularly in London. The duplicity of the monarch with the apparent connivance of MPs had enraged the rank and file in the army and a large section of the officer corps, and made a well-founded peace in which citizens could have confidence seem highly remote. To all intents and purposes, the country had many of the characteristics of a failed state and the circumstances were ripe for a highly motivated group to promote a new agenda.

The catalyst for the purge was the decision to continue negotiations with the king and the civilians' obvious reluctance to hold him personally to account for his part in perpetuating the civil war. As Cromwell had written to Hammond in late November, Newport meant that 'the whole fruit of war (was) like to be frustrated'. He was not alone in his apprehension, Lucy Hutchinson noting in her *Memoirs* that Newport 'so frightened all the honest people that it made them as violent in their zeal to pull down as the others were in their madness to restore this kingly idol'.[1] That the basis of the army's intervention was not the *Remonstrance* was no doubt to the chagrin of its principle contributor Henry Ireton, but it reflected the more practical and soldierly instincts of Fairfax at that moment.

Those MPs considered for removal from the Commons were instead identified by their adherence to the Newport process and, perhaps more seriously, by their open endorsement of the Engager invasion in the summer. Ireton had been in favour of a forced dissolution, which put him at odds with the Levellers but far more importantly, with his own commander-in-chief. Now a group of MPs met with a deputation of the Council of Officers to further emphasise that dissolution of the current House would lack any legitimacy and place the full onus of achieving a settlement on the army. However, radicals like Marten and Ludlow recognised that the mood of bitterness in the military could be exploited to help them drive out their toughest opponents amongst the Presbyterians. The decision was therefore made to purge about thirty of those MPs most enthusiastic to pursue a personal treaty with the untrustworthy monarch.

On the morning of 6 December 1648, Pride flooded the precincts of Westminster with heavily armed New Model troops. There was some concern that the London-trained bands might rally to their masters in the Commons but Philip Skippon, although a Presbyterian of conviction, was a soldier first and ordered them not to intervene. Nonetheless, the action over the two days contained many elements of improvisation and farce which ensured that the event took on a complexion that was completely unintentional but of long-lasting significance. Pride was only recently back from the campaign in Lancashire and had no other intelligence than a list. He was therefore reliant on Lord Grey of Groby to act as the cat's paw for the coup. Groby was an MP and a soldier, but he was not infallible. As the soldiers desperately tried to put their list of names to faces, a number of members refused to identify themselves while others managed to creep into the chamber by unguarded doors and had to be winkled out protesting loudly at the monstrous breach of parliament's privilege. Some were arrested while more than a hundred were merely turned away. Predictably, William Prynne created a terrific rumpus and had to be wrestled to the ground in an undignified scrum of flailing limbs, cloaks and broad-brimmed hats. Amid shows of great indignation by the MPs and of vilification by the soldiers, around forty members were eventually escorted or shoved into a large cook house adjacent to a store room in the precincts, respectively known later as 'Heaven' and 'Hell'.

Some were speedily released on the orders of Fairfax, including Nathaniel Fiennes, the son of Viscount Saye and Sele, and (much to the exasperation of Ireton) Prynne himself. Over succeeding days, the majority were set free on parole but some were held and a number were rearrested and incarcerated at St James's Palace. These were considered to be the most irreconcilable members of the Presbyterian faction and included Sir William Waller, Sir John Clotworthy and Edward Massey. Denzil Holles, the biggest prize of all, managed to evade arrest and escaped to France but his colleagues were to face a number of years in detention without trial. Meanwhile, a deputation of vexed and frightened MPs attended the lord general to demand an explanation, an approach which the soldier politely but laconically parried.

Fairfax was too canny an individual to get intimately involved with Pride's chaotic piece of theatre but the over-emphatic denial of knowledge contained in his *Short Memorials* published after his death strains credulity. The *Memorials* were carefully edited and produced to a purpose which distorted the testimony of the soldier, who was himself describing events well after they had occurred. His recollection is also contradicted by the *Memoirs* of Ludlow. Far from being a dupe of the radicals, in late 1648 Fairfax may be seen as being guilty of no more than a determined partiality towards his soldiers and officers. His actions were consistent with his behaviour the previous year in an atmosphere that was just as charged. However, the application of his integrity on this occasion was unsuccessful. That the lord general was a demonstrably gifted and admired soldier was not in doubt but his political judgement was far less well developed. For by allowing the army to be used to drive out a caucus firmly attached to a personal settlement with the king, Fairfax alienated a much larger group of moderates and waverers, and ensured that only the most radically inclined remained to dictate events in parliament.

Over the next two months a small core of about seventy MPs

remained active in what was later derisorily referred to as the 'Rump'. While some attended the Commons out of a residual sense of duty to their constituents, a group of highly energised militants that included Henry Marten, Thomas Scot and Thomas Chaloner seized the initiative. Critically, the larger group that had provided parliamentary support to the New Model Army and weight to the Heads of Proposals was now driven apart from the soldiers by the unconstitutionality of the purge. Even Henry Vane, who had been for so long a stout defender of the army and who had publicly doubted that a personal treaty with the king could be effected, now absented himself from the Commons. For these outcomes Cromwell too shared some responsibility, notwithstanding that he had been absent on campaign as the political tension in the capital grew. The number of serving soldiers within the House of Commons was material but Fairfax was particularly dependent on Cromwell for his leadership of this group and for his political impact amongst the civilians. Somewhat distrustful of the abstract intensity of the verbose Ireton, the commander-in-chief was more inclined to rely on the older soldier, with whom he shared a close professional relationship that contained much personal respect.

Yet Cromwell had hesitated when ordered back to London, unenthusiastically endorsed the purge once it had taken place and spent the next two months acquiescing in events rather than using his enhanced authority to help Fairfax to mould them.[2] As in 1647, Fairfax was personally disinclined to provide political direction, still less dictate the terms of a settlement, which he saw not as his job but the responsibility of parliament and the king. Cromwell was loyal to Fairfax but was far more minded to await the signs of God's providence, fortified in his belief by the serial success the Almighty had granted him and his troops on the battlefield. However, by acquiescing in the opposition to the Newport process and purging the Commons, the responsibility which Fairfax and Cromwell had wanted to avoid (albeit for different reasons) was left in the hands of the radicals in the Rump and a Council of Officers which was ill-equipped to deal with it. Seeking to build a coalition by other means, some officers treated with the Levellers and discussions were held at Whitehall in the second week of December.

As recorded by Clarke, Ireton was again in commanding but dogmatic form. Lilburne mistrusted Ireton, whom he called the 'alpha and omega' of the army, and preferred to deal with Harrison, whom he perceived to be more sympathetic to the Leveller ideals. An updated version of the *Agreement of the People* was debated but as with the *Remonstrance*, Ireton only seemed interested by Leveller contributions where they coincided with his own. Lilburne appealed directly to Fairfax to resolve the 'tedious tug we had with Commissary General' but the commander-in-chief was disinclined to get involved and both Overton and Lilburne walked away from the discussions within a few days. To officers like Hardress Waller, debates about the franchise in the new dispensation were beside the point. What mattered was to bring the king speedily to justice and to that end Charles was brought to Windsor in the last week of the month. Now all the debate centred on the conditions of Charles's confinement, the charges to be brought against him and the desire of many officers to have him executed for his perfidy. On all these issues Cromwell was an unpersuasive voice of caution against the zeal of his son-in law, the radicals in the Commons and those of intermediate military rank like Waller, Pride, Okey and Hewson who articulated the vengeful mood in the Council of Officers.

In the bleak Christmas season, the streets of London were wreathed in speculation and recrimination. The royalist press had been driven underground by the tightening of the war regime but following the example of the Levellers it managed to covertly print and distribute opinion, news and rumour. Cromwell had been a habitual target of attack on account of his profile astride the military and civil divide. Now open season was declared on Fairfax, whose prestige and authority had hitherto been almost unassailed. Notwithstanding the public support given in sermons by the sectaries and by army chaplains like Hugh Peter, the purge was angrily attacked by the Presbyterian clergy, which still dominated the religious hierarchy of the capital.

One, Thomas Watson, even had the courage to preach before the diminished body of the Commons in St Margaret's, Westminster, prophetically declaring that they were no parliament. The soldiers were elsewhere denounced for their presumption and vainglory.

Intellectual justification for the purge was thin on the ground. In his well-attended parish church in Coleman Street, the Puritan divine John Goodwin offered exculpation of sorts in a pamphlet entitled *Right and Might Well Met*. Goodwin was no ordinary pastor but a thoughtful and large-spirited theologian who confounds contemporary notions of the Puritans as narrow-minded dogmatists. To him, individual reason and judgement rather than blind obedience were the keys to spiritual enlightenment and the reception of God's grace. His temerity in thus challenging some of the harsher aspects of Calvinist faith had seen him barred from the Westminster Assembly and his apparent unsoundness provoked unjustified denunciation by Edwards in his vituperative work *Gangraena*. Now he declared that the soldiers were merely responding to a primal law of nature that superseded anything put in place by man, by warding off the imminent destruction of the citizenry.

It was all to little avail and by the end of a joyless and working Christmas Day both Fairfax and Cromwell seemed to have concluded by separate processes of logic that the purge had been a fiasco whose further ramifications were nonetheless unstoppable. Far from being constrained by the shadow of the sword, the radicals were happy to strike out on their own. Cromwell had already counselled against the mood to execute Charles (believing that such a course of action would make him a martyr), and in a final attempt to shake the king from the attitude of resignation that he had displayed at the formal close of the talks at Newport, the Earl of Denbigh was despatched to Windsor with the grumpy approval of a majority in the Council of Officers. But the charge sheet that the soldiers had insisted on sending was unopened by the monarch, who refused to see the earl. The following day Cromwell made his famous surrender to the militants in the House of Commons, seeming to attribute the will of the Lord for his diminished appetite to offer leadership in this crucial hour.

Now that the high command had ceded the initiative, the radicals in the Commons proceeded with alacrity.[3] Cromwell was co-opted onto the committee charged with planning the king's arraignment but it was the fired-up Marten who acted as spokesman. The ordinance for the trial commenced with a sententious blast not only against the 'notorious' Charles Stuart but also against the 'many encroachments' of his predecessors. The implication that it was uniquely the current parliament which had had the wit and the courage to finally stand up to the dynasty and their numerous calumnies added a thick layer of self-righteousness to the fervour of the radical MPs. Conscious that the running of a tyrannical government was as much a matter of opinion as of legal fact, the king was specifically charged with high treason. The tiny caucus of aristocrats which still doggedly attended the Upper House were far less impressed with this line of argument. Marshalled by the Earls of Northumberland and Manchester, the peers pointed out that charging a sovereign with treason was oxymoronic and was no legal basis on which to conduct a trial. Nor could Charles be arraigned under Common Law as he was not a subject. In an extraordinary passage of scepticism, some peers even questioned whether it was not in fact the parliament rather than the king which had started the conflict in the first place. After all, the monarch's right to both call and dissolve parliament could not be disputed in law. Having placed their well-reasoned reservations on the record, the peers made themselves scarce rather in the manner of Pilate washing his hands of Christ.

The Scots too were alarmed by the direction of travel and instructed their commissioners in London to protest in the strongest terms. Their pleas were echoed by a Dutch delegation under Adriaan Pauw, one of the senior statesmen of the United Provinces. The Scots were affronted by the assault on the dynasty which they claimed as their own and pointed to the Covenant wherein the inviolability of the king's person was taken, as with the document's other particulars, as sacrosanct. Their attachment to the monarchy was no hypocrisy but an expression of profound belief in an institution that was at the core of their national identity – after all, in comparison to the royal line north of the border, the Normans and their successors were relative parvenus.

It was a time of prophecy and portents. The Council of Officers went into a conclave with Elizabeth Poole, a gentlewoman from Oxfordshire who claimed to have been vouchsafed visions entirely relevant to the proposed treatment of the king. The cult of millenarianism also seemed to be an acceptable way in which women could be permitted to publicly articulate their innermost fears and thoughts without being branded as insubordinate or heretical, or worse still, a witch. The wars had already provided the example of Anna Trapnel in London's East End, who vividly characterised the enthusiasm of those who anticipated a new epoch of rule by the saints with the fervour of her witness.[4] Katherine Chidley had gone further still. Prominent among the separatist congregations of London, she had challenged the intolerance on display in *Gangraena*, dismissing its assertions as those that 'a man of understanding would not meddle with'.[5] Elizabeth Poole herself had a strong insight into male psychology and won the soldiers' attention by describing her vision of the realm as a weak and ravaged woman that would be saved by the masculine army. It was right that the king be tried, but not that he be executed. Vengeance was a matter for God alone. The Council was impressed enough to ask the clairvoyant to return for a second consultation; the lady was asked what would happen if the king refused to co-operate with a trial by his subjects. Alas, Poole appeared not to have been acquainted with the finer points of law by the Almighty and she was respectfully sent on her way.[6]

The Commons were impervious to either legal reasoning or prophecy. The demurral of the peers and the hesitations of the soldiers had merely placed a dent in the plans for a trial, not stopped it. The unco-operative aristocrats in the Upper House were removed from the proposed list of the king's judges, and on 6 January 1649 the Commons took the penultimate step towards the turning of Great Britain and Ireland into a republic. Having already declared parliament to be the supreme authority in the land, the House of Commons decided by the tiniest quorum of its depleted membership that it could now do without their lordships as co-legislators. Further, the Commons would henceforward issue acts rather than ordinances, thus giving themselves the constitutional power to make law in their own right. Once more, Cromwell spoke up as a voice of caution by urging harmony with the peers but again he found himself among the minority. A list of 135 commissioners who would form the High Court of Justice to try the king was published and the weaknesses of the arrangements were further exposed. The attempt to achieve a broad range of representation was undermined by the decision to set a quorum for the court at twenty members – on that basis the New Model Army alone would have been able to condemn the king, as over thirty soldiers were on the list. The legality of the court was further undermined by the refusal of both of the chief justices, Oliver St John and Henry Rolle, as well as of the head of the Exchequer Court, to have any part in it.

The decision of St John was particularly serious as he had close links with the army, was related to Cromwell and had been a leading member of the Independent grouping in the Commons. Henry Vane also dissented. Fairfax's name headed the roll of commissioners and he attended the initial meeting of the court in the Painted Chamber of the Palace of Westminster. It was the last time he was to do so, at considerable cost to his later reputation. Under the circumstances, his behaviour was perhaps in accordance with what he perceived as his honour and his duty. All his instincts would have urged caution about associating himself with a process the legality of which was thoroughly flawed. That first meeting would have confirmed his foreboding: barely one-third of the commissioners attended and those that did were treated to a well-argued speech by the precocious Algernon Sydney, who amplified the earlier scepticism of the lords.

Fairfax's belief that it was not the job of the army to offer the constitutional lead remained intact and he was certainly not going to do the dirty work of the radicals and militants for them. Despite the misgivings of senior officers like Philip Skippon and Sir William Brereton, the conqueror of Chester, the overall mood of the Council of Officers was supportive of tough retribution. Fairfax was well acquainted with the king's double-dealing and to call a halt to proceedings at this stage would have risked splitting the army and reigniting civil war. It is perhaps difficult to blame Fairfax for weighing his doubts against a near certainty and coming to a conclusion that was both practicable and honourable. His abstention has been illogically and unfavourably contrasted with the apparent leadership now shown by Cromwell at this late hour, although the latter's behaviour could be better described as growing connivance in a denouement that he was able to justify to himself as being God's will.

It took a further week to settle on the charges, in the process of which the new attorney general, Anthony Steele, excused himself on account of illness. John Bradshaw, a little-known but passably competent judge of the Sheriff Court of London, was appointed as lord president of the commissioners. The duty for presenting the prosecution in court in the absence of the attorney general was delegated to three relative unknowns including a Dutch scholar who had taught at Cambridge University. Also chosen was John Cook, a committed and radical lawyer who made up in zeal and enthusiasm what he perhaps lacked in forensic skill. He had previously represented John Lilburne but was also entirely sympathetic to what he perceived as the godly mission of the army. In the depths of the second civil war he had published the pamphlet *Unum Necessarium: or, The Poor Mans Case* which argued for social reform, including free medical provision for the destitute.

Of greater impact than the selection of parliament's advocates was the decision to hold the trial in public in Westminster Hall, despite the obvious security risks. Although goodwill towards the person of the king had been severely tested, London contained many royalist sympathisers and during the long-drawn-out peace negotiations, Charles himself had frequently demanded that he be heard in the capital to exploit this well of support. So the stage management of the king's arraignment was an act of some boldness. If the king denied the authority of the court then the commissioners were determined that at least it look like one and there was no question that a process in the name of the people would be held *in camera*: this was to be a symbolic piece of theatre as much as a judicial occasion.

Charles was brought to face his accusers on 20 January 1649. It was a Saturday. The carpenters had worked night and day to prepare the venue and the king was to confront the serried ranks of his accusers from a small dais behind which was erected a screen, ostensibly to shield him from the public beyond but more likely to deter any last minute attempts at rescue. As the heavily guarded monarch entered the cavernous court on the cold winter afternoon with the light beginning to fade, his senses would have been assaulted by the oppressive gloom and the smells of freshly cut timber and tar mixed with the faintly sour odour of the large press of people who had gathered in the public galleries that were laid out on three sides. The diminutive monarch was dressed in simple but dignified attire; around his shoulders was a thick cape upon which was embroidered the enormous star of the Order of the Garter.

Beneath his large-brimmed hat however, Charles's features were careworn and his expression tired. His hair was longer and his full beard was now heavily tinted with grey: he looked far older than a man in his forty-ninth year. Surveying the scene, his hooded eyes would have taken in the presence of scores of heavily armed musketeers under the command of Colonel Axtell, who regarded him with a mixture of curiosity and hostility. To his right, sitting in tiers, were the commissioners, nervously aware of their role in a drama for which there had never been a rehearsal, but all trying hard to look authoritative and appropriately severe. In the middle sat Bradshaw, his eyes darting nervously from beneath his armour-plated hat. With measured step, Charles walked towards the dais with its velvet-covered chair that was more than a seat but far less than a throne. Disdainfully declining to remove his own hat, the king gathered his cape and sat down.

If there had ever been any doubt about Charles's personal courage, there was none now. Barely acquainted with the freshly minted charge sheet, the king defended himself alone over the following week with both spirit and aplomb. After a weak start in which he disingenuously asserted his sincere attachment to the Newport process, he soon showed his mettle and the habitual stutter that had plagued his speech deserted him. The battle revolved around the king's refusal to recognise the court and the commissioners' fruitless attempts to get him to plead. In the monarch's view, the Commons were 'never a court of judicature' and by no stretch of the imagination could the present one be said to represent the 'Commons of England and of all the people thereof'. Barely half the number of commissioners appointed to attend the trial did so and those that did represented merely a rump of the Rump Parliament. In the face of Bradshaw's bluster, Charles effectively challenged the whole legal basis of the proceedings, exposed as preposterous the court's assertion that he was an elected king and laughingly scorned the charges of treason and tyranny. There was no precedent for his accusers' thesis that the sovereign was responsible to the Commons rather than the other way around. He had no need to expose the political motivation of his accusers and the inappropriate role of the military in a civil judicial process, which he anyway denied. Instead, he attacked their usurpation of the law: 'For if power without law may make laws, may alter the fundamental laws of the Kingdom, I do not know what subject he is in England that can be sure of his life, or anything that he calls his own.'[7]

These were palpable hits and to the further consternation of the commissioners, the mood of the public in court was becoming more animated. On the first day of the trial when the roll-call of commissioners had been called, a veiled lady in the public gallery had loudly exclaimed that the lord general had more wit than to attend the proceedings, before being bustled out by her companion. As the trial progressed and the king's self-defence became more spirited, there were murmurs of approval at Charles's interjections and even the occasional 'God save His Majesty'. Now, as Bradshaw struggled to land a blow, the heckler in the gallery had returned. So when the court president again demanded that the monarch answer the charges in 'the name of the people of England' a high piping voice full of confidence and scorn rang out 'Not half, not a quarter of the people of England. Oliver Cromwell is a traitor.' It was all too much for Axtell, who ordered his men to train their muskets on the offending section of the audience, and as the spectators dived for cover the lady was again spirited away. High on his dais among the judges however, Cromwell shifted in his seat with evident embarrassment: he had recognised the voice of the wife of his commander-in-chief.[8]

In desperation, the commissioners decided that the king's refusal to plead was sufficient reason to condemn him. After seven days of fruitless skirmishing and with a looming sense that the end was near, Charles requested that he be heard before a joint session of both Lords and Commons. There was a brief wavering among some of the commissioners, but after a short recess a resolute Bradshaw delivered the sentence. It was a lengthy performance. The president of the High Court had evidently given a great deal of thought to the matter and his preparation suggested that he was not expecting any demurral from his fellow commissioners. The king derived his authority from parliament and hence from his people – parliament held the rights given in *Magna Carta* in trust and was, he asserted, the ultimate court of justice. Revealing the coronation act of anointment by God as a bit of hocus pocus that need only have calamitous effects on those that received the unction, he reminded Charles that there were a number of precedents for the removal of defective monarchs. Eventually however, the nub of the matter was finally and decisively made plain for posterity. Charles had failed to protect his people, thus breaking the intangible compact between sovereign and subject: he had to go.

The warrant for the king's execution was signed by fifty-nine of the commissioners, forty-three of them members of parliament, the majority of whom had been elected during the course of the wars. A solitary nobleman, Lord Grey of Groby, also appended his signature. The received wisdom is that Cromwell overbore the waverers to ensure that the sentence proceeded smoothly to execution, but much of this testimony came from those (such as the soldier MP Richard Ingoldsby) who were anxious to disassociate themselves from the whole process when they were eventually called to account and after Cromwell had attracted much opprobrium as head of state. The contemporary diaries of Lucy Hutchinson, wife of the regicide Colonel John Hutchinson show, *per contra*, that all who signed had the freedom to do otherwise. Her husband, a staunch Puritan, was no admirer of Cromwell and had been disdainful of the recent 'usurpations' of the army. Certainly, not all of the commissioners who attended the trial put their name to the death warrant, but the majority did. Even John Downes, who had momentarily spoken up in favour of the king's right to be heard by the whole of the parliament seemed to resolve his doubts such as to sign the document in a firm hand.

The most notable absentee was the lord general himself. Laconically aloof but troubled by the whole passage of events, it had been left to his wife with her spirited interruptions from the public gallery while the trial was in progress, to express the discomfort he undoubtedly felt. Lady Fairfax's influence on the thinking of her husband has perhaps been under-appreciated in an age when women were supposed to be subservient to their menfolk. A devout and committed Presbyterian, she had accompanied Fairfax into the field and had indeed been briefly taken prisoner by the royalists after the battle of Adwalton Moor. Her antipathy towards the activities of the sects amongst the men under her husband's command was well known and she distrusted Cromwell on account of his supposed toleration of them. Neither she nor apparently the lord general was content that she be Caesar's wife and it is possible that he sanctioned her outburst at the trial, if not her choice of words. But for all that, Fairfax was keeping his own private counsel. He had been bombarded from all sides to come off the fence, but in the end the one thing that might have moved him – an appeal for clemency from the sovereign himself – never came.

Instead, Charles met his end with all the frigid dignity that he had maintained in the face of outsiders for most of the entirety of his reign. His composure had very briefly left him at the end of his trial when he had been denied a final word and been bustled from the court exclaiming indignantly. Now he was once again in control of himself and, after saying a tender goodbye to his children Princess Elizabeth and Prince Henry (which included a short digression on the dangers of popery), he was led to the Banqueting House at Whitehall on 30 January.[9] The Palladian splendour of the building, designed by Inigo Jones, had been much dilapidated by the conditions of weather and war, and its environs were laid out as if in preparation for an imminent assault. Inside, the gloom concealed the magnificent ceiling painting, the *Apotheosis of King James I* by Rubens, which had been commissioned by Charles to celebrate the dynasty and its unification of the isles and kingdoms of Britain. Everything else was boarded up. The king had been up since dawn but now there was an unconscionable delay as it was realised that no one had given thought to the declaration of a new sovereign, which would happen automatically once the axe had fallen. A Bill forbidding such a thing was rushed through the Commons and after a sepulchral meal of bread and wine in a small antechamber, Charles was escorted onto the scaffold.

It was a cold day and he had put on two shirts under his doublet and cape. His chaplain intoned a prayer as Charles gathered his hair away from his neck under a small cap. Apart from his minister, he was entirely alone amongst his enemies. Nonetheless, the king then made a short statement which would probably have been audible only to the dense crush of soldiers around the platform. Further back a large crowd had gathered in the chilly air, their faces a mixture of anxiety, anticipation and curiosity. In a remarkable act of composure, he chose this mortal moment to remind his audience of the essence of the relationship between sovereign and subject. His words were a last instance of Stuart assertion. The sovereign then lowered his body to the level of the block. A short distance away, in a room where only the light from a candle pierced the shuttered gloom, the lord general was on his knees too, his hands clasped in prayer. Moments later it was all over and, as the heavily disguised executioner held the sovereign's severed head aloft, the crowd emitted a groan of resigned disgust, the noise that people make when they witness something appalling but which they feel powerless to prevent.

An execution of such significance created sincere outrage in the courts of Europe, but its practical effect was nugatory. The Continent was beginning its convalescence from the Thirty Years War and there was neither the energy nor the will to back the denunciations with acts of hostility. France was in the middle of an uprising of its own and Henrietta Maria received the news of her husband's death in a cold and besieged Paris. Her son, the putative king, read about it in the news-sheets. Only the Dutch and the Scots had put a serious effort into commissions that had the purpose of saving Charles's life. The Scots were particularly aggravated by their exclusion from the whole process, a point that was emphasised when the new Great Seal of the Commonwealth was produced. On its reverse was shown the truncated outline of England, Wales and Ireland; Scotland was nowhere to be seen. The estrangement was complete and once more its representatives returned in high dudgeon to Edinburgh. There the dead monarch's son was shortly declared King Charles II (subject to him taking the Covenant), despite the lurking presence of English troops.

The process of government had to continue and to be obeyed, notwithstanding the profound doubt about its legality – amongst the outrage expressed by the Presbyterians, William Prynne immediately circulated a pamphlet proclaiming Charles II as king. It was a principled and brave stand by a man who had been so savagely treated by the institution he sought to defend and his profound shock was felt by many. A small committee of members of the Commons, not all of them regicides, was tasked with drawing up a list of appointees to a new Council of State. There was evident determination to ensure that senior military representation was kept to a bare minimum and of the initial membership of forty-one, only three (Fairfax, Cromwell and Skippon) were judged acceptable: both Ireton and Harrison were rejected. Ireton had further spoilt his chances by proposing a somewhat blood-curdling oath of office that emphasised the absolute rightness of cutting off the king's head and fealty to the court that had condemned him. Now, the preferred rubric was loyalty to the directions of parliament and Ireton was too compromised by his association with the purge of the previous December to be admitted. Cromwell initially presided, but he was shortly afterwards replaced by Bradshaw. A number of peers were also appointed (in the teeth of opposition from a sceptical Henry Marten), but only three participated, on the understanding that they would later gain admission to the Commons.

Marten was, however, to have his satisfaction when the House of Lords (if not the peerage itself) was abolished by statute on 19 March, having been peevishly dismissed by the Commons as a 'a great inconvenience'. Attention was also given to the judiciary as it was an article of faith that a functioning and accepted system of justices of the peace was critical to rebuilding confidence in law and order in the country at large. But changing the names of the courts was one thing, building loyalty to the new dispensation quite another, and of the dozen senior Common Law judges, only half accepted their new commissions. The change of regime was also accompanied by a further clear-out of office holders deemed to be hostile to it. Eminent Presbyterians headed the list – the Earl of Warwick was again relieved of his command of the navy, and Sir Gilbert Gerard and Sir Robert Harley were turfed out of their respective positions as Chancellor of the Duchy of Lancaster and Master of the Mint. For noisily refusing to propagate the new regime, the Mayor of London (Abraham Reynardson) was imprisoned.

However, there were just too few active members of the Commons to give legitimacy to the nascent Commonwealth or to continue the business of government now that parliament had declared itself the source of both legislative and executive authority. There was fear too that unless there was a process of conciliation of moderate and otherwise undecided MPs, some would be tempted to throw in their lot with the royalists and civil strife be renewed. The immediate need was to put the purge behind it and to reassert the primacy of the Commons over the military. Accordingly, around sixty members were readmitted in February on condition that they affirm their disapproval of the Newport process. It was an astute formula, conceived by the members themselves, that saved both face and honour, and allowed the immediate return of a large number of MPs that included Vane, Sydney and Whitelocke, who had supported neither the purge nor the execution of the king.[10]

In time, about 200 members were eventually to take their place on the benches of the Rump, many late arrivals having 'repented' their vote in favour of continuing to treat with the king. In the meantime, one member among many who neither resumed nor even took their seat was Sir Thomas Fairfax. On appointment to the Council of State, he had been swiftly elected to the constituency from which he had been so murkily excluded two years before. In the new circumstances of fundamental change being made by a very narrowly representative establishment, he was now playing his cards closer to his chest. His continuing and taciturn abstention hinted at growing alienation.[11]

8

'The restitution of our shaking Freedom'

Salisbury

He shewes the peasant and the Clowne
But poor guardians of a Crowne
And Princes do but tottering stand
Who pull the power out of their hand

Anon., seventeenth century

As winter subsided, the much-depleted Commons took the final step in the creation of a republic. On the day that Charles's body was taken back to Windsor, the MPs debated the abolition of the monarchy. For the radicals who presently held the initiative in the Rump, it was a logical outcome in light of the execution of the king and the decision to forbid the proclamation of a successor. An Act of Abolition was passed into law on 17 March 1649, two days before the deletion from the constitution of the House of Lords. The royal regalia that had been assembled under the Plantagenets was broken up and sold for scrap: the only piece to survive was perhaps the most sacramental of all, the spoon that was used to pour the oil of anointment, the symbolic unction joining sovereign with God. The metaphysical compact with the Almighty had sustained Charles throughout his reign. Yet now royal power and authority had not merely been recalled and placed in trust with another, but ended altogether.

Change was taking place at breakneck speed and as the self-interested Whitelocke ruefully noted, everyone 'endeavoured or expected to have his private fancy put into motion'. Cromwell too lamented that 'our passions were more than our judgements'.[1] The debate was not confined to parliament alone. In the north country, the governor of Newcastle, Arthur Hesilrige, received a petition from a Mr Norwood addressed to 'all ingenuous Protestants of the late King's party' which argued that natural authority resided with the head of individual families and not with a monarch, and that a council of representatives of these independent people was the most just form of government. With many satisfied that the death of the king had at last secured the country for Protestantism, Norwood went on to claim bizarrely that the English monarchy was all part of a Roman Catholic plot, got up at the great papal Council of Trent in the previous century, and much the better for being extinguished.[2]

Among others with a ready-made agenda was the caucus in the Council of Officers grouped around Ireton. In the absence of the Leveller leaders, a committee had drawn up an army version of the *Agreement of the People* which was shorn of those Leveller assumptions that were likely to cause controversy. A new House, reduced in size, was to be elected by all men over the age of twenty-one who were proprietors in their own right. Many of the proposals for social amelioration contained in earlier Leveller manifestos were endorsed but the unbound religious dispensation envisaged by Overton was laid aside; there would be no free-for-all but instead a non-compulsory national Church with ministers maintained at public expense, although not by tithes. The current parliament was to wind itself up within a year. Ireton's document was laid before the Commons, somewhat inauspiciously on the same day that the king's trial opened. The MPs were not minded to be rushed into any of its particulars and certainly not the one relating to their self-extinction; the same Act that abolished the monarchy also envisaged a dissolution when 'the safety of the people that hath be-trusted them permitted it'. It was an open-ended commitment that was to be of continuing significance.

The Levellers too were indignant that their programme had been hijacked by a military junta. The execution of the king and establishment of a new executive authority before a properly representative body had been chosen confirmed their worst fear that they were dealing with the same oppressive regime, albeit with different masters. In angry disappointment, John Lilburne penned *England's New Chains Discovered*, which demanded the immediate dissolution of both the current parliament and recently chosen Council of State, and took a thinly disguised swipe at the high command in general and Cromwell in particular. More was to follow. Richard Overton took up the cause of a small group of soldiers that had petitioned the Council of Officers in defiance of military discipline. Following a court martial, five were cashiered in a humiliating ceremony. In his pamphlet *The Hunting of the Foxes from Newmarket and Triploe Heath to Whitehall by Five Beagles late of the Army*, Overton wittily attempted to run the junta to ground by accusing 'the conclave of officers' of a new tyranny and Cromwell of aspirations to monarchy. Fired up with righteous indignation but not quite convinced that his earlier denunciations had fully resonated with the reading public, Lilburne published an encore to his earlier effort, prosaically entitled *The Second Part of England's New Chains Discovered*.

It was all too much for the new authorities and the Leveller leaders Walwyn, Overton and Lilburne were hauled before the Council of State accused of sedition. As recorded by Ludlow, Cromwell's *amour propre* was thoroughly aroused by the drubbing he had received in print and he frustratedly shouted his denunciation of these vexatious agitators, to whom he had displayed much individual sympathy in the past. His colleagues must have taken a small measure of *Schadenfreude* in his discomfiture as the Leveller leaders were consigned to the Tower to await trial by the slenderest of votes. Once again, imprisonment proved to be no impediment to output and the pamphlets continued to pour forth, including a final version of the *Agreement of the People*.

All this may not have made much of a difference had it not coincided with a renewed mood of militancy amongst the ranks which illustrated the distance between the soldiers and some of their more politically distracted officers. The men were bored, fed up with the lack of progress in meeting arrears and indignant at the continued hostility of their civil hosts upon whom many were still billeted. Outbreaks of ill-discipline and clashes with civilians were becoming more frequent. They had been inflamed too by the literature of the Levellers. The plan to reduce the army to a home establishment of some 30,000 troops coincided with the decision to send a force equivalent to nearly half this number to Ireland. Such was the sensitivity attached to the programme of redundancy and overseas service in 1647, it was considered safer to choose the eight regiments for Ireland by lot, and the resultant force included the cavalry regiments of Ireton, Scrope (another regicide) and Lambert, and four of infantry including Hewson's.

Almost immediately, a mutiny broke out in London amongst Colonel Whalley's regiment. The unit had avoided the draft for Ireland, but Leveller agitation gave rise to an anxiety that their pay would be sacrificed in favour of those on the expedition. There were calls too for a recall of the General Council of the Army. Fairfax personally intervened with assurances but the ringleaders were dealt with severely. One, a trooper called Lockyer who had served at Edgehill aged sixteen, was shot and became an instant Leveller martyr. There followed mutinies amongst the men of Ireton and Scrope, who were encamped in the large garrison area centred on Salisbury and earmarked for Ireland. Scrope's soldiers had access to the Leveller printing press, published a petition and started electing their own officers. There were accusations of bad faith by the regimental commanders and the claim that the soldiers had been forced to renege on their *Solemn Engagement*: 'Wherefore we are now resolved no longer to dally with our God, but with all our endeavours to pursue what we have before promised in order to the settling of this poor Nation and the restitution of our shaking Freedom and redeeming ourselves out of the hands of Tyrants.'[3]

This was as big a threat as the attempted splitting of the New Model Army by the Presbyterian faction two years before. It was a make-or-break moment for the high command which risked losing its authority altogether among the large concentration of troops. Sidelining the son-in-law, Fairfax and Cromwell raised a disciplined force in London and set off in hot pursuit of the malcontents, which now included a large splinter group from a unit whose own mutiny had been barely suppressed by its commanding officer. Catching the 'delinquents' by surprise near Burford, Fairfax persuaded most to surrender and had the good sense to keep reprisals to a minimum. Instead, apart from a tiny handful of ringleaders who were shot, the troops who had taken part were herded together and treated to a series of crossly worded and admonitory sermons by regimental chaplains.[4]

While the so-called Leveller mutinies in the late spring of 1649 have captured attention, the loyalty of the troops who suppressed them and the relative ease with which this was done has been less remarked upon. After nearly ten years of almost continuous warfare, many soldiers would have contemplated a return to a disrupted and depression-struck civil society with barely a sense of recognition, still less enthusiasm. The camaraderie engendered by shared dangers, the singing of psalms and religious self-identification was a powerful glue, and it was a particular skill of Cromwell's to be able to exploit it, as he had done in similar circumstances in Wales the year before. The New Model Army had become a social institution in its own right and its more motivated members saw themselves as part of the vanguard of the new order, whether it be by fighting the ungodly and the Irish, dealing with mutinous colleagues or by suppressing Christmas celebrations. The priority of maintaining the cohesion of the army as a disciplined unit did, however, effectively retard the New Model Army as a source of political innovation – in the view of Fairfax and Cromwell, and the majority of their officers, the flirtation with the Levellers had added unnecessary kindling to a situation inflamed by prospective service in Ireland and lack of pay. As a protest movement against the injustices of the war regime, the

Levellers' attitude to the military had always been ambivalent and the defeat of the mutinies ended any residual hopes they had had for leveraging the army as an agent for their agenda.

The former monarch had been buried in the middle of a heavy snow-shower on 8 February, although he was denied the Anglican obsequies at his interment. Windsor was felt to be sufficiently remote and secure to ensure that the Stuart grave would not become a scene of pilgrimage or devotion. Charles was laid to rest next to Henry VIII and the most personally beloved of his six wives, Jane Seymour. The cycle of change initiated in the previous century remained unfinished: Charles had been determined to conclude the reformation of the national Church begun by the Tudor king, originally to extricate the realm from the residual authority of Rome. A harmonious balance between religious consciousness and manners, and the state's demand for social cohesiveness and obedience had more or less eluded all his predecessors in the interval, and Charles paid for his own attempt to achieve it with his life. His loyalty to his Anglican faith was posthumously embellished by the appearance, on the same day as his execution, of a publication that purported to be the work of the king himself. The *Eikon Basilike*, a compilation of prayers and reflections on his Majesty's personal Calvary, was an instant sensation, whilst the record of duplicity in Charles's own hand in *The King's Cabinet Opened* and at Newport was conveniently forgotten. In spite of the efforts of the authorities to suppress it, the book went through thirty subsequent reprints and was popular in Europe. Its tone of injured piety and lengthy enumeration of thwarted good intentions hindered an objective understanding of the king's motives, and the main impact of the book was to implant the idea of Charles as a martyr, thus adding to the residual mystique of the monarchy whilst seeming to diminish its responsibility for the recent wars.

This was the toughest cultural edifice that the Commonwealth, formally proclaimed in the spring of 1649, had to overcome. The state was no stranger to regicide but the institution of monarchy itself had thus far survived, come what may. Its durability had depended on the successful exploitation of an intangible authority that transcended the subject's individual beliefs and status in order to generate collective identification and endeavour, particularly in times of national danger. The sense of shock at the execution of a monarch anointed by God was profound. Replacing this totem of national loyalty was not going to be easy. In fact, the demoralised 'cavaliers' of England were to be the least amongst the new regime's immediate challenges. The religious allegiances which had provided the impetus to the rebellion against Charles were not so easily reconciled to the events at Westminster. Only the Baptists and independent congregations seemed to greet the Commonwealth, buoyed by the hope that it would generate a genuinely tolerant dispensation and give them protection. The Presbyterians maintained their rhetorical assault on the sectarian influences in the army and denounced the execution of the king. Clerical opposition to the regime from ministers such as Christopher Love, Thomas Cawton and Tom Juggard was particularly pronounced in London, the north-west and the West Country. In response, an Act was passed forbidding clerical interference in politics, and recalcitrants were referred to the Security Committee of the Council of State. In January 1650, an Act required all citizens to declare their allegiance to the Commonwealth by way of an 'Engagement'. A special parliamentary committee dominated by republicans was also formed to 'undeceive' the measure's opponents, of which there were many.

Whereas the Levellers had run into the military might of the army, the breakdown of the ecclesiastical court system and wilting of the authority of the Justices of the Peace meant that new devotions and heresies were able to flourish more easily – to the Presbyterians, the wars and the new regime had opened a Pandora's Box. The temper of the times favoured heterodoxy and was now more strongly echoed in the Commons by the disposition of those like Ludlow and Vane who favoured Church disestablishment and toleration, and those such as Henry Marten who had argued that theology was 'a matter for a university, perhaps, not for a kingdom'.[5] For those susceptible to the apparent power of prophecy of the Bible, the trial of the king was seen to be analogous to the Day of Judgement and his execution a sign of great portent: the rule of the saints was at hand. Put in these terms, the Fifth Monarchists provided an uplifting vision of the righteous coming into their own, an idea that had a strong appeal in the army. The vision of its adherents sprang from their interpretation of the Book of Daniel that the four empires of the ancient world would be succeeded by the Kingdom of Christ. The movement had grown upon the millenarian sensibility sown and nurtured by the violently epochal nature of the wars, and amongst the new establishment which considered themselves in the vanguard of the changed order it was embraced by senior soldiers such as Thomas Harrison and Robert Overton, and the regicide John Carew, a Cornish MP. But its seed contained the idea that the world would be run by a new Elect, even more favoured and hallowed than the existing godly elite.[6] The civil wars had barely commenced when the Nonconformist preacher John Simpson began denouncing (via the code offered by Scripture) the intrinsic rottenness he saw in the existing social hierarchy from the vantage point of his pulpit at the Church of All Hallows the Great in London.[7] So even as the wider coalition of the godly prevailed against the king, the Fifth Monarchists perceived future disappointment and the millenarian minister Christopher Feake pondered how the existing habits of government could be reconciled with righteousness. A petition early in the year had asked, 'How can the Kingdom be the Saints' when the un-Godly are electors and elected to govern?'[8] In time, this pessimism would provide the rationale for a more political agenda, and challenged a commonwealth to which the Fifth Monarchists had initially attached so much faith.

The spirit of Nonconformity gathered strength; understandably so as social discipline had been badly shaken. If the Fifth Monarchists saw events as signifying an escape by England from its Babylonian captivity, to others it seemed as if the country was still stuck right in it. For the Ranters, the prohibitions occasioned by the war regime were intolerable and the breakdown of the state and its Church had robbed it of its authority to dictate how men and women should behave. Abiezer Coppe had already been imprisoned for his pamphlet the *Fiery Flying Roll*, and his challenge to the hypocrisy and inequality he perceived in the agenda of Puritan manners was taken up by Laurence Clarkson in his own tract, *A Single Eye*. He argued that in God's design, black could indeed be white and vice versa; sin was purely in the eye of the beholder and Clarkson's message that 'There is no act whatsoever, that is impure in God' was taken up by a band of followers eager to cast off the restrictions of the war years. This found its most overt expression in a culture of free love which reminded people of the happy paganism of folk traditions that had been suppressed in the interests of Puritan conformity. But the promiscuity captured in quaint woodcuts of priapic men dancing around naked females to the accompaniment of a fully clothed fiddler scandalised an establishment which, whatever its other differences, was alert to sin and the corrosive impact of licentiousness.

The Ranters have often been seen to be at the margins of the Republic but they were regarded as heretics and blasphemers, and thus attracted a civil reaction that was arguably more ferocious than that accorded to the Levellers. Although the Commonwealth was slowly persuaded over time to loosen the more institutional aspects of the Puritan regime such as fast days and the compulsory attendance of parish churches on the Sabbath, it was also far tougher with what it regarded as displays of immorality and impiety. Adultery was made a capital offence, although the sanctions were more severe for women than for men – a husband who broke his marriage vows with a single woman was guilty of no more than fornication. The sense that it was Eve who had led Adam astray was very firmly embedded in the psyche of the devout.

The Blasphemy Act was likewise toughened with an onerous scale of fines that reflected the deeply embedded understanding among the elite about the proper gradations of society; the well-bred were accordingly charged more for slips of the tongue than the commoner sort of folk and women (who were judged to be the responsibility of their male kin) got off the most lightly. Women were finding their voice in other ways, aided by the spread of literacy. The arrest of the Leveller leaders in the spring of 1649 prompted a large demonstration by their womenfolk. Led by Mary Overton and Katherine Chidley, a protest was organised at Westminster which vented the exhaustion of families with the social and economic consequences of the wars. The MPs greeted this effrontery with magisterial condescension and the women were commanded to return to their 'huswifery' and leave matters of 'higher concernment' to the men. The king might well have had his head removed, but to many MPs the organised disobedience of women would have seemed an intolerable inversion of their social assumptions.[9]

The last royalist redoubt at Pontefract was finally captured by forces under John Lambert after a nine-month siege. In the meantime, other cavalier notables and renegade officers of the army of parliament who had taken part in the insurrection in Wales had been tried and executed. Having served his king so ineffectually, the Duke of Hamilton achieved authentic nobility at his end; he had refused to implicate his sovereign in the Engager invasion (despite Cromwell's best efforts to get him to do so) and he met his execution with calmness. Holland too behaved with a final dignity, the pleas for clemency from his elder brother the Earl of Warwick having been rejected. But beyond the small group of principals whose complicity in the genesis and conduct of the second civil war could not be denied, capital retribution against civilians on the losing side at the termination of hostilities was scarce. The burden on the royalist 'delinquents' in England was economic. Sequestered of their estates and properties throughout the later stages of the wars, many spent years 'compounding' by the payment of fines to reclaim a portion of that which they had originally owned. The Commonwealth was to make great play of royalist plots and disturbances to keep the new body politic in a state of vigilance and to justify the bankrolling of the regime by the defeated. But there was no denying that royalist military power, at least in England, had been destroyed.

The Commonwealth could not, however, rely on broken spirits to ensure acquiescence from the defeated or loyalty from everyone else. As the pulpit was presently such an unreliable platform from which to build legitimacy, the news-sheets took on greater importance. The royalist press had been driven underground but still attracted wide readership with its highly personal vilifications. *Mercurius Elenticus* was especially virulent and Cromwell ('the proudest rebel in the pack') was singled out as the exemplar of the new and supposedly alien elite – his motives and behaviour were subject to continuous attack. His looks too ('Nose Cromwell') were the subject of ridicule. Belatedly the Commonwealth moved to license the press in the autumn of 1649 but, given the sheer number of publications, placed the responsibility for enforcement on the stationers who supplied the raw materials – official state censorship was to come much later. The first item to be starved of paper and ink was an English version of the Koran.

In the meantime, the larger part of a thriving press effectively proselytised in the regime's favour, led by John Rushworth's *A Perfect Diurnall* and Marchamont Nedham's *Mercurius Politicus*, which used clever satire and ridicule to undermine opponents. Nedham's ambition was to be a sophisticated commentator rather than a crude polemicist and his career revealed a number of swerves in editorial direction. He had written for both sides in the main civil war news-sheets, supplying copy for the standard-bearer for the opposition, *Mercurius Britannicus*, before taking editorial control of *Mercurius Pragmaticus*, an unashamed organ of royalist propaganda. Unfreighted by too much ideological baggage, he decisively plumped for the winning side of the wars in 1650 and founded *Mercurius Politicus* in the summer of that year. Quickly pinning his stylised colours to the mast, he asked in its first edition, 'Why should not the Commonwealth have a fool as well as the King had?'[10]

The times called for a public intellectual who could provide a secular perspective in the absence of religious consensus and a clear definition of the 'liberty' that had been acquired with the ending of the monarchy. Anthony Ascham argued for acceptance of the de facto authority of the regime in his work *The Bounds and Bonds of Public Obedience* and was rewarded with the ambassadorship to Spain. But a more advanced sensibility appeared in the works of

John Milton, a devout Puritan and lyrical poet who provided a non-sectarian justification for the regime. He was born in December 1608 at a house in what is now part of Cheapside in London. Milton's precocious intelligence, sceptical curiosity and growing mastery of Latin, Greek and Hebrew marked him out as a budding intellectual from an early age. His formative output was prodigious and his work *On the Morning of Christ's Nativity*, written just after his twenty-first birthday, had the mythical element that distinguished his later masterpiece *Paradise Lost*.

The power and intensity of his poetry has perhaps been coloured by the perceptions of Milton as a public servant and in that capacity he is sometimes regarded as a mere polemicist for the new regime. Yet despite his obvious and deep passion, he was hardly doctrinaire and produced work that articulately anticipated the later Enlightenment. He is perhaps as well known for his moving defence of the freedom of the written word in *Areopagitica* as for his later epic poem of Satan's revolt. His scepticism of the intrusive institutional aspects of religious authority was aimed at Catholics, Anglicans and Presbyterians alike. In 1646 he had penned the sonnet *On the New Forcers of Conscience under the Long Parliament*, which contained his famous admonition that 'New Presbyter is but old Priest writ large'. With the onset of the second civil war, his disenchantment with the failure of institutional wisdom became more marked and his views more radical – his sonnet in honour of Fairfax expressed dismay at the factionalism of parliament and he favoured the subsequent purge. The execution of the king provided the occasion for him to attract wider public notice with his work *The Tenure of Kings and Magistrate*s, which refuted the Presbyterian denunciations and claimed biblical justification for both the trial and death of the monarch. Here was a novel doctrine – it was right not only to dissent but also actively to resist a wayward monarch. But in justifying the new regime, he drew a distinction between liberty and licence. As with Ascham, he was rewarded with public office and became a secretary and translator for the new Council of State on a salary of £200.

Now aged forty, Milton was beginning to suffer the degeneration that eventually made him go blind. The discovery might have caused a temporary flagging of his creative spirit for *Eikonoklastes*, his rebuttal of the *Eikon Basilike*, was a densely structured and occasionally pedantic work that completely failed to match the circulation of its flawed adversary. Milton was, however, no careerist. His antagonism towards the superstitious respect given to institutions that did not deserve it and to political cant were of a piece with his Nonconformist thinking. He was sympathetic to the Levellers and declined the Council's invitation to deploy his skills against them. In *The Tenure of Kings and Magistrates* he had already written that no one 'can be so stupid to deny that all men naturally were born free, being the image and resemblance of God himself'.[11] It is possible that he admired the energy of the demotic Lilburne but more probable that he was better attuned to the sensibilities of Walwyn, who produced his *Just Defence* while awaiting trial. In it, the conscience of the Leveller movement charged the government to find an authentically Christian purpose. 'I do think it one main end of Government to provide that those who refuse not labour should eat comfortably,' Walwyn wrote.[12]

In the end, Lilburne was, however, able to score a moral victory of sorts. While languishing in the cold and gloomy depths of the Tower, the Leveller mutinies broke out in London and Wiltshire, and official attitudes towards the incarcerated leaders hardened. Further implicated in a royalist plot to exploit the Leveller agitation to undermine the new Commonwealth, Lilburne was now charged with high treason. He was tried at the Guildhall in the autumn of 1649 by the same process which had been used against the former sovereign, with the exception that the verdict was delivered by jurors rather than the court commissioners. These commoners were not impressed by the weight of the hammer being used to crack the now diminished Leveller nut and a 'Not Guilty' verdict was delivered after minimal discussion. The celebrations were noisy and prolonged, and the regime made to look ridiculous as Lilburne was shouldered and carried through the streets when eventually released. But by now the firebrand was a very debilitated man, both physically and financially. He took the new Engagement to the Commonwealth and on a wave of goodwill, was elected to London's Common Council. But a spirit of priggish pride and official vindictiveness prevailed, and his election was declared void. It was not an auspicious moment for those who looked to the Commonwealth to initiate some overdue reforms in a spirit of justice and conciliation.

Walwyn's challenge to the perception that society was unalterably composed of the damned and the saved was mounted in a different way by the work of another skilled communicator. Gerard Winstanley, born in Lancashire, was a former London cloth merchant who had been ruined by the wars. As with the Levellers, the so-called Digger communities that he represented also suffered appropriation by posterity, in their case as proto-communists. The anachronism is made worse by being inexact; the Diggers were perhaps closer in spirit to the later Distributist philosophy of Chesterton and Belloc than the determinism of Marx and reflected the needs of the rural poor that worked in an overwhelmingly agrarian economy. The Levellers had called for a restoration of the social institutions that were supposed to protect citizens and believed that all men possessed equal natural rights. The Diggers shared the second idea but inferred a revolutionary outcome, namely the equality of property. As Rainsborough had laid claim to the franchise, so Winstanley exponentially advanced it in respect of property, by asserting 'The poorest man hath as true and just right to the land as the richest man.'[13]

So, in his work *The True Levellers Standard Advanced*, Winstanley argued that the rule of the saints be prepared by a renunciation of lordship and, effectively, proprietorship. He went further still in a work that he dedicated to Cromwell.

In *The Law of Freedom in a Platform* the vision of a propertyless Commonwealth was laid out with some rather authoritarian rules about how people should behave in the new utopia. In contrast to the libertarians, Winstanley held strongly repressive views about the sexual act, and he was thoroughly put out when he found out that a gang of horny Ranters had infiltrated one of his communes to 'cause scandal'.[14] He was certainly regarded as an unhelpful and competing polemicist by the Levellers and was crossly denounced for pilfering their label by Lilburne, who was annoyed to find the flank of his own agenda so unexpectedly exposed. But in practical terms, Winstanley's millenarian project was a flop. The first Digger land-grab near Windsor was treated by the soldiers sent to investigate as a gathering of harmless eccentrics. Certainly, Fairfax would have been politely surprised to learn from Winstanley when he came before him that his followers did not want to restore the 'ancient laws' but the 'pure law of righteousness before the Fall'. But the rural communities whose interests Winstanley claimed to represent were not best pleased with such a disruptive experiment. The half dozen Digger communities that set to tilling and planting common land in the shires around London were eventually driven off by those who resented the occupation of the spaces supposedly open to all and by freeholders who feared their property was at risk of appropriation. The spirit of the Clubmen movement was still strong; local communities had suffered quite enough already from the wars without a new group of outsiders muscling in to establish unauthorised allotments all over the place and telling them how to live their lives.

The men who served on the benches of the Rump, and in whom supreme authority was now vested, operated in unfamiliar territory. The abolition of the monarchy, far from heralding a wider inversion of society and its hierarchical assumptions, acted as a catalyst for conservatism, most immediately in the area of public morality. Over time the Commonwealth was able to project its own ethos and generate a measure of pride in its achievements as a non-monarchical state, but the MPs who returned to parliament after the purge were less enamoured of abstract theories of government than motivated by the practicalities of the management of it. The republicans like Marten had made a fundamental change to the constitution but now the priority was the restoration of stability. The coalitions of the last few years no longer seemed so relevant. The achievement of a republic had gone way beyond the ambition of many who had identified with the Independent interest, and the enthusiastic heterodoxy represented by those like the Ranters and Levellers seemed to cross the line between private conscience and ambition, and public morality and stability. In the reaction to perceived sin and ungodliness, the viewpoint of former antagonists in the parliament gradually began to converge. The rhythms of government under the Rump would not be dominated by those who had signed the king's death warrant, but by pragmatists like Vane and trimmers like Whitelocke. The radical energy behind the republican regicides was sublimated as the Rump engaged with practicalities.

Above all loomed the presence of the army, and the sense that the Republic rested on the blade of a sword was pervasive. With the neutralisation of the Levellers, the political activities of the soldiers became more internalised, particularly amongst its intermediate and junior officers. The religious radicalism of those like Harrison presented a dimension of the army as a social institution and in early 1650 the proselytising character of the New Model found an outlet in the Rump's sanction of the Commission for the Propagation of the Gospel in Wales. Harrison and other army officers headed the list of commissioners whose job was to seek out 'delinquency, scandal, malignancy and non-residency' amongst the parsons, vicars, curates and schoolteachers of the former principality. Wales had been staunchly royalist, and the Commission was expected to ensure religious assimilation and to foster loyalty while providing a useful diversion for millenarians and radical Puritans in a suitably remote part of the Commonwealth.

Although a soldier of colourfully expressed faith, Harrison was no administrator and the details of the Commission of which he was nominally the head were very much left in the hands of others. The organising spirits were the radical New Model Army chaplain Hugh Peter and Vavasor Powell. Educated at Jesus College, Oxford, the thirty-three-year-old Powell had become an itinerant and unauthorised preacher, an activity for which he had been imprisoned. He refused to be ordained as a Presbyterian minister but received dispensation from the Westminster Assembly to continue his own ministry and came to preach before the Rump. He impressed enough to be invited to act as an adviser to the Commission and was the guiding hand behind the 278 ejections that took place in the Welsh ministry between 1650 and 1653. Most of these were for 'moral lapses' and 'malignancy' rather than for doctrinal differences and certainly the zealous work of Powell, and others, lent weight to the belief of the Fifth Monarchists that Christ's mission was now being fulfilled by his earthly saints.

Back at Westminster, the detached position of the commander-in-chief had ensured that the trajectory of the new constitutional settlement was set by the civilians. He had won the war for parliament and suppressed the Leveller militants but he was no republican law giver, still less a dictator, and his role had been more analogous to that of a Cincinnatus. Such was his prestige, the cohort of the army's senior officers and representatives in parliament were of a similar disposition. But the spirit of Ireton lived on and there was, too, a clear desire among the junior ranks that the state that emerged from the wars should pay due regard to the godliness of the men who had done the fighting. The new regime thus faced a difficult conundrum – how to benefit from the security conferred by the army while keeping it out of politics. While there were still enemies to be fought, addressing this pivotal issue could be deferred.

9

'The righteous judgement of God upon these barbarous wretches'

Drogheda

And now the Irish are ashamed
To see themselves in one year tamed

> Andrew Marvell, *An Horatian Ode*

These unhappy people, when they saw they could not
make war, but were beaten as often as encountered, would
not yet make peace; or if they did they no sooner made it
than broke it.

> Edward Hyde, Earl of Clarendon,
> *The History of the Rebellion*

The war against the Celt continued. Ireland was in a delicate state
of equilibrium with none of the armed, ethnic, political and religious groupings of sufficient size to overwhelm the others. Loyalties
remained fluid and alignments of temporary convenience commonplace. The island was divided by the fiefs of various warlords, of whom
the most powerful was presently the Marquis of Ormonde. He had
continued faithfully to serve his Stuart master and had adroitly managed to assemble an improbable coalition which presently offered

the youthful Prince of Wales perhaps the best chance of recovering the throne by way of this deeply rebellious part of his patrimony. Ormonde's ranks had been swollen by the forces under the command of Lord Inchiquin. A chieftain of Munster, Inchiquin had fiercely fought against the Catholic rebels in the south; indeed, he had inflicted upon them a crushing defeat at the battle of Knocknanuss in late 1647. Of ambiguous and fluid loyalty, which he disguised as a matter of 'honour', his interest as a Munster landowner trumped all other allegiances and he had sided with the English parliamentarians until it became obvious that they could not reliably support him, at which point he threw his lot in with the royalists.[1] Ormonde also cemented his position by concluding another treaty with the Confederacy with sufficiently sincere promises of a parliament and the ending of impositions on Catholics. He also encouraged desertions from the Covenanter army under the Munro clan in Ulster. Like their brethren in Scotland, they had been appalled by the execution of the king and the powerful Belfast presbytery had fiercely condemned it. Ormonde thus achieved the unlikely feat of uniting Protestants and Catholics in the royalist cause to drive out the small garrisons of English parliamentary troops.

The opportunity offered by Ireland appealed to the advisers around the exiled Charles, particularly those like Sir Edward Hyde who had not reconciled themselves to the part that the Scots had played in the original rebellion against the dynasty. Furthermore, the defeat of the Engagers suggested that the route back to the throne lay via Dublin rather than Edinburgh. Prince Rupert too was excited by the military possibilities, and swiftly swapping an army command for a naval one he led the royalist squadron to Kinsale (suffering appalling seasickness en route). In the meantime, many English royalists preferred exile in Ireland to living with the uncertainty of the new Commonwealth and were heartened by the circumstances they found there. Ann, Lady Fanshawe, wrote 'For six months we lived so much to our satisfaction that we began to thinking of making our abode there during the war for the country was fertile and all provisions cheap and the homes good . . . My Lord of Ormonde had a very good army and the country seemingly quiet; and to complete our content, all persons were very civil to us.'[2]

For the parliamentary garrisons, the situation looked unpromising unless they were reinforced. Yet they had a unity of purpose that was far more robust than the fragile coincidence of interests under Ormonde, among which were many recent antagonists. In Ulster, the Commonwealth's forces were led by George Monck. A forty-year-old Devonian of mercenary inclination whom Hyde later condescended to describe as 'a gentleman of very good extraction', he had fought in the Netherlands against the Spanish and had also held a commission in the royal army. Thickset and with an inscrutable manner, Monck had been captured by the parliamentarians in 1644 and was incarcerated in the Tower. There were a few consolations during his imprisonment – within the precincts of the forbidding Norman fortress the swarthy-looking warrior met a seamstress called Anne Clarges, who later became his wife.[3] Bored by his otherwise inactive life, he inveigled his way into an appointment with the New Model Army. A practical soldier with firm Presbyterian convictions, he justified his volte-face by acceptance of an Irish commission so he could fight against the hated Catholic rebels.

In early 1649, however, he found himself walled up in Dundalk with only the most slender of links to the other garrisons in Derry and Dublin, where Colonel Michael Jones held the perimeter. His predicament seemed to justify extraordinary measures and in the spring he was authorised to conclude an armistice with the one major warlord that Ormonde had been unable to entice, the leader of the Catholic Irish rebellion in Ulster, Owen Roe O'Neill. The aging chieftain was slowly being ground down by illness but he still had a sizeable force at his disposal. The armistice concluded with Monck rendered this army inert, and robbed Ormonde of precious momentum as he tried to shepherd a coalition for the royalists.

Although it caused great anxiety to the supporters of parliament, in practical terms Ireland had made itself far less felt in the civil wars on land in Great Britain than had the Scots, or even arguably the Welsh. For the nascent Commonwealth however, it remained unfinished business and was regarded as a colony that had to be brought back under firm Protestant control. Quite apart from the royalist threat, there were sound political and financial reasons for Ireland to be prioritised. It gave an opportunity to build loyalty to the new regime in the face of an unambiguous external enemy, and a Catholic one to boot. Additionally, the Adventurers' Act had been conceived as a commercial incentive to reconquest, with the cost of suppression of the Catholic revolt which had broken out in 1641 to be met by the confiscation of the lands of the rebels. The plantation of the island with loyal Protestants was to be accelerated: Cromwell himself had subscribed to the scheme. For the politicians, the deployment of a significant portion of the army overseas would also have the added benefit of splitting it up, thus rendering those officers like Henry Ireton less able to meddle in domestic affairs. With his military reputation burnished by his success in Wales and at Preston, Cromwell was regarded as the natural choice to lead the campaign while Fairfax retained larger responsibility for the army as a whole. Nonetheless, the arrangements for the expedition proved to be anything but straightforward.

Cromwell was at first reluctant. Ireland was a difficult and inhospitable place in which to conduct military operations and it had claimed the reputation of many before who had been sent to pacify it. His better attuned political antennae as an MP also made him aware that the constitutional arrangements of the Commonwealth and the legitimate aims of the army were far from settled; indeed before he sailed he argued that the Rump's numbers should not be swelled in his absence by the 'recruitment' of additional and potentially hostile members. But his immediate concerns were more practical and he insisted that the campaign was fully underwritten, with substantial cash delivered up front. To that end the sale of ecclesiastical lands was accelerated and the Excise Tax mortgaged for a year in advance.[4]

The organisation of the regiments to go to Ireland was even more problematic and the Leveller-inspired mutinies that broke out in the spring of 1649 prompted a widespread purge of the ranks of the New Model to ensure that the expeditionary force was both disciplined and cohesive. Here at least there was a clear coincidence of interest between the members of the Commonwealth Parliament and the high command: the Levellers were already distrusted by the proprietor class, but the dispassionate championing of the Irish natives by those like William Walwyn put them completely beyond the pale. There was much joy at their suppression by Fairfax and New Model officers were feted and feasted by the grateful civilians. With Henry Marten a brave and solitary voice of dissent in the House, the organs of propaganda were unleashed as Irish awfulness and barbarity were advanced as justification for the expedition. Even Milton abandoned his reason by wading in against the 'mixed rabble, part Papist, part fugitive and part savages'.

The assumption of Irish cultural inferiority was not just confined to supporters of the Republic; it was a mindset that pervaded Protestant English attitudes more generally and which crossed political and social differences. Although comfortably hosted by her Anglo-Irish connections, Ann, Lady Fanshawe, firmly deprecated, 'the great superstition of the Irish and the want of that knowing faith that should defend them from the power of the Devil which he exercises amongst them very much'.[5]

As preparations in England continued, the disparate forces under Ormonde occupied Dundalk and captured the strategically important town of Drogheda astride the main route between Dublin and Ulster. At last, towards the end of July, Cromwell left London to join his gathering forces at their embarkation point in Wales. His departure took on the aspect of a royal progress as the Commonwealth tried to imitate some of the iconography and majesty of the regime that it had replaced. The *Moderate Intelligencer* gushed enthusiastically that Cromwell 'went forth in that state and equipage as the like hath hardly been seen . . . with trumpets sounding . . . and such a guard as is hardly to be paralleled in the world. If you say "Caesar or nothing" they say "A republic or nothing".'[6]

The man in whose name battle in Ireland was about to be joined was presently living in the tolerably comfortable shadow of the court of his brother-in-law, William of Orange. Charles was eighteen and already the object of sexual intrigues and the conflicting agendas of the ragged group of Stuart loyalists and constitutional royalists that surrounded him. Principle among these was his mother, Henrietta Maria, who did not share the hostility of those devoted Anglican courtiers like Sir Edward Hyde towards the Scots. Buffeted by the divergent opinions of his advisers, the energetic young prince's attention was more agreeably diverted by female companions. His royal good looks and exciting predicament were powerful aphrodisiacs. Many sought his attention and among his lovers, Lucy Walter soon bore him an illegitimate son who was shortly bundled off to Paris to be looked after by the household of the prince's mother. He also enjoyed the company of the likes of the twenty-one-year-old Duke of Buckingham, whose free-spirited antics and insouciant temperament appealed to his future sovereign, with whom he had been brought up.

But a life of itinerant action and considerable danger had also honed those innate qualities that were to make Charles a sharper political practitioner than had been his father. His first serious negotiations were with the Scots, whose state was being hollowed out by the fratricidal power struggle that had been ignited by the Engagement. The Act of Classes had prompted a thorough purge of religious and political 'malignants' and had allowed the powerful party that adhered to the more zealous wing of the Kirk to gain ascendancy. But the wider attachment to both Covenant and a king was deep and sincere. Writing in anguish to his cousin in early 1649, Robert Baillie said, 'If his Majestie may be moved to join us in this one point, he will have all Scotland readie to sacrifice their lives for his service: if he refuse, or shift this duety, his best and most usefull friends, both here and elsewhere, will be cast into inextricable labyrinths, we fear, for the ruine of us all.'[7]

Above the hostile factions, the Marquis of Argyll exercised an uneasy pre-eminence. At heart a patriot, he was also the most prominent noble who understood that in the face of the new republic and the sectarian army that sustained it, a royal keystone (if properly shaped) was the only thing likely to keep the various blocs of the Scottish state from crashing to the ground.

Accordingly, a commission was despatched to Holland, arriving on Easter Monday 1649. It was led by the Earl of Cassilis, a Calvinist noble of unbending rectitude who had played a significant role in both the Westminster Assembly and the so-called Whiggamore Raid in September 1648 that had attempted to oust the Engagers from power in Edinburgh. The commissioners' dourly uncompromising agenda would have been familiar to anyone who had been acquainted with the manner of Charles I' s treatment at Newcastle and it would have been unusual had his heir not harboured a resentment against them. He parried their insistence that he take the Covenant not just for Scotland but for all his realms by arguing that it would need the authority of the English and Irish parliaments for him to do such a thing. The Scots returned unsatisfied, but some of their number gained a favourable impression of Charles, with Robert Baillie opining that 'In this conference I found the King, in my judgement, of a very meeke and equitable disposition, understanding and judicious enough, though firm in the tenets his education and companie has planted in him. If God would send him among us, without some of his present counsellors, I think he might make, by God's blessing, as good a King as Brittane saw these hundred years.'[8]

With his preparations complete and cash in hand sufficient for at least three months of late summer campaigning, Cromwell was ready for departure with his invasion force of 12,000. He briefly met with George Monck, en route to Westminster following his eviction from Dundalk. In London, the former royalist was publicly upbraided by the Rump for his brief armistice with the Catholics, notwithstanding that it had bought the Commonwealth time and had been done with the connivance of Cromwell and the Council of State. Monck appeared to accept his dressing-down, but he was not to forget the humiliation and the civil state thus forfeited an opportunity to cement the loyalty of one of its more wily and able military commanders. Now, at the last minute, came the astonishing and welcome news that the numerically inferior Commonwealth garrison under Colonel Michael Jones had rushed out of Dublin to inflict a crushing defeat on the levies of Ormonde at Rathmines, a short distance to the south of the capital. The marquis had made that fatal mistake common to men of action by doing something unnecessary when he should have been watching and waiting, ready to attack the invasion force wherever it landed. Instead, by sending Inchiquin into Munster, he needlessly split his forces and ensured that Cromwell's well-signalled arrival would be unopposed.

By the second week of September, Cromwell's army and siege train were well dug in before the walls of Drogheda; he had arrived in Ireland determined on a swift campaign. Although he had given a public instruction to his troops that there was to be no pillaging, the 'barbarous and bloodthirsty Irish' could expect little mercy if they continued to resist God's providence and the English parliament, the source of their 'favour and protection'. As Cromwell had told the Council of Officers in the spring, the Irish were the most disdained of the enemies of the state, well below the royalists and the Scots. Now, however, he was faced by a mostly Protestant and English garrison of about 3,000 behind the thick walls of this strategic point at the mouth of the River Boyne. It was commanded by the one-legged Sir Arthur Aston, a peppery soldier of Roman Catholic faith who had nonetheless raised an English regiment for the Protestant King Gustavus Adolphus of Sweden in the Thirty Years War. He had also held various commissions in the army of Charles I, amongst them command of the garrison at Reading. There were many other royalists beside who had also seen action in the king's service in England, including one called Ned Verney.

The *Memoirs of the Verney Family* is considered to be one of the most evocative of the sources that describe the impact of civil war on family relationships, and the conflicting loyalties that it engendered. His father, Sir Edmund, had been the Knight Marshal of England who had lost his life defending the royal standard at the battle of Edgehill. Sir Edmund, one of the more sympathetic characters of the period, had been no admirer of Charles's religious policies but in the end had been impelled by a sense of honour and loyalty to serve his wayward sovereign. He had sat in the Long Parliament with his elder son Ralph but they had gone their separate ways at the outbreak of the war in England. The younger son, Ned, had followed the inclination of his father and was now holed up in Drogheda, where it was hoped that Cromwell's army would be tied up in a futile siege until Ormonde could outflank him in the field.

There were a number of attempts to get the garrison to surrender – indeed Aston's own grandmother, Lady Wilmot, tried to get him to do so before being crossly ejected from the town. But morale was high, relief expected and there was hope too that the Commonwealth forces would be more badly affected by their immobile predicament than the defenders. On 11 September, after a week of fruitless parleying and skirmishing, Cromwell attacked Drogheda in earnest and his siege guns rapidly made a hole in the town's southern walls. Taking many casualties, including the death of a regimental commander, the New Model troops fanned through the breach before coming under a murderous fire from a small fort within the walls atop St Michael's Mount. There were now more than 2,000 of Cromwell's soldiers surging through the town, their bloodlust inflamed by their hatred of the Irish 'reptilia', the earlier goading of their chaplains and the death of their comrades. In the melee and confusion, the bridge across the Boyne which linked the town's two halves was captured intact and the soldiers erupted into the densely packed northern section. The slaughter was terrible. Anyone caught bearing arms was likely to be killed on the spot, whether offering surrender or not. A number of the defenders fled into the supposed sanctuary of St Peter's Church, which was promptly fired by the enraged attackers. The screams of the trapped men tore through the air as they were burnt alive. The mayhem continued for hours with the murder of unarmed prisoners. Ned Verney, amongst those singled out by the orders for decimation, was run through in Cromwell's presence in the smouldering aftermath. Others, including priests, were rounded up and ruthlessly bludgeoned to death (or 'knocked on the head' in Cromwell's careful phrase for the squeamish): Sir Arthur had his skull crushed with his own wooden leg. The surviving soldiers were later shipped off to the plantations of the New World.

By this stage of the civil wars there was nothing unusual about military encounters, whether in the field or at sieges, creating carnage. But that at Drogheda was on a bigger scale than had been the final assault on Colchester in England, although it was very nearly surpassed by Monck's later assault on Dundee in Scotland. The main eyewitness account came from Cromwell himself, who reported to parliament that in his estimation about 2,000 defenders had been put to the sword. His letter to the Speaker, William Lenthall, contained the barest of regret for his soldiers' actions although he expected the massacre to have a salutary effect on the regime's enemies and hoped that it would hasten their surrender. Above all, however, he was persuaded that the events at Drogheda had been the 'righteous judgement of God upon these barbarous wretches who have imbrued their hands in so much innocent blood'.[9] This was proof of the divine sanction that the new regime so earnestly sought and Cromwell's bloody victory was lauded from the pulpits. A public holiday was declared. Royalist morale was rather harder hit, although it was more in sorrow at the diminution of the Prince of Wales's cause than tenderness towards the victims. Amongst a busy list of engagements with exiled royalists and Anglican divines in France, the diarist John Evelyn recorded that on 15 September 'Came news of Drogheda being taken by the Rebels and all put to the sword which made us very sad, forerunning the loss of all Ireland.'[10]

Ormonde had said that he feared Cromwell's capacity for bribery as much as his troops, but the payment and provisioning of his own soldiers was a bigger priority in the latter's mind. Orders came from the Council of State that all captured rebel estates should be exploited as soon as possible in order to pay for his campaign. Next, Cromwell turned southwards towards Cork and Munster. Among his staff was Roger Boyle, Lord Broghill, who was the expedition's Master of the Ordinance. Broghill was a son of the Earl of Cork and elder brother to his ultimately more renowned sibling, the chemist

Robert Boyle. His political impact was, however, to be significant. He had been suborned by Cromwell, who had cajoled him to place his faith in the Commonwealth rather than the Confederacy under Ormonde. The scion of the Old Protestant tradition did not need too much persuading. Broghill's influence lay among his fellow peers and landowners in Munster, most of whom he persuaded to join him, not least more effectively to protect and augment their wealth. In the meantime, the English army moved further to protect its own seaborne flank and supply line to the south of Ireland by securing Wexford. Once again, Cromwell attempted to persuade the predominantly Catholic garrison to surrender, an interval Ormonde used to reinforce the town. The cynicism of this manoeuvre enraged Cromwell, although his troops were spared a full-frontal assault when an Irish traitor let them through a key part of the defences. As at Drogheda, so too at Wexford, the English troops ran amok and Cromwell's report put the butcher's bill at some 2,000 souls, mostly civilians, among whom were a mere twenty of his own army.

As another Irish winter approached, Ormonde retreated to Kilkenny in the heart of Leinster to consolidate his forces. These were still numerically stronger than the invaders but they had been serially worsted. Yet he was able to reinforce the port garrison at Waterford, which successfully resisted the combined efforts of both Henry Ireton and Michael Jones as the weather grew harsher. There, the Irish under Viscount Tara were to hold out until the summer of 1650. By now the Commonwealth's army was severely debilitated; dysentery and a strain of malaria had set in, to which Cromwell himself fell prey, and the number of troops available for active operations dropped to a quarter of the force that had arrived in Dublin in August. Fortunately for the invaders, the efforts of Broghill were highly influential in neutralising the main towns of the south-east. Cork itself was secured when the Protestant citizens expelled the small royalist garrison. Those members of the Fanshawe family that had taken refuge there were taken by surprise and Lady Ann who, upon 'hearing lamentable screams of men, women and children, I asked at the cause. They told me they were all Irish, stripped and wounded, turned out of town and that Colonel Jeffries (and his supporters) had possessed themselves of the town for Cromwell.'[11]

The English warlord next protected his landward flank with the surrender of Ross. Here, the Catholic defenders under the command of Sir Lucas Taaffe were allowed to disperse peacefully and the residual citizenry promised safe harbour. But by now the troops of the New Model Army were, in their commander's words, 'fitter for a hospital than the field' and as the heavy rain turned the ground to slush and brought movement to a standstill, Cromwell shepherded his remaining troops into winter quarters. Meanwhile, his letters back to the civilians in London kept up the steady barrage of requests for continued logistical support and reinforcement, which arrived only after much cajoling.

The truth was that the Irish campaign masked the growing importance of what was ultimately to become a greater strategic priority, namely command of the ocean around the new Commonwealth and protection of the sea lanes upon which so much of its vital commerce depended. After the execution of the king, fears about security were heightened by the animosity of the other European powers, notwithstanding that two of them (France and Spain) were still locked in hostilities. Piracy in the waters around Britain was also out of control. On the other side of the Atlantic in the New World, only Massachusetts (which had sent troops to the mother country to fight in parliament's cause) was reliably loyal. Virginia was under the sway of a royalist governor (the playwright Sir William Berkeley) as was the commercially important island of Barbados. The loyalties of Maryland, named after Henrietta Maria, hung in the balance. Here the governor was the Roman Catholic Lord Baltimore, who was engaged in a delicate balancing act between his co-religionists and Protestant sectaries fleeing Puritan authoritarianism in New England. Above all else the commercial interests of London, its value as a centre of finance for the Commonwealth and its close association with the merchant fleet and trade, needed protection.

Metaphorically surrounded, the new regime ordered an expensive ship-building programme in one of its first acts. There was too a clear determination to make the navy more professional. The dismissal of the Earl of Warwick had been followed by the appointment of three Generals-at-Sea. Of the triumvirate, Edward Popham was more obviously a political appointment. Both Richard Deane (one of the regicides) and Robert Blake had, however, served with distinction in the New Model Army. The former was a skilful artillery commander who had fought at Naseby and was much admired by Cromwell. Robert Blake was the elder of the three and had been born in Bridgewater in Somerset in 1598, one of thirteen children. Educated at Wadham College, Oxford, Blake was (like Cromwell) to secure greatness without the thick and downy coat of earlier patronage. Despite his brains, he failed to gain a fellowship at the university and was also thwarted in his attempt to win election to parliament in 1640. Blake was unusually tall and powerfully built compared to contemporaries and he sublimated his energies as a soldier, playing a notable part in the campaigns in the West Country. As with Rainsborough and Monck, he was later to swap his army commission for a naval one.

It was his treatise *Laws of War and Ordinances of the Sea* that attracted political notice and the work was later endorsed by the Rump as official naval policy. Blake was placed in command of a New Model naval squadron with orders to run down Prince Rupert, whom he blockaded off the south-east coast of Ireland, preventing the royalist from interfering with Cromwell's August landing. Theirs was an epic duel. The prince managed to break away from the jaws of the Commonwealth hunters in a storm and headed for the Iberian coast. Blake set off in hot pursuit, both men learning the skills of naval manoeuvre and seamanship as they went along. Prince Rupert led his force into the mouth of the Tagus where he was promptly shut in by his antagonist, notwithstanding the protests of the Portuguese government of King John IV. After much dithering, the Portuguese sent their own ships to see off the English, but in a sign that the new English Commonwealth was in deadly earnest, Blake ruthlessly attacked them first. His intended royal target used the pandemonium to slip anchor and sail into the Mediterranean as the year drew to a close. Once more, Blake set off on the chase, leaving a smoking Portuguese fleet behind him. Rupert spent his thirtieth birthday aboard his flagship (the ironically named *Constant Reformation*), grabbing unwary vessels where he could but losing just as many as he tried to outrun his pursuers. Eventually he was caught just off Malaga but managed once more to escape. By now, Rupert would have seen the hand of Providence moving more equitably: emboldened by his good fortune, he set sail for the wider Atlantic. He was to remain under the mast for another three years.

While Prince Rupert kept the royalist cause alive at sea, a romantically charged but ultimately doomed campaign on land was planned by the Marquis of Montrose. Now in his late thirties, James Graham had been in exile since his defeat by Leslie at Philiphaugh in 1646. His grief at the execution of the king, expressed in highly lachrymose verse, had apparently been sincere. He had been forced to watch from the sidelines as his great rival Argyll consolidated his precarious ascendancy over the various factions back home. However, Montrose's distance from Scotland did nothing to diminish the bitterness felt towards him on account of his savage Highland campaign. Back in the service of the late king's son, he now made himself useful by trying to recruit soldiers made redundant by the ending of the Thirty Years War while conducting a brief dalliance with his patron's aunt, Elizabeth, the widowed Winter Queen. The youthful Prince Charles saw the opportunity to introduce a little grit into the dynamic of his relationship with the Covenanters and granted Montrose the title of his Lieutenant. Scottish sensibilities were outraged and the Cassilis mission made it a condition of support that the marquis be dismissed.

The unbending suit of the Scots was, however, given a lift by the unpromising developments in Ireland, where Cromwell was rapidly delivering the *coup de grâce* to royalist ambition. Heralding the renewal of his campaign as snow hit the ground in January 1650, he delivered a tremendous broadside against the Roman Catholic clergy whose bishops, in an act of religious fervour that was devoid of political sense, had declared holy war against the invading troops at Clonmacnoise at the beginning of the previous Advent season. Equally symbolic, but of doubtful military value, was the appointment of the Bishop of Clogher to lead the Catholic army in Ulster, in place of Owen Roe O'Neill, who had finally succumbed to his infirmities. His reason distorted by self-righteous anger and messianic cultural supremacism, Cromwell denounced the political meddling of those whose 'covenant was with death and hell' and who had provoked the act of rebellion against Englishman who 'had good inheritances, which many of them purchased with their money . . . from you and your ancestors'. He came not to destroy men who held their Catholicism as a matter of sincere personal belief (although the open celebration of the mass was not to be countenanced), but to assert the rule of English law as a guarantee of peace.[12]

The first target of the new year's campaigning season was the Confederate capital of Kilkenny, which surrendered without a fight. Once more, the garrison was allowed to disperse peacefully. By now, large numbers of royalist troops were surrendering and Catholic rebels melting away. Inchiquin's force had already begun to disintegrate, a process that was accelerated by a truce in which Cromwell offered free passage to those that would leave Ireland altogether or move to areas under his control. The Protestant warlord took the opportunity to leave for exile, although the armistice was disdainfully rejected by Ormonde himself. The options of the marquis were limited, although there were still a number of large garrisons that could threaten the English and their supply lines. Cromwell knew that these would have to be reduced if a long-drawn-out guerrilla war was to be avoided. Accordingly, the assault was resumed against Waterford and a force marched to Clonmel, one of the most imposing fortresses in Munster. This was commanded by 'Black Hugh' O'Neill, a kinsman of the eponymous Ulster chieftain, who had nearly 2,000 men at his disposal, including a force of cavalry. The position of the town, surrounded as it was on three sides by marsh and river, meant that it could only be attacked from its northern flank. Nonetheless, from this direction the garrison was overlooked by higher ground.

Cromwell lost no time in installing his artillery on this spot and once it became clear that the Irish were going to make a fight of it, the bombardment commenced. The English had an almost unimpeded view of the effect of their shells on the town, yet the reduction of the northern walls proved to be hard work. Using the cover of darkness, O'Neill's troops constructed a secondary defensive position behind that section of the outer wall through which the enemy was expected to make their breach. Cannons were placed in enfilade and the upper storeys of the surrounding houses fortified. On 17 May, a terrific barrage finally blew a hole in the ramparts and through the smoke and dust the Irish could hear the sound of singing coming from the English. As the words of the psalms drifted forward, the New Model infantry advanced, led by dragoons on horseback who picked their way through the rubble. In the eerie silence, the attackers pressed forward until, in the clearing smoke, it became obvious that their route forward was blocked. There was a moment of terrible realisation as the soldiers at the front started to turn back. By now there was a terrific crush with Cromwell's officers urging more of them through the breach. Suddenly there was a roar as the concealed Irish cannon burst into life. From upper windows and embrasures volleys of small-arms fire cascaded down. The carnage was terrible: limbs flew as deadly chain shot was blasted at waist height, and men were scythed down in the hail of musket balls and shrapnel. There was no way out except backwards and as the thinning ranks of English retreated through the hole, they were to leave nearly 2,000 of their comrades behind, many screaming in agony from their appalling wounds.

In terms of numbers killed, Clonmel was the biggest reversal ever suffered by the New Model Army in a single action and Cromwell was aghast. But for the Irish, it was something of a pyrrhic victory: Ormonde's field force had disintegrated and he was in no position to turn Clonmel into a decisive engagement. More prosaically, O'Neill had run out of ammunition and his last fusillade was composed mostly of glass beads, nails and silver coins. Realising that his garrison could do no more, he spirited away his troops in the night, leaving the mayor to make the surrender. Under the circumstances of such losses, the English soldiers might have been expected to behave as they had done at Drogheda but Cromwell intuited that Irish resistance was almost at an end and although furious, he was inclined to be merciful to the civilians left behind. He was also under increasing pressure from the Council of State to return. The politicians in London had viewed the relatively swift subjugation of Ireland with surprised delight but their joy soon gave way to anxiety at the thought that Cromwell now had the victory and the means to carve out a substantial and potentially rival fiefdom for himself. Former royalists and Protestants of influence like Broghill were joining his banner. He was, too, beginning to exercise the patronage of a conqueror by making a number of appointments to the civil administration of Ireland: John Cook, the radical lawyer who had conducted the arraignment of the king at Westminster was offered the role of Chief Justice of Munster. Accordingly, the Council now firmly ordered their general home, despatching the new frigate *President* to collect him. Leaving Ireton in command of the army, Cromwell left Ireland on 29 May 1650, never to return.

10

'Think it possible you may be mistaken?'

Dunbar

God hath a people here fearing His name, though deceived.

Oliver Cromwell, Dunbar Despatch

Your own guilt is too much for you to bear: bring not therefore upon yourselves the blood of innocent men deceived with pretences of King and Covenant, from whose eyes you hid a better knowledge.

Oliver Cromwell, Letter to the General Assembly

Besides the force it has to fright
The spirits of the shady night
The same arts that did gain
A power, must it maintain.

Andrew Marvell, An Horatian Ode

The denouement in Ireland left the Prince of Wales with little option but to pursue further negotiations with the Scots, who were themselves thoroughly divided. He had sailed to Jersey in antici-pation of joining a victorious Ormonde, but Cromwell's campaign and Blake's dispersal of the royalist squadron under Prince Rupert had put paid to that. Sir Edward Hyde had been sent away to drum up military support from a politely indifferent Spain. Making little headway with the polished courtiers of Philip IV, Hyde wandered off to console himself with the altogether rougher spectacle of a bullfight. He was to return to his master empty-handed. With the option of Ireland fading, Charles was more easily persuaded to write to the Estates and to the General Assembly to propose that talks be reconvened back at Breda in the Netherlands.

The Kirk party baulked at this. The Stuarts' motive was mistrusted and besides, the Act of Classes had purified the way towards the theocratic state run by Old Testament elders for which the fanat-ics had so devoutly prayed. Even the army was now subject to the discipline of the civil Presbytery and lay patronage of ministerial appointments had been abolished. The Kirk's fervour for disci-pline went right to the apex of society too and for the first time in living memory, members of the aristocracy found themselves on trial for adultery. Argyll could see the traditional dominance of the Scottish state by the nobility and his own authority dribbling away. It was time to take a stand and in this there was a coinci-dence of interest with the residual Engager blue-bloods gathered around Charles. After fierce debate, the nobles (with the exception of the dissenting Cassilis) persuaded the parliament to send the commissioners back.

But now the terms were significantly hardened. The teenager was to take the Covenant, confirm all acts made by his father's oppo-nents, abrogate the Irish treaty brokered by Ormonde, and replace his court and council with approved Calvinists. As before, the commissioners were especially insistent that Montrose be cashiered, lest he perpetuate the civil discord at home by reigniting the war. But the bloodthirsty chieftain was one of the few assets Charles had left, and the Highlands north of the River Tay were far from settled and obedient. Fully aware of talks that might ultimately lead to his undoing but urged on by the prince, Montrose laid out a quixotic plan to reinvade his homeland. He issued a ringing declaration from the Continent that his countrymen should metaphorically come out with their hands up. His correspondence too gave strong hints of a death wish and there seems little doubt that he was motivated by an intense attachment to the idea of the romantic cavalier. His motto, 'Nil Medium', spoke of a life lived at the intersection between ecstasy and doom. Charles was as impressed by the theatricals as he was interested in hedging his bets, and sent his warrior the insignia of the Garter. Nonetheless, he was honest enough to hint to Montrose that he might not live to enjoy it.

The marquis landed in the Orkneys in the early spring of 1650 with a motley collection of Swedish and German mercenaries. He was joined there by a small bevy of confused and leaderless Highlanders whose own chieftain, the Earl of Kintoull, had died a short while previously, leaving them without a plan. As they were gathering, the talks at Breda matured, although the prince and his advisers were determined that the commissioners would not get everything their way. The Irish issue was deferred and the Prince of Wales maintained his loyalty towards those Engagers, such as Lauderdale and Lanark, at his court. He remained elusive in committing to Presbyterianism but at last conceded that he would sign a declaration attached to the Covenant, although not the document itself. It was just enough. The Scots commissioners could now plausibly claim that they had a covenanted sovereign, an outcome that they had never achieved with Charles's father: the prince had a route back to at least a part of his inheritance. But the lack of sincerity on each side was palpable and there were few illusions. Among the commissioners, Alexander Jaffray gloomily noted, 'We did both sinfully entangle and engage the nation ourselves and that poor, young Prince to whom we were sent, making him sign and swear a Covenant which we knew from clear and demonstrable reasons that he hated in his heart.'[1] In haste, a letter was despatched to Montrose ordering him to stand down. He was never to receive it.

The royalist war party had already crossed the Pentland Firth, with

the aim of provoking a wider rising. However, news of the rapprochement between the Stuart faction and the Covenanters was spreading
rapidly and this cut the ground from beneath Montrose's feet.
Unbelievably, he was still able to draw in a few additional supporters
to what could now plainly be seen as a suicidal mission. Marching
towards the Dornoch Firth, his tiny cosmopolitan army was taken
by surprise and decisively dispersed in the last week of April, just as
Charles was about to sign the treaty. The marquis himself escaped
but was later turned in by a fellow Highlander for the prodigious
sum of £20,000 and carted off to Edinburgh in ignominy. Having
already been condemned *in absentia*, his enemies declared there to
be no need of a formal trial. Nonetheless, he was subjected to the
full scorn of the more fanatical of his adversaries in the setting of the
parliament building. To his credit, Argyll disdained to take part in all
the ritualised humiliation and was absent as Montrose was led to his
death. His execution became as celebrated in fable and poetry as was
the beheading of the former Stuart sovereign. Dressed with greater
than usual care and attention (as if for his wedding day, according
to one eyewitness), he was hanged from an enormous gibbet on the
afternoon of 21 May 1650. His lifeless body was dismembered, and
the limbs and head distributed around the major towns of the north
as a salutary reminder of the perils of vainglory. It was an end that
the marquis himself had anticipated in verse on the eve of his death
and with the same grim relish with which he had often regarded his
opponents:

> Let them bestow on every airth a limb
> Then open all my veins that I may swim
> To Thee my Maker in that crimson lake;
> Then place my parboiled head upon a stake
> Scatter my ashes, strew them in the air
> Lord, since Thou knowest where all these atoms are
> I am hopeful Thou'lt recover once my dust
> And confident Thou'lt raise me with the just.[2]

One month later, far away from his champion's decaying head, Charles Stuart landed on the shore of the Moray Firth.

The homeland to which Cromwell had returned was a drab and subdued place. As in Scotland and Wales, the husks of destroyed and dilapidated buildings still littered a landscape made more forlorn by economic depression. The scenes of destruction were most prolific in the western part of England and in the Midlands, where much of the campaigning had taken place. These mute legacies of war were not just to be observed at cannon- and mortar-blasted castles like Corfe in Dorset, or in the massive royalist forts thrown up around Newark. Towns and villages too were still disfigured by earthen ramparts, now covered in weeds, which had been ordered by military command or erected by local communities in acts of self-defence. Those larger towns such as Worcester, Newark, Chester, Oxford, Colchester, Exeter and Taunton which had suffered prolonged sieges were particularly badly damaged, and Leicester (which had been subjected to a double sacking either side of the battle at Naseby), was reduced to a shell, many of its wooden dwellings having burnt down. At Taunton, a local divine had lamented the colossal task of clearing up the wreckage of his town with 'her heaps of rubbish, her consumed houses, a multitude of which are raked in their own ashes. Here a poor forsaken chimney and there a little fragment of a wall.'[3]

The economic dislocation was just as bad. A large number of these towns, such as Banbury which was noted for its large community of shoemakers or Leicester which was a centre for garment-making, were dominated by particular crafts or manufactures, and many took time to recover their commercial zest not least because communities had been dispersed and turned into refugees, many of whom had converged upon London. The disruption of so many centres of high-value activity presented a huge challenge to the authorities as they looked for new sources of revenue to meet the crippling liabilities of a heavily armed state, as well as the costs of repairing all the damage.

The most sorrowful sights were the skeletons of once beautiful houses like the late Elizabethan manor at Moreton Corbet in

Shropshire, or the former home of the Harley family at Brampton Bryan, and those more formidable dwellings such as Basing in Hampshire. While many had been damaged or destroyed during the actual fighting, a good deal more had been 'slighted' or deliberately rendered uninhabitable to deprive them to the enemy. The well-bred and wealthy were able to flee to safer ground but for the poor there was little respite, and many of the charitable hospitals and almshouses that had only just started to recover after their reduction during the Reformation period were flattened or spoiled once again. The indigent had nowhere else to go.[4]

Well over 80,000 people had been killed in England as a direct consequence of the fighting and a similar number had been left maimed by injury. Some of these, as revealed by petitions to local law officers at the Quarter Sessions, were horrific: a Somerset man called John Middlewick had been wounded in 1644 and 'had received a cut from the enemy throughout his face . . . his bowels trod out by a horse and was then run through with a Turk to the unparalleled hazard of his life'. Local parishes shouldered the main responsibility for the payment of pensions to the incapacitated and to widows, but the system was haphazard, roughly bureaucratic and often dependent on the personal intervention of a notable to ensure care was taken. James Swann had been maimed in both upper limbs fighting for parliament in 1642 but nearly a decade later it took the intervention of Edmund Ludlow with the Wiltshire magistrates for his claim to be upheld.[5] However, those who had fought for the king were not so lucky and 'delinquents' were excluded from relief, further handicapping the process of reconciliation and causing resentment.

A stern public morality was being imposed too, and spies and informers run by the ruthless and shadowy MP Thomas Scot kept watch for any resurgence of royalist activity. John Evelyn, returning briefly from exile to his home in Surrey reported a country 'much molested by soldiers' and the London pulpits 'full of novices and novelties'. His travel was authorised by a forged pass in the name of Bradshaw, it being 'so difficult to procure one of the Rebels without entering into oaths, which I never would do'.[6] Even Andrew

Marvell's *Horatian Ode*, composed in honour of Cromwell's great Irish victory, was threaded with a melancholy at the order that had been lost and the grim logic of a militarised state driven by a new and restless Caesar. Cromwell had been greeted warmly by his commander-in-chief, yet Fairfax seemed aloof from the Commonwealth.

However, the Treaty at Breda was concentrating minds in London and the threat which had seemed so ephemeral since Preston once more loomed large with the arrival of the dead king's heir on Scottish soil. It seemed clear enough that the erstwhile allies were determined to impose the Stuart dynasty in the Kirk's garb. A subcommittee of state that included Cromwell, Lambert and Harrison was appointed to deal with the preparations for a struggle that many considered inevitable. If the Commonwealth was to survive, the feared military power of the Scots would have to be broken. As lord general, it was beyond question that Fairfax would lead the army but, in a pivotal moment, he demurred. An anguished conference took place in Whitehall in which his senior colleagues, including Cromwell, pressed him hard to exercise his command in a pre-emptive invasion. But Fairfax did not think the probability of a Scottish attack sufficient reason to invade a country that he personally considered still nominally bound to England by the sacred oath of the Solemn League. As recorded by his wife, Colonel John Hutchinson also detected the hand of Lady Fairfax in the lord general's refusal. Sir Thomas 'expressed his opinion that God had laid him aside as not being worthy of more . . . this great man was then as immoveable by his friends as he was pertinacious in obeying his wife'.

At the last, he resigned his commission, enigmatically citing 'debilities both in body and mind' for his decision.[7] He was just thirty-eight and had been one of the most successful military leaders ever produced by the British state. Leadership of the expedition and the title of lord general now passed to Cromwell, with Harrison appointed to command the home army in England.

In Scotland, the ascendant militants of the Kirk were more exercised by the need for national purification than preparation for the coming clash of arms with the schismatic English. The zealous divines were determined to root out 'blasphemy, profanity, adultery, bestiality and buggery'. In the scorching heat of messianic fervour, trials for witchcraft (a distinctive feature of both English and Scottish culture during these years), exploded in number. There was to be no back-sliding and no sooner had he arrived than Charles was escorted to Falkland Lodge in the Lomonds, a remote hunting lodge built by his great-great-grandfather, James V. There he was subjected to a regime of indoctrination that followed the script that had been pursued at Newcastle with the late king. In the face of opposition from Argyll and other nobles, the Engagers of his court were removed and the young prince was exhorted to abjure his father. A more impression-able person may have succumbed to this barrage, but Charles had inherited the will of his parents to add to his own innate intelligence. Perceiving the growing despondency of Argyll, Charles allowed the thought to be entertained that he might one day marry one of the marquis's elder daughters (a conceit that his mother in France later smothered). With his insight, he used his considerable charm to woo the more rational among the Covenanters while maintaining con-tacts with those sympathetic to the Stuart cause in the Highlands.

Meanwhile, David Leslie continued to gather his army, an exer-cise that had been in progress ever since the state had been placed in a 'posture of defence' following the execution of Charles I. By now he had assembled a force of some 15,000 men and, although it contained a number of professional fighting men of long experience, its *esprit de corps* and composition had been seriously undermined by the purges. Long on numbers, their level of military competence was, however, poor. With the New Model Army on the march, Charles was advised to take the opportunity to visit the Scottish army in person, an initiative of morale-building that was so well received that the General Assembly immediately pushed for a further inqui-sition of 'malignancy' in the ranks. In a climactic of Old Testament hysteria, another 3,000 men were weeded out, to be replaced by sons of the Presbytery whose Calvinist ardour was but little compensation for their lack of military training and skill.

The mobilisation of an English army to fight the Scots had been a swifter exercise than that against the Irish, and Cromwell's arrangements were completed within two months of his return to London. In advance of the invasion, the Scots received *A Declaration of the Army of England*, which denied that the Covenant required the imposition of Presbyterianism across all the former realms and warned that the serial successes of the New Model Army meant that God was obviously on the side of the English. Thus justified, Cromwell recrossed the Tweed with a fired-up army of 16,000 men on 22 July 1650. A transport fleet under Deane was organised to keep him supplied from the sea. With him on land as senior commanders went Lambert and Fleetwood. Monck too was in the advance guard, although his appointment proved controversial to those English soldiers who could remember his service for the royalists. Cromwell had nonetheless kept faith with him for taking the opprobrium of the O'Neill armistice and he was given command of a scratch unit of men recruited from the borderlands of northern England, the genesis of a unit that one day would become the Coldstream Guards. But now, the Scottish Border landscape into which the army crossed was deserted and barren of any item that might be of use to the enemy. Leslie and his forces had melted away.

While the Scottish commanders kept their forces tantalisingly out of range, the Kirk maintained a barrage of propaganda against the invaders. In *A Seasonable and Necessary Warning*, its commissioners urged the faithful to fast and warned them against the 'insolent and strange actings of that prevailing party of Sectaries in England these years past' and their 'monstrous blasphemies and strange opinions in Religion'.[8] These claims were rebuffed in a declaration from the non-commissioned officers and soldiers of the English army which showed the depth of the ordinary rankers' attachment to independence in matters of Protestant faith and expressed dismay at the inflexible spiritual authority claimed by the Kirk. In some exasperation, Cromwell followed this two days later with his own broadside against the presumption and hypocrisy of his co-religionists. In his 3 August letter sent from Musselburgh to the General Assembly he memorably challenged their dogmatism: 'You take upon you to judge us in the things of our God, though you know us not', he thundered, before demanding 'Is it therefore infallibly agreeable to the Word of God, all that you say? I beseech you, in the bowels of Christ, think it possible you may be mistaken?'

The thought of its being in error had not crossed the Kirk's collective mind and Cromwell's blunt enquiry was primly rejected. With its divines determinedly occupying the moral high ground, there followed a month of military feinting and parrying as Cromwell tried to draw the Scottish army into a decisive engagement. The approaches to Edinburgh were strongly fortified by mutually supporting positions, and the lord general had had his fill of sieges. But all the marching, countermarching and inconclusive skirmishes in the wet summer conditions were beginning to take their toll on the troops, who were poorly protected from the elements. As in Ireland, dysentery began to make itself felt in the unsanitary conditions. Within a short space of time, fewer than 10,000 men were left who were fit for operations and the decision was taken to start withdrawing towards the army's logistics base at Dunbar, with its narrow, protected harbour. Leslie saw his chance and with a force swollen to nearly 25,000 men, he left his forts and made a rapid march across the Lammermuir Hills on the English southern flank. On 1 September he drew up his army on Doon Hill, a steep and virtually unassailable piece of high ground that loomed over the town and harbour two miles away. In the distance could be seen the chill waters of the Firth of Forth and the land of Fife beyond. The English were very nearly trapped, and as they began to embark their sick and wounded from the harbour jetties, both senior commanders knew that the decisive battle was at hand.

Leslie's army comfortably outnumbered the English and he saw immediately that his debilitated opponents would be neither mad enough nor desperate enough to attack him uphill. But if he was to destroy Cromwell's force, he was going to have to manoeuvre his own troops into a position where they could engage it at closer quarter. It did not need the numerous and implacable divines amongst his troops to point out the obvious and all his senior officers agreed that the Scots redeploy to the lower ground, thus completely closing the route south to Newcastle. With a great clattering of claymore, musket, halberd and pike, a seemingly remorseless wave of Scottish soldiers now rolled down the steep slopes. But there was no immediate attack. Instead, Leslie ordered his troops to turn in for a night's rest in preparation for battle the next day: the English were cut off. In the fading light and drizzle, Cromwell knew that he would have to make a stand but also perceived that Leslie's move had overextended his force across a much longer front around the New Model Army. With great insight and resolution, he ordered a night move which substantially shifted the bulk of his cavalry under Lambert towards the Scottish right wing, now occupying the muddy ground astride the low road back to England. In the darkness, the horses were quietly followed by an infantry brigade under Monck. The artillery was wheeled to the centre of the line to keep the rest of Leslie's force pinned down.

As the sun began to rise in English faces in the early hours of 2 September, Lambert commenced his assault. Achieving near total surprise among the clearly silhouetted Scots, whose infantry barely had time to stand-to, he fell upon the disordered ranks as they frantically tried to get into formation. The fighting on this part of the line was intense as the Scottish cavalry rallied. With the crucial extra support of infantry under Colonel Goffe, Lambert and his troopers finally managed to force their way through the bristles of Scottish pikes to the open road to England; but they knew that ultimate success would depend upon the cavalry keeping the two wings of the Scottish army from rejoining. As in all battles, the critical moment had been reached and Cromwell (with superb timing) deployed his own right wing to engage the Scots on their depleted left flank around a low ravine in which Leslie's troops could barely manoeuvre. The carnage amongst the Scottish troops was terrible as they were subjected to a sustained and highly disciplined assault by the numerically inferior Ironsides. Within an hour, the battlefield belonged to the English.

With minimal English casualties, Dunbar was, in the lord general's words, 'a signal mercy'. He triumphantly wrote Hesilrige in Newcastle that 'The Kirke has done its doo' and hoped that 'Wee may find opportunities both upon Edenburgh and Leith Starling Bridge or other such places as the Lord shall lead unto.'⁹ But for the Scots, it was a catastrophe. Militarily emasculated by the rout, it required little imagination to see that the battle was the hinge upon which swung Scotland's continued existence as an independent state. Over 3,000 of their soldiers were cut down and more than 5,000 taken prisoner. There was no parole now; the captives were marched south in atrocious conditions towards Newcastle, many falling by the wayside and scores succumbing to their injuries. Most of the survivors faced a life of slavery or indenture in the cane and tobacco fields of the New World, and few saw their homeland again. Others managed to make their way northwards towards the vastness of the Highlands where Anne, Lady Halkett, recorded their misery en route. Berthed at Kinross House, this lively royalist aristocrat had played a major part in the escape of the young Prince James, Duke of York, from his father's enemies when she had spirited him out of his confinement at Saint James's Palace disguised as a teenaged girl in 1648. Now she was on hand to help the injured teeming from the battlefield. Among the horrors was 'a youth of about sixteen that had been run through the body with a tuke. It went under his right shoulder and came out under his left breast . . . but his greatest prejudice was from so infinite a swarm of creatures that is incredible for any that were not eye witness to it.'¹⁰

But the Scottish command could not afford to dwell on these losses. Showing some skill in the face of calamity, Leslie gathered up the remnants of his force and withdrew in good order to Stirling, leaving a tiny garrison holed up in Edinburgh Castle. On 7 September, with their horses' shoes clattering noisily on the cobbled streets, Cromwell's troops entered the otherwise undefended city.

The wider psychological and political impact of his victory on his opponents was profound. Ahead of the battle, the Scots thought that they had been thoroughly cleansed of their sins but the Almighty had spurned them. Repentance was again the order of the day and Leslie was denounced from the pulpit. Urged on by Wariston and the fundamentalists, a section of the residual Scottish army broke away to form the Western Association. Under the auspices of the Glasgow Synod, the dissenters then issued a remonstrance in the first week of October. Amidst much hand-wringing, it was doubted that the Scots should ever have placed their faith in the young Stuart prince and 'his corrupt principles'. But nor were they minded to seek an accommodation with the heretical English invaders. Charles himself regarded Dunbar with understandable *Schadenfreude*. Emboldened by the humiliation of those who had sold his father at Newcastle for thirty pieces of silver, he tried to rekindle the royalist flame in the Highlands. He rode northwards, hoping to stir his followers in the glens of Angus. But in an embarrassing episode known as the 'Start', the loyalists whom he approached were too disorganised to give him effective support and he was run to ground while hiding in a shepherd's hovel and returned to semi-captivity. Argyll was back in charge.

The disarray among the Scots did not, however, make the consolidation of English control of the Lowlands any easier. At the political level, it was not at all clear with whom the Commonwealth should be dealing. Lambert was sent off to neutralise the military threat posed by the Western Association and in an impressive *coup de main*, he lured them into an ambush and defeated them at the battle of Hamilton. Monck faced a guerrilla campaign in Lothian and the Borders where renegades and former mercenaries known as 'moss-troopers' harried English supply lines and engaged in general banditry. Although having had no truck with the Catholic establishment in Ireland, Cromwell was however motivated to conciliate his Calvinist opponents in Scotland and called together a number of divines to find common ground in a prayer meeting at Glasgow. But in the new year he succumbed to serial bouts of dysentery and fever; the months of virtually uninterrupted campaigning were taking their toll on his health. After Dunbar, his vigour began imperceptibly but remorselessly to drain away. The Scots managed against the odds to re-energise themselves in the cause of national liberation. The destruction of the military power behind the fanatics had allowed a more rational approach to survival to be taken and in December 1650 at Perth, a series of 'Resolutions' were adopted which permitted repentant royalists, Highlanders and other 'malignants' to return to the colours.

With the Kirk split, a more professional army of the Kingdom of Scotland being recreated and the Prince of Wales chastened by the debacle of the 'Start', there was sufficient impetus to rally round the Stuart cause. Accordingly, on New Year's Day 1651, Charles was crowned at the ancient site of Scone Palace. In a ceremony which would have been entirely alien and repugnant to his father, the twenty-year-old cast aside the presumptions of his dynasty and submitted to his tormentors. He accepted the crown from Argyll and endured a sermon of inordinate length from the Moderator of the General Assembly of the Kirk. Taking the crowning of Josiah as his theme from the Second Book of Kings, Robert Douglas reminded the assembled company of the vainglory of the institution of monarchy and implicitly seemed to question the fitness of the young sovereign. Baillie later recorded Charles's heartfelt recollection that 'I think that I must repent too that ever I was born.'[11] Affirming his allegiance to the Covenant on his knees and with tears in his eyes, the young man played his part in the whole charade with a panache that convinced the onlookers of his sincerity and which was further displayed in a royal progress around the Highlands in the weeks that followed. Consolidating this remarkable turnaround from the ignominy of the 'Start', Charles then tried to bolster his political position by pressing for the readmission of former Engagers to the Committee of Estates as well as to the army. By the early summer, the divisive Act of Classes had been repealed and former 'malignants' began to re-enter civil public life. The rule of the fanatics seemed to be at an end.

Although Cromwell's victories in both Ireland and Scotland in the two years following the execution of the king had mortally wounded the Commonwealth's Celtic and Scots opponents, the mopping-up operations were prolonged. In Ireland, his son-in-law made heavy weather of defeating residual Irish resistance in the River Shannon valley and he became bogged down in the siege of the strong point of Limerick. It was Ireton's misfortune that, once again, his expedition faced 'Black Hugh' O'Neill, the resourceful commander who had inflicted such pain on Cromwell at Clonmel. The authorities back in London moved swiftly to reassert control of the island's administration and the youthful republican Edmund Ludlow was despatched with the rank of Lieutenant General of Horse and full plenipotentiary powers to settle affairs with his fellow commissioners. Although an admirer of the exploits of the New Model Army, Ludlow represented the persuasion that the military caste was subordinate to the civil magistracy and it did not take long for arguments to develop over the soldiers' authority and the share of the spoils to be enjoyed by the men who had done the fighting. Very soon he was crossing metaphorical swords with the old sweat Hardress Waller. It was an inauspicious omen.

Among the exiled royalists, the news of yet another defeat was taken with weary resignation. John Evelyn had managed to get back to Europe after a Channel crossing in which he was chased by pirates and very nearly drowned. The country of his refuge was as disordered as the one he had fled: France was still at war with Spain and the state was beset by the Fronde, a rebellion among its judicial and aristocratic elites. His journey back to Paris was across a landscape over which large bodies of soldiers of uncertain allegiance roamed freely, plundering the population and making everyone's life a misery. As from the bleak conditions of the civil wars back home, there seemed to be little hope of escape. His certainties had taken a battering but this was not the time to be provoking the Almighty, who after all moved in mysterious ways. 'Men had no faith' he mourned, 'for though we prayed for the restitution of our estates and defeat of our enemies, yet we must not think of self-revenge or go on in luxury.'[12] Whilst attending punctiliously to his Anglican devotions, Evelyn also found as firm a spiritual refuge in aesthetic beauty and the 'neat and well contrived' order that could be found in architecture and well-crafted interiors. He rarely seemed to miss an opportunity to admire the art and artefacts of his connections. In his melancholic gaze, the parqueted floors of the Palais d'Orléans and of the Tuileries had a solidity and harmony that seemed entirely lacking in the affairs of his fellow men.

11

'The pure light of God dwelling within you'

Worcester

Yet much remains to conquer still, peace hath her victories no less renowned than war.

John Milton

What ever hath been said by any yet concerning Him is but opinion.

Henry Marten

For we believe that the outward Law and powers of the Earth is only to preserve men's persons and Estates and not to preserve men in opinions.

Edward Burrough, *Declaration of Quaker Faith*

After Dunbar, Cromwell sent nearly 200 banners and Scottish regimental colours to London, and his prisoners were paraded through Newcastle. His reputation as the English nation's pre-eminent military commander of the moment had been sealed, not least because the New Model Army had prevailed against seemingly overwhelming numbers. With the withdrawal of Fairfax, the new lord general felt a heavier burden of responsibility to speak for the concerns of his tired troops. In his letter sent to the Speaker of the Commons in the aftermath of victory, it was clear he was also thinking of a wider canvas. God had cleared the way with the victory on the Scottish coast, but it was now up to the MPs to ensure that the long years of war were given some meaning. But Cromwell apprehended the likely fruits of victory only very vaguely: the politicians were exhorted to have a sense of responsibility; to 'curb the proud and the insolent', to 'Relieve the oppressed' and to 'reform the abuses of all professions'.[1] His more authentic voice came through as he defended his men against the perceived religious snobbery of their political masters – 'It would do you good to see and hear our poor foot to go up and down making their boast of God' – but his exultant frame of mind could now contemplate an England that would 'shine forth to other Nations, who shall emulate the glory of such a pattern'.

The MPs who formed the residual of the parliament that had sat since 1640 were much relieved by military victory and respectful of the skills of the soldiers who had achieved it. The apparently decisive victory over a much-feared military power was extraordinary and the delighted members voted a special commemorative medal to be distributed to officers and other ranks. But they had originally gone to war over the fundamentals of the Protestant Church and the monarch's abuse of his authority. In their minds, the struggle had been about neither legal nor electoral reform, nor about many of the other particulars identified in the *Agreement of the People*. Their primary concern in the wake of victory over the king had been to ensure that the religious dimensions of the Commonwealth were settled and public order restored. The prejudices and inclinations of the disparate groupings in parliament had gradually coalesced in the campaign against impiety and immorality. The sense too that the differences among well-bred men of God had been an unfortunate aberration was articulated by influential members like Sir James Harrington, who wrote that Presbyterians and Independents were but 'two children contending in the womb of the same mother'.[2]

Moreover, the war against the Irish and Scots helped to reconcile the Presbyterian opponents of the Commonwealth in the cause of English patriotism against the perfidious Celts.

There were some Rumpers, among them Henry Marten, Alexander Rigby, Cornelius Holland and Thomas Chaloner, who had Leveller connections and whose priority was the consolidation of constitutional change and, for Rigby, the amelioration of social deprivation. Algernon Sydney was busy burnishing a growing intellectual conviction that, absent a successful monarch, a republic was the only true exemplar of governance. But these agendas were lesser priorities, as religion and public morality took centre stage in the earliest preoccupations of the Commonwealth. The Anglican model and its 'popish' Arminian doctrines had been swept away and many of its leading practitioners had fled into exile. Dunbar had delivered God's verdict on the theocratic state of the Scottish Kirk. Although the Blasphemy Act had blunted the activities of the Ranters, there was pressure to recognise Protestant independency. Accordingly, the Commons were grudgingly minded to pass a Toleration Act, which relieved citizens of the obligation to attend Sunday observance in a consecrated church. As a nod to the huge proliferation of 'gathered congregations', the measure was passed more in recognition of the facts on the ground and to the temper of the New Model Army than as a retreat from theological orthodoxy. Suspicion and barely concealed hostility towards the sects remained, and while a spirit of conciliation towards English Presbyterians gathered wind a fierce pamphlet war was maintained against Nonconformity in matters of doctrine if not of manners. William Prynne was soon at work at another piece of vituperation in *Independency Examined*.

But by now, a new interpretation of God's love and grace was making itself felt in the Protestant canon, and this one was to prove one of the most enduring of all. In his late teens, George Fox had performed service in the parliamentary army and it is enjoyable to imagine that he might have stood shoulder-to-shoulder with John Bunyan at Edgehill, another who was later to leave a profound cultural mark with the poetic expression of his devotion. Fox came from an artisan background that was sufficiently of means to enable him to leave both military duty and home in 1643.[3] Setting off as a prototypical drop-out, Fox wandered around the north and the Midlands engaging in passionate debate and proselytising a version of God's grace that manifested itself as a profound 'inner light'. As with many sects of the time, he was animated by interpretations of the Book of Revelation and strongly opposed both tithes and the concept of an official ministry. He converted many, including Edward Burrough, a Cumbrian ten years his junior and who was to become one of the itinerant preachers of the age.[4] The beauty of his and the later Quaker message was that it was shorn of that spirit of compulsion that often hardened into dogma in such a large number of alternative belief systems of the period. The free-spiritedness implied by the 'inner light' rapidly caught on and even attracted a number of adherents among the officer class of the army. It seemed of far gentler persuasion than the hard determinism of the Fifth Monarchists and the licentiousness of the Ranters.

In its earlier days, the movement shared too many of the aspirations of those Levellers like William Walwyn who deplored the social consequences of the wars and its impact on the weaker members of society. A strong strain of egalitarianism was also apparent and the refusal of its adherents to adhere to the norms of deferential behaviour in a graded society attracted much derision and later hostility. The Quaker habit of refusing to doff the cap in respect of their supposed betters and persons of authority was deemed to be particularly insulting. But the movement was also careful to stay on-message as far as the military was concerned and it endorsed the idea that the soldiery was fulfilling prophecy in the doing of God's work. But what really aggravated more orthodox Protestants was the further challenge that the concept of the 'inner light' presented to the doctrines of predestination and damnation. Reliance on the 'pure light of God dwelling within you' also denied the need for a ministry or even Scripture, a disposition that attracted increasing hostility as adherents became practised at noisily disrupting churches and other congregations with their 'quaking' and general hullabaloo. Soon, the 'inner light' was seen as a threat to public order, not just to accepted manners.

The attitude of the Rumpers cannot just be dismissed as the condescension of the ruling elite towards those who were seen to express their inferior social status by religious difference. The campaign for public morality and conformity was sincere, and the MPs were quite capable of turning on their own – a majority of members successfully called for the expulsion of the regicide Gregory Clement for adultery. Heresy was arguably taken more seriously still and of all the theological obsessions of the period, the doctrine of the Trinity was perhaps the most sacrosanct. The Socinians (later Unitarians) denied this belief and challenged other sacred cows such as predestination and the doctrine relating to the exercise of free will. They believed that God's grace was given freely and in general, not to the individual alone. In subverting the concept of an Elect, the Socinians echoed the Arminian philosophy that had caused such aggravation to Puritan sensibilities. For those who believed that belief in the Trinity was the only way to perceive sacred truths, this denial was too heretical to be tolerated.

In early 1649 the trial of the king had been disturbed by a rumpus in which one of the commissioners, an MP from Dorset called John Fry, was accused by another of denying the divinity of Christ. With momentous events taking place in Westminster Hall, the MPs nonetheless took time off to debate this shocking allegation of what was a capital offence. Fry dissembled an explanation but was angrily booted off the Commission and suspended from the House pending further investigation. Shortly after, he affirmed his belief in the Trinity and was grudgingly readmitted as a member. But with his heterodox convictions overwhelming a sense of discretion, he was soon back penning more pamphlets which suggested a recantation of his recantation. His work *The Clergy in their Colours* was the final straw and his observation that true enlightenment could only come from the lowest rungs of society seemed particularly subversive: 'It hath been the pleasure of God in all ages, to confound the wise and mighty by poor and despicable instruments in the eyes of the World.

Witness many of the Prophets, Christ's Apostles and Disciples in their times.'[5]

Led by the regicide William Purefoy, there were calls for Fry's formal arraignment and his works were publicly burnt by the hangman. The errant member was defended by Nedham in *Mercurius Politicus* and although the editor acknowledged the need for the Church and the clergy to be controlled by the state he was far more critical of that Puritan zeal that demanded conformity of conscience. Henry Vane urged clemency too, but it was not enough to save Fry from expulsion in February 1651. However, the scepticism of the main tenets of Calvinist faith, identified in his works and in those of his fellow Unitarian John Biddle, was to live on and flourish.

Vane himself was emerging as one of the leading spirits of the Commonwealth and even drew the grudging admiration of Edward Hyde. Milton had eulogised him as 'that sage counsel old, than whom a better Senator never held, the Helm of Rome' and he was an effective practitioner in the Rump's committees devoted to trade, the sequestration of royalists and the Admiralty. Happily his own passionate religious inclinations, so murkily expressed in print, were sufficiently opaque to frustrate any imputation of heresy. But his attachment to freedom of religious conscience, forged from his experience of Puritan intolerance in the New World, was nonetheless sincere. He was far less forgiving where matters of conscience compromised public security and he was in the forefront of the Rump's vigilance towards those Presbyterians who remained unreconciled to the regime. In the spring of 1651 the clergyman Christopher Love was tried for treason. Love had been an outspoken critic of the Commonwealth from the pulpit but, at a time when England was still at war with Scotland, his correspondence with the government in Edinburgh and the royalists in exile was considered damning. While the soldier MPs Skippon and Fleetwood urged clemency, Vane was implacable that miscreants be executed as a powerful deterrent. Love was led to the scaffold that same August.

Vane had also been tasked with consideration of ways that the Rump could be brought up to the strength of a full parliament.

Barely one-fifth of the MPs who attended the House could trace their mandate back to the parliament that had been called in 1640 and few debates were attended by more than fifty members. Many excluded by the Purge did not return and for those exiles who died in the meantime, it was felt appropriate to hold by-elections. But sitting Rumpers and regicide MPs who died were not so replaced. Vane's committee reported back that it favoured so-called 'recruiter' elections where the Rump itself would be responsible for the addition of representatives. But there was an insufficiently strong consensus about this proposal and it was laid to one side, although remaining dormant. The army was particularly suspicious of any arrangement that would allow royalist or Presbyterian interests to reassert themselves. It also baulked at incumbents having their tenure perpetuated.

The mood of the soldiers was reinforced too by the conviction of Thomas Harrison that only men of complete probity and godliness could direct the nation. The intensity of this extroverted soldier's zeal had been such as to frighten the normally imperturbable and erstwhile monarch, who thought Harrison had been sent to assassinate him on his journey to captivity at Windsor. Now the king was dead, the rule of the saints was at hand and the current incumbents of authority were too tainted by factional interest and personal greed to guide the nation to the promised land. As if to emphasise the point, Harrison added the scalp of Lord Howard of Escrick to that of Gregory Clement when the former was charged with embezzlement. Ruthless personal enrichment at the expense of the defeated was a hallmark of the period but the Yorkshire knight was the only Rumper to be so pilloried. Yet Harrison was in deadly earnest and his contention that soldiers rather than civil ministers made better spiritual guides echoed the chiliastic temper of the army. The disposition he represented was cemented upon his election to the Council of State: in the same ballot secular republicans like Marten, his ally Herbert Morley and Ludlow were displaced.

The task of godly reconstruction went hand-in-hand with the rebuilding of the state, although here the priority was financial and commercial rejuvenation rather than social justice; indeed, the requirement that the defeated subsidise the new regime precluded such a thing. At last, the monarchy's opponents had all the levers of state funding in their hands and the mounting cost of the army and navy provided the spur for the optimisation of revenue. By the time of Cromwell's victory at Dunbar, a purge of local Justices of the Peace and officials had improved the collection of taxes, and the authority of the government's agents was strengthened by the attention given to the county militias. Able commissioners, such as John Pine in Somerset, were soon able to create local administrative fiefdoms. Regicide MPs John Venn and Miles Corbet sublimated their energies in the causes of naval administration and trade. Together with Isaac Pennington (MP for the City of London) and Francis Allen, who had both sat at the king's trial, they formed the nucleus of a powerful commercial interest group in the Rump.[6] Venn had been a founder member of the Massachusetts Bay Company and Pennington was governor of that for the Levant, whose charter had originally been granted by Elizabeth I. With an eye to a more systematic approach to moneymaking, in the late summer of 1650 the Rump established a Commission of Trade under Henry Vane to look at all matters pertaining to the regulation of commerce, manufactures, fisheries, customs and the plantations.

Of all the territories of the New World, the island of Barbados was perhaps the most important. Its economy had been transformed by the growing of cane, and the manufacture and trade of sugar, an industry that had been established with the expertise of the Dutch. By 1650 the population was nearly equal to that of Massachusetts and Virginia combined and the tiny island's economy was generating the prodigious sum of over £3 million. An ocean-going vessel was attaching stern and bow lines to its harbour walls every three days. The serious business of making money had ensured that relations between royalist and parliamentarian sympathisers had been cordially maintained during the long years of civil war back home. Parading one's allegiance in such a close community was considered the height of bad form.

However, the execution of the king had led to a hardening of attitudes and the royalist faction on the island now saw an opportunity to add to their fortunes by driving out their neighbours. Sympathisers of the Commonwealth, including the sugar pioneer Sir James Drax, were fined and had their estates sequestrated. Others were arrested and physically mutilated – some were branded. The arrival of Lord Willoughby, appointed by the Prince of Wales as governor of the Caribbean Islands, put a stop to the worst excesses; but the damage had been done.[7] The exiles were soon back in London spreading the tale of their outrageous treatment. Fearful that Virginia and the islands of Barbados, Antigua and Bermuda were on the verge of becoming fully armed royalist colonies, the Rump passed an Act in October 1650 prohibiting trade with these plantations and extended the embargo to cover the ships of any other foreign nation. Barbados itself was to be physically subdued and preparations were accelerated when Lord Willoughby declared the island's independence.

However, in the loose wording of the trade embargo lay the seeds of the later conflict with the Dutch. The long struggle for independence from Spain had gone hand-in-hand with an enormous accretion of the power and wealth of the United Provinces based on the carrying capacity of her merchant fleet. Largely at the expense of Portugal, the Dutch had extended their trading empire around the globe. Whether in spices and silks from the East Indies, slaves from Africa, sugar from the north-east coast of South America and the Caribbean, or in metal ore, grain and timber from the Baltic, the Dutch exerted an impressive commercial dominance relative to the modest size of their nation. Their sophisticated bourses, centred on Amsterdam, allowed the efficient aggregation of capital to support this complex machine and the means of exchange to oil it.

Although a fellow Protestant power, relations with the United Provinces had been uneasy. Quite apart from the commercial rivalry between the two maritime nations, the Court of the Stadtholder in the Hague had provided a refuge to the Prince of Wales. Soon after the trial and execution of the king, Isaac Dorislaus (who had been on the prosecution team with John Cook), had been murdered in its environs by royalist assassins. William of Orange was Charles I's son-in-law, and the Dutch were indolent in bringing the killers to justice. Within their dominant trade to the English plantations of the New World, they were also known to be supplying arms and powder to the royalist outposts. But in December 1650, William died of smallpox, leaving a newborn son as heir to his titles.

The death of the Stadtholder, which was an elective office, saw power in the United Provinces swing back to the patrician class of 'regents' whose authority largely derived from their commercial and business connections and economic clout. In their background, education and outlook, members of this class provided exemplars of the liberal, Protestant merchant that dominated the Dutch 'Golden Age'. Something of their elitism, but also their occasionally smug complacency, was slyly captured for posterity in the works of Rembrandt. Their success seemed to arouse admiration and resentment in almost equal measure. The reorientation of power away from the monarchist and Calvinist 'Orangists' back towards the merchant republicans appeared to offer an opportunity for the English Commonwealth, newly energised by a famous victory over the fanatics of Scotland, to engage with the Dutch. They were perceived as sympathetic co-religionists with the same blueprint for a successful state, and Cromwell was a particular enthusiast for the forging of closer ties.

Accordingly, an enormous delegation of 200 under the leadership of Oliver St John was packed off to the Hague in the early spring of 1651. They carried an ambitious proposal: no less than an economic and political union of the two states cemented by common rights of citizenship. The Commonwealth presented itself as a new but triumphant republic, eager to spread its enthusiasm and experience. The embassy was, however, a humiliation born out of English hubris. The Hague was a bastion of 'Orangist' sympathy and the rougher citizens made their feelings known as St John and his colleagues processed through the town's streets on the way to present their suit. To shouts of 'St John's bastards', the delegates were rudely jostled and insulted.[8] Worse was to follow. Their official hosts were not sure what to make of these representatives of a boorish nation still at war with itself. They dissembled polite interest in the economic proposals but were far less enamoured of the constitutional ones. The United Provinces had not spent nearly a century of struggle against the overlordship of Spain only to see the fruits of their liberty diluted in an implausible arrangement with the palpably hard-up, but more numerous, English. Struggling to mask their condescension, the Dutch allowed the talks to dribble into the sand. St John had a sharp mind but was somewhat thin-skinned and he took the slight badly. The Dutch seemed in defiance of the spirit God had ordained for the age. He and his delegation returned to England in high dudgeon.

A war with one Protestant power and the rebuff of another helped to infuse the culture of the Republic with a markedly more Anglo-Saxon patriotic spirit and pragmatically assertive outlook towards the rest of the world. In the wake of the failure of the Dutch mission, polite society was gripped too by a brief mania for the model of republicanism represented by Venice. The small maritime state seemed to punch well above its weight while its public culture, nominally Catholic, had an independent spirit that disdained the temporal or spiritual lordship of mightier powers. A series of articles in *Mercurius Politicus* extolled the benefits of this exemplar while excoriating the Dutch. Milton too drew a comparison between the civic greatness of Venice and the republican glory of ancient Rome.

Nor did religious orientation get in the way of a more cordial relationship with England's old antagonist of the Elizabethan era. After all the revulsion caused by the king's execution, Spain had been the first of the major European powers to recognise the new Commonwealth. Notwithstanding the murder of the new English ambassador (Anthony Ascham) by royalist renegades before he had even presented his letters of credence, Philip IV perceived that the Commonwealth could provide some useful ballast for the creaking Habsburg empire in the aftermath of the Thirty Years War. In Alonso de Cárdenas, the Spanish had a wily and sophisticated representative to the 'Parliament of the Republic of England', a title that was expected to be punctiliously observed by all foreign nations. On behalf of his sovereign, Cárdenas had taken early and astute advantage of the Commonwealth's dispersal of the magnificent Stuart art collection (a lot of it at knock-down prices) and he was to form an unlikely but abiding friendship with the picaresque Henry Marten.[9] He was also soon stressing the mutuality of English and Spanish interests vis-à-vis the French and Dutch, who continued to shelter royalist exiles.

The security of England depended upon Scotland being subdued. Cromwell's appetite for conciliation based on religious accord was soon superseded by military realities. Leslie had managed to rebuild his forces over the winter months and by the summer of 1651 had assembled another army of around 18,000 men grouped around Stirling, the landward gateway to the Highlands. Fearing a reprise of Dunbar, he avoided a full-on engagement with the far more battle-hardened English. His force was comprised of amateurs and enthusiastic Highlanders and islanders from the Inner Hebrides but was simply too large to be ignored by a fitfully convalescent Cromwell. Showing once again great tactical imagination, he conceived an amphibious assault across the Firth of Forth at its narrowest point to the west of Edinburgh at Queensferry, to outflank his opponents from the east.

Again the highly dependable Lambert was put in charge of the operation and by midsummer had got nearly 5,000 men over to the Fife shore. The disconcerted Scots detached what was, for them, an elite force to head him off and the two sides met on the hills above Inverkeithing on 20 July. In a familiar pattern, the disciplined and aggressively led New Model soldiers worsted the brave but tactically naïve Highlanders, who suffered over 2,000 casualties. In the epicentre of the fighting were found the bodies of nearly 800 clansmen from Mull grouped around the inert figure of their chief 'Red Hector' Maclean of Duart; a mere thirty-five of the islanders had survived.[10]

Inverkeithing was not, however, decisive. But the continued sense of precarious stalemate allowed the old Engager party to exert a firmer grip on the direction of Scottish strategy. With Argyll's influence diluted, Charles was soon persuaded by Middleton and Lauderdale to mount an invasion of England if ever he was to restore the full realm of the Stuarts. They were joined by the executed Duke of Hamilton's brother, the Earl of Lanark, who had succeeded to the title. Hyde recorded his approval: 'He was in all respects to be much preferred before the other, a much wiser, though it may be a less cunning, man: for he did not affect dissimulation, which was the other's masterpiece. He has unquestionable courage, in which the other did not abound.'[11]

Their argument was that the well of royalist sympathy in Scotland had been fully exploited. Now it was time to drain the English one. Leslie too was persuaded to adopt an offensive approach and despite his earlier antagonism to the Engagers, he was now in the service of a crowned monarch, albeit an ambiguously covenanted one. Accordingly, a large Scottish army slipped camp around Stirling and for the third time in a decade crossed the border in force on 5 August 1651. A day later, Charles was proclaimed King of England.

Notwithstanding what was a wager of high risk by the Scots, allowing their army to break away southwards was a considerable gamble for the English too. Fortified by his now unshakeable belief in God's providence, Cromwell issued confident, if somewhat vague, assurances to the nervous civilians back in London. Although recent royalist attempts at insurrection had been nipped firmly in the bud, there was no guarantee that Charles would not be able to galvanise support in the north of England. Fleetwood was ordered to screen the capital and the newly reorganised county militias were efficiently mobilised. Fairfax cast aside his inhibitions and retirement to command the levies of Yorkshire against the invaders. Once more, the Scots took the western route, this time advancing in a more compact formation to deter any assault on their flank whilst on the move. There were the usual squabbles amongst the royalist notables. The youthful Duke of Buckingham kept pressing for overall command, which Charles crossly refused and which prompted a prolonged sulk from the disappointed nobleman. With Monck left to subdue remaining resistance north of the border, Lambert was ordered to follow behind Leslie's force while Cromwell advanced down the east side of the Pennines lest the invading host changed course.

Any hope that Charles had placed in the citizenry flocking to his colours and the Covenant was rapidly disabused. The propaganda of *Mercurius Politicus* did its work: the invasion was a clear act of aggression by one state against another and the number of Englishmen who were prepared to take up arms for the new (Scottish) king or swear to the Covenant were few. The Earl of Derby managed to gather a few brave retainers from his estates around Manchester, but they were effortlessly brushed aside by Lambert on his line of march and the earl taken prisoner. In the third week of August, the royal army reached and occupied Worcester without a struggle. Leslie and his 16,000 men were now a very long way from reinforcements, but the town offered a stout defensive position, was surrounded by waterways that would be obstacles to the New Model Army and had good routes to the Welsh hinterland if a withdrawal was ordered. Among his subordinate commanders was Edward Massey, who had returned from Holland, now fully committed the royalist cause, having escaped there after a brief imprisonment following Pride's Purge. Massey knew the surrounding countryside well, having led the parliament's forces in the area before their disbandment. If the English could be lured into a siege with its inevitable frontal assaults, Leslie's odds would improve.

But news reaching the Scots from their homeland was not encouraging. Monck had used his independent commission and 6,000 troops to emphasise his growing military indispensability. Following the departure of the main body of the Scottish army, he rapidly secured the strategic position of Stirling, which surrendered after a brief bombardment, and sent Colonel Okey to pacify Glasgow. Lacking the sensibilities of Cromwell, he saw his duty as to focus on the practical mission in hand and to be neither diverted nor delayed by other considerations. Accordingly, he set off in ruthless pursuit of the residual Scottish government under the Earl of Loudon. After outrunning the English they were finally rounded up in Angus, but not before spiriting the Scottish coronation regalia to Dunottar Castle, a remote fortress on the Aberdeenshire coast.[12]

Monck had the good sense not to waste energy with encroachments in the vast tracts of the Highlands and instead fixed his attention on the only remaining large town of any military significance, Dundee. As Cromwell was making his dispositions outside Worcester, Monck commenced his siege of this former bastion of the Episcopalian interest in Scotland. The garrison commander refused to surrender after two attempts to get him to do so. The long-winded parleys that had been Cromwell's style in Ireland were not in Monck's nature and with a phlegmatic shrug he commenced a vigorous assault: he was not going to ask again. The walls were soon breached and there then followed an episode of terrible barbarity. Monck considered the civil population to be as fair game as the garrison which had foolishly squandered the summons to surrender and his troops were authorised to take a terrible revenge. Over a thousand civilians were murdered in cold blood, including many women and children as the town was sacked.

A few days later in the West Midlands of England, the last great military confrontation of the civil wars on British soil commenced in earnest. It was an enormous engagement. Cromwell's army had swollen to over 31,000 men, having been reinforced along his way south. He had also assembled a powerful artillery train which he deployed on the high ground to the east of the city as well as a vast quantity of picks, shovels, planking and powder, for mining and breaching operations. Leslie had had the good sense to plan a demolition of bridges across the rivers Severn and Teme in order to frustrate English attempts to encircle Worcester and to protect his southern flank should he need to retire to the Welsh Marches, but Lambert, travelling in a wide arc south of the city, came across some undamaged piers across the lower reaches of the Severn which his engineers were able to turn into a span. Within a few hours the New Model Army was across. Frantically, Massey rode south with the cavalry to head him off before he could capture the Teme bridges intact but in a furious engagement the former parliamentary commander was severely wounded and his troopers forced to withdraw.

Cromwell still had to cross the Teme at its confluence with the Severn if he was to complete his encirclement efficiently. Leslie's soldiers managed to do sufficient damage to the remaining crossings such that his adversary now chose to throw pontoons across the rivers at points least visible to the defenders in their redoubt two miles upstream. Intuiting Cromwell's move but lacking the artillery support to stop the English on the riverbanks, Leslie ordered his Highlanders to move into positions where they could ambush Cromwell's troops when they made it to the defenders' side. On the morning of 3 September 1651, Fleetwood's troops surged across the pontoons while Deane crossed the Teme in force half a mile to the west. The Scots put up a murderous resistance; hundreds of miles from home, they threw themselves into a fight to the death that they knew they absolutely had to win. The English were thrown off-balance and Cromwell had to use his reserves to stop a reverse turning into a rout. At this moment, the defenders in the town perceived an opportunity. Charles was nearly as brave as his father, but his keener intelligence was not yet augmented by experience of command against overwhelming numbers. With more bravado than judgement, he chose this moment to launch a counterattack on the artillery position to the east of the city on Red Hill and at Perry Wood. After a quick parley with the equally inexperienced Lanark, each man led separate squadrons out of the city's gates to attempt an encirclement of their tormentors. With the lanky sovereign exhorting his troops, the royalists panted up the steep slopes and managed to force the surprised New Model artillerymen and infantry backwards.

The critical moment of the fight had been reached. Charles's impetuosity had opened a tiny window of advantage for the besieged. Leslie's residual cavalry stood nearby, but whether through lack of co-ordination or faulty orders, they failed to exploit the improbable momentum gained by their colleagues on Red Hill. Seeing their opponents hesitating, the New Model soldiers counterattacked and now made their preponderance in numbers count. The royalists were relentlessly pushed back and they began to retreat to the town. On the other side of Worcester, the Scots continued to inflict heavy casualties in the close-quarter fighting, but they too were being ground down by the sheer weight of the enemy. There was no option now but to fight it out within Worcester's walls and a bloody hand-to-hand struggle continued until dusk, when the heavily outnumbered Scots tried to make good their escape. They had lost another 3,000 men and the remainder went into Cromwell's bag, including Leslie, Lauderdale and the other leading commanders. A badly mangled Lanark succumbed to gangrene from a hideous wound that severed the lower part of one of his legs, and the bleeding Massey also fell into Commonwealth hands. But the king himself managed to escape.

At well over six feet tall, the rather recognisable monarch was vulnerable to betrayal and capture, and little time was wasted in deploying patrols to find him. Showing great presence of mind, Charles dismissed his retinue the better to preserve his slender anonymity. In imitation of his father's seemingly random wanderings after Naseby, the young king was then spirited about the country by an unlikely cast that included Roman Catholic priests, local tenant farmers and royalist officers still keen for some derring-do. More heavyweight support was lacking as the notables in the counties through which he passed preferred discretion as the better part of valour: the Stuart cause was no longer worth the risks. Nonetheless, Charles was eventually smuggled out of the country by brave sympathisers, like the Catholic Penderel family, by way of the Boscobel Oak, Bristol Docks and a voyage aboard the aptly named *Surprise* from Shoreham-on-Sea. After this real adventure, which he later himself described with great enthusiasm and colour, the dishevelled and famished sovereign arrived back in France in October with torn and blistered feet. But the hinge upon which had swung the independent Scottish state had finally snapped.

A Stuart anointed by God. King Charles I coronation medal 1633, attributed to Nicholas Briot
(National Galleries of Scotland)

Great Britain and Ireland's *Leviathan*? Oliver Cromwell, attributed to Samuel Cooper
(National Portrait Gallery, London)

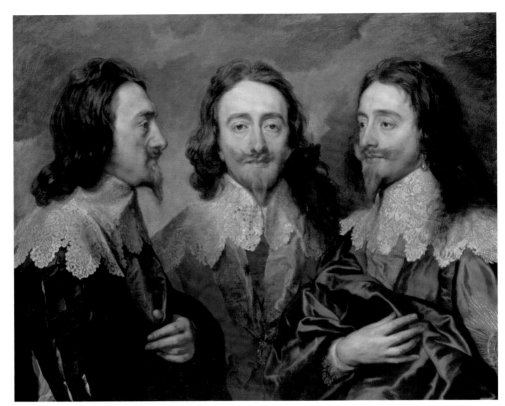

Above. Monarchy as an
aesthetic phenomenon.
King Charles I, attributed to
Anthony Van Dyck (Royal
Collection Trust
© Her Majesty Queen
Elizabeth II 2020)

Right. The uncrowned
consort. Queen Henrietta
Maria, attributed to Anthony
Van Dyck (Royal Collection
Trust © Her Majesty Queen
Elizabeth II 2020)

Towards a state under the Covenant. Archibald Campbell, 1st Marquis of Argyll, attributed to David Scougall (National Galleries of Scotland)

The royalist guerrilla. James Graham, 1st Marquis of Montrose, attribution unknown (National Galleries of Scotland)

'Black Tom'. Sir Thomas Fairfax, attribution unknown (National Portrait Gallery, London)

The 'Penman General' of the New Model Army.
Henry Ireton, attributed to George Harding after
Samuel Cooper (Bridgeman Images)

The pulse of the Republic. Henry Marten, attributed to Peter Lely
(Bridgeman Images)

A dissenting Christian. William Walwyn, attribution unknown (National Portrait Gallery, London)

Author of England's written constitution. John Lambert, attributed to Francis Place
(National Portrait Gallery, London)

The adaptable Stuart prince. King Charles II, attributed to David des Granges
(National Galleries of Scotland)

An acerbic Puritan diarist. Lucy Hutchinson, attributed to Samuel Freeman (National Portrait Gallery, London)

Towards a new sensibility. Katherine Philips, 'The Matchless Orinda', attributed to William Fairthorne (National Portrait Gallery, London)

The gentle Lord Protector. Richard Cromwell, attribution unknown
(National Portrait Gallery, London)

A champion of civil magistracy. Sir Arthur Hesilrige, attribution unknown
(reproduced by kind permission Lord Arthur Hazelrigg)

The grey eminence of the Restoration? General George Monck, attributed to Samuel Cooper
(Bridgeman Images)

12

'Winning all by fight'

Dover

The government of the Commonwealth and that of its trade are exercised by the same individuals.

Venetian Ambassador

The English are about to attack a mountain of gold; we are about to attack a mountain of iron.

Adriaan Pauw

Six weeks after Worcester came the news of O'Neill's surrender at the plague-bound Limerick after a lengthy and intermittent siege that had lasted more than a year. In the meantime, a naval expedition under the command of Sir George Ayscue was in the process of recapturing Barbados for the Commonwealth and a fleet had been despatched to ensure the compliance of Virginia. But where Cromwell's steady occupation of the Lowlands of Scotland had been accompanied by attempts to conciliate co-religionists, Ireton's progress had been a hard and bitter slog in which violence driven by cultural hatred was given and reciprocated in full. Over the course of the campaigns between 1649 and 1652, the New Model Army alone sustained over 8,000 fatalities, mostly to disease. It was an astonishingly high casualty rate of nearly one-fifth. The Irish had been at war for over ten years, a somewhat shorter period than had been the case for the Scots. But their losses were proportionately and absolutely of a far greater magnitude than had been endured by the citizens of Great Britain. By the end of the fighting, approximately two-fifths of the country's pre-war population had disappeared. To the military deaths could be added the victims of score-settling by neighbours, destitution, famine and disease. It was to the latter that Ireton had himself succumbed in November 1651 and his body was shipped back to England in the company of the Irish leader, on his way to the Tower to join the notables captured at Worcester.

The death of Ireton deprived the army of one of its strongest Puritan intellects. Both Fairfax and to some degree Cromwell had been troubled by his intensity and irritated by his legalistic verbosity, and he had found it hard to build and sustain alliances, such was the earnest single-mindedness of his convictions. But he had had a logical vision of the sinews of peace that the soldiers wanted to see emerge from the corpses of the civil wars while his personal probity would have commended itself to the increasingly influential Fifth Monarchy men in the army. In a mark of the esteem in which he was held by his colleagues, his funeral was an elaborate state occasion, but, in a neat symmetry, his death had coincided with the apogee of the reputation of his far less intellectual father-in-law, undisputed conqueror of the Scots and Irish. The serial and spectacular success of the former minor squire of Huntingdonshire seemed to be a powerful sign of God's will. Now that Fairfax too had withdrawn, there was no one with the record, prestige and authority to match his own. Parliamentarians like Marten, Hesilrige and Vane might outweigh him in intellectual capacity, but none had had such an impact on the delivery of victory.

Yet Cromwell was not entirely trusted by the Commonwealth establishment. In theory his membership of the Council of State and position as lord general made him a servant of the civilian masters of the nation but as Hyde observed, 'yet his entire confidence was in the officers of the army'.[1] His championing of the peaceful expression of men's consciences and aversion to uniformity were well known – had he not declared that he would rather that 'Mahometanism' be permitted than that one man be persecuted by following his own spiritual path to God's grace? He did not belong to any 'gathered church' but rather to the unchurched body of the army, where the temper of independence was not just a matter of private conscience but vigorously expressed by unauthorised preaching. His public expressions of his own faith had a messianic quality that seemed to go well beyond the bounds of quiet conviction. God's apparent sanction, manifested in serial success on the battlefield, made Cromwell less tolerant of the moral failings of others and his capacity for angry disappointment was disturbing.

His political views, where they were not waiting upon God's providence, were driven by pragmatism and expediency. To Hyde, this approach was no more than dissembling hypocrisy; Cromwell, he believed, 'never did any thing, how ungracious or imprudent soever it seemed to be, but what was necessary to the design; even his roughness and unpolishedness . . . was necessary'.[2] But this judgement seems unfair and misses the deep sincerity of the soldier's faith. To Cromwell, the institutional arrangements of government were but 'dross and dung in comparison of Christ' and he seemed to believe that the grace of the Almighty was itself sufficient to guarantee that the custodians of the state would ultimately behave with integrity. In his own mind, he had justified the deletion of both king and the House of Lords from the constitution on the grounds that they had each serially betrayed the trust reposed in them by God. Yet to the doubters and his opponents, this begged the question as to what might happen if the Commonwealth too was found as wanting as the regime it had replaced? The anxiety he inspired was only partly mollified by the satirists:

Of Noll's nose my muse now sings
his power, force and might
subduing kingdoms, murthering kings
and winning all by fight.

Noll's mouth devowers king's crownes and powers
his gullet stretches wide
his stomach good as Kentish wood
old Mallet and young Pride.

But out behinde flew such a winde
from his back-doore with powder
that Bradshaw Jack quak'd at the crack
and said he neere heard lowder.[3]

Cromwell's views on the constitution were as rudimentary and the similarity of the sentiments he had publicly expressed after each of the battles of Naseby and Dunbar suggested little evolution in his thinking about the purposes of national stewardship.

Across Great Britain and Ireland there were now over 70,000 men under arms who needed managing as the fighting ended. Those senior men involved in public duties who had military experience could not be classed as a distinctive ideological bloc as they included convinced regicides and republicans like Ludlow, but also many of a Presbyterian disposition like Skippon, and those conservatively inclined in matters of religious doctrine and manners like Colonel William Purefoy. Most of the regicides who were professional soldiers were neither MPs nor had responsibilities outside their military ones. But among the contingent of commissioned officers retaking their seats in parliament, Major-General Thomas Harrison had a vision of a godly state that was inflamed by millenarian zeal. Among the junior officers and men who had been fighting for over a decade, there was too an expectation that change should not be long delayed now that hostilities had ceased.

In an attempt to head off the growing whiff of Caesarism, the civilians voted that the presidency of the Council of State should henceforward be held for one month only before being passed to another, and shortly after took the opportunity provided by Cromwell's resignation of the office of Lord Lieutenant of Ireland to abolish the post altogether. But the conclusion of the civil wars highlighted the provisional nature of the Rump and in an uneasy compromise the parliament that had been called by Charles I in the autumn of 1640 decided (by thirty-three votes to twenty-six) to terminate its sitting no later than the end of November 1654, a three-year extension that placed the onus on the House to deliver on a myriad of aspirations. Exercising his personal authority, Cromwell convened a meeting of soldiers and civilians in the December that followed Worcester to discuss the way ahead.

As recorded by Bulstrode Whitelocke, who was amongst those in attendance at the house of Speaker Lenthall, the tone of the meeting suggested that few of its participants were completely at home with the republican rubric of the Commonwealth, not least Cromwell himself. A consensus emerged that the laws and traditions of England were more compatible with a monarchical state, a proposition from which the lord general did not demur although it was not a dispensation that would have been recognised by the Stuarts. Once again, the idea of settling the crown on Charles and Henrietta Maria's youngest son, Prince Henry, was mooted. The sprightly and robust eleven-year-old was now the only remaining member of the immediate royal family in custody. Brought up in the care of strictly Protestant notables, he had famously declared on the eve of his father's execution that he would rather be pulled apart by wild horses than be made king at the expense of his elder brothers. Of greater relevance, the institution of regency had had a problematic history and the name of Stuart was too much of a hex to be a realistic option. But the apparent equivocation angered those members of the Council of Officers who were part of the debate and Cromwell's brother-in-law, the soldier John Desborough, demanded to know with some passion why England should not be a republic in perpetuity. To them, a restoration was out of the question. The 'Good Old Cause' had been well justified and was now an article of faith within the military establishment.

If the conference had revealed something of Cromwell's agnosticism towards the constitution, he was much clearer on the need for legality if there was to be a lasting settlement. Accordingly, with Marten and Lambert, he was a sponsor of the Act of Oblivion passed early in the new year. This was less an exercise in humanity and goodwill than an attempt to clarify ambiguities in the status, in law, of victors and vanquished. The soldiers were also motivated by the knowledge of the numerous local armistices during the wars where royalists had surrendered in good faith on condition that they kept their property. Apart from those guilty of treasonable deeds, the hatchets of the 'late differences' were to be buried. However, the terms of the Act were too open-ended to allow a line to be drawn and the memory of the recent wars in England was still raw for many of those with experience of royalist outrages. As important, the upheaval in land ownership caused by conflict and the subsequent economic depression was far from complete. Across the spectrum of participants on the winning side, the idea of restitution and a fair division of the spoils of victory ran deep. Just as Cromwell and Marten were inclining towards forgetting, if not forgiving, a case which was emblematic of the problem was reaching its denouement.

Sir Arthur Hesilrige enjoyed a status as an icon of the earlier rebellion against the arbitrary rule of Charles I. Not everyone was a wholehearted admirer – Ludlow acknowledged his sincerity but otherwise described the parliamentarian as a 'man of disobliging carriage, sour and morose of temper'.[4] With the disgraced Holles in exile, Hesilrige was the sole survivor in parliament of the five members whose arrest the king had spectacularly bungled in January 1642. As a leading principal of the Independent grouping in the House, he had supported the creation of the New Model Army and had spoken in its favour during the great confrontation with parliament in May 1647. Yet his attachment to the supremacy of civil magistracy was equally sincere and he had been appointed governor of Newcastle after command in the field. Quick-witted and ruthless, the 'Bishop of Durham' used the opportunity of his position to accumulate a sizeable portfolio of land in the north-east, much of it originally sequestered from royalists, episcopal estates and cathedral chapters. Economic recession gave an opportunity to pick up bargains from distressed sellers in addition to property gifted by parliament for services rendered to the cause.

His ownership of some collieries did, however, bring him into conflict with the wider family of John Lilburne, which also claimed title in furtherance of a grant from parliament. As so often in his career, the size and reputation of his intended target seemed to re-energise the old firebrand and Lilburne was soon locked in polemical public dispute. Once again, he took on the very people whose goodwill he needed if he were to prevail. The members of the Rump's Sequestration Committee were softened up by a public attack on their integrity before Lilburne presented them with a petition of his case. A larger group of MPs then found against him. Lilburne was fined and exiled, but in ridding the state of the Leveller, the Rump fed the perception that the benefits accruing from the wars were most inequitably distributed.

The unsteady domestic progress of the Commonwealth was overshadowed in the spring of 1652 by the outbreak of hostilities with the United Provinces. In the previous November the Rump had passed the Navigation Act, which sought to achieve greater ownership and control of the carrying of trade to and from the mother country and its overseas plantations. Henceforward, imports to the Commonwealth and colonies had to be brought directly from their country of origin and carried in either British ships or those of the exporting country. The mercantilist measure was squarely aimed at the competitive superiority enjoyed by the Dutch carrying trade and that country's position as a finisher and re-exporter of goods. Additionally, the English asserted their rights to the fishing grounds around the whole island by forbidding the landing of salted fish and oil except where caught by native ships. The herring industry of the North Sea was of great importance to the Dutch and at the time was estimated to engage, in the various parts of its value chain, fully one-fifth of the population. Naturally, the Navigation Act was only going to be as effective as the means used to enforce it and in overseas waters it was relatively easy to circumvent – Sir George

Ayscue had found several Dutch merchantmen trading in defiance of it and the earlier Act when he eventually arrived in the waters of royalist Barbados.

However, the Commonwealth had put a great deal of resource and energy into the growing of the New Model navy. Since Charles's head had lain upon the block, the size of the fleet had been more than doubled. Financed by disposals from the royal estates, twenty new warships had been built including the *Fairfax* and the *Speaker*, which each displaced over 775 tons and carried nearly sixty guns apiece. In addition, some twenty-five ships had been purchased or captured and refitted. The most immediate priorities of the expanded force was to assert control of the waters around the British Isles and the reduction, if not elimination, of the scourge of piracy. English assertiveness was not aimed exclusively at the United Provinces – William Penn spent the early part of the year harrying French vessels and privateers in the Mediterranean. Further to its strategy, the Commonwealth attempted to strike a deal for control of Dunkirk, which would have given it a naval base on the other side of the Channel. Notwithstanding that the town was under siege by the Spanish at the time, the French government baulked at the terms offered, whereupon Blake attacked and dispersed a squadron sent by it to relieve the town from the sea. The act of pugnacity was a further demonstration that the English were deadly serious about what they regarded as their sea lanes.

Although the Navigation Act provided an economic rationale, it was in fact English naval aggression that was the catalyst for the clash of arms with the Dutch. The waters between Great Britain and the Low Countries were a natural choke point which the Commonwealth exploited to interrupt trade flowing to the great Dutch entrepôts. In the aftermath of the legislation, the navy further asserted its power to stop and search vessels suspected of contravening the Act or carrying war materiel to hostile countries like France. It also more aggressively enforced the ruling that foreign vessels strike their flags and topsails in recognition of Commonwealth sovereignty when they passed through British waters. In one such incident in May, shots were exchanged when an English vessel attempted to impound a Dutch ship which was part of a convoy returning from Genoa. When news of another interception reached the United Provinces fleet under Admiral Marten de Tromp, it proved to be the final straw. In a showdown off Dover, the Dutch sailed into British waters and refused to observe the punctilio expected by Blake. Notwithstanding the size of the flotilla against him, the Englishman held his station and fired warning shots, whereupon Tromp unleashed a full broadside. The melee lasted over four hours as the vessels barged into one another and many men were killed, but it was Tromp who retired first, having lost two ships.

The Dutch 'regents', who already had sent another delegation to London to find a way around the threat to their commerce, were horrified by the developments. Cromwell himself was understood to be equally dismayed by the prospect of war against another Protestant power which seemed more congenial than had been the Scots and whose hospitality he was keen to deny to the Stuarts. But as with the team despatched the previous winter to dissuade the English from the Navigation Act, their hosts were intractable. Not that the Dutch sailors were fearful of further blows; in Tromp they had a belligerent commander who had cemented his reputation by destroying a Spanish fleet under the impotent gaze and cheering voices of Charles's sailors off the Downs, an anchorage in British waters, in 1639. Together with his fellow admiral, de Ruyter, Tromp was a highly experienced and resourceful mariner of 'Orangist' persuasion, who firmly believed that the English should be taught a lesson.

In spite of the preponderant size of her navy and merchant marine, the Dutch suffered a number of disadvantages. Among them was the relative size of the opposing naval vessels. Dutch fighting ships, few of which displaced more than 450 tons, were designed to accommodate the shallower waters around her coasts and estuaries, and were therefore smaller and more lightly armed. Most were converted merchantmen. Their tactics relied on superior seamanship and numbers to close with an enemy, disable their ship, board and capture it. The British relied on momentum under sail and much heavier firepower at greater ranges. The Dutch were also handicapped by a divided command structure, as each of the maritime provinces had their own naval boards which were jealously guarded. Whereas the British had one aim, namely the disruption of Dutch trade, the Dutch had two which were difficult to co-ordinate – the protection of their convoys (particularly the silver fleets) and the destruction of their foes.[5]

The next engagement was prosaic in a military sense but of great economic importance to the United Provinces: the dispersal of their herring fleet in the North Sea. Blake and Penn forged north with sixty ships, easily overpowered the trawlermen's escorts and maintained their course to intercept a Dutch convoy that was sailing around the north of Scotland to avoid the perilous English Channel. Ayscue was left behind to provide a screen off the south-east coast and he successfully attacked another convoy while eluding a frustrated Tromp, who knew that only the destruction of Blake's main fleet would be decisive. Accordingly he raced northwards to intercept the English between the Orkneys and Shetland. The sortie was a disaster. Hoping to settle the conflict in an afternoon, the opposing forces ran into a ferocious summer storm blowing from the north-west in which the shallower draughts of the Dutch ships were unable to cope as well as the English. The Dutch lost sixteen vessels, many driven onto the rocks of the islands. The Dutch had failed in their aims and a disconsolate Tromp, who had already upset his political masters by his earlier peremptory action off Dover, chose to resign his commission.

The sailor from Zeeland was replaced by Witte de With, who was from the province of Holland and much more closely associated with the 'regent' class. Aggressive and bad-tempered, de With was unpopular with his largely civilian 'Orangist' crews but in October he made a rendezvous with de Ruyter off Ostend and managed to surprise Blake, whose fleet was lying in an extended anchorage at the mouth of the Thames. The resultant battle in the shoals of the Kentish Knock was a disorderly scuffle in which two of the heaviest ships in the English line, the eighty-eight gun *Sovereign* and the sixty-six gun *James* immediately ran aground as they manoeuvred to face the Dutch tacking in from the north. But it was the Dutch fleet that proved the more difficult to control. A truculent Zeeland crew on the flagship *Brederode* refused to let de With come aboard and he was forced to conduct the battle from a much less powerful vessel. In the confused encounter that followed, the Dutch were once again worsted and as night fell, part of their fleet sailed off without orders. Overcome by the strain, de With had a nervous breakdown and Tromp was recalled. But Blake had little cause for satisfaction. Unlike the Dutch, the New Model navy suffered from a desperate shortage of manpower and its strength was augmented by armed merchantmen commanded by civilian masters who took a discretionary view of any orders given by their military colleagues. Overseen by an enthusiastic but largely inexperienced parliamentary committee, the supply of the fleet was unsatisfactory and in the hands of monopoly suppliers in the former royal dockyards. It was taking far too long to man the fleet and to turn around the ships that were being damaged in the fighting.

Two months later, the adversaries met again. Tromp was escorting a vast outbound armada of some 300 ships destined for French ports and the West Indies when he encountered Blake sailing off the south-east tip of the Kent coast. Shielding his merchantmen from the English fleet, which chose to hug the shoreline upwind of their opponents, the Dutchman entered a tacking race with Blake down the Channel, both fleets divided by a length of shoals known as the Rip Raps. The convoy used Tromp's cover to sail off on a southerly bearing out of harm's way. Blake now perceived that his line of vessels was extremely vulnerable to interception by the more numerous Dutch as the English emerged, one by one, from the narrower band of water on their side of the shoals. With the wind almost directly in their faces, the two fleets were now very close hauled and Blake realised he would have to keep the weather gage if he were to stand any chance against his opponents. Accordingly, leading with the *Triumph*, he brought the van of the fleet around in a sharp turn to port to take the wind as he emerged from his side of the shoals. Thundering towards him, the Dutch ran up their blood-red battle flag aboard the *Brederode*. It was the signal to engage. The ships of the two admirals came together, Blake attempting to deny the Dutchman a broadside while optimising *Triumph*'s own by sailing across Tromp's bows. Another chaotic fight ensued in which the Dutch were unable to make their superiority count decisively. Nonetheless, Blake was himself injured and the English lost five warships as the bulk of his fleet meandered about, seemingly keen to avoid engagement. Tromp appeared to have mastered the Channel.[6]

The defeat off Dungeness had a big and long-term impact on the English navy. In the wake of the battle, a number of commanders were cashiered for their lacklustre performance, including one of Blake's own brothers. The naval committee of parliament was purged of its amateurs, including the regicides Marten and Chaloner, and its administrative duties taken over by six competent commissioners including Vane, Maurice Thomson (the main author of the Navigation Act) and the Fifth Monarchists John Carew and Richard Salwey. On the advice of the professionals, control of the fleet was improved by the phasing-out of the use made of armed merchantmen, the navy was divided into three divisions (Red, White and Blue) to make it more manageable in combat and a ferocious discipline was enforced under the *Laws of War and Ordinances of the Sea*. To deal with the chronic shortage of manpower, rates of pay and shares of prize money were improved, and the army was ordered to make 1,200 men available to serve alongside the matelots.[7] More ships were ordered. The additional financial burden was shouldered in a further round of sequestration of 'delinquent' estates, which reached a peak as the year ended. Causing great bitterness and giving the lie to the Act of Oblivion, a royalist balladeer ruefully noted 'For where there's money to be got, I find this pardon pardons not . . .'[8]

In the interval of the hostilities at sea, whether against Dutch or French, the progress of the reforms identified as priorities in the army version of the *Agreement of the People* encountered heavy weather. To a majority of the House, which included many regicides, freedom of conscience emphatically did not mean freedom to express a heretical theological opinion. But while the MPs were alert to errors of doctrine, the consensus about what the new national Church should look like was far less strong. Parliament cleaved to the *Directory for Public Worship* less from settled conviction than as a bulwark against religious anarchy. In the wake of the Toleration Act, the Roman Catholic community had felt emboldened to present a petition to the Rump that was nonetheless given short shrift. The (modest) lifting of penalties for Nonconformity did not mean that people were now free to do their own thing by right – the Mass was absolutely proscribed and priests that were found in defiance of it were imprisoned, deported or executed. Attempting to settle an evangelical rubric, the dean of Christ Church, Oxford, was tasked with producing ideas for a national catechism. Of a somewhat angelic countenance, John Owen was a Puritan divine and a protégé of Cromwell's whom he had accompanied as a chaplain on both the Irish and Scottish expeditions. Indeed, it was the lord general's patronage that had secured his university appointment.

The minister had preached before the New Model Army against religious persecution and his work *Of Toleration*, published in 1649, had argued that liberty of conscience was founded on natural law rather than theology. Owen's advisory committee included Philip Nye, who had been such an articulate exponent of congregational independence at the Westminster Assembly. It won favour by damning the 'blasphemous errors' of the Socinians but it also castigated John Milton in his capacity as a government censor for having allowed their propagation in the first place. The author of *Areopagitica* was affronted by this barb and in a crossly worded sonnet, urged Cromwell to 'Help us save free conscience from the paw of hireling wolves whose Gospel is their maw'. Milton nonetheless lost his role. The ministers drew up a list of sixteen 'Fundamentals', each backed by copious references in Scripture which seemed to offer a *via media*. These would provide an anchor to recognised Protestant congregations which would then be able to associate freely around a national Church – indulgence was even to be extended to Arminians. But to Vane, Owen's 'Fundamentals' sounded much too like a new official orthodoxy while his proposals about preaching and public ministry that would have excluded the Fifth Monarchists (as well as the Roman Catholics), upset Harrison and the millenarians.

The issue of tithes, a form of poll tax by which local clergy were remunerated, was more vexatious still, bearing as it did on people's pockets. Based on a fixed proportion of the parishioner's income, the impost was highly regressive. The breakdown of ecclesiastical authority and the proliferation of independent congregations, sects and alternative belief systems had, in the minds of many, rendered tithes anachronistic and oppressive. Their ending formed a key plank of the agendas of the army, the Levellers and Nonconformists. Although there was some acceptance among the radicals that another form of payment should be substituted for the maintenance of God's ministry, it was ironically the Toleration Act which seemed to undermine the case for a national subscription altogether. Yet the attachment to tithes proved hard to shake – if men stopped paying them, they might stop paying rents and other dues. They were thus considered to be a form of property that had the sanction of Scripture and were part of the web of patronage by which notables of the laity could have a direct hand in the direction of their local parishes and clerical appointments. Reluctant to lance the boil, the Rump sanctioned their continuation in April 1652.

Earlier in January, the MPs had appointed a committee under the jurist Matthew Hale to consider the 'inconveniences' and 'mischiefs' of the law. Hale was a Puritan born into a legal family in the first decade of the century. Despite his defence of notables of the former regime like the Earl of Strafford and his spirited advocacy on behalf of Archbishop Laud against a charge of treason in 1644, he was not considered to be a doctrinaire royalist but rather a distinguished jurist of complete probity. The chaos of the wars was associated with an increasing arbitrariness of justice – the ending of abuses and the more inhumane aspects of the legal system were perhaps of greater moment to the anti-war protests of the Levellers than reform of the franchise. The seemingly indiscriminate and increasing use made of prison was a particular bugbear in an age where acceptance of the death penalty for a range of misdemeanours was more settled. It was the Levellers' championing of relief for the multitude of imprisoned debtors that had greatly appealed to Henry Marten, whose own expensively unorthodox lifestyle would have given him no protection against his creditors once he ceased to be an MP. There was also widespread disenchantment with the Court of Chancery, and its slow and often inadequate processes for registering title to land and weeding out fraudulent transactions. In the proliferation of army pamphlets, the soldiers took as jaundiced a view; the regicide Colonel Thomas Pride angrily declared 'that it will never be well in England until mercenary lawyers' gowns were hung up by the Scotch trophies'.[9]

To outsiders, the vested interests of a parliament that contained a great many lawyers seemed like an egregious blockage against change. Whitelocke's *Annals* give a good sense of how the arcane and labyrinthine legal system conferred huge advantage on its practitioners.[10] On the other hand, conservatively minded Rumpers that included Sir Thomas Widdrington and the Provost of Eton, Francis Rous, and those like Sir James Harrington on the Council of State (who had opposed the king's trial), were much less inclined to tamper with a framework that provided the main bulwark to parliament's own legitimacy. Some changes were however made: Norman French and Latin were dropped as the language of court process in favour of English, and relief from prison was given to some of those unable to settle their debts. Throughout the spring of 1652, Hale and his colleagues produced sixteen bills that covered various aspects of the law, including better protections for defendants and the amelioration of penalties such that punishment was seen to be more proportionate to the crime. But the best turned out to be the enemy of the good. Among Hale's colleagues, the army preacher Hugh Peter excoriated 'obsolete precedents' in favour of laws sourced directly from the word of God, Moses and Solomon, which to him was but 'sound reason'. But to the MPs whose understanding of the legal state was distilled through the lens of the Common Law, such sentiments were greeted with profound scepticism, if not incredulity. Hales's proposals lay fallow.

The Council of Officers again reasserted itself as the invigilator of change with a petition that was sent to parliament on 2 August. Presented by Colonel Whalley at the bar of the House, the document followed the agenda of previous public statements by the New Model Army, which only emphasised how little progress had been made in the eyes of the soldiers. Threaded through the exhortations for a 'new representative', removal of tithes and the settlement of arrears, was an unmistakable skein of bitter suspicion. The demand for a national treasury with transparent accounts and the call for an end to the abuse of the Excise suggested a deep mistrust of the civilians' stewardship of the financial aspects of the Commonwealth settlement, particularly the distribution and use made of sequestered estates and the fair treatment of landless soldiers who were being demobilised into a depressed economy. There was also a call for the independent examination of monopolies by men who were not serving MPs. The influence of Harrison and the Fifth Monarchists showed itself in their complaint that too many men in authority were morally unfit and that the propagation of the Word of the Lord was in a state of neglect. The Rump speedily convened a committee of the great and the good to consider the petition headed by the Fifth Monarchist John Carew and which included Cromwell, who had not himself signed the document. The Committee on Elections under Vane was brought out of hibernation and given a specific mandate to work with the Council of Officers to settle the manner by which the new parliament would be elected. Progress was slow as, among other matters, the politicians had their minds on the Dutch.

The defeat of the fleet off Dungeness did little to improve the army's temper, as it seemed to confirm the ineptitude and dishonesty of the civilians who had stewardship of it. The New Model Army was in the midst of another drawdown and despite an increase in the monthly Assessment, many of the remaining soldiers were behind on pay and sensitivities were inflamed by the perception that the navy was being favoured. The situation was made worse by the new Sequestration Act in which the army considered its honour to be at stake. Among the particulars of the petition presented in the summer, the Council of Officers had asked that the terms of the various armistices negotiated during the fighting (the so-called 'articles of war') be upheld. Yet the new assault on royalist and 'delinquent' estates was in flagrant contradiction of these arrangements and of the earlier Act of Oblivion which the soldiers had helped to broker. At the back of the officers' minds too was the anxiety that they themselves might ultimately be held to account for this perfidy.

By early 1653 the three Generals-at-Sea (Popham had been replaced by Monck) were back in the Channel. On 18 February contact was made with a large incoming convoy of 150 merchantmen with 80 escorts under Tromp, just off Portland Bill. The wind was blowing strongly from the north-west and this time the Dutch had the advantage of the weather gage as Blake started to gather his forces, which had been dispersed across the widest part of the Channel in a reconnaissance line. Trying a repeat of the tactics that had delivered the earlier victory, Tromp detached his warships from the convoy to charge down Blake's Red Squadron and to allow the merchantmen to escape to the shallow waters of the Flanders coast unmolested. The English were still spread over a large area: Monck frantically tacked towards the imminent action from further south but in its eagerness, Penn's squadron overshot the tail of the Dutch convoy altogether. Tromp was now bearing down strongly in four lines with the wind behind him. With no time to reconnect with his scattered ships, Blake's only option was to turn head-to-wind, heave to and form a compact, box-shaped formation to take the brunt of the assault. This time, there was a far better understanding of the likely shape of the battle by the English commanders. As Blake's ships blasted away at the smaller Dutch vessels crowded around them, Penn and Vice Admiral John Lawson sailed back towards the fighting from the south-west and caught the following lines of opposing warships in the flank. In the strong winds, many of these lighter vessels began to show their hulls below the waterline which the English gunners wasted little time in attempting to hole.[11]

There were now over 150 warships engaged over a wide area of sea, and the noise and smoke was tremendous. The Dutch sailors employed their usual tactic of trying to board the English ships with swarms of sailors, having shot at their rudders, sails and rigging to disable them; yet these frenzied assaults were mostly repulsed in spasms of fire and iron. Meanwhile, the merchantmen continued their ponderous progress, the most heavily laden of them barely making two knots. Tromp was faced by an agonising decision – with the battle shrouded in thick smoke, it was not at all clear who was getting the better of whom but in the meantime the convoy remained a very tempting target. Cutting his losses, he broke off to protect the merchantmen. These had by now begun to scatter and over the next two days he fought a desperate rearguard action to keep the English from picking them off. In the end, he marshalled the survivors through the narrows around Cap Gris Nez, where the waters were too shallow for the English to pursue them. But the battle had ended with severe losses for the United Provinces: nearly a dozen warships and over sixty merchant vessels were either sunk or captured in the rout. Despite heavy damage to a number of the fleet, only one English vessel had been destroyed.

Once again Blake was wounded, this time more severely, and many sailors had been killed; but the English learnt valuable lessons from an engagement which in its initial stages could have gone either way. The importance of disciplined drills that had to be executed under pressure had been validated and these were distilled as *Instructions for the Better Ordering of the Fleet in Fighting*. For the Dutch, the knowledge that they needed bigger ships was reinforced, but there was much squabbling amongst the provinces as to who was going to pay for Tromp's ambitious ship-building programme and in the meantime they were again forced to sail more of their convoys by the circuitous route around the north of Scotland to avoid the Channel. The English press was cock-a-hoop, the *Weekly Intelligencer* crowing that the battle (the noise of which had been heard as far away as the South Downs) would 'serve all Christendom for discourse'.[12] The civilian Rumpers too were delighted; here was another sign of God's favour and a victory that they could plausibly claim was more closely connected with their own planning and resolution. The irony of a victory over a power whose religious manners they were happy to share was apparently overlooked in the moment of exaltation. But Blake had burnished the Rump's prestige and thus seemed to justify its continued existence.

13

'I say you are no Parliament'

Westminster

There must be civil and military power in the hands of the
saints . . . before the day of Christ's appearance.

John Tillinghast

None stir out of their houses, so ridiculously were they
abused by knavish and ignorant star gazers.

John Evelyn

I had there occasion to meet and be acquainted with many
godly men, 'though I can say little of any good we did at that
Parliament; yet it was in the hearts of some there to have
done good for promoting the kingdom of Christ.

Alexander Jaffray

In November 1652, with leaves on the ground and apparent stalemate at sea, Cromwell had taken a morose walk around St James's
Park. The Commonwealth had stalled. It had been ushered in by a
small radical minority of the Long Parliament who were dependent
on the soldiers, but whose just deserts they nevertheless seemed

unable or unwilling to satisfy and whose ethos they did not share. Nearly a whole year had passed since the conclave in the lord general's quarters had attempted to give some further definition to a state which rested on force of arms alone. The constitutional status of both Scotland and Ireland within the Commonwealth was not settled. Little progress had been made with reforms, deciding the method of electing a new 'representative' or of determining the interim arrangements between the ending of the old parliament and the birth of the new.

The hiatus was not entirely due to the inertia and indecision of the civilians. Although less direct than their action in late 1648, the Council of Officers continued to take a hand in political and constitutional matters. But although there was unanimity in disappointment with the Rump, there was a conflicting spectrum of opinion across the most senior of its members about the direction of the Republic. Lambert was well respected and had a renewed interest in constitutional issues, but his political judgement had been coloured by a very public humiliation at the hands of the Rumpers when they abolished the position of Lord Deputy of Ireland, an appointment he had been expected to fill. Lambert had gone to some expense in preparation for the formerly vice-regal role and probably saw the opportunities there as a justifiable reward for his distinguished military service. In his pique, he turned down command of the army in Ireland which went instead to Charles Fleetwood, who further inveigled his way into the commander-in-chief's retinue by marrying the widowed Bridget Ireton. Lambert spent more time at his magnificent home at Wimbledon House pursuing his interest in botany and where, according to Lucy Hutchinson, he also nursed his grievance.

As his profile waned, that of Harrison waxed. The Fifth Monarchy movement was taking firmer root, particularly in London where there were huge evangelical rallies of an almost obsessive temper as the year drew to a close. The early spring of 1652 had seen an eclipse of the sun, hardly an unusual event but one to which the zeitgeist attached a special significance. Harrison had been active in the earlier institutional workings of the Rump and had given impetus to the Commission for the Propagation of the Gospel in Wales, where the garrison commanders looked to him for leadership and inspiration. He was also strongly in favour of the Dutch war, about which Cromwell had anguished doubts. But his chiliastic temper meant that he took an increasing aversion to the Republic to which he had helped give birth – the preoccupations of the 'new' state were just too like those of the old one ever to measure up to the visionaries of the Fifth Monarchy. He had sponsored various ministers to preach before parliament, and the MPs had not been best pleased to have their worldliness criticised, albeit in biblical terms. As the Norfolk pastor John Tillinghast put it, 'It is the special duty of the Saints to declare for God . . . though others count it rashness, hastiness and over-forwardness.'[1] To a certain cast of mind, however, the antics of the sects were as socially embarrassing as they were theologically suspect.

Cromwell seemed disinclined to take a lead and if he did aspire to the highest position in the civil state, as so many of his detractors claimed, he was being extremely dilatory about it given his prestige. His approach to politics was as visceral as it was cerebral. God had shown the way and who was he to meddle? It was up to the politicians to deliver on 'those good things that had been promised . . . from their own ingenuity'.[2] He was no secularist and his absolute belief in providence was shared by many of his compatriots who lacked the mental geography to make the kind of choices that seem logical to those of a later and more enlightened age. As he wandered beneath the slowly dying canopy in the London park, he fell in with his fellow MP Bulstrode Whitelocke. His frustration was plain: the army was beginning to have a 'strange distaste' for the civilian politicians, and who could blame it? He would have been aware too that the mood among the sects in London, agitated by talented stirrers of the spirit like Christopher Feake at his Blackfriars congregation, was becoming impatient. Whitelocke cavilled at the undue pressure the army was applying to the civil state through its constant petitioning. It was not appropriate that the soldiers should be seen to be giving orders to parliament and his lawyerly qualification of Cromwell's responses began to get up the lord general's nose.

At the back of his mind, Cromwell would surely have contemplated the possibility that the inertia and 'self-seeking' of the Commonwealthsmen as they addressed a domestic settlement would lead to backsliding. In such circumstances, the return of the institution of monarchy before reform had been properly embedded would be the lesser evil to all but the small grouping of MPs who were convinced republicans. Skilled trimmers like Whitelocke would come to the fore and the army would then be highly vulnerable to retribution. Seen in this light, the lord general's question to the MP ('What if a man should take upon him to be king?') takes on a different meaning. Cromwell's own sense of the attractiveness of 'something monarchical' was well known to Whitelocke and his later insinuation that the lord general had proposed a fully-fledged Cromwellian dynasty seems disingenuous. Indeed, only months before, the soldier had raised again the idea of offering the crown to the young Duke of Gloucester. The infelicitous expression of the lord general rather contained the idea of an interim monarch who could oversee changes before the rightful dynasty was restored. But if Cromwell was groping towards the type of coalition that had got behind the Heads of Proposals, he was to be sorely disappointed.

Blake's victory off Portland was a rare bit of good news. Inflation was rising as an economic cost of the war at sea, and in a cold and foggy London the price of coal delivered by barge to the energy-starved capital more than doubled. There was no organised Leveller movement now to mobilise discontent with the costs and dislocations of the war regime, and Harrison and the radical Fifth Monarchists were compromised by their support of it. Back in Westminster, the Council of Officers was preoccupied with the electorate and the shape of the new parliament. Although Harrison had been given charge of the committee previously overseen by Vane, the radical soldier seemed disinclined to apply himself to these detailed issues. To him, the details of the franchise and conduct of the election process was irrelevant to rule by the saints – what mattered was the selection of a cohort of 'men fearing God and of approved integrity' as stewards of the state.

But arguably, the appointment of Harrison by the Rumpers was done as much in the expectation that he would make a mess of it as it was a concession to the chiliasts of the army. With the Fifth Monarchist otherwise engaged, Sir Arthur Hesilrige (who like Vane had not been appointed to the Carew Committee), determinedly started to build the coalition in the Rump that aimed to keep the decisions about the 'new representative' in more worldly hands. The reinvigoration of the Justices of the Peace and of the county militia commissions was gradually restoring the influence of those persons of 'quality' which had been lost to the hated County Committees of the war regime: Hesilrige was not going to allow the magistracy of the men of 1640 to be derailed by a new parliament chosen by the soldiers or the militant sects.

Harrison was further outflanked by the decision to wind up the Commission for the Propagation of the Gospel in Wales, the army's favourite mechanism for proselytising the word of God. Within the context of the continued failure to settle decisively the nature and shape of the national Church and the method of funding it, this seemed like a gratuitous provocation. But the Rumpers had had enough of the Commission being used as a back door to implant radicalism and perceived heresy in the provinces. A campaign against the Nonconformist press was also reinvigorated and this time the popular army-supporting news-sheet *The Faithful Scout* was caught by Commonwealth disapproval. The debate about the Rump's successor plodded on and in exasperation at the Rump's suggestion that those with military commissions take a pay cut to fund the navy, the Council of Officers again demanded an immediate dissolution. Cromwell urged caution and managed to persuade his fellow MPs to bring forward the date of dissolution by one year. At last the basis of the franchise was settled on men of property worth £200 a year. It was a far cry from the manhood suffrage envisioned by John Lilburne and Thomas Rainsborough, and was essentially the inflation-adjusted qualification of the old regime. However, at least the Rumpers had been weaned off the idea of 'recruiter' elections under which sitting MPs would ensure their perpetual personal tenure.

Hesilrige was, however, determined to ensure that the transitional arrangements to the new parliament did not cement army influence in the successor regime and he was determined to keep serving officers out of the new House. On its side, the Council of Officers were anxious that the current proposals would allow the election of 'neuters', royalists and unreconciled Presbyterians. 'Thus, as we apprehended', said Cromwell later, 'would have been thrown away the liberties of the nation into the hands of those who had never fought for it.'[3] To break the building impasse, the officers recommended a form of caretaker government in the shape of a Council of forty members. To Hesilrige and his allies however, this proposal looked like a junta that might prove impossible to shift – after all, the Rump had proved adept at extending its own sitting. Tempers started to rise.

Cromwell used his prestige to call together a group of notables to the Cockpit, his lodgings in Whitehall. On the evening of 19 April 1653, leading Commonwealthsmen and officers got together in the cramped accommodation to discuss the transitional arrangements. It was scarcely a meeting of minds and the arguments went on to the point of exhaustion. But as the civilians cleared up their papers, the soldiers were given the impression that the passage of the Bill for Elections would be halted until such time as the MPs had given full attention to the interim arrangements and to those who would control the vetting and selection of future members. The following day the officers continued their fretful discussions and were then surprised by the news from Colonel Richard Ingoldsby that contrary to the assurances that they believed they had been given, the MPs were bringing the debate on the Bill to a conclusion in the House. If the Rumpers voted for an adjournment to mark the end of their sitting, there would be no constitutional need for a transitional regime before the new parliament met. The army was being outflanked.

Issuing swift orders for the gathering of troops, Cromwell rushed off to Westminster. Far from the motley assembly of forty to fifty MPs that could usually be found when the House was in session for important debates, Hesilrige and his confederates had whipped-in over a hundred. The backwoodsmen might be undecided on matters like the established Church and the law, but they knew a threat to their seats when they saw it. There was a palpable sense that a show-down was upon them. Taking a seat, the lord general appeared to listen politely to the debate but when his own turn came to speak, he built himself into a rage and launched a blistering attack of denunciation. Even Harrison, who was sitting nearby, whispered that he was perhaps overdoing it. But Cromwell was now riding at the gallop, charging at his enemies on the benches around him: his temper had got the better of him. His tirade was no forensic dismantling of the inadequacies of governance under the Rump. Instead the MPs were loudly accused of moral failing, inebriation and nest-feathering – they were no more than a bunch of reprobates. Vane, Chaloner, Marten and Scot all received a tongue-lashing. Blinking with embarrassment and indignation, the MP Peter Wentworth struggled to his feet to protest. In an attempted reprise of the speech that his grandfather had given to the House against the abuse of the royal prerogative by the Virgin Queen, he too was rudely cut short, this time by Cromwell who suddenly had an access of genius as he stood on that delicate cusp between carrying the day and looking a complete idiot.

'You are no Parliament,' he bellowed. 'I say you are no Parliament. I will put an end to your sitting.' It was an emphatic statement of fact, not an opinion that invited refutation, but one which did not deny parliament as an institution. By personalising the inadequacies of the Rump, the soldier completely removed the opportunity for the stunned MPs to defend themselves in constitutional terms. As they sat with their mouths opening and shutting noiselessly, Cromwell ordered in his troopers. Colonel Worsley, who had helped draft the army petition of the previous summer then marched in and carried out his duty. After a feeble demurral, the Speaker was hauled out of his chair and led away. One or two members made a theatrical show of protest: the witty republican Algernon Sydney held his seat with his arms primly folded until he too was ushered out. Vane attempted a statesmanlike rebuke which nonetheless came out as mere bombast

– Cromwell batted him away as he might a foolish schoolboy. As the MPs were shown the door, Cromwell quietly pocketed the offensive document that had caused all the rumpus in the first place; it was not to be seen again.

The lord general then marched off to give an account to the Council of Officers, whose members might have been individually surprised at finding themselves so precipitately placed back in the constitutional saddle. Attempting self-exculpation, he attributed the hand of God to his fury – this conveniently blunted any imputation of premeditation, at least among his subordinates. The civilian members of the Council of State were not so easily persuaded. Bradshaw lacked the wit to refute Cromwell in the sort of biblical terms that the lord general was in the habit of minting for his own use and asserted that the supreme authority of parliament, which had been claimed a mere four years previously, was not exceeded by any 'power under heaven'. Hesilrige and Scot also crossly scolded the soldier but in his second coup of the day, Cromwell splendidly allowed the gathering to continue to meet as private persons, notwithstanding their authority had been removed with the ending of the Rump. Good manners and forbearance were beginning to reassert themselves after a trying afternoon. Six years after having mooted the idea, the New Model Army had at last achieved the dissolution of the Long Parliament.

As the Huntingdonshire soldier-squire eased himself between the sheets of his bed that night, it would as likely have been with a sense of dread as a feeling of elation that he was now the de facto arbiter of the British state. That part of his character in which lurked the overbearing but sensitive reactionary had been laid bare by the torment of his fellow, yet irresponsible, MPs. But those qualities which made him such a zealous and inspirational soldier were going to be of limited use now that the political fallout of the second military coup in five years had to be faced. Laying a paw of Puritan benediction on the brow of his wife, he may have considered the likely reaction of his old commander, Fairfax, to the events in London.

Rumours had swirled of a return of the victor of Naseby. The aura of Fairfax's reputation rested in part on his taciturn intellect and unde-monstrative but deep integrity, attributes which were far less evident in Cromwell. What is more, it was difficult to imagine the younger man blowing his top in the manner of his former subordinate before his fellow MPs. It was all very vexing.

A few miles away in Fetter Lane, Thomas Hobbes might also have wondered if *Leviathan* had at last found the exemplar of the leader that he had identified in his eponymous book. His great treatise on the nature of civil society, and the need for a figure of authority if men's lives were to be anything other than 'solitary, poor, nasty, brut-ish and short', had been published in 1651.[4] Hobbes had been born in the April of the year of the Armada, his mother's labour brought on by fright of the dreaded Spaniards. Her son later claimed that she had been delivered of two children – him, and fear. Yet despite the straitened circumstances of his upbringing (his father had been deprived of his living as a minister of the Church, accused of her-esy), Hobbes developed as a sprightly polymath. He wrote the first English translation of Thucydides' epic *History of the Peloponnesian War* when he was forty. Briefly a tutor of mathematics to the Prince of Wales, he spent the period of the civil wars abroad contemplating the 'naturall condition of mankind' and writing his thesis.

When it was eventually produced, his apologia for the authoritar-ian state caused uproar amongst the exiled royalists and Anglicans in France. Like Henry Marten (who was also a bit of a show-off), Hobbes seemed to enjoy confounding those in the elite whose views he was assumed to share. The treatment of his father and his later work on Thucydides would have made him question the role of a benevolent God in the affairs of men, but in *Leviathan* he went further and denied that the authority of kings was indivisible from that of the Almighty. In a further challenge to the world-view of the former monarch, he also identified ecclesiastics as subversive of the state's authority, for 'This power regal under Christ, being challenged by Assemblies of Pastors of the place comes to be so passionately disputed, that it putteth out the Light of Nature and causeth so great a Darknesse in mens understanding, that they see not who it is to whom they have engaged their obedience.'[5]

This was all too much for his fellow exiles and, badly shaken by charges of rank disloyalty and by outright hostility, Hobbes fled back to Britain from Paris. But while others might have claimed to be able to find at least something that they liked – the Levellers would have been happy with his premise about the natural equality of all men, for example – *Leviathan* was essentially a work born of pessimism. The condition of man was rooted in fear and the achievement of civic order required men mutually to 'lay down this right to all things' and submit to the sovereign authority, whatever their estate.[6] In contrast to the can-do spirit of that Commonwealth identified in Milton's *First Defence of the People of England*, Hobbes was much more circumspect about the exercise of individual liberty and conscience, and he condemned as seditious the doctrine 'That every private man is judge of good and evill actions.'[7]

Yet the later idea that *Leviathan* might be seen as the blueprint for a dictatorship is unpersuasive. The purpose of men's renunciation of their natural rights in favour of the sovereign 'is not meant a bare Preservation, but also all other Contentments of life, which every man by lawfull industry, without danger, or hurt to the Commonwealth, shall acquire to himself'.

Nor need the supreme authority be a despotic one, as public peace and freedom from fear was to be achieved not just 'by care applying to individuals . . . but by a general Providence, contained in Publique Instruction, both of Doctrine and Example; and in the making, and exercising of good Lawes, to which individuall persons may apply their own cases'.[8]

To Hobbes, the key to a settled state was an indivisible supreme authority which guaranteed protection and security. A person did not even have to read his book however, to discover the philosopher's implicit denial that the former king had provided such protection for his subjects; from the beautifully engraved frontispiece of the first edition stared out a sturdy looking figure who bore only a very fleeting resemblance to the soulful countenance on the front of the

Eikon Basilike. Closer inspection would have suggested that the resolute titan rising above the swarming multitude was a hairier version of the lord general with a crown on his head.

That the monarchy was still such a powerful icon of authority two years after the proclamation of a republic showed perhaps how little the Commonwealth had progressed in turning sullen acquiescence amongst the citizenry into active allegiance. Cromwell might have looked like Hobbes's avatar, but the army he led represented the very forces that had torn the country to pieces. How was civil society to flourish if it was to be so burdened with an expensive militocracy? Two years on from the execution of the king and the country was still at war, a state of affairs that had been in place since 1639 when the fighting started in Scotland. Cromwell had proclaimed his conviction that the Lord's flock needed a godly peace tempered by the justice of man's ingenuity. His faith had been tortured by the struggles against fellow Protestant states and his hopes diminished by the wrangling of the Rump. Yet in the days that followed his bit of theatre at Westminster, he would perhaps have been heartened by the comparative lack of hostility it had aroused beyond that small elite which he had displaced: 'There was not so much as the barking of a dog, or any general or visible repining at it,' he noted. A mood of passive fatalism was not, however, to be confused with endorsement.

A few days later, the Council of Officers issued a declaration. One of the many special-interest-group effusions that littered the age, its significance has perhaps been understated. For the first time, the army offered a *post facto* justification for its action in which its tone of injured righteousness could not erase the soldiers' culpability. Much more importantly, the army effectively undertook to settle the state itself by 'finding men of approved integrity' so that the 'people might forget monarchy . . . without hazard to this glorious cause, or necessitating to keep up armies for the defence of the same'.[9] But if the army was in its own estimation ultimately unnecessary, with what legitimacy other than force of arms could it claim to order the country? It was a spectacular misjudgement and one which it is hard to see the soldierly parts of the brains of either Cromwell or Fairfax making in the field. Cromwell had allowed himself to be boxed in with the New Model Army whose existence, by its own admission, was thoroughly resented.

The first task was to square the navy. Blake was a Commonwealth hero whose exploits had given a badly needed patina of success to the Rumpers, but he was now laid up by his injuries sustained in the hectic fight off Portland and, in the interim of his recovery, Deane and Monck ensured that the coup was presented to the sailors as a piece of administrative shuffling that need not interfere with their aim of seeing off the Dutch. A new, smaller Council of State was convened which contained four regicides and eight former MPs of the Rump who were considered reliable. Lambert was in favour of this compact and self-directed group running the affairs of the state until such time as it was safe to call an election, but the thought of such an open-ended and narrowly based government did not appeal to Cromwell. His military career had not completely severed the roots of his parliamentary one and he was not going to follow a path that seemed in direct opposition to the way indicated by God's providences. Lambert's scheme bore too much of a resemblance to the personal rule of Charles I, albeit without the formal title of 'King' for its first citizen. The idea of a regency was again discounted; the young Prince Henry was allowed to leave England to join his family in Paris, with £200 authorised for his expenses.

Instead, the lord general leaned towards a model of governance based on the Jewish Sanhedrin that was presently in vogue with the Fifth Monarchists, especially Harrison. In reaction to the *coup d'état*, their preachers John Spittlehouse and John Rogers had loudly hosannaed the actions of Cromwell as that of a new Moses. Accordingly a proclamation went out from the Council of Officers, under the lord general's signature, summoning approved persons to a new assembly. There is some evidence of localities submitting nominations to London but, to all intents and purposes, it was an army show.[10] The authority of the Nominated Assembly was, however, immediately undermined by the provisional nature of the role allocated to it: the notables would sit only until the first week of November 1654 (the original date of termination for the rump of the Long Parliament), whereupon it would appoint its own successor. This body would in turn sit for no longer than a year, during which it would prepare for what was assumed to be a definitive parliament. Cromwell's intention seemed to be that these surrogate parliaments would carry through a programme of reform before the real one met, but little thought was given to binding the hands of the successor bodies lest they unpick what went before. However, it was confirmed that the new Council of State would be subordinate to the Nominated Assembly and that the latter would contain no serving officers, an echo of the Self-Denying Ordinance.

While preparations continued for its initial meeting, the fleet under Monck and Deane engaged the Dutch in one of the biggest and fiercest engagements of the war at the Gabbard, a bank of shoals off the Suffolk coast. In terms of numbers, the two fleets were almost identical in size, but over the course of three days English firepower overwhelmed their opponents while their more disciplined battle drills under a unified command prevented the Dutch from deploying their favourite tactics. The United Provinces lost seventeen vessels, of which six were sunk, and many prisoners were taken. Monck submitted a typically terse report, in which it would have been difficult to discern that nearly 200 warships had been engaged in another colossal fight.[11] He laconically noted too that General-at-Sea Deane had lost his life on the first day of the action when he was hit by a cannonball. At his death, Monck had ordered the body of the distinguished soldier to be covered in a sailcloth, lest the sight of the mangled talisman upset the sailors' morale. Yet the victory allowed the navy to tighten its blockade of the Dutch ports and soon the United Provinces began to suffer real hardship. As maritime activity shrank, unemployment rose and the coastal towns began to run out of necessities. In vain, the Dutch had tried to settle the conflict before the battle, but had met with a rebuff from the Council of State whose terms were both egregious and uncompromising.[12]

It was with a palpable sense of relief that Cromwell welcomed the Nominated Assembly to the council chamber at Whitehall on 4 July

1653. One hundred and forty had been summoned, including seventeen representatives from Ireland, Scotland and Wales, but a number failed to show, while others such as Fairfax declined to become involved. Edward Hyde might scoff from exile at the inferior social status and lack of 'quality' that he perceived amongst its members, but in fact the new assembly bore many similarities to the make-up of the old – indeed eighteen of its total number were former Rumpers. The main problem was their lack of experience. The army had tried to avoid a body composed of argumentative and querulous lawyers, but a good number of them had been selected. There were, too, a large number of newly energised Justices of the Peace and Sheriffs, as well as two peers, four baronets and four knights. As the men sat or stood, eager and expectant – some dissembling serious surprise at having been invited in the first place – the lord general swept in to deliver a pep-talk.

It was a long-winded performance and as they shifted uncomfortably in the stuffy heat of the hall, some might have wondered at Cromwell's state of mind. If any had expected a closely reasoned list of expectations and responsibilities, they were to be disappointed. Instead, the members were treated to a prolix exculpation of the actions of the army in the form of a history lesson about the 'strange windings and turnings of Providence'. But as his peroration developed, the lord general's voice rose, his speech became more messianic and tears of intense emotion welled in his eyes. Quoting freely from Hosea, Samuel, Isaiah and the New Testament, he exhorted them towards fulfilment of their biblical mission – 'Therefore I beseech you – but I think I need not, have a care of the whole flock.' Theirs too was the sacred task of the saints and 'God hath owned you in the eyes of the world and thus by coming hither, you own Him.' There were some vague references to those practical issues which might feature on this special journey, but at least it seemed clear that Cromwell was delighted to be handing over responsibility, notwithstanding the sceptical glances of some of the officers gathered to witness this return of authority to the civilians.

Thus fired up, the members of the Nominated Assembly set about their assumed mandate by immediately departing from that part of their script that had been set in stone. Despite the stern admonition that only an elected body could call itself a parliament, by a vote of sixty-five to forty-six they adopted the title which had been forbidden them. The uncomfortable chamber within Whitehall was also abandoned in favour of the symbolic and more agreeable premises back at Westminster. The septuagenarian Provost of Eton, Francis Rous, was elected as Speaker. A man of learning with special interest in theological matters (he had been a lay member of the Westminster Assembly), Rous was an experienced if aged parliamentarian who had followed the Presbyterian line before finding greater sympathy with that of the Independents. Amongst the first acts of the assembly was the decision to increase the size of the executive Council of State to thirty-one, and it was joined by Viscount Lisle (son of the Earl of Leicester) and Sir Anthony Ashley Cooper.

Like Rous, Ashley Cooper was from the West Country and he had served as an officer in the royal army until changing sides in 1644, ostensibly on account of pernicious Roman Catholic influence at court. Born in the summer of 1621, he came from a wealthy family of gentry, was educated at Oxford and later at Lincoln's Inn. Although he took some part in parliament's military campaigns in the south-west, he was more admired as an administrator and he sat on the County Committee for Dorset. He had a strong commercial streak too and astutely invested in the economic recovery on the island of Barbados. Thus his acumen and apparent godliness were commended to the Council of Officers as they considered the Nominated Assembly, and Ashley Cooper was invited to join as the representative for Wiltshire. Articulate, and with a subtle and wide-ranging mind, he came to the particular attention of Cromwell (who referred to him as 'the little man with three names') and was part of that committee given responsibility for overseeing the process of law reform.

In spite of the opprobrium attached to it, 'Barebone's Parliament'[13] addressed the process of reform with a greater sense of zeal and energy than had been observed in the Rump. In its five months of existence, it passed thirty statutes, including that which instituted civil marriage and civil registrations. Committees were established to look at the effectiveness of poor relief and the better protection of tenants. A number of these initiatives, including the one requiring marriages to be solemnised in front of a Justice of the Peace, were attempts to deal with the civic malfunctions of the civil war years. The assembly comprised a broad range of opinion, although the main difference that emerged at its start was around the pace rather than the direction of travel. Despite the yearnings of Harrison, only thirteen clearly identifiable Fifth Monarchists took part in its proceedings, but there were many other sincere and devout members of other Nonconformist groups and congregations whose intensity and righteousness nonetheless came to alienate their more worldly and conservative colleagues. Once again, the two subjects of the law and the national Church caused the most controversy. The Hale Committee was revived although the more radically inclined members were soon demanding that a new model of the law be contemplated which followed the code practised in Massachusetts. Their opponents did not deny the need for change, but argued that the radicals' agenda would lead to a wholesale upending of the body of the law as it then stood. The *casus belli* turned on the issue of the Court of Chancery where the proposal for its abolition was defeated by the casting vote of Rous as Speaker. The Hale Committee continued its deliberations but now it was shadowed by a separate one composed of radicals, which single-mindedly pursued a different agenda.[14]

Resolution of the issue of tithes and the stewardship of the national Church proved equally elusive, and the religious debate generated its own brand of heated denunciation by opposing factions. The harmonious enjoyment of freedom of conscience envisaged by Cromwell turned out to be anything but, as the followers of rival interpretations of the Protestant Church insisted that their own brand trumped all others. In vain did Cromwell and John Owen plead with the leading protagonists that the authentic Bible was not just confined to the Book of Daniel or Revelation.[15] In such

an atmosphere, both within and without Westminster, the achievement of consensus proved impossible. The debate about tithes had
advanced only in so far as they were now defended for practical
reasons and out of respect for property rather than as things that
were sanctified by their longevity alone, with authority conferred
by Magna Carta and Scripture. Owen's scheme for commissions of
'Triers' and 'Ejectors', which would be responsible for the vetting
of publicly maintained ministers and the removal of those who fell
below the required standard, was revived. But this confirmation that
there would be a national Church affronted those who believed in
the right of congregations to appoint their own pastor and angered
those who did not want to pay for a national ministry to which
they were not affiliated. At his Monday meetings in his church at St
Anne's, Blackfriars, Christopher Feake stirred the Fifth Monarchy
Elect into a state of ecstatic condemnation and there were emotional
demonstrations on the streets, as well as the usual downpour of
crossly worded and accusatory pamphlets.

At sea, the Dutch had suffered a further defeat. The plan to produce larger ships that could take on the more heavily armed English
vessels was far behind in its execution, but Tromp was determined
to break the enemy blockade with the resources at hand in what he
hoped would be a decisive encounter.[16] A month after the battle of
the Gabbard, he made a rendezvous with de With's smaller flotilla off
the Hook of Holland. The combined fleet ran into an almost equally
sized battle group sailing from the West under Monck. The soldier,
who still found the naval vocabulary rather more taxing than the
straightforward orders he was used to delivering on dry land, nonetheless seemed to be making a successful transition from command
on the battlefield to one on the water. Once again, the Dutch were
severely worsted losing twenty-six ships, and Tromp was killed by a
musket ball fired by a sailor in the English rigging. The loss of their
admiral had a profound effect on Dutch morale, but unbeknownst
to them their defeat was to coincide with the ending of the blockade.
Victory was seen as vindication for the religious radicals who had

embraced the conflict as a clearing of the seas to prepare for Christ's coming, but Cromwell had tired of it.

The lord general had been an early enthusiast of the proposals for a grand coming-together with England's Protestant neighbour across the North Sea and was far less persuaded by the economic rationale for the war. At his behest, diplomatic channels with the United Provinces had been maintained over the summer of 1653 although there was still a great distance between the English hopes for a civic union (plus a demand for reparations), and the more pragmatic agenda of the Dutch, whose urgent priority was a return of uninterrupted free trade without compromise of their sovereignty. Cromwell's promotion of the grandiose terms that made sense to him was also thwarted by Harrison's continued and militant advocacy of the campaign against the United Provinces. The lack of consensus on the Council of State was a sign that the bonds of comradeship that had been forged in battle were far harder to maintain in the army's present predicament. The cooling of his relations with the army's religious radicals was mirrored in his dealings with Lambert. All three men had been invited to sit with Barebone's as a matter of courtesy, but none made a notable appearance. Cromwell had spoken before about the need for the civilians to be seen to deliberate without soldierly interference, a scruple which now looked ironic but which he nonetheless maintained. His colleagues were, however, as antagonistic towards the body that their superior officer had brought into being as they were towards each other. As the summer lengthened, both men became more detached from the political process at Whitehall and Westminster.

The mood on the streets of London darkened that of a government which was already distracted by signs of incipient royalist insurrection in the Highlands. The costs and dislocations of a seemingly interminable state of armed conflict and of the huge military establishment that it sustained were again reaching the bounds of tolerance – even the members of Barebones chafed at the inequitable impact of the Excise and the mounting deficit of the naval struggle. With standards of living under renewed pressure from the disruption of trade and commerce, outbreaks of violence and disorder increased, inflamed by the latent antagonism between artisans, apprentices and congregations which supported the war.

Physically debilitated but with his sense of drama and self-righteousness undimmed, John Lilburne returned from exile, where he had received the attention of the Duke of Buckingham and those who appreciated his value as a thorough nuisance to the regime. The law prescribed the death penalty for any who broke the terms of their banishment, but 'Freeborn John' was not known for his dread of the capital sanction and he denounced his punishment by a parliament whose illegality had been proven by its forced dissolution. He was arraigned once more and, although his guilt was established, the jury found him not culpable of any misdemeanour that was worthy of death. Even the soldiers in the packed courthouse cheered and there were large demonstrations in the streets to celebrate the verdict. The establishment was not going to endure further loss of face and so he was consigned once more to the Tower. Knowing how resourceful his wife had been in keeping up her husband's profile while he had been behind bars, and to be on the safe side, Mrs Lilburne was incarcerated with him.

As the bickering on the benches at Westminster continued, the Council of State had to deal with outbreaks of mutiny in the dockyards of Chatham and Harwich. Predictably, the catalyst for the disobedience was arrears of pay and the denouement was a march by sailors to Whitehall where they were bloodily dispersed by army units in October. In the middle of it all stood Monck, waving his sword and swearing oaths at the men whom he had just led to victory. It was a depressing moment that hardened the attitudes of those conservative and moderate members at Westminster who yearned for a quiet life and a return to normality, if any could remember what that looked like. The debate on the national Church came to a head: by a vote of sixty to forty-three the motion to end lay appointment to clerical benefices was carried by a coalition of radicals and those who sincerely favoured the autonomy of congregations to appoint their own leaders. For those committed to some form of national Church, which included many in the Council of Officers, the proposed reformation of tithes would be crucial. In the unstable atmosphere, the Venetian ambassador wrote home to say that a change of government was imminent. At last the committee charged with their review produced its recommendations. The result was a fudge: tithes would be maintained as an interim measure, although provision was made for conscientious objectors to make their case in front of Justices of the Peace and a Commission of Twenty-One would be empowered to vet the clergy. This time it was the conservatives who very narrowly carried the day on the grounds that the scheme was simply unworkable.

The stalemate at Westminster and disorder on the streets was getting on everyone's nerves. The debates about the Court of Chancery and tithes portended a much wider attack on property. The moderately inclined members at Westminster were fed up having to take responsibility and opprobrium in equal measure. In any event, the frightful bit of constitutional hogwash with which they had been lumbered was only ever supposed to be temporary. If the chief citizen had scruples about annulling his own Nominated Assembly, then they would do it themselves. Early on Monday, 12 December, a large party of the discontented, which included the Speaker, gathered in the Chamber. As was their wont, the zealots and radicals were at private prayer or attending to their devotions amidst their congregations. With a brisk wave of his hand, Rous gave the floor to Sir Charles Wolseley, an admirer of the lord general who was also married to a daughter of the Independent grandee Viscount Saye and Sele. Sir Charles, whose family motto was *Homo Homini Lupus* ('Man is a wolf to fellow man'), got to the point at once: the proposed amendment to the system of tithes was an assault on property itself, plain and simple. A change of such fundamental importance at the behest of a bunch of amateurs (he seemed to imply) was not to be tolerated and the only solution was for the House to hand back its authority to whence it came. Prompted by the appearance of some of the radicals who had started to drift back in, Rous remembered his lines and quickly called a vote. The motion was carried, and grabbing the mace the Speaker trotted off with his fellow conspirators to tender their resignations and those of their colleagues to the lord general. Shortly afterwards, the remaining members were cleared from the Chamber by troops. Cromwell's experiment, conceived in a mood of rash piety, but not properly planned, had not been a success.

14

'The inhabitants perishing daily from want'

Galway and Edinburgh

Thus our General Assembly, the glory and strength of our church upon earth is by your soldiery crushed and trod under foot

Robert Baillie

It is the interest of the Commonwealth of England to break the interest of the great men in Scotland and to settle the interest of the common people upon a different foot from the interests of their lords and masters . . .'

Colonel John Jones

Her safety rescued Ireland to him owes
And treacherous Scotland to no interest true
Yet blessed that fate which did his arms dispose
Her land to civilise as to subdue.

John Dryden, *Heroic Stanzas*

The longest piece of legislation produced by Barebone's Parliament was the Irish Land Act, passed two months before its own self-dissolution. Many narratives of the period focus on the fright-fulness of the outcomes of the sieges of Drogheda and Wexford, but the true animosity of the republican Commonwealth towards the conquered of Ireland is perhaps best observed in the settlement that followed the main fighting. After the fall of Limerick, 'Black Hugh' had been lucky to escape with his life: but while there was no systematic programme for the extermination of the island's Roman Catholic elites, neither Broghill nor Ireton suffered qualms in executing bishops as well as priests, as the campaigns of subjugation reached their denouement. Instead, Ireland was to be dealt with by way of a programme of massive economic reallocation and the displacement of its civil population.

As war was about to break out with the United Provinces, the remaining royalist and rebel garrisons of Roscommon and Galway surrendered. To travel the road north-west from Clonmel through Tipperary to the Shannon and beyond was to experience a via dolorosa of blackened hovels, barren fields, dead animals and roadside gibbets from which swung the condemned. Ludlow and his fellow commissioners had already proceeded to rebuild the apparatus of justice and civil administration, and had begun too the process of disbandment. Yet even they were forced to admit that the country had been blasted for vanquished and victors alike. In a letter back to the Council they warned that 'This country is like to be a sad place this ensuing year for want of bread, many of the inhabitants perishing daily from want, and the common food of them in many places being horseflesh, grass and green ears of corn, so as there cannot be any considerable supply of bread or other provisions for our forces.'[1]

But the most immediate challenge was to satisfy the demands for land for the victors. The new Commonwealth had inherited a lengthy list of creditors, principally those who had subscribed to the Adventurers' Act of 1642. The scope of the original Bill would have resulted in the confiscation of nearly a fifth of all the profitable land in Ireland in settlement for those who had advanced hard cash for the suppression of the 1641 rebellion. But as the civil war broke out in England and military costs rose, the original Adventurers were persuaded to make a modest increment to their original investment in return for a proportionately larger slice of conquered territory. By the end of the fighting, the new regime was on the hook for well over a third of the land of Ireland: the Adventurers had waited for rather longer than had originally been anticipated for their investment to mature, and now they demanded that it be redeemed.[2]

There were approximately 33,000 troops (three times the number that had initially been brought over in 1649), who had also been promised parcels of land in lieu of pay for their service in Cromwell and Ireton's campaigns.[3] Soon, bad-tempered missives were passing between Dublin and London as the commissioners tried to deal with the competing demands of soldiers and civilian investors for timely restitution. In its initial response, the Rump of the Long Parliament had passed an Act for Settling Ireland in August 1652. The first task was to establish the guilt of the defeated and the tariffs to be imposed. The long years of hatred and propaganda attached to the rising of 1641 had left their mark; all those who had led or participated in the original rebellion were considered beyond due process and were to face summary execution and their property forfeited. A distinction was made for those armed combatants who had later taken orders from the Confederacy and who had surrendered in good faith with other royalist soldiers. These were to lose two-thirds of their property, while landless prisoners-of-war were offered a choice of either exile or indenture in the New World.[4] A large number of senior leaders and commanders (including Ormonde) were, however, exempted from these more lenient provisions – they too were to lose their lives. Arguably the most sinister clause of the Act was the one that related to non-belligerents; these and others of the 'inferior sort' had to have 'manifested their constant good affection to the Commonwealth of England' to escape retribution. Where any had to be relocated for reasons of public safety, they were to be compensated with land to the west of the River Shannon.

The settlement had a strongly sectarian flavour. The Roman Catholic Church was singled out for special sanction – their clergy were exempted from pardon and in January 1653 the commissioners ordered all priests to leave the country by the end of the following month. On the other hand, Protestant rebels who had surrendered by the time that Cromwell had left Ireland in May 1650 were exempted from the property provisions upon payment of a fine, while the Engagers of Ulster were arguably treated the most leniently of all. Although their clergy were driven out, there was be no attempt at conversion or assimilation of Catholics; one of the features of a faith that was built around the concept of an Elect was that its adherents felt no responsibility for those whose souls were inevitably damned. This was particularly true of the 'idolatrous' natives and their 'anti-Christ' pope.

In late 1652, the Rump appointed sixty commissioners that included Lord Broghill to adjudicate on those held responsible for the rebellion and their Protestant victims. Justice for the accused was complicated by the consideration that had to be given to those combatants who had surrendered and been given their parole in the latter stages of the war. Indeed, the offer of clemency had played such an undoubted part in persuading a good many to surrender that it had become an informal policy to hasten the end of the conflict. In the end, the desire for revenge trumped honour: Phelim O'Neill, the leader of 1641 rebellion who had earlier been released, was recaptured and hanged, drawn and quartered in Dublin. Meanwhile the High Court of Justice established in Dublin and in the major Irish towns had to deal with the enormous backlog of claims for land, not least by New Model soldiers and officers. To speed the process, Catholic landlords who faced partial expropriation were ordered to move by May 1654, to land west of the Shannon in Connaught and Clare where they would be compensated for the residue of the property they had been forced to vacate. Wary of creating a ghetto that would threaten the security forces in these areas, Barebone's Parliament further decreed that no Roman Catholic would be permitted to enter any town, port or garrison area in these counties. A large portion of the indigenous landowning classes and their connections was to be sealed off in bucolic exile.

In September 1653 the members of Barebones completed the settlement initiated by the Rumpers with the Irish Land Act. Priority was given to the Adventurers, who were given territory in ten of the most fertile counties to the east of the line of the Shannon. The investors drew lots for the parcels of property that were allocated to them, although the boundaries and acreages had to await confirmation by an official survey: for the time being, the spoils were divided up with a high degree of guesswork. To the chagrin of the New Model troops whose lives had actually been at stake, their entitlements were largely settled by way of promissory notes or discounted debentures. For many of the private soldiers who wanted to go home or whose allocations were too small to make settlement feasible, the only option was to sell up, with some accepting discounts of over three-quarters of the debenture's face value.[5] Officers did correspondingly better amongst those 7,500 former soldiers who later had their title confirmed by the restored monarchy.

The transplantations initiated by the English Republic were as ruthlessly executed as they were poorly planned. A member from Munster in Barebone's Parliament, Vincent Gookin, genuinely saw them as the best way of preserving communal peace by creating distance between those of different faith and allegiance. But the trauma of the dislocations on the Irish national psyche and economy only added to that of the war which preceded them. Disappointed with their share of the spoils, the army under Fleetwood was not minded to enforce the terms of the settlement with forbearance, still less mercy. Their harsh measures and intolerant radicalism even managed to alienate indigenous Protestants. As the exodus of the expropriated gathered intensity, incoming proprietors found their land denuded of those labourers that would be required to work it. Some of the dispossessed thought so little of the compensation that they were to receive in the west, or were so tied to the ground which they had previously owned, that they elected to stay put and become tenants of the newcomers instead. It was not to be the basis of a happy relationship. Depressed by the evidence before him, Gookin later wrote a pamphlet detailing the inhumane effects of the implementation of the policy, and was highly critical of the army's attitude as well as the agitation of those who argued for even harsher terms that would have seen the entire Roman Catholic population relocated.[6] In the slender leniency that some have perceived in the English Republic's attitude to its own native Catholic citizens, it is hard to find much mitigation for the experience of Ireland.

Whereas the Commonwealth addressed Ireland as a problem to be solved by suitably severe economic and cultural measures, its approach to Scotland was political, although in the loss of its statehood the consequences for the former realm were no less significant. In the aftermath of Dunbar, the presence of New Model units had resulted in a regime of martial law in the areas they occupied. However, following Cromwell's decisive victory at Worcester and the collapse of organised resistance north of the border, the Rump moved swiftly to assert its civil authority over the neighbouring state and, although the language of conquest was less pronounced than in Ireland, the direction of travel soon became plain. There was to be no federal union as conceived by James I and VI – England's northern neighbour was to be incorporated. By contrast to Ireland, where the Catholics were made to shoulder a cultural burden of collective guilt, in Scotland the Commonwealth singled out the thickly layered aristocracy and the political wing of the Kirk as those sources of trouble to the British state which were to be bridled.

In the bending of Scotland to its will, the Commonwealth was undoubtedly helped by the profound divisions within the Presbyterian clerical establishment and amongst its laity. Despite the best efforts of more magnanimous spirits like Alexander Jaffray, the Remonstrant and Resolutioner wings of the Kirk remained unreconciled. Indeed, the loose grouping around Lord Wariston, which included former 'Whiggamores' and the influential divines Patrick Gillespie and James Guthrie, had even considered accommodation with the English as a way of better shielding the purists of the Kirk from the 'malignancy' of the royalists and the backsliders within the ministry. Alas, the tiny impulse of compromise with the sectarian invaders was entirely smothered by the oath of the Covenant, from which neither wing of the Kirk would resile. While the Remonstrants might recoil from the Stuarts and their hated malignant supporters, they were at least united with the Resolutioners in their firm attachment to the institution of monarchy which had been so impiously cast aside in England.

Barely eight weeks after Worcester, the Council of State produced the blueprint for the settlement of Scotland. Political union of the kingdom with the Commonwealth would be effected with 'convenient speed'. Former adversaries would be subjected to the usual fines and expropriations, but the net was less widely cast than it had been in Ireland; only those who had continued to resist after the battle of Dunbar would be subject to expropriation. Thus the aged Earl of Leven, who had led the Scottish army to the aid of the English parliamentary rebels and who had commanded the combined army to victory at Marston Moor, was deprived of his estates. As far as religion was concerned, all those able to preach 'in a Gospel way' would be allowed to do so and there was no specific reference to Presbyterianism – in the eyes of the Commonwealth, there was no reason for the Kirk to enjoy a monopoly.[7] On the other hand, there was to be no requirement for citizens to abjure the Covenant – a sign perhaps that the English now considered this to be a dead letter. Loyal citizens would be freed of feudal and tribal bonds and the Commonwealth offered protection to all proprietors below a certain threshold of value. In this way was the residual grip of the aristocracy and clan chief to be prised from the people. Unlike Ireland, where the rubric of peace was couched in terms of punishment, the Scots were to be given a less rough incentive to see where their best interests lay. The obtuse would be reminded by the presence of the New Model Army.

English commissioners that included Vane, St John, Lambert and Salwey were appointed, and they made their Scottish headquarters at Dalkeith, in a castle owned by the Duke of Buccleuch. The plan of the English was not made public in Edinburgh until February 1652, a good four months after its principles had first emerged from the Council of State, and its broad provisions were then amplified by the *Tender of Incorporation*. The burghs and counties were instructed to send representatives (to be chosen by a process ordained by the commissioners), to discuss the terms. No member of the nobility was involved and, in the event, only three of the eighty-nine constituencies formally recorded their dissent.[8] The English could have left it at that, so as to at least foster the impression that the Scots had delivered a majority verdict of their own accord; but the Commonwealth wanted no trouble, and troopers were sent to overawe the recalcitrant. Shortly thereafter, they had unanimity.

The Scots' views on the *Tender* were recorded in the form of 'Desires'. The Presbyterian clergy were outraged by the religious aspects of the settlement, but not enough to reconcile its two warring wings. The split had undermined the Kirk's wider authority and the presence of the evangelicals of the New Model Army had fostered a modest interest in religious independence amongst the defeated. Their manners and congregational practices might be different, but did they not all believe in the same Protestant God?[9] Above all, people yearned for peace and justice. The last meeting of the Court of Session, Scotland's highest judicial authority, had been as far back as February 1650, and in the meantime the legal order had been fitfully maintained according to the rough rules of the New Model Army. By the time the commissioners returned to London, the administration and foundations of Scottish justice had been significantly altered.

Barony courts which had provided judicial underpinning for feudal customs and obligations were abolished. Sheriff courts were given new powers and the Court of Session was replaced with a High Court of Justice in Edinburgh, presided over by seven senior jurists, four of them English, who were paid twice as much again as their Scottish colleagues. But the willingness of the latter to accept the supreme legal authority of the Commonwealth and become employees of the new British state pointed to a shifting of attitudes amongst the Scottish elites. The authority of High Sheriffs in their localities was similarly shared between a Scotsman and an Englishman. While the system was overhauled, English justices moved throughout the country, settling disputes and adjudicating in civil and criminal cases that had been long delayed. While some regard was paid to the intricacies of Scots law and custom, the primacy of law sanctioned by the Commonwealth was made plain. The justices applied leniency to alleged witches and were appropriately sceptical of suits motivated by score-settling. But any manifestations of royalism were dealt with severely. The *Diary of Public Transactions* by John Nicoll recorded a man having his ears ('lugs') cut off merely for drinking the king's health, but otherwise praised the English for their speedy and generally disinterested application of the law.

A Bill for the union of the two states was ready for the approval of the Rump in the spring of 1652. As with other numerous matters under its attention, the MPs seemed to lack the means or inclination to apply themselves with a sense of urgency or focus, and were accordingly happy to wait for the arrival of commissioners from north of the Tweed to deal with the finer points and practicalities. Scotland was not a priority. By the time their representatives arrived in London in October, the political situation in London had deteriorated and the English were otherwise detained by the Dutch war. The commissioners were treated with scant consideration – their credentials were questioned and they achieved only limited access to their English counterparts, who by now included Cromwell, Sydney, Hesilrige and Harrison. Eventually, one of the main sources of their anxiety, namely the level of Scottish representation in the new state, was grudgingly answered: Scotland would get thirty MPs only.

The constitutional settlement of Scotland *de jure* was further delayed by the dissolution of the Rump and the subsequent outbreak of unrest in the Highlands led by John Cunningham, Earl of Glencairn. The most consequential of the magnates, the Marquis of Argyll, had made his peace with the Commonwealth the previous summer. His advice against sending the army south in 1651 had been ignored and he no longer trusted the prince that he had crowned. The long struggle for political mastery had virtually bankrupted him but his loyal clansmen were still a force sufficient to cause trouble in the lands of the west of Scotland if they had a mind to do so. In exchange for allowing him to retain his title, and with a promise of money, the English secured the compliance of the Campbells. The exception was Lord Lorne, Argyll's son, whose truculence was condemned by his father as tiresome, if dangerous, showing off. It was more difficult to achieve acquiescence elsewhere. The legal assault on the feudal duties of the connections of the magnates created widespread resentment, while the terms attached to the expropriation of land declared forfeit were so vaguely drawn as to alarm all but the most compliant of the nobility. Charles had appointed the Earl of Glencairn as his agent, pending the return to Scotland of the more militarily experienced Middleton, who had escaped following the debacle at Worcester. The noble was a loyal lowlander who had remained at large following the dispersal of the Scottish government by Monck in late 1651. With discontent among the Kirk and Scottish peers rising once more, Glencairn saw his opportunity to foment resistance.

But aristocratic and clerical antipathy towards the alien Common- wealth, and general grumbling, did not make for a successful insurrection. Argyll deprecated the uprising and Charles had been so depressed by his brief experience in Scotland that the chance of his return to act as rallying point was considered vestigial. In consequence, Glencairn found it difficult to organise the quarrel- some clan chiefs and nobles, and the so-called rising only gained purchase because of the relative weakness of English forces now under the command of Colonel Robert Lilburne. As in Ireland, the Commonwealth's hope was that the cost of maintaining security would be borne by the local population, but Scotland was so abso- lutely and relatively impoverished by the wars that its contribution to the Assessment was barely half the level implied by the size of its population. The army was being drawn down so that resources could be released for the navy, and Lilburne was only able to follow a policy of containment. However, the soldier was clear about one thing, and that was the power of gatherings of religious leaders to provoke unrest. Accordingly, he suppressed the General Assembly of the Kirk, whose two wings had continued to meet separately, in the summer of 1653. It was not to meet again for nearly four decades. England and Scotland had been united, but not as the signatories to the Solemn League and Covenant had ever intended.

15

'Oh ye tyrants, who shall be your lord protector?'

Whitehall

A Caesar he ere long to Gaul
To Italy an Hannibal
And to all states not free
Shall climacteric be.

Andrew Marvell, *An Horatian Ode*

But what can tend more to the honour and glory of any country than the restoration of liberty both to civil life and to divine worship?

John Milton, *A Second Defence of the English People*

Therefore it is unlawful for us to consent to any government but the King; Or take any engagement or oath of allegiance to any: But it is not unlawful for us to submit to them by living quietly in our places and to make use of the Courts of Justice established by law, yea and to demand protection from the Usurper.

Richard Baxter, *Reliquiae Baxterianae*

As Sir Charles Wolseley's speech in December 1653 to Barebone's Parliament had an almost instantaneous effect, it may be seen as one of the most influential in British parliamentary history. His words contained a succinct if partial defence of the link between the holding of property and a share in secular and clerical government, and it prompted the immediate self-destruction of a body that had had the backing of the most powerful citizen in the state and which had, in turn, mostly been selected by the army. Shortly afterwards, Lambert brought forward a more detailed blueprint of government which he had determinedly advocated to his colleagues in the Council of Officers since the demise of the Rump. Cromwell's waiting upon God's providence was no longer a viable strategy, while Harrison's 'prophecies' were past due: it was time for some proper political planning and for the authority of the state to be applied with a more efficient smack than had been achieved by the unruly and unfocused civilians. The *Instrument of Government* was England's first written constitution and leant heavily on the earlier proposals of Ireton. Primacy was given to the principle of conciliar government, led by a lord protector working with a reformed parliament. Although the idea of King Oliver was discreetly canvassed, Cromwell would not scruple to it and the matter, if not dropped, went into hibernation. But in convincing the Council of Officers of his wider plan, John Lambert brought off a significant personal coup.

Unlike the former Privy Council under the monarchy, the reformed Council of State was to occupy a much more powerful position in the Protectorate. The will of one man was replaced by conciliar rule. Composed of no more than twenty-one members, it would appoint the lord protector and his successor, who would serve for life. Decisions of peace or war were no longer reserved to the first citizen, but would be determined by majority vote of his council. In furtherance of which, the gaffe committed in the army's declaration following the dissolution of the Rump was airbrushed away; now the military establishment was given permanency as the first charge on the state's resources. The New Model Army would be kept at its post-Naseby strength of 30,000 soldiers, and there was to be a 'convenient number of ships'. Control of the armed forces (which included the militia), an issue central to the men of 1640, was reserved to the lord protector and his Council when the MPs were not sitting, and shared when they were.

Perhaps the most significant break with the post-war Commonwealth settlement was the role given to the Protectorate parliament. As befitted a man of action, Lambert's plan did away with the endless talking-shop of government by parliamentary committee. There was to be neither a complete return to the rhythms of the Elizabethan and Stuart parliaments, as legislative power was now unequivocally shared with the protector; but nor was the unicameral parliament to be the sovereign body as understood by Bradshaw, Ludlow and Marten. Instead, it was to be reduced in size, with elections held every three years on the property franchise approved by the Rump and Council of Officers. Once assembled, the protector could not order parliament's dissolution until at least five months had elapsed. In the interim of its sittings, the Council would have the authority to raise funds and to issue ordinances which the MPs would later have the power to confirm or annul. The protector would only be allowed to veto legislation that contravened the *Instrument of Government*. But while the MPs were to retain a measure of legislative initiative, Lambert was determined to reduce the influence that they had previously enjoyed over the executive in the Commonwealth regime. Henceforward, the parliament would only be permitted to make recommendations for membership of the Council. Its composition would ultimately be determined by the lord protector after a vetting process conducted by his conciliar colleagues: the rigmarole of the semi-annual elections to Council was abandoned.

The parliament envisaged by Lambert was also to be an agent of change beyond that achieved by the individual acts of the Commonwealth. Regard was given to officers' versions of *The Agreement of the People* but the Leveller aspiration of a franchise for all men over twenty-one (bar servants and dependants) was attenuated. The House was shrunk to 400 seats for England and Wales, and 30 each for Ireland and Scotland. Growing towns like Durham,

Manchester and Halifax were to be represented for the first time. In the prior debate about the franchise, the army had championed a redistribution of seats away from the boroughs towards the counties and this was done with the new ratio set at two to one. The power of patronage to produce potentially unfriendly MPs in the 'rotten' boroughs was diluted and the army's areas of recruitment, where its own brand of religious independency had been gaining ground, received more representation. Yet these were also areas where political capital was determined by land ownership and the arrangement pointed to a more socially conservative body. It made it harder too for the Council to exercise patronage in a way that could influence the vote.

The intended composition of the new House reflected the desire of the lord protector for representatives of a pious and 'well-affected' citizenry (known royalists were excluded from the first three assemblies), but Lambert was alert to the possibility of unintended consequences by reserving the right to vet the membership of parliament to the Council. A similar desire for peace and order was observable in the outline for the settlement of the national Church. Citizens were permitted liberty of worship, provided their religious manners did not breach the peace, but Ireton's conception of religious toleration contained in the *Heads of Proposals* was much abridged. The use of the Book of Common Prayer was unambiguously banned, as was 'popery' and prelacy, and tithes were to be retained until such time as a better method for remunerating the ministry could be devised.

In a self-consciously downbeat ceremony on 16 December 1653, Cromwell was installed as lord protector. The place chosen for his formal appointment was the premises of that same Court of Chancery whose existence had caused so much aggravation in the debates of the Commonwealth. In the first conundrum to be faced by the new head of state, the stage management of an ostensibly civic event suggested the need to downplay the military context of the proceedings whilst also showing that the new regime meant business. The general opted for a plain worsted suit of black and grey, an outfit that was saved from near invisibility only by the addition of a gold band and trim to his hat. After some appropriate incantations, Lambert presented his commander-in-chief with a sword of state that looked like a dagger in comparison to the meat cleaver that Cromwell had used by habit as an Ironside. There followed a few civic hosannas and a musket salute, the noise of which was strangely muffled in the cold winter air. Then Cromwell and his retinue processed to the Banqueting House watched by sparse and seemingly indifferent knots of citizens. To the recently arrived French ambassador, Antoine de Bordeaux, it all looked a bit glum and a world apart from the splendid ceremony and cavalcade which marked the end of the minority of his sovereign Louis XIV and which had been rhapsodised in the *Diary* of John Evelyn.[1]

But Cromwell's apparent reluctance in accepting his office cut little ice with his detractors. The disdain of the Hutchinson household at Owthorpe was undimmed by Colonel John's peaceful enjoyment of a swelling portfolio of ex-royalist land and his wife caustically damned the lord protector's perceived lack of integrity in her *Memoir*. Although his position was underwritten by the vast majority of the serving officers of the armed forces, the *Instrument of Government* also marked a parting of the ways with Thomas Harrison and his other Fifth Monarchy lieutenants, the firebrand chaplain Vavasor Powell and senior commanders such as Nathaniel Rich and Robert Overton. The general refused to swear loyalty to the new regime, was cashiered and sent to internal exile at the house of his father in Staffordshire.

To other millenarians, this sharp detour on the road to the Second Coming was a disaster and there was a cacophony of denunciation from the sects, although it split the Fifth Monarchists.[2] In London's East End, Anna Trapnel fell into a stunned trance and Cromwell was roundly condemned as a 'dissemblingest perjured villain' from the pulpit of Christopher Feake.[3] The generals were excoriated: 'Oh ye tyrants, who shall be your lord protector in the day when Jehovah's fury shall be poured out like fire?'

Immediately showing the regime's limits to the new religious toleration, the preacher was arrested for his insolence. But the sense of disenchantment and demoralisation among the religious radicals, and amongst those soldiers and civilians who cleaved to their Leveller beliefs, was more long lasting. After service to the Commonwealth as an ambassador to the rebels in France, the former army agitator Edmund Sexby drifted towards the royalists. The compliance of John Lilburne was considered unlikely and, within three months of Cromwell's installation, he was exiled to Jersey.

In Yorkshire, another soldier was also trying to achieve a peaceful space. Sir Thomas Fairfax had retired to his home, the former priory at Nun Appleton overlooking the River Wharfe. Here he spent his time supervising his estate, taking part in county affairs and composing poems. His was now a quieter life of soldierly reflection surrounded by his garden with its views of the tranquil water meadows beyond. It was not an existence of total ease as he was still afflicted by stones and episodes of painful gout. The former were agony and although no stranger to injury, he seemed to have foregone the rudimentary and gory surgery for their removal, a procedure which Evelyn graphically described in his *Diary*. His reverential contemplation of the Psalms and the strict Presbyterianism of the Lady Anne would have been disturbed by the religious fervour and novelty of the times. Like many men of his wealth and degree, he yearned for an ordered state and the quiet enjoyment of his faith, his kin and his property. He had been prepared to be ruthless to protect what he held dear, as the Leveller mutineers had discovered to their cost. He had done his duty, but had it been enough?

In 1650 the poet Andrew Marvell, now in his thirtieth year, had come to Nun Appleton to take up an appointment as tutor to the Fairfaxes' only child, the spirited teenager Lady Mary. Marvell had been somewhat star-struck by the celebrity conferred on the victorious soldiers, a thrill possibly enhanced by his own lack of participation in the fighting. He had a lively mind and personality, and within two years the secluded life of his patron had begun to pall. He set off to pursue a career closer to the centre of active power in London, but not before he had composed *Upon Appleton House*, his epic poem of nearly a hundred stanzas. His admiration for his young charge, with whom he might have been a little bit in love, was plain. However, the encomium was far more ambiguous about Fairfax himself; unlike the Cromwell of the *Horatian Ode* who had forsaken his own 'private gardens where he liv'd reserved and austere' to fight the Irish and Picts, his patron seemed content to repine amidst a space laid out in serried ranks of flowers and topiary forts. It was true that the former soldier did 'with his utmost skill, Ambition weed but conscience till', but the poet seemed to regret the general's withdrawal as almost a dereliction of duty; the world continued to look upside down – where men 'like Antipodes in shoes, Have shod their heads in their canoos' – and needed righting.

After Barebones, the government did now have 'something of the monarchical' about it and the title assumed by Cromwell recalled English regencies of the past. Nonetheless, a strong link to the 'Little Parliament' was maintained in the Council of State, which was comprised of many of those who had headed the list of the last annual election before the self-dissolution. It was notable for its large cohort of individuals who were joined by kinship or connection to the lord protector himself: his son-in-law Fleetwood, his brother-in-law Desborough, his former landlord Henry Lawrence, and Richard Mayor, whose daughter Dorothy was married to Cromwell's eldest son. Colonel Philip Jones, who had superintended the lord protector's estates in South Wales and who had served on the Commission for the Propagation of the Gospel, was one of a number of serving soldiers which also included Lambert and the unbending Presbyterian Philip Skippon. There was also a heavy sprinkling of other knights such as Wolseley and the plainly aristocratic Viscount Lisle. They were joined by Anthony Ashley Cooper and Edward Montagu, a younger cousin of Cromwell's former antagonist, the Earl of Manchester.

As befitted his new position, the lord protector was accorded somewhat grander accommodation than were his cramped former digs at the Cockpit. The erstwhile royal apartments at Whitehall were redecorated under the supervision of Surveyor General John Embree, a protégé of Inigo Jones. There his household was supervised by his chamberlain, Sir Gilbert Pickering, who also held a seat on the Council and was related to Montagu. Royal art and artefacts that had not been dispersed by the Commonwealth sale, such as Raphael's cartoon *The Acts of the Apostles*, were taken out of storage and displayed. Many items that had been sold were repurchased, although care was taken to avoid any representations considered too lascivious or superstitious for the republican aesthetic. Artemisia Gentileschi's *Bathing Bathsheba* was considered sufficiently chaste (despite the voyeuristic presence of a ghostly-looking King David), to be chosen for the household's gaze.

The boards were taken down in the Banqueting House and once more James I and VI could be seen in his contortion of ecstasy among the angels; beneath him, the lord protector received foreign dignitaries and ambassadors. Even grander in scale were the renovations at Hampton Court, which Cromwell selected as his country seat, being near the army headquarters at Windsor. The hard-up Commonwealth had already sold off adjoining parkland and meadow, and these were now bought back to better ensure security and privacy. In all, the prodigious sum of over £55,000 was spent on restoring these centres of the Protectorate nervous system, outlays that drew sceptical questions even from the Council of State. Yet there was little hypocrisy in these appurtenances that recalled the former regime – the need to project the prestige of the state, whether a monarchy or not, was well understood.

The Rump and Barebones had been excised, but the Council realised that the Protectorate regime needed to seize the initiative while the population at large remained in a state of uneasy bafflement. Opponents such as Scot and Marten had been banished from the centres of power while some like Ludlow were sufficiently remote from it in Ireland. Indeed, Marten had fallen prey to his many creditors, who insisted on his imprisonment. Whitelocke, who was judged by Cromwell to be too much of a fair-weather friend, was rusticated as ambassador to Protestant Sweden, tasked with the exploration of mutual interests of state with Queen Christina and her grey eminence, the first minister Axel Oxenstierna. The regime could also count on the strong desire for stability from amongst the professional classes of lawyers, merchants and ministers which had each been threatened by the disruption perceived in the programme of the saints. It was this desire that the regime's popularist, Marchamont Nedham, used to justify the new dispensation in his propaganda *A True State of the Case of the Commonwealth*.

A key priority for the regime was security. Disappointed doctrinaire republicans were to be left in peace provided they did nothing seditious, although Edward Montagu and Henry Cromwell, the protector's younger son, were sent to report on the political reliability of the navy and of the officer corps in Ireland respectively. The navy was a particular concern – Admiral Lawson had publicly condemned the army's dissolution of the Rump, and Montagu was sent to take the temperature of Blake. The Commonwealth Oath was replaced as a touchstone by a new Treason Ordinance that had the safety of the lord protector at its centre. The seemingly complete victory over the royalist cause at Worcester, and the extraordinary personal powers attributed to Cromwell, obscured the anxiety that was felt by the regime about clandestine plots and open disobedience. Some, such as the Presbyterian divine Richard Baxter, thought the protector too keen to 'conjure up at pleasure some terrible apparition of Agitators, Levellers or such like, who . . . shall affright the people to fly to him for refuge'.[4]

However, as 1654 dawned, the Republic was still at war with the Dutch, the 'young man' remained at large on the Continent and the Highlands of Scotland were unpacified. In England, a shadowy royalist organisation called the Sealed Knot had sprung up in the autumn of the previous year. It had been founded by ex-officers of the king's army (including Lord John Belasyse, who had doughtily defended Newark against the Scots) and stirred up a number of disorders and insurrections, none of which did serious damage to the Republic in England. Armed opposition in Scotland and Ireland was met with bloodthirsty ruthlessness, but in England the ephemeral nature of the threat required a different approach. A military presence was maintained throughout in the army garrisons that dot-ted the country and some officers also served as Justices of the Peace. But the Council also preferred to work through the spy network that had been inherited from its creator, the shadowy Thomas Scot, under the Commonwealth regime.

This was placed in the hands of John Thurloe, who had been appointed as secretary to the Council of State under the Rump at the age of thirty-six. Thurloe was the son of an Essex minister and his half-brother was one of the regicides. Although a public servant at the time of the civil wars, he was unconnected with the king's trial and enjoyed the patronage of Oliver St John, whom he had accom-panied on the abortive diplomatic mission to the Hague in 1651. Legally trained, he was a diligent and reliable administrator whose contemporary portrait is hardly suggestive of the aura of menace con-veyed by that of his Elizabethan predecessor, Francis Walsingham. The rack and the thumbscrew were not Thurloe's style, and there was no official policy to use either torture or the court-martial of civilians. The extraordinary justice dispensed so lavishly in Ireland by the High Court was meted out far more sparingly in England.

In helping to maintain security, Thurloe and his agents were undoubtedly assisted by the amateurishness and ineptitude of their royalist opponents. In vain had Hyde, by now Charles's chancellor and principal adviser, counselled sympathisers to adopt an attitude of 'quiet' – the regime was just too strong for their activity to do any more than discredit their sovereign. Royalist organisations were soon thoroughly penetrated, a process facilitated by Thurloe's employ-ment of a gifted mathematician called John Wallis who managed to break their codes and ciphers. Messengers and other agents were 'turned' and even the Leveller Richard Overton eventually offered his services to the rather benign-looking spymaster. Thurloe man-aged as well to plant a mole at the centre of the exiled court, and Henry Manning (who came from a Roman Catholic family) was to do severe damage to the royalist networks back home. The passions that could be stirred by latent royalism or other opposition were sub-dued by the limiting of rights to assembly for anything unconnected with worship or godliness. Theatres remained closed and all public performances forbidden. The sanguinary sports of cockfighting and bear-baiting were also suppressed – men needed to control their baser instincts. So was horse-racing, admittedly a more wholesome activity but one which was perceived to provide an opportunity for large crowds to be exploited by 'delinquents' stirring up trouble. In an attempt to suppress the violence that often went hand-in-hand with the protection of personal honour, duelling was also forbidden. But nor did Puritan sensibility permit more harmless practices and the maypole remained banned lest it arouse pagan instincts and the sort of licence associated with the Quakers and Ranters.

There seemed no hurry to reconvene a 'new representative' – the calling of a parliament was put back once more to the autumn. In the meantime the Council issued a blizzard of ordinances, a number of which merely reactivated parliamentary measures that were soon to expire or had already done so. Some were genuinely enlightened, such as the one which ensured that demobilised soldiers could enter any profession that they chose and could not be excluded by the 'closed-shop' practices of the trades guilds. The rubric of the *Instrument* had however, been ambiguous about the status of these measures. How were Conciliar directions passed on grounds of 'necessity' to be reconciled with the legislative role of parliament? The realisation of one obvious flaw was followed by a proclamation that the law-making power of the protector and his Council would 'lapse' as soon as the new parliament met. Nonetheless, features of the new dispensation that were to provoke profound disagreement remained, of which the most contentious was the ability of the executive to raise funds in the absence of the MPs. The *Instrument* had effectively placed the hated Assessment in the hands of Cromwell himself, a measure that managed to be both constitutionally contentious yet fiscally insufficient. The outgoings of the military establishment and the Dutch war far exceeded revenue and in March 1654, with the income from fines and the sequestrations nearly exhausted, the Excise was extended to cover many more items of consumption.

As well as finance, the regime was obliged to address the Church and the law, issues with which its predecessors had struggled inconclusively. The treasury might be empty but the citizens of the Republic were far from doctrinally exhausted. Cromwell was still seen by many as the protector of independency as well as of the state, and the congregations had welcomed the demise of the Rump and Barebones in the same spirit as they had praised the suppression of the Levellers. In January, a letter circulated through the Independent and Baptist congregations of London that urged support for the new dispensation lest the 'Blackfriars prophets' bring God's ordinances and magistracy into disrepute. But there was still a distance between those who perceived the threat of disorder in the free expression of conscience, and the complete independence of worship that had been envisaged by Philip Nye and Thomas Goodwin at the Westminster Assembly. On the Council, Philip Skippon remained as staunch in his intolerance of toleration as he had been determined as a soldier in the parliamentary cause. The Church brought into being at the Assembly was not disestablished, and Cromwell wanted neither more Presbyterian 'martyrs' like Christopher Love nor sectarian disorder. But equally, the form of Presbyterian Church government envisaged by the Assembly had never properly satisfied parishioners who wanted a greater say in their choice of divine and of those who preached to them. Accordingly, it was decided to sponsor a more inclusive style of ministry.

The basis for Protectorate policy towards the national Church had already been outlined by John Owen and his collaborators. In the spring of 1654 an ordinance was passed by the Council establishing a Commission of 'Triers' which was to vet all new appointments to the clergy. This was a central body composed, in a spirit of pragmatic ecumenism, of Independents, Presbyterians and a sprinkling of Baptists. The commissioners' remit was confined to the determination of fitness by reference to competence and probity. There was no rigorous doctrinal test, rather a simple requirement that candidates be well-grounded in the 'essentials'. In its pragmatic approach, the policy was one of the regime's successes and was supported at the grass-roots level by the appearance of local ecumenical associations of the Protestant faith that encouraged those seeking ordination. Eventually more than a dozen counties had such a body, including Richard Baxter's in Worcestershire.

Lay patronage, which had been abolished by the 'Little Parliament' was restored and in August of the same year, local initiative in clerical appointment was reinforced by the establishment (again by conciliar ordinance) of Commissions of 'Ejectors'. These had the power to remove incompetent or negligent clergymen (and teachers) with the aim that the religious and the devout got the ministers they wanted. Desborough had roughly demanded of the Council that Nonconforming clergy be 'thrown out' without ado and certainly there were instances of overbearing zeal by local commissioners. In Somerset, a local minister was found guilty of 'profaning the Sabbath day, frequenting inns and ale houses and drinking to excess . . . and in associating himself with severall persons who were chief actors in the late Insurrection'.[5] Nonetheless, the system introduced by Owen was not nearly as autocratic as its terminology suggests and the number relieved of their ministry was a small proportion of the turnover experienced during the tumult of the wars when the campaign to purge the ministry of Arminians, royalists and the ungodly was at its height. Although a champion of orthodoxy, Baxter was moved to express his qualified admiration of the system – 'Yet to give them their due, they did an abundance of good for the Church: They saved many a congregation . . . tho' there were many of them somewhat partial for the Independents, Separatists, Fifth Monarchy Men and Anabaptists . . .'[6]

A process of conciliation without surrender to the millenarians and radicals was also observable in the Council's approach to law reform. Matthew Hale managed to swallow his scruples about the usurpation of parliamentary authority and accepted his commission to achieve incremental improvements. There was to be no move to novelty – as Thurloe put it, the state was to remain circumscribed by the 'good old laws' – but some of the worst aspects of the law's operation were ameliorated. The Chancery Ordinance of August was designed to produce simpler procedures and lower fees, and to end the lottery of the order in which a case was heard. Capital punishment was to be reserved solely for acts of murder or treason. Naturally, there was a good deal of resistance to the proposals for administrative reform from the lawyers, who resented the dilution of their privileges, and the Council frequently found that its ordinances (particularly where they related to property matters), were subject to challenge until such time as they were confirmed by parliament.

In Scotland, direct intervention in the affairs of the Kirk at the local level was considered to be too sensitive to handle systematically. Instead, the Protectorate tried to effect a more compliant ministry by ensuring that its finishing schools at the universities were directed by those sympathetic to the regime. The Remonstrant Patrick Gillespie, whose previously unyielding Calvinism had developed a flex, was won over by being placed in charge of Glasgow University; there his zealous collaboration and attempts to reorientate the political loyalties of the ministry drew the ire of Resolutioners such as Robert Baillie, who thoroughly objected to what they perceived as the Protectorate's agenda of stealthily laicising the clergy. But elsewhere, something of an ecumenical balance was achieved by appointing a Resolutioner as principal of Edinburgh University (Robert Leighton) and an Independent at Aberdeen (John Row).

In the field, Scottish submission was more energetically pursued following the return of George Monck, fresh from his triumphs over the Dutch. Monck was nothing if not meticulous in his preparations and while waiting for a consignment of cheese for his forces before moving north, he wrote to Cromwell with his misgivings, noting on 22 April that 'Upon enquiry into affairs here found that the design of this insurrection is more universal than I expected.'[7] The protector was receptive: the union between Scotland and England had been passed by ordinance and there was a determination that the Stuart cause be rubbed out for good. Monck was given reinforcements (including a regiment under Colonel Pride) and much more financial and logistical support than had been enjoyed by his predecessor.

Although those rebels under arms were not as ubiquitous as his report supposed, Monck saw plainly that geography was not in his favour if he was ever to contain and defeat the insurrection. He decided on a policy of isolating the Highlands from the Lowlands, thus protecting his rear as he moved into the remote and forbidding glens and passes north of the River Tay. He swiftly established numerous fortified garrisons which could dominate the surrounding area, such as Ruthven in the Spey Valley, or which could provide choke points, such as at St Johnstouns in Perth. Thus he aimed to limit the movements of the royalist forces now under the command of Middleton, the Engager cavalry commander whose record in both the Preston and Worcester campaigns had been somewhat undistinguished.

Incentives other than just brute force were also offered. An English ordinance of 'Pardon and Grace' gave an amnesty to all those who laid down their arms and, crucially, removed the ambiguity in the earlier policy relating to forfeiture of rebel land. Twenty-four nobles were relieved of their estates and seventy-three others were fined, a far more lenient punishment of rebellion than was observed in either England or Ireland. Continued disobedience was to be treated harshly however, with the property of wider kin groups at risk if individuals persisted with resistance. With soldierly pragmatism, Monck also recommended to Cromwell that the warlike temper of the Scots could profitably be channelled by allowing local regiments to be raised to serve against the Republic's enemies abroad, 'the people here being so generally poor and idle that they cannot live unless they be in arms'.[8]

But despite the carrot-and-stick approach, Middleton continued to lead the English troops a far from merry dance all the same. Monck was forced to march up and down the main lines of communication in the glens, ruthlessly ordering cattle to be driven away and for stores of grain, or anything else that could be of use to the enemy, to be burnt. He also ordered ships and boats that could be used for flanking attacks from the Highland's extensive network of lochs and waterways to be destroyed.[9] But with English troops (which had just laid waste to Caithness) pressing down from the Dornoch Firth, Middleton was eventually cornered with his diminished royalist force in July 1654 at Dalnaspidal on the north shore of Loch Garry. There, the Stuart monarch's supporters were thoroughly routed.

Monck's iron grip and a growing sense that the new relationship with England might lead to economic and commercial improvement persuaded more of the Scottish laity into a grudging acceptance of the Protectorate. Argyll had gone one step further and used his Campbell soldiers to support English operations in areas in which he had an interest, but there was, too, a realisation that it had been the old politics and religious dogmatism which had led Scotland to its present state of infirmity. More and more royalists like Sir William Lockhart and Covenanters like Sir James Hope and Sir John Swinton perceived that the Stuarts were a lost cause or, if not, then not to be trusted. Accordingly, a larger number of notables were happy to take the English shilling. The tenuous influence which the young king exerted on the affections of his supporters at home was further weakened by the straitened nature of his own circumstances. Prince Rupert had returned from his long odyssey at sea (minus his much-loved younger brother Prince Maurice, who had drowned during a hurricane) to find a court very much down-on-its-luck and hard-up. His face now a mask of weather-beaten leather, the exhausted cavalier soon became disillusioned by the pointless intrigues and animosities that enlivened the community of impoverished exiles in which his outspoken temperament was unwelcome. Shortly after his arrival back in France, he took his leave of his cousin.

The vexation caused by his relatives (of whom the worst offender was his mother, who was determined to reorientate the dynasty in a Roman Catholic direction), was perhaps the least of Charles's problems. The Continent was becoming a less friendly place for the exiled monarch as the European powers reached accommodation with the English Republic or actively sought its collaboration. The French state, whose government, led by Cardinal Mazarin, was getting to grips with insurgents, heretics and the predations of the Habsburgs, was determined to ensure that the military power of England was not used decisively to tip the balance of fortune against the young sovereign, Louis XIV. Accordingly, his representatives entered a diplomatic bidding war against those of Philip IV of Spain for the favour of the Protectorate as the year progressed. In such circumstances, Charles thought it prudent to decamp to Cologne, whose citizens seemed to be far more receptive to the now somewhat ersatz star-quality of the Stuart sovereign than the cynical and worldly French. Reluctantly leaving his young brother Prince Henry in the problematic Catholic care of his mother, the king loaded his meagre possessions onto a cart bound for the Rhine – as Hyde ruefully noted, he could no longer afford even a carriage.

In responding to the overtures of both Spain and France, Cromwell appeared more guided by the rougher tactics he had learnt as a soldier than by the strategic impulses of a natural statesman. His worldview was founded on his Protestant sympathies and by confidence in God's providence. More than once did he protest a desire to lead his Continental co-religionists in a Protestant union that would have the added benefit of giving employment (and continued justification) to the well-tried forces of the English Republic. He would, too, have remembered the serial disappointments of an earlier period of Stuart diplomacy and the way in which this had contributed to the low esteem in which the monarchy had fallen before the outbreak of civil war. Although the agenda of his foreign policy was frequently concealed by a series of feints and bluffs, it was conducted in a spirit of aggressive opportunism leavened with religious zeal. But it is difficult to detect the systematic approach that some have identified with the beginnings of a British Empire; the commercial thrust at the core of the Rump's foreign policy had been discredited in Cromwell's eyes by the war against the United Provinces. The lord protector was motivated less by economic considerations than by narrow financial ones – the state needed hard cash.

The first task was to settle the expensive quarrel with the Dutch. In spite of the scale of its military defeat, the United Provinces emerged from the Treaty of Westminster in the spring of 1654 with better terms than might have been expected. While they agreed to salute the flag of the Republic in British waters, they refused to acknowledge its wider sovereignty over the seas and rejected Cromwell's proposals for a closer union: the Dutch were far more interested in restoring their trade than in signing-up to some nebulous anti-Catholic league. They also regained access to the lucrative fishing grounds of the North Sea without having to pay dues. In return, the United Provinces agreed to pay compensation for British losses resulting from their successful counterblockade of the Baltic (in alliance with the Danes), which had seriously limited British access to naval stores, timber and iron. Although unable to persuade the English to repeal the Navigation Act, they managed to circumvent it by the simple expedient of disguising the beneficial ownership of their vessels. The Dutch also preserved the trading monopoly of their own East Indies company by the payment of an indemnity to the English one. However, they refused point-blank the proposal that the fleets of the former antagonists be used in joint operations against the Spanish, who had in the course of a generation gone from being hated overlords to valued trading partners and customers.

But Cromwell was satisfied, nonetheless. At the last minute he persuaded the dominant province of Holland to exclude the young William III, Charles's nephew, from the title of Stadtholder. This secret annex to the treaty caused an uproar in the other states when it was eventually revealed, but it removed another option from the Stuarts while blocking the House of Orange, to the benefit of the 'regent' class which dominated Dutch affairs. When the ink was dry, the representatives from each side sat down in brotherly Protestant concord. As reported by Thurloe, the Dutch envoy Jongestall observed 'The lord protector had us into another room . . . where we had also music and wine and a psalm sung which his Highness gave us and told us that it was yet the best paper that had been exchanged between us.'[10] Nonetheless, the Dutch had learnt their lesson and used the peace to rapidly expand and improve their fighting fleet: the next time they clashed, they were not going to allow themselves to be out-muscled by the English navy.

Peace with the Dutch had released English forces to cause mischief elsewhere, and Cromwell and his Council spent the summer encouraging ever higher competing bids from Cárdenas and Bordeaux as the price of English acquiescence. As a way of extorting funds for the payment of the British military establishment, the approach had some merit. France was a more obvious antagonist – it presently sheltered the Stuart court, was connected to royalist conspiracy at home and English sailors were still locked in a brutal struggle with French privateers in the Channel and Mediterranean that had been going on for years. The lord protector also saw the literal meaning of his title extending to French Protestants, whether they wanted his tender care or not. But the French state was now asserting itself against the rebels of the Fronde while fighting the Spanish to a virtual standstill: a Catholic power itself, it was nonetheless determined to thwart the dynastic ambitions of its co-religionists under the Habsburgs. In Marshal Turenne, an almost exact contemporary of Fairfax, it had, too, a soldier whose growing reputation was providing stiff competition to that of the English warlords. By contrast, the power of a heavily indebted Spain was clearly on the wane.[11]

The lord protector perhaps lacked the caution and guile that had marked the foreign policy of his Elizabethan predecessor. He had a grander vision and was keen to project the Republic in the service of the Protestant communion in Europe. Over the course of the summer, his preference for an opportunist campaign against Spain in the Caribbean began to harden. At home, an attack on such an overtly Roman Catholic power would protect his flank against the militant sects and Fifth Monarchists as well as cheering up the Presbyterians. Logistically, any expedition to the West Indies would largely be self-funded by the seizure of a strategic island athwart their trading routes and, better still, by the interception and capture of Spain's fabled treasure fleets. Indeed, there was an expectation that the campaign would turn a profit. In a sign that the Protestant settlement of Ireland was proceeding far from smoothly, the expedition to the West Indies was additionally justified by the prospect of a repopulation of the godly further afield. In the Council, the plan (the so-called 'Western Design') was received enthusiastically and the aggressively tempered Desborough was placed in charge of preparations. However, Lambert was far less certain and viewed the operation as a sign of hubris and the waste of an opportunity to take peacefully some of the enormous trade the Dutch enjoyed with her former imperial master for the English.

The 'Western Design', so clear on paper, turned into something of a shambles that had a number of unintended consequences – in its inadvertent seizure of Jamaica, the campaign perhaps provides the genesis of the idea that the subsequent British empire was acquired mostly by accident. As originally conceived, the expedition's target was Hispaniola, an enormous island off the south-east coast of Cuba that was almost two-thirds the size of England. But Cromwell's large hand had been cast over a very small map. Although acting under faulty intelligence that described the Spanish garrisons there as an ill-led crowd of lazy nondescripts, the English planned to assemble an overwhelming force of several thousand men under the command of Robert Venables, a veteran of the Irish campaign. In charge of the naval side of the operation was William Penn, who had distinguished himself alongside Blake and whose job it was to transport the soldiers. It was a large undertaking, eventually comprising a force equivalent to nearly a fifth of the home army's entire strength and over eighty vessels. But the last time the British state had conducted such a large combined-service operation (the Duke of Buckingham's expedition against the Île de Ré in the summer of 1627), the result had been a costly fiasco.

The initial auspices were not good. Venables was not at all impressed by the quality of his troops mustered in England. The army was still demobilising and many of the regular regimental and garrison commanders used the expedition as a way of off-loading their least-valued soldiers. Neither officer was given overall command of the operation, although its very scope and the latitude given to the officers to set their objective once they were in theatre suggested the navy took the lead. The lack of unity was compounded by the presence of civilian commissioners, including the aged Edward Winslow who had sailed with the Pilgrim Fathers. The fleet set off from Spithead on another working Christmas Day at the end of 1654. Among the crowded soldiers, mostly unknown to one another and muddled together in makeshift regiments, Venables installed his wife; he anticipated a long tour of duty. But her presence caused resentment amongst the men who had been forced to leave their womenfolk behind. A month later, the already quarrelsome joint-venture landed at Barbados.

The island had surrendered early in 1652 – the torrential rain and oppressive heat made conventional fighting uncongenial and Charles's governor, Lord Willoughby, had thrown in the towel after a few drinks with the Commonwealth commanders at a local tavern. The English squadron under Ayscue had been accompanied by an armada of planters including James Drax, all eager to get their hands back on their highly lucrative estates of tobacco and sugar cane. In the intervening years before the arrival of Penn's fleet, the island had continued to flourish in contrast to the unsettled economy back home. The Republic's governor Daniel Searle quickly realised how to exploit the island's resources and Barbados continued a brisk trade with the Dutch, notwithstanding the provisions of the Navigation Act – when Penn eventually tried to come alongside at Barbados's harbour pier, his way was blocked by a large concourse of merchant-men from Britain's former adversary.

Although one of the civil commissioners to the 'Western Design', Searle was keen to get the expedition off his island as soon as possible – there were just too many additional mouths to feed and he was nervous that the surly and disagreeable tourists threatened public order. Venables's plan rested on the assumption that he could get reinforcements from among the settler communities of the Leeward and Windward Isles. Accordingly, his ranks were swollen with volunteers from Barbados and the island of St Kitts. Amidst the smallholders and labourers (who were struggling to improve their lot amidst the wealthy planters) were formerly indentured men who had been taken as prisoners-of-war in the Scottish campaigns. Eager to escape the stifling heat and back-breaking toil of work in the sugar-cane fields, they and many of the English soldiers they joined saw the expedition primarily as a route to plunder and freedom, rather than colonisation. Yet no sooner were all aboard than the civilian commissioners announced that the 'Western Design' was for the advantage of the Protectorate – this was to be no free-for-all. Morale began to fall.

The expedition landed on Hispaniola in April 1655, some way from its intended objective. The harbour of Santo Domingo was one of Spain's earliest settlements in the New World and was only reached after a gruelling march across unfamiliar terrain. En route, the troops vented their frustration on a chapel and on the effigy of a Madonna dragged from within, a 'popish' juju they then proceeded to pelt with oranges. The small garrison of their intended target proved to be far more competent and aggressive than Venables had been led to believe. In the heat, his poorly equipped troops succumbed to dysentery and thirst (the promised issue of water bottles had not materialised) and soon the famous warriors of the New Model Army lost all cohesion and shape. Short of drinkable water and shelter from the tropical thunderstorms, the soldiers' assaults on the harbour's bastions were bloodily rebuffed; Venables proved himself to be a poor commander and at one point 'very nobelly rune behind a tree being so very much prosesed with teror that he could harlie spake'.[12] Within three weeks, the attempted conquest of Hispaniola was abandoned.

Reputations were now at stake and eager for something to show after this humiliation, Penn and Venables agreed to press on to Jamaica, a smaller target whose demanding topography was populated by only a few thousand souls who eked out a living alongside the swamps and steep ravines of the island's southern coastline. Vastly outnumbered, the Spanish quickly came to terms but when Venables insisted that they quit the island they fled into the mountainous hinterland and conducted a vicious guerrilla war against the invaders, whose main priority now was to find food and water. By the summer, both senior commanders had scuttled back to Britain, leaving their exhausted and malaria-ridden men in the charge of subordinates. Each was eager to give their separate accounts of the debacle but

Cromwell was so appalled that he had both men thrown into the Tower and later cashiered. The weakened garrison managed to retain a toehold on the Caribbean island, but the 'Western Design' seemed to confirm the limitations of state-sponsored expeditions to faraway places and arguably had a profound influence on the shape of later manifestations of British empire-building. However, Cromwell and his councillors were more concerned about the metaphysical rather than practical implications of the failure: for the first time, God had unambiguously spurned them.

16

'A man whom pride hath overcome'
Oundle

Liberty of conscience is a natural right; and he that would have it ought to give it.

Oliver Cromwell

The natural magistracy of the Nation, was it not almost trampled underfoot, under despite and contempt, by men of Levelling principles? I beseech you, for the orders of men and ranks of men, did not that Levelling principle tend to the reducing of all to an equality?

Oliver Cromwell

Cavaliers fell in with the Presbyterians against you and the government and the spirit is generally bitter against swordsmen, decimators and courtiers and most of those chosen to sit in the ensuing Parliament are of the same spirit.

Major-General Kelsey, letter to Cromwell

Before Penn and Venables departed on their ill-starred venture, the lord protector had faced his first parliament. With the national debt now exceeding the state's annual revenue and the sources of income exhausted, the Council understood that the calling of a parliament to sanction further taxes was now unavoidable. The armed forces were still a huge drain, notwithstanding Cromwell's agreement to drop the hated Assessment by a quarter. A triennial parliament had been promised in the *Instrument* and writs were issued for an election on the new franchise that proceeded, as Thurloe noted, with surprisingly little rancour. In the first week of September 1654, the new House assembled. The army was well represented: Thomas Harrison was returned as were (for the first time) other New Model regicides including William Goffe and Hardress Waller. A large number of the thirty seats allocated to Ireland were filled by serving officers; but Scotland failed to meet its quota altogether, a consequence of the disruption that had been caused by the rising in the Highlands. Although elected, Fairfax once again declined to take his seat – his enigmatic abstention was now beginning to look like certain disapproval.

In advance of the gathering, the Council had exercised its right of veto by drawing its metaphorical red pencil through the names of eleven undesirables, including the Leveller John Wildman and others thought to be crypto-royalists or insufficiently godly. Nonetheless, the vote also brought back a large number of MPs who had gone through the purges and who were entirely unsympathetic to the shape of the new regime, among the most determined of whom were Arthur Hesilrige and Thomas Scot. Within a week of the hopeful opening by the lord protector, the MPs began to unpick the constitution that had brought them together. The Council was disconcerted when Justice Matthew Hale, now an MP for Gloucestershire, proposed that government 'should be in a Parliament and single person limited and restrained as the Parliament should think fit'. This was less of a personal challenge to Cromwell than a sincere attempt to address one of the glaring omissions of the *Instrument*, namely what was to happen if the executive and legislature could not agree?

From his exile in Paris, Hyde grudgingly conceded the 'strange dexterity' with which the lord protector moved. Yet in his relations with parliament, Cromwell appeared to have learnt very little from the constitutional crisis of late 1648. His determination to see that the law was reformed and that peaceable Protestant consciences be allowed free exercise was genuine, but he seemed to lack the will to manage the political aspects of his office. He had proved himself to be both zealous and a capable reactionary whenever the dynamics of a situation reached the point of crossing God's manifest will, but he appeared curiously detached from those processes of political manoeuvring that are designed to head off a crisis in the first place. Although not lazy, he had attended barely a third of the Council meetings in his first year of office – which showed an unusual degree of diffidence given the need to bed-in the regime and the relative inexperience of his councillors. On the other hand, he was often energised by individual cases which a more focused leader would have left to subordinates. Moreover, these interventions were frequently unsuccessful (such as trying to preserve the estates of the Irish aristocrats the Earl of Westmeath and Lord Ikerrin in accordance with the articles of war), to the detriment of his prestige.

Cromwell's reaction to the debates about the *Instrument* and the question of its legitimacy began to show a grim consistency. On 12 September 1654, the Members arrived at the House to find it surrounded by troops. Offering fulsome apologies, the first citizen explained to them that by some oversight he and the Council had forgotten to bind the stewards of the state by an oath. This was now to be rectified by parliament making an 'Act of Recognition'. Hale had made a decent stab at addressing the ambiguity in the *Instrument*, but the lord protector preferred a rubric which placed government in the hands of one person and a parliament, not one which placed the office holder in a subordinate position. Despite the naked show of force, over fifty members simply refused to make the required obeisance and eventually more than eighty of them were excluded. It was an unhappy start.

Soon after, parliament introduced a Bill 'for the restraining of atheism, blasphemy, damnable heresies . . . or any thing contrary to the fundamental principles of doctrine'. Although his father had been re-elected to the House, Henry Vane was not around to beat the drum for toleration, and the conservative coalition reasserted itself. Allowing people to skip church was one thing, allowing them to say and do what they liked in matters of the Protestant faith was quite another. In this, there was a degree of unanimity with the protector, who had shown that he had grown tired of the 'blasphemies' of the sects, their intolerance towards one another and their threat to public peace. Had not Cromwell referred approvingly to the settled order of the ranks of society and the abuses that were being made of liberty of conscience in his opening address? Certainly, the Fifth Monarchists seemed irreconcilable and Harrison was briefly rearrested for alleged sedition. But rather than divide and rule amongst the myriad strands of religious inspiration, Cromwell seemed to think that he could bring round many of the antagonists and his own detractors by means of the personal interview. At various times a number of the more celebrated divines were sent before him, including the millenarian minister John Rogers (who had scolded the protector for taking the crown off Christ's head and placing it upon his own), John Simpson (the preacher at All Hallows who accused Cromwell of treason), Christopher Feake and George Fox.

Fox had enjoyed a successful evangelising mission in the Midlands, as had Edward Burrough in London, but by 1654 the local authorities had had enough. The refusal of the Quakers to defer to those in authority was thoroughly irritating, but they were also serial and noisy disruptors of church services and their penchant for semi-nakedness was an affront to decent Puritan society. In Edinburgh, the diarist John Nicoll had been scandalised by the sight of these fervent mendicants wandering around the city in only their shirts. It was time to get a grip of the *sans-culottes* and neutralise their threat to public peace. Parliament passed an Act forbidding interruptions in church and Fox soon found himself bundled off to London for a stern lecture from the lord protector. But whereas a metaphorical pre-caning homily from the regime's headmaster frequently resulted in a term in jail, Fox seemed to charm him enough to get an invitation back to preach to the Whitehall household. It was this sort of benediction that continued to confuse his political opponents and supporters alike. The MPs wanted a tougher line: shortly afterwards, the Socinian John Biddle was imprisoned and they further reserved the right to determine what was heretical and blasphemous without recourse to the inconsistent protector.

Battle was also resumed with the recalcitrant Members on the issue of the control and financing of the military establishment. With its widespread commitments across Great Britain and Ireland, and with the 'Western Design' under planning, the army still numbered over 55,000 men. There were demands and resolutions that Cromwell and his Council stick to the terms of the *Instrument* and the authorised Assessment was cut to only half the amount needed to keep the armed forces at its present strength. A Council of Officers reconvened at St James's angrily to denounce the move (payments were again in arrears), but the quarrel highlighted the acute problem of how otherwise the regime was legally to raise money without the ultimate sanction of parliament. At about the same time, an emblematic and extra-parliamentary challenge came from a citizen called George Cony. A wealthy merchant who was an acquaintance of the protector, Cony had refused to pay customs duty on some imported silk on the grounds that an impost levied by ordinance did not have the sanction of law. Rebuffing the bailiffs sent to collect it, he was imprisoned. His case became a cause célèbre – he was eventually to submit, but not before one of the chief justices adjourned the case while parliament sat and then resigned rather than try it.[1]

In the interval of these disputes, the lord protector was badly hurt in an accident that served as a metaphor for both the nature and fragility of his authority. He had accepted a gift of some horses from northern Germany and, anxious for some diversion and a desire to see their worth, he had them harnessed up for a carriage ride around a London park. Setting off with Thurloe in the seat beside him, Cromwell got carried away with his whip, the horses bolted and both men were thrown to the ground. The lord protector, his legs tangled in the traces, was then dragged along by the over-excited beasts. Worse still, both men were armed and in the melee a pistol went off, narrowly missing them both: the underground pamphlets of the royalists had a field day and the hapless duo were widely lampooned. Equines were not the real problem, however; the regime simply seemed unable to build necessary support amongst the establishment.[2]

Reflecting Chief Justice Rolle's reticence in the Cony case, many law officers were deeply unhappy about enforcing rules that did not yet have parliament's approval and, in one extreme instance in Warwickshire, Sir Peter Wentworth sought to expunge his humiliation at Cromwell's hands during the dissolution of the Rump by having the collectors of the Assessment in his bailiwick arrested. Cromwell had also set his heart on law reform, but when the commissioners of the Great Seal of the Republic were ordered to give effect to the Chancery Ordinance of 1654, two of them (Sir Thomas Widdrington and Bulstrode Whitelocke) refused to do so. Just as ominous, the cohesion of the army was splintering again. Inspired by the excluded Member John Wildman, three New Model officers (Colonels Alured, Saunders and the regicide John Okey) produced a petition in October that denounced the *Instrument* as giving Cromwell more powers than the former king. The soldiers were court-martialled and cashiered but their rumblings were echoed in the navy by Lawson, whose prestige seemed presently too high to risk having him taken into custody. In Scotland too, some disaffected officers gathered around the Fifth Monarchist Robert Overton, whose arrest on trumped-up charges was speedily ordered by Monck. He was to languish in jail for four years.

Another crisis was coming to a head as well. At the end of the year, there was a further proposal that Cromwell be made king, presented to the MPs by the regicide Augustine Garland. As with Lambert's earlier recommendation, this too was withdrawn, although the motivation of the soldier was most likely different. In the general's case, he would have remembered his contribution to the Heads of Proposals and his desire for the right ordering of an efficient state with familiar signposts. But there was also a growing sense that it was only by offering the Crown that the regime could be brought back to a semblance of that in which Charles I had been shorn of his powers and by which the over-mighty aspects of the *Instrument* could be curtailed. There was certainly a determination to exert greater control over the Council of State. Early in the new year a Bill was introduced which sought to make it more explicitly accountable – the lord protector's right to appoint the Council was confirmed, but his choices would have to be approved by parliament and be subject to further approval by succeeding triennial assemblies. When the MPs next voted to bring the militia under their sole control it proved to be the final straw. In the third week of January, Cromwell crossly dismissed the representatives; as with the Rump, the MPs had failed in their 'trust'. They had sat for barely five months.

In the early spring of 1655, the regime dealt with a series of royalist disorders, the most serious of which was the so-called Penruddock Rising. Looking for some diversion from the bickering of his courtiers, and with a clear sense that Cromwell was beginning to flounder, Charles appointed Henry Wilmot, Earl of Rochester, to stir things up back in England. For all the security implied by its secretive name, the main royalist organisation proved less of a Sealed Knot than a leaky sieve. Thurloe's agents were taken to be everywhere and the principals were understandably timid about taking on the might of the New Model Army, notwithstanding that a large proportion of it was presently engaged in Ireland, Scotland and the West Indies. Nonetheless, in March a former royalist colonel, John Penruddock, taking advantage of local fury at the transportation of royalist prisoners to the Caribbean, bravely managed to stage an insurrection in Salisbury.

As at the time of Charles's escape after Worcester, notables who had been assumed to be keen to lend a hand were more than happy to keep their heads down. Penruddock's little gang was hotly pursued into the West Country where it was squashed with minimal fuss by Desborough, now rapidly cementing his reputation as the regime's irascible enforcer. In a sign that the disturbances were seen as more of a serious inconvenience than an existential threat, the perpetrators of this and other disorders were tried by the local assizes rather than by the full might of the High Court. Thirty-nine were sentenced to death, of which fewer than a dozen were eventually executed. The condemned were mostly spared the gruesome fate of hanging, drawing and quartering that was usually reserved for traitors – a dignified Penruddock was cleanly beheaded in Exeter.

The course of the narrative suggests that it was the royalist rebellion and other discontents which prompted the regime to usher in the so-called 'rule of the major-generals'. Certainly, a good deal of anxiety is revealed in Thurloe's papers for this period although a reader might be forgiven for thinking that the spymaster derived a vicarious pleasure from all the skulduggery involved in keeping an eye on his fellow and foreign citizens. However, nearly six months were to elapse before this step was taken and in the meantime the burdens of state demanded a more systematic form of governance than had been provided by the *Instrument of Government.* As time had passed, the Protectorate Council discovered (as had their predecessors), that it had neither the resources nor the bureaucratic infrastructure to run the country either effectively or securely. The shady networks operated by Thurloe were not enough. Nedham had tried to popularise the practical aspects of the regime through pamphlets and broadsheets, but arguably the Protectorate needed a more uplifting rationale than had been provided by Hobbes.

Milton had lent his intellect to finding its justification beyond the duties of obedience commended in *Leviathan*. In his *Second Defence of the English People*, published in the summer of 1654, the now very dimly sighted bard focused on the moral case for the protectoral arrangements. Writing in Latin, the poet devoted most of his piece to giving another lashing to those who remained unreconciled to the trial and execution of the king, and who, in his view, were slandering both him and the regime. In his purple prose it was not entirely clear which Milton regarded as the greater affront. Nonetheless, he confirmed his attachment to the principles of *Areopagitica* and rhapsodised a state that was based on probity and pureness of spirit, in which corruption and all the grubbier aspects of government would eventually wither. But, in a small sign of his flagging confidence, he plaintively urged the protector to do the right thing: 'Honor this great confidence reposed in you, honor your country's singular hope in you. Honor the faces and the words of the many brave men, all those who under your leadership have striven so vigorously for victory.'[3]

Yet arguably his plea was misdirected. Cromwell too remained frustrated that the stewards of both the state and the religious ministry had, in his own words, serially failed to bring forth a settlement where mercy and truth might prevail and 'righteousness and peace kiss'.

The rule of the major-generals may be considered as a further attempted iteration of the godly state of the well-affected that had proven, thus far, to be so tantalisingly out of reach, despite the best efforts of Owen and Puritan reformers like Baxter and John Goodwin. Godliness would only be embedded in the national culture and psyche where it was supported by a strong magistracy. The soldiers would supply that strength. Accordingly, England was divided up into cantons of two or more aggregated counties, and the first ten appointments to oversee them were made in August 1655. The catalyst for their creation was a reorganisation of the militia, specifically the raising of local cavalry formations that, it was hoped, would be a cheaper way of providing home security than the standing army. As defined by Lambert, the primary role of the major-generals was to be the maintenance of (godly) law and order, but their taking of control of the county militias immediately put them at odds with the convention that these should be in the hands of civilian law-officers, not regular soldiers. Their remit was greatly expanded such that they were also made responsible for enforcing the social measures of the regime and supporting the religious ones via the Commissions of Ejectors. Further, they were given authority to purge local corporations, the backbone of civic rule in the towns.

Whilst Lambert's approach to governance was narrowly soldierly and pragmatic, the major-generals were almost immediately saddled with the reputation for being mini-dictators and somewhat joyless enforcers of Puritan manners. From a different angle, they were also attacked by the religious radicals and in *A word for God . . . from . . . Wales*, Vavasor Powell whipped his confederates into a denunciation of a Protectorate which was in danger of forgetting the Almighty just as the Israelites had done after their deliverance from Egypt. In their letter to Cromwell they recorded their dismay: 'For as much as you have caused great searching of heart and divisions among many of God's people by a sudden, strange and unexpected alteration of government and other actions, to the great astonishment of those who knew your former public resolutions and declarations.'[4]

Some seemed actively to court their unfavourable reputation. From Oundle, William Boteler oversaw a domain that encompassed Northamptonshire, Rutland, Bedfordshire and Huntingdonshire. He had served in the second civil war with a commission in the cavalry and had taken part in the suppression of the Leveller mutinies in the spring of 1649. Boteler was not going to take any nonsense from the community for which he was now responsible and was soon taking firm action. He was clearly not an easy man to please, having observed to Thurloe he had 'met with many malignants, though but few commissioners, and some of them not very hearty in our worke neither'.[5] He proved to be a zealous scourge of both Catholics and Protestant sects alike, especially the Quakers; Fox denounced him as 'a man whom pride hath overcome'. His finer Puritan sensibilities were however displayed in Cobthorne, the residence that he built in the middle of the town and an impressive example of the 'Commonwealth' style. Today, it serves as the headmaster's house for the local school. With distinctive double gables and a roof that resembles the famous Puritan stove-pipe hat, Cobthorne was an example of a new confident architectural method that paid attention to the neoclassical arrangements of Inigo Jones without being subservient to them.

Others reconciled themselves to the zeitgeist in a different way. Katherine Fowler had been in her teens when the second civil war reached its ferocious zenith and achieved an early maturity in the 'world turned upside down'. Born in London, at sixteen she was married to the parliamentarian Colonel James Philips (a man nearly four decades her senior), and settled in Carmarthenshire at a former priory in Cardigan. Intensive study of the Bible was fostering a growing literacy among women of all degrees, but Katherine Philips was slowly to turn her back on her Puritan upbringing and its more unattractive dogmas, which reached into all areas of family life. She used her poetry to attack the purges of the Welsh ministry conducted by Vavasor Powell. Instead, Philips sought spiritual solace in the cultivation of friendships shorn of religious dogmatism and conformity. In the quest for a sensibility unsullied by the neuroses of the age, she resembled in some ways Robert Herrick, and she too is regarded as a royalist poet. Philips is perhaps as famous for the coterie assembled in her 'Society of Friendship' and the unusual names which they gave to one another as for her verse. Styled 'Orinda' (her otherwise invisible husband was referred to affectionately, if fleetingly, as 'Antenor'), she attracted a group of like-minded spirits who venerated the Platonic ideal in the relationship between men and women, and whose subtle hierarchy was determined by the depth of their individual good natures rather than their religious scruples.

The famously erudite Edwardian poet and critic Edmund Gosse hailed Philips as the 'first sentimental writer in the English language', but he meant it in the original sense, and her exaltation of empathy and human understanding was expressed with great clarity and economy:

> The hearts thus intermixed speak
> A Love that no bold shock can break
> For Joyn'd and growing, both in one
> Neither can be disturbd alone.

. . .

That friendship hearts so much refines,
It nothing but itself designs
The hearts are free from lower ends,
For each point to the other tends . . . [6]

Gosse was, however, perhaps wide of the mark in inferring a sapphic relationship between her and Anne Owen ('Lucasia'), the local beauty about and to whom Gosse's 'ruddy cockney' wrote reams of verse. In fact, the 'matchless Orinda' was breaking the mould of an aesthetic that had been almost entirely dominated by males. Among the sophisticated, Sir Philip Sidney's *Arcadia* was still one of the most popular pieces of fiction of the age (although Milton had given it short shrift in *Eikonoclastes*) and was given a further boost by the posthumous publication of a life of the soldier-poet by his great friend Fulke Neville in 1652. Yet despite the renown of Sir Philip, 'Orinda' was able to successfully articulate an alternative to the critique of Puritan sensibility that had been achieved by the saucy Elizabethan. Her success in her circle was an early instance of a woman getting proper recognition for her intellect as much as her piety.

Whatever his own aesthetic preferences, however, Boteler was a punctilious enforcer of the Decimation Tax that was introduced by ordinance at the end of October. The rule of Cromwell's 'bashaws', as opponents described them, turned out to be more expensive than originally calculated and the Council was now working with a reduced level of the Assessment. Perturbed by the royalist disturbances earlier in the year, Cromwell retreated from the instincts that had earlier informed his support for the Act of Oblivion and sanctioned a new 'emergency' levy equivalent to an annual payment of one-tenth of the value of the property and land of known royalists and other members of the class of 'disaffected'. Thurloe primly observed that there was nothing unreasonable about making the royalists pay for the maintenance of peace after their earlier disorders and he believed that the first duty of the major-generals was to get the cavaliers to cough up.[7] But the measure hit well over 14,000 families and caused real hardship. Coming on top of the sequestrations, many were driven to near penury and the Council was soon flooded with petitions for mercy and relief. A number of these were sanctioned, thus undermining the major-generals who had to take the opprobrium for collecting the levy on the ground.

Ludlow, recently returned from Ireland, denounced the tax to Cromwell and Lambert – 'decimation' would destroy any hope of reconciliation with royalists and the regime of the generals was in any case a 'detestable project'. The state, he insisted, could only be governed by consent. Cromwell not unreasonably pointed out that consensus preceded consent and that this could only be achieved slowly while opinion was so divided between the 'prelatical party, Presbyterians, Independents, Anabaptists and Levellers'. Lambert took a firmer approach, insisting that the republican post a bond for good behaviour and when this was refused Ludlow was rusticated to East Anglia and ordered to stay away from his political base in Wiltshire. The major-generals were less fussed about the constitutionality of their position or the tax however, and, at Oundle, Boteler maintained an uncompromising line. Although not authorised to do so, he imprisoned many defaulters including the Earl of Northampton, in whose arrest Boteler may have felt further justified by the fact that he was related of one of the founders of the Sealed Knot.

But clearing the streets and lanes of vagrants, bearing down hard on blasphemy, drunkenness and other signs of profanity, and ensuring the closure of brothels and swathes of out-of-town alehouses, neither endeared the broader population to the innovation of governance under the major-generals nor prompted a widespread change in public culture beyond resentment. Amongst that section of the population that felt itself entitled by 'quality' and 'degree' to have a commanding role in local magistracy and ministry, the major-generals were regarded as parvenus and interfering busybodies. Again, this was less to do with narrow social prejudice than profound discomfort at the inversion of the cause for which the men of 1640 believed they had been fighting. Whether a major-general, a Leveller, a Ranter or a Quaker, all were considered as unnatural novelties with little or no part in a settled Protestant state. One great irony of their rule was that they attracted the most disapproval in those areas that had spawned the deepest aversion to the royal regime, opposition that was enhanced by the disappointment of the men who had dominated the County Committees of wartime and their successors, and whose authority was now much diluted.

The magistracy of the major-generals as a consistent instrument of state in England was further undermined by the varying agendas and personalities of the individuals who held the office. While Boteler was ferociously chasing Quakers and Fifth Monarchists around the south-east Midlands, James Berry was giving them succour in Wales and its borderlands, and was happy to see some of Fox's followers serve in his forces. His affiliations were somewhat atypical of the most senior level of the Council of Officers: hailing from a community of the ironworks that dotted Shropshire, he had had close associations with the army's 'agitators' and was believed to have strong Leveller sympathies. Amongst Cromwell's kith and kin, Desborough and Edward Whalley also had contrasting styles. The choleric brother-in-law had charge of the south-west, which held a large proportion of royalist sympathisers amongst its communities of devout Puritans. Like Boteler, he was a punctilious enforcer of what he perceived to be his mandate. Although his troops had been barely troubled by Penruddock's ineffectual insurrection, he took a dim view of the royalists and argued that the Decimation Tax should be made a permanent levy. Cromwell's cousin, Edward Whalley, who served in the Midlands, was arguably the most pragmatic, although his somewhat breezy reports to Thurloe suggest that he had less hard a time of it than his colleagues. Although a regicide, he had been personally thanked by the sovereign for the sensitivity which he brought to his brief role as the king's gaoler; neither this nor the mutiny amongst his troops in 1649 seemed to harm his prospects. A known Independent, he nonetheless conciliated local Presbyterians and firmly supported the idea of a national

Church as a defence against the impact of the religious radicals and sectaries.

Unlike those major-generals like Boteler who saw their role as being to stir things up, a different rhythm was observed among the Republic's representatives in Ireland and Scotland. The old Protestant interests shared by those like Broghill had been thoroughly alienated by the disruptive approach to Irish settlement adopted by the New Model soldiers under Fleetwood, and they were dismayed too by the soldiers' religious radicalism. While Ludlow was privately denouncing the Protectorate as a betrayal of the victory over Charles I, many of the indigenous Protestant community welcomed it as a way of getting the interlopers under control and the Irish commissioners in Dublin off their backs. To them, the Act of Union with England was seen as a way of regularising the status of Ireland on a par with that of Scotland. Alas, the Protectorate parliament was on the cusp of debating this very thing when Cromwell dissolved the assembly.

Instead, Henry Cromwell was sent back to Ireland as major-general of the army and deputy to the malleable Fleetwood, who was himself recalled. In his mid-twenties, the junior Cromwell was a younger son who had seen service with his father in both the north of England and in the Irish campaign of 1649. A contemporary portrait reveals him as a thick-set and tough, if somewhat wary-looking, individual. His cardinal quality was absolute and vigorous loyalty to the head of the family and the lord protector had sent him on a brief tour to take the political temperature of Ireland in 1654. Here, he quickly formed an adverse opinion of both Ludlow and those of his fellow officers who were Anabaptists. Surrounded by the swarm of idolatrous papists, many of these men had honed a fervent and uncompromising edge to their faith which became part of their *esprit de corps*. In Fleetwood, they found shelter under one of the most evangelical senior commanders in the army, but the younger Cromwell perceived their fanaticism as an impediment to peace, a view shared by the landed elite. Indeed, the divisions were made plain in the elections to the first Protectorate parliament which saw

Irish Protestant gentry pitched against commissioners and soldiers for the available seats. When Henry Cromwell returned in the summer of 1655 he showed his colours by refusing to serve in the pocket of the army (as Fleetwood had done), and focused instead on building a political and social coalition in support of his father from amongst the elites whose counterparts were being so alienated back in England.

As revealed by his correspondence to Thurloe, the younger Cromwell was nonetheless a constant worrier who seemed to find equal vexation in matters large and small. The land survey conducted by the polymath and statistician William Petty had brought a greater degree of rigour, if not justice, to the apportioning of land away from vanquished to victor, but Henry Cromwell found it difficult to square the need to conciliate those sections of the Protestant gentry whose previous royalism he was inclined to pardon with the legitimate demands of the soldiers for land in lieu of arrears. Not that the regime was finished with sectarianism as a coercive policy of state management; indeed, various schemes, including the forcible removal from their parents of Roman Catholic children under the age of fourteen to serve as indentured servants in Jamaica, were adumbrated on the younger Cromwell's watch.[8] Attempts too were made to entice some of the colonists of New England to return to augment the godly communities of Ireland as well as those in the Caribbean, but this had limited success. As shown by such petitions as that submitted by the town authorities of Gloucester in December 1656, throughout the Protectorate period Ireland was seen as a source of compensation for anyone on either side of the Irish Sea who could claim, however implausibly, that they had suffered from royalist or Catholic depredations during the long struggles.

Broghill himself was sent as the head of a new civil council for the running of Scotland. There had been some chafing at the no-nonsense style of Monck and the financial burden of the military establishment, but there was also much relief at the return of law and order. One English observer recalled that 'A man may ride all

Scotland over with a switch in his hand and £100 in his pocket which he could not have done these [past] 500 years.'[9] The general was hardly a martinet. He had, for example, proposed that the Assessment should be collected by the Scots rather than the English to soften the blow of necessary compliance, and had argued that local chieftains should be allowed to raise men to help keep the peace. But now Monck's influence on the civil administration was diluted by his inclusion in the membership of an eight-man council that included two Scots, Lockhart and Swinton. Broghill had familial connections in Scotland and pursued a policy of conciliating the local elites while also building bridges with the grandees of the wider Presbyterian political interest.

Electing to serve for twelve months only, he had an early success in his new commission when he persuaded the majority of ministers of Resolutioner persuasion to abandon their prayers for the king. It helped that Broghill had himself signed the Covenant, but his relationship with its more extreme adherents was more problematic. Here his tactics were complicated by the visceral partiality of the lord protector to the Remonstrant wing. Cromwell was attracted by their animosity to the Stuarts and by sympathy for their religious sincerity – indeed the diehard Wariston was later co-opted into the protectoral administration. But Broghill was helped by a growing division amongst the Remonstrants themselves, who baulked, like the divine James Guthrie, at the powers that Patrick Gillespie seemed to enjoy which allowed him to influence the local clergy through the syllabus at Glasgow. Others, such as Alexander Jaffray, weary at the interminable feuding and hair-splitting, took themselves off to become Quakers. But, in a departure from his attempts at conciliation, Broghill (as did Monck) developed a strong aversion to Argyll, whom he mistrusted in a way that was enhanced by the deep understanding of their shared background as landed magnates.[10] He did everything possible to reduce his residual power until the marquis threw himself on the mercy of the protector to save him from ruin, a correspondence that later proved damning when the noble went on trial for his life. In the meantime, Cromwell took him on as (another) special case and the Scottish nobleman was awarded £12,000 towards the payment of his debts, a sum which attracted much grumbling.

Whatever the prejudices of the major-generals, the effort to stimulate a more godly disposition amongst the local populations for which they had responsibility was an uphill struggle. The Council was bombarded with missives from the most zealous, like Boteler, or from the most vexed, such as Robert Lilburne (who deputised for Lambert in the north) and Goffe, complaining about both the lack of money and the ragged moral fibre of the community of officials, ministers and Justices of the Peace with whom they had to work. There was also a great deal of paranoia – one recorded his fear of a 'profane, malignant, disaffected party' and even Whalley spoke of 'irreconcilable enemies'.[11] To some, however, it did not seem as if the major-generals were being allowed to be tough enough, and from the Sessions of Flintshire came the lament that there were simply not enough of the well-affected to deal with 'vice and profaneness . . . Sabbath-breaking, whoredom . . . and other enormous crimes . . . to the great dishonour of God, scandal of government and prejudice of the peace and welfare of this country'.[12]

The ethos of the military caste simply inhibited an understanding of the subtler rhythms of compromise that were needed to achieve civil consensus, and a number of the major-generals personally struggled with their wide remits. For the Council of State, this was doubly unfortunate as it had a high expectation that its representatives would exercise a decisive influence on the outcome of the 1656 election which, it was assumed, would produce a more co-operative Protectorate parliament than the one that had assembled in 1654.

Once again, the motivation for calling the election was financial. The Assessment and Decimation Tax, both at the direct disposal of the lord protector, proved to be insufficient to pay for the regular army, the standing militia of cavalry, the navy and the cadre of salaried officials brought into being since the dissolution of the Rump. The efforts to raise income took on the appearance of desperation as the regime resorted to measures that recalled the worst finagles of the personal rule of the former monarch. With its treasury replenished by the terms of the peace treaty with the Dutch, the East India Company was prevailed upon to make a 'loan' in exchange for some emollient reassurances about the status of its charter. The Excise was extended to Scotland as a sort of quid pro quo for being brought within the beneficial terms of the Navigation Act, and the number of consumables to which it applied was increased. At the local level, the major-generals themselves came up with ruses to raise cash, with Desborough issuing 'bonds' secured against good behaviour in the south-west, but it was still not enough, and in the summer the major-generals were ordered to arm-twist a prepayment of the Assessment for the first half of 1657.

The election for the second of Cromwell's parliaments was thus a far livelier and more bad-tempered affair than the one conducted for the first. The leaky censorship arrangements of the Commonwealth had been hardened in 1655 such that now only two broadsheets had official sanction, *Mercurius Politicus* and the *Publick Intelligencer*. But in spite of the articulate toadying of Nedham, who edited both, the polls rapidly turned into a referendum on the Protectorate. In the highly charged atmosphere unauthorised pamphlets and publications, some originating from within the army itself, challenged the state's fundamental legitimacy. Henry Vane's withdrawal from front-line politics after the dissolution of the Rump had been followed by a change in the direction of his career towards that of a speculative polemicist. In his treatise *A Healing Question*, Vane brought his somewhat mystical and obscure prose style to bear on the shape of the Commonwealth, as he had done earlier on matters of religious faith. Fleetwood was so beguiled by the work with its pleasing postscript approval of the 'Good Old Cause' that he presented it to his father-in-law, but the general's naïve recommendation landed with a thud: Cromwell was neither impressed by Fleetwood's enthusiasm nor by the challenge to authority that he perceived within Vane's cobweb of argument.

The anger against the 'swordsmen' and 'decimators' was, however, palpable. The major-generals did their utmost to ensure that only supporters of the regime were returned – Boteler even went so far as to round up the most prominent electors on a remote piece of heath and to read them their 'choice' (which included himself) at the point of a sword. Acts of chicanery stopped dissenters such as Bradshaw and John Hutchinson from standing altogether and high-profile opponents such as Vane were dealt with by the simpler expedient of putting them in prison for the duration of the campaign. But others within the regime were more alert to the looming embarrassment. Goffe wrote thanks for the help he had received from Richard Cromwell 'tho he did not thinke fit to putt my name into any of the lists he gave out, yet he was so tender of my reputation, that his counsell was, that I were better not be named than receive a baffle'.[13] In the end, the number of the regime's supporters were indeed much reduced by the polls and Goffe was left to lament the success of the 'disaffected party, much to the grief of the honest party and . . . their designe to have no soldier, decemator or any man that hath salary' as their representative.[14] While all but one of the serving major-generals were returned, so too were many diehard opponents. Cromwell was furious and upbraided his officials for failing to fix the election which they themselves had persuaded him to hold against his better judgement.

17

'*I feare little will be done for the future*'

Bristol

Know assuredly that if I have an interest, I am by the voice of the People the Supreme Magistrate.

Oliver Cromwell

There was nothing practical preached or that pressed reformation of life but high and speculative points and strains that few understood, which left people very ignorant and of no steady principles.

John Evelyn, *Diary*

While Lambert had been planning the regime of the major-generals, the lord protector was occupied with the Republic's relations with the European powers. The 'Western Design' had not been accompanied by any general declaration of war against Spain, and while the majority of the Council waited with bated breath for the interception and capture of the treasure fleet which gave the expedition much of its rationale, Cromwell's attention was attracted to an issue much closer to his heart and which gave a better insight of his whole approach to foreign policy. Within France, the Waldensians had been one of the earliest of the medieval sects in Western Christendom to be persecuted for heresy, but by the seventeenth century these tenacious *devots* had become assimilated to the Calvinist tradition. Granted relief by the Edict of Nantes of Henri IV in 1598, they nonetheless co-existed in uneasy harmony among their Catholic neighbours in the mountainous areas of Savoy and the Jura that abutted Switzerland.

Although they were largely confined (by agreement) to ghettos in the uplands, by early 1655 the Catholic Duke of Savoy had determined on a campaign of brutal suppression of these proudly long-lasting Nonconformists. What followed became known as the 'Piedmont Easter'. The news of subsequent Catholic atrocities caused genuine outrage in London and elsewhere in Europe, and prompted Milton to take up his pen in the service of the persecuted in his poem 'Avenge, O Lord, thy slaughter'd saints'. It also drove Cromwell into a frenzy of diplomatic activity (the Swiss and even the Transylvanians were encouraged to stir for their co-religionists) and he contributed £2,000 of his personal wealth to the large public subscription organised for the relief of victims. The government of Louis XIV's first minister, Cardinal Mazarin, was bombarded with missives from the Council demanding action, and orders were prepared for Blake to intensify his operations against French interests in the Mediterranean by a blockade of Nice.

Beyond sincere religious sympathy, Cromwell saw the plight of Waldensians (as with the Huguenots) as a further catalyst for his grand conception of an anti-Catholic alliance across Europe in defence of the godly. Frustrated by the Dutch, who had more material priorities, the lord protector had invested more time in trying to draw in Protestant Sweden to underwrite his ambition. Until she abdicated in the summer of 1654, Sweden was ruled by the unmarried Queen Christina, daughter of Gustavus Adolphus. Intelligent, creative and wilful, the young queen ruled in uneasy partnership with her first minister, Axel Oxenstierna, who had also been regent during her minority (her father had died shortly before her sixth birthday). Rumours had circulated that the monarch entertained a chaste admiration for the Englishman whose exploits so closely resembled those of her father, albeit on a more modest scale. Certainly, Cromwell seemed happy to play the coquet, and the Whitelocke embassy had been packed off with an orchestra to woo her and her court. Later, he even sent her a miniature of himself suitably embellished with some bombastic lines by Marvell, addressed to the *Bellipotens Virgo*.[1]

But, in spite of the diplomatic fluttering of eyelashes across the North Sea and Baltic, the initiative yielded little fruit. Christina had become bored and frustrated with her own bossy male advisers and their constant importunities for her to marry, and she decided to stand down. In an elaborate ceremony of abdication and succession planned by the queen, the crown was placed on the head of Charles X, a cousin four years her senior. Of sternly martial inclination, the new king was determined to rectify what were regarded as the somewhat inadequate spoils of victory that had accrued to Sweden for its part in the Thirty Years War. In particular he was determined to get control over those territories that comprise modern Poland and to assert Swedish power over the Baltic against the irritating rivalry of Denmark. However, he was not at all interested in the sort of pan-European crusade in the mind of Cromwell, and as a crowned head he was certainly not inclined to place himself in a position of subservience or even of obligation to a republican. Mistaking the protector's overtures as a preliminary to the offer of English troops for his own dynastic ambitions, he cautiously sanctioned further discussions. As Denmark was an ally of the United Provinces, he reasoned that the English would see the benefit of fostering a good relationship with Sweden as a way of protecting its own commercial interests in the Baltic.

Thus, when his ambassador arrived at the protectoral court, there was a sense of mutual incomprehension. In any event, greater French efforts to pacify the disorders on their border with Switzerland seemed to mollify the English and steps towards a deeper rapprochement were also cemented by the overdue reaction of the government in Spain to the incursions of the English at the fringes of their empire in the New World. News of the unsuccessful attack on Hispaniola and then of the landings on Jamaica finally prompted Philip IV to recall Cárdenas and formalise the large-scale heist in the Caribbean as an act of general war. Blake, who had only recently revictualled his fleet in Spanish ports, was ordered to break off his harassment of the French and his sorties against the Muslim pirate enclaves of the North African coast (which had led to the release of many captive English mariners), and concentrate instead on preventing the Spanish from reinforcing the Caribbean. But by now Blake's command was in a poor way after a lengthy period at sea and after missing an opportunity to engage an outbound Spanish squadron off Cádiz, he brought his ships home for a badly needed refit.

Towards the end of the year, Mazarin was able to bring off a rapprochement with the Republic, which was at something of a low ebb. Blake had returned empty-handed to England only a few months after Penn and Venables had each given their versions of the fiasco in the fabled area of the Spanish Main. The country had been disturbed by royalist insurrection and the major-generals were beginning their processes of governance that were to further alienate an establishment which was far from reconciled to the *Instrument of Government*. So the commercial treaty signed in October 1655 represented something of an opportunistic triumph for the French as it would neutralise the English should they revive themselves, and brought forward the tantalising prospect that, in time, they might be induced to widen their operations against their now mutual antagonist, Spain.

Further to the agreement, each side promised not to give succour to the enemies of either state. English support to the rebels of the Fronde grouped around the Prince of Condé had never got much further than desultory talks, but on the French side, Mazarin undertook to withdraw existing support from the Stuarts. Such was the paranoia induced by Thurloe's vigilance and discoveries of widely ramified plots and designs against the regime, the closing-off of French aid for Charles might have seemed significant. But in truth, the condition of the young king was of no practical threat. Entirely dependent on the handouts of the Rhenish princes among whom they dwelt, the royal courtiers had watched with dismay as the rebellion in the spring of 1655 was snuffed out. Once more, the more aggressive amongst them were compelled to adopt the attitude of 'quiet' that had been strenuously argued by Hyde. A small glimmer of hope was seen in the summer of the following year when the Spanish co-opted the otherwise redundant monarch in the Habsburg stratagems by offering safe harbour in the Spanish Netherlands, a modest pension and the promise of men and ships should he ever be able to put together a realistic plan to regain his homeland. In the meantime, his younger brother James swapped his French commission (he had commanded a regiment of Irish volunteers under Turenne) for a Spanish one.

Marvell, Milton and even Hyde had all in their own ways imagined and extolled the anxiety that Cromwell struck into the hearts of Britain's European neighbours, but it could be argued that by the end of 1655 the Republic had seen an inadequate return on its foreign policy for the amount of resource that had been cumulatively devoted to its military capacity. It had fought and vanquished its co-religionists, the Dutch and the Scots. Rather than exercising authority in an all-Protestant European alliance, a reunified Britain had thrown itself onto the embers of the dynastic struggles of the Thirty Years War. It was now the putative ally of one Catholic power against another. Nor had the commercial advantages that went with the ownership of a powerful fleet been properly exploited.

In the new year, the Council again put its faith in the interception of a Spanish bullion convoy – the silver was badly needed. Still worried about the political reliability of the fleet, however, Edward Montagu was appointed general-at-sea (in Monck's absence), thus thwarting the ambitions of Lawson, who was highly regarded by the sailors but thought of as out of countenance with the regime. In some disgust, the admiral decided to resign his commission rather than accept a lesser command, and was followed by a number of other officers. But, by appointing the youthful aristocrat, the Council made a happy choice. By any measure, Montagu had enjoyed a meteoric rise. Born in the summer of 1625, he had been raised at Hinchingbroke which had, by coincidence, once belonged to one of Cromwell's more senior relations. From the evidence of his journals, Montagu had been praised for a quick and enquiring mind, and had served with distinction in the field, commanding a regiment at Naseby alongside Philip Skippon. Of independent spirit, he had broken with his royalist father and had raised troops for the Eastern Association before his twentieth birthday. He handed back his commission after the New Model Army's great victory and secured a seat in parliament. Although he withdrew from the Commons after the purge of late 1648, he was well-enough regarded within the army to be co-opted for Barebones and he joined the caucus that handed the Assembly's authority back to Cromwell. Although no sycophant, he was very much a favourite of the protector, and his war record, energy and intelligence were thought essential to ensure the loyalty of the much older Blake.

The naval campaign of 1656 was a frustrating affair. The refit of Blake's ships had been unsatisfactory and drawn out – the bulk of the fleet from the Caribbean had arrived back at port at around the same time, and the naval commissioners were soon struggling to pay the chandlers and shipwrights for their services which caused 'great disrepute and prejudice to the service of the navy'.[2] Taking advantage of the forced inaction, the Spanish had resumed their convoys to the New World unimpeded, and the English spent most of the spring and early summer fruitlessly sailing around southern Spain hoping to make contact with a prize worthy of the effort. Montagu soon tired of the rigmarole of having to communicate securely with London in code whilst aboard a heaving vessel, and tartly signalled Thurloe that 'I have written so much in cipher that I am wearye of it and I doubt it will cause you too much trouble . . . wherefore I shall proceede by words at length.'[3] Then, in September, the English got a break when a reconnaissance group under Richard Stayner surprised a flotilla of treasure-ships sailing unescorted towards Cádiz. In the unequal contest that resulted, an enormous haul of loot was taken and caused much excitement when the news broke at home. At last, the Protectorate had something to galvanise the loyalty of its second parliament that had just assembled at Westminster.

In the third week of September, the newly elected members arrived in London in a spirit of resolve to discover that their admission past the soldiers to the Chamber would be determined by their possession of a ticket. Once more, the Council had exercised its right to vet the intake: unlike the House that had assembled in 1654, there were now ten times as many MPs of which the regime disapproved. In addition to the Commonwealthsmen that included Hesilrige, Scot, Herbert Morley and Sir Henry Mildmay (who had served on the High Court that had tried the king, but did not sign the death warrant), a covey of crypto-royalists and Presbyterian 'neuters' such as Sir John Gore and the exotically named Sir Harbottle Grimston were all excluded. In a sign that the protectoral caucus was beginning to fragment, Anthony Ashley Cooper, who had been elected as a county MP for Wiltshire, was similarly denied his place.

Ashley Cooper had stood down from the Council unhappy with the dissolution of the first Protectorate parliament and his misgivings about the direction of the regime had hardened with the advent of the major-generals. He joined the list of over 140 MPs that were either 'excluded' or who subsequently declined to take their place in protest and it was of note that by far the higher proportion of MPs thus barred came from areas that had previously been in the forefront of the opposition to the personal rule of Charles I – half the MPs from both Lincolnshire and Kent were denied entry, as were seven of the thirteen representatives selected for Sussex. In an instance of further embarrassment, the Council even tried to exclude some of the Protestant gentry (courted so assiduously by Henry Cromwell) that made up the Irish list.

Faced with so much indignation, the lord protector distanced himself from the whole process, thereby undermining the Council. Instead, he gave a rambling address of welcome to the members which was distinguished by its combination of circumlocution, personal bathos and an almost incoherent discourse on the dangers presented by malignants and Spain, once more cast as England's 'providential' enemy. He defended too the regime of the major-generals, although the lord protector fluffed his lines when it came to account for the strain the whole exercise was placing on the Treasury. On and on he ploughed in the autumn heat of the Painted Chamber with the MPs trying to ease the pressure on their bottoms as they were held for what seemed an inordinate length of time. There was much nervous coughing and shuffling as the protector claimed for himself the role of Supreme Magistrate and exhorted the MPs to be in union with him as he pursued Christ's 'peculiar interest in the world'. To many of them, Cromwell's interpretation of what the Lord wanted for the state was too peculiar by half, while the conflation of his executive role with a higher judicial one suggested overweening ambition that had gone too far and needed restraint – perhaps the excluded Hesilrige was right?

The MPs were enthusiastic to endorse the war against Spain and did so unanimously – there was no mileage in pointing out the apparent contradiction of the alliance with Catholic France with the members in this temper – but they were far more circumspect when it came to the matter of funding it. They were happier debating the religious context for the hostilities and a new campaign was launched against Catholic 'recusants', who were ordered to take an Oath of Abjuration. If Cromwell had misgivings about this latest assault on the peaceful exercise of a religious conscience, he did not pursue them. Indeed, he had already attacked that community for its supposed loyalty to Spain in terms that suggested it was a genetic trait. He was, however, far more exercised by the case of the Quakers, one of whom was to experience the full venom of the House's hostility towards Nonconformity.

James Nayler was in his late thirties when he was hauled in front of the MPs. He had served as a quarter-master in the New Model Army before being invalided out of the army after the battle of Dunbar and had subsequently undergone a conversion while peacefully tilling his plot of land in Yorkshire. Such was the intensity of his experience, he went walkabout without even telling his wife and children. But like Fox, his itinerant campaign to spread the word of personal witness and obedience to 'the Christ within' was intoxicating to those who were inclined to question, or felt excluded by, the whole concept of an Elect. Unlike Fox, whose ingenuous spirit had so beguiled the lord protector, Nayler had a more highly developed social agenda and he produced numerous pamphlets as well as a book, *Spiritual Wickedness*, which had been published in 1653. Amongst the many injustices he perceived in society, he attacked the law as a giant racket by which the 'envious' rich took 'revenge' upon the poor and denounced the new establishment for being as greedy and self-aggrandising as its predecessors.[4] For all the talk of a regime of the godly, the people had yet to find 'the Righteous One'.

The critique was similar to that laid out by both Lilburne (who had himself become a Quaker) and Gerard Winstanley, but Nayler's religious views, as disclosed in pamphlets such as *A Public Discovery of the Open Blindness of Babel Builders*, were considered too heretical to countenance. His assertion that predestination was hogwash and that the 'inner light' was of itself sufficient for salvation was bad enough, but his denial that the Bible was the word of God caused outrage. In the late summer of 1656 the former soldier visited Fox (who had been taken into custody for stirring up the Quakers in the south-east) and was himself briefly incarcerated in turn. But despite the cautious advice of his younger colleague, Nayler treated his own release with some exuberance and bullishly staged a rally with his supporters by entering Bristol in the manner of Christ entering Jerusalem on Palm Sunday.

Intended as a bit of evangelical theatre to be enjoyed by the citizens, the Quaker was instead grabbed by the shocked local authorities and ordered before parliament accused of blasphemy. The majority of MPs were determined to make an example of a man who was considered to be the leader of this disruptive and by now national movement. They were egged on by major-generals Goffe, Whalley and Boteler, and on the Council too, Skippon urged that Nayler be executed.[5] Others among his colleagues argued for a more lenient sentence, but William Sydenham was the voice of the minority in favour of clemency, as he warned that the members' ire was contrary to justice. The punishments contemplated for Nayler were, he said, a gross breach of the liberties for which they had fought and were thus thoroughly unpatriotic. It was an uplifting formulation, but unavailing. After a lengthy inquisition, Nayler narrowly escaped a sentence of death and was ordered instead to be flogged in both London and Bristol, and for his forehead to be branded and his tongue bored. The excruciating public torture was carried out in the Advent season. After a public whipping through the streets of the city, the preacher was permitted barely a day to recover before being locked in the stocks where two assistants held his head in a vice-like grip and forced apart his jaws as the hangman plunged a red-hot poker inside his mouth before branding the unconscious Nayler below the crown of his head. It was an appalling scene of judicial barbarity as well as an act of questionable legality and Cromwell bitterly demanded to know by what authority parliament had behaved thus.

For the grounds of Sydenham's intervention did in fact obscure the more immediate political truth. The MPs had reached their verdict without the consent of the protector ('the Supreme Magistrate'), with whom they shared authority, a jurisdiction that had been reasserted in the aftermath of the Biddle case. More fundamentally, the objection to judicial power being exercised by those who also made the rules had been one of the main planks of the opposition to Charles I's regime, an issue also skilfully exploited by the early Leveller movement in its campaign against the House of Lords as the royal apex of authority crumbled. The case also reopened the issue of the imposition of Protestant orthodoxy at a time when the settlement mandated by the *Instrument of Government* was showing progress in taking some of the heat out of the debate about the national Church. Nayler's treatment had a personally depressing effect too on the lord protector, whose physical powers and morale were waning.

Cromwell was by now spiritually and physically debilitated. Brought low by the death of his mother and the illness through cancer of a favourite daughter, he was afflicted by gout, stones, boils and the fevers of the lingering ailments he had contracted while on campaign: unbeknownst to any, but perhaps suspected by some, he had less than two years to live. He had laboured, by his lights mostly in vain, for toleration within the broadening and highly diverse Protestant communion but had been unable to surmount the dogmatism of the establishment or the self-righteousness of the sects. To him, the stewards of the state were behaving no better than those unblinking zealots of the Kirk with whom he had had to contend for over a decade. The sects were as inflexible, individually insisting that their version of revealed truth was the only right one.

Most notably Fox, whose character despite his gentle philosophy also contained a strand of intolerance, had opposed the plan to settle a new university at Durham. Intended as a modest diversification within an educational establishment monopolised by Oxford and Cambridge, Fox urged rejection of Durham on the grounds that it would extend the university system as a way to train men for the official ministry, of which the Quakers disapproved. Yet away from the radicals and amongst the conservatively inclined, Cromwell's approach had met a mood of exasperation – the protector seemed wedded to the idea of a national Church, but his sympathy towards the Nonconformists simply undermined it. To these men, the protector's attempts at conciliation had alarming ramifications: if men were allowed to believe and to act as they saw fit in matters of personal faith, they might question the law, property and the whole social construct.

The war with Spain and accompanying outburst of moralistic fervour at least drew parliament's attention away from the major-generals. The regime of Lucy Hutchinson's 'silly mean fellows' continued, but the Council concluded that the settlement of their financial position should no longer be delayed – after all, that was the primary reason why the parliament had been recalled one year earlier than stated in the rubric of the *Instrument of Government*. On another working Christmas Day and exploiting a House that was denuded of many members who were away experiencing yet another season without celebration, Desborough craftily introduced a Militia Bill. The measure was designed to give permanency to the Decimation Tax and the general attempted to sweeten the pill by suggesting that it might be offset (and thus be better targeted against the regime's enemies) by a reduction of the Excise.

Desborough had in fact argued that the Decimation Tax be higher still but was overruled by more cautious colleagues. In the event, the proposal (to which was appended a clause indemnifying the major-generals for past actions) achieved a modest majority on the thinly attended benches for its first reading, with over eighty MPs voting in favour. But as more of the members drifted back from their localities, resistance to the measure began to harden. There was widespread aversion to any tax based on property – the Excise was irksome, but at least its regressive nature gave some relative protection to the better-off – and opponents expressed scepticism about giving carte-blanche to the regime with an Act of Indemnity. There was too a new-found enthusiasm for the Act of Oblivion, of which the Decimation Tax was a clear breach.

The numerous lawyers on the benches stirred with indignation. John Glyn had been one of the eleven members forced out by the New Model Army in 1647 and had briefly suffered imprisonment in the Tower while his colleagues fled. But he had managed to survive the Council's screening processes such that he sat in both the first and second Protectorate parliaments for a Welsh constituency. A well-regarded jurist, his and others' doubts about the Militia Bill were allowed an airing by Sir Thomas Widdrington, a fellow lawyer who had recently been appointed as the new Speaker. These arguments gathered sway and were publicly supported too by those with more acutely attuned antennae such as Broghill and the self-interested weathervane, Bulstrode Whitelocke.

As with other contentious measures previously before the House, the arguments both for and against were couched in references to Scripture with the Exeter MP Thomas Bampfield warning that in overturning the Act of Oblivion, the MPs risked the famine visited upon the Israelites when King Saul broke his treaty with the Gideonites: 'We have sworn unto them by the Lord God of Israel – now therefore we may not touch them.'[6] The measure was just as firmly supported by the regime's architects, with Lambert insisting that recent events and the perfidy of the Stuarts (now in alliance with Spain) showed that the royalists were irreconcilable. Others argued that leniency towards royalists would only dishearten the godly. But as the debate reconnected with the actions of some of those major-generals for whom the tax was supposed to provide the funding, tempers became more heated, with two of Cromwell's close relatives publicly admitting their lack of enthusiasm for Lambert's brainchild.

In the middle of these deliberations, Thurloe attempted to trump the sceptics by revealing that a plot against the life of the protector had been foiled. In a conspiracy involving the former army agitator Edmund Sexby, a zealous royalist called Miles Sindercombe had planned to gun down Cromwell and Lambert on their way to open the parliament. Thwarted by the heavy presence of the military around the precincts of Westminster Hall on the day, the desperados had resorted to a plan to blow up Whitehall (with the first citizen in it) as an alternative. Accordingly, an unfeasibly large quantity of tar and explosives was to be smuggled into the palace past the huge security detail and detonated as Cromwell was settling himself on the floor above. Once again, some of the principals got cold feet and the plot was betrayed. The sense of relief in the establishment seemed quite genuine (a service of thanksgiving was ordered), and Cromwell himself was gruffly moved by the obvious concern for his well-being. Sindercombe however, showed no contrition and took poison rather than face the gruesome and lingering death that was prescribed for convicted traitors.

On 29 January 1657, the Council's Militia Bill came to the decisive vote. Over a hundred MPs chose discretion as the better part of valour and failed to appear, a worryingly high rate of abstention amongst those whose credentials had been endorsed by the Protectorate's vetting processes. Thus, by a vote of 124 to 88, the Bill was defeated, although the following day the members separately voted for £400,000 to be raised by way of a general tax to finance operations against Spain. It was a significant reversal and there was a sense that the Protectorate had perhaps reached an existential moment of truth. Thurloe wrote anxiously to Henry Cromwell of the vote that 'the truth is, it hath wrought such a heate in the house, that I feare little will be done for the future'.[7]

For the sum voted was an inadequate increment and the financial plank under the major-generals, if not completely removed, had at least been withdrawn by several feet. To insist that the tax be collected now without the authorisation of parliament would negate one of the main reasons for taking on the Stuart regime in the first place. Cromwell took the news pretty calmly and expressed disappointment that Desborough and his colleagues had risked such a vote of confidence when the major-generals had seemed, on the face of it, to be set fair. But the vote revealed a perceptible hardening of the sense among the more conservatively and moderately inclined that things would have to change if the state was to achieve a durable settlement between the civil and military castes.

18

'A feather in a hat'

Hampton Court

The Providence of God which governs the World
has so ordered it that England is returned into a
Commonwealth. Do what you can, you cannot make
it otherwise.

Sir Arthur Hesilrige

Who made thee a Prince and a judge over us? If God
made thee, make it manifest to us. If the people, where
did we meet to do it? Who took out subscriptions? To
whom deputed we our authority?

William Allen

In the autumn of 1656 as the parliament had been reassembling,
the censors seized from a printer in London a book entitled *The
Commonwealth of Oceana*. Its author was James Harrington, a well-
to-do, middle-aged Northamptonshire gentleman whose life to
that point seems to have been that of a well-travelled dilettante. As
a member of those local gentry who had extended a welcome to
Charles I during his stay at Holdenby, he had been honoured to serve
a brief spell as a groom of the bedchamber to the former monarch.

Harrington seems to have baulked when asked to be an informer for the king's enemies and he was relieved of his duties as the army's custody of its Stuart prisoner became more beadily intrusive. In the intervening years he devoted himself to the serious consideration of political philosophy, of which *Oceana* was the product.

Unlike the speculations of Milton and Vane, which had a metaphysical character, Harrington's work seemed firmly rooted in the present and indeed reflected a number of practical ideas that had already been developed by the Levellers and Diggers, as well as by those like Algernon Sydney, who had developed their own alternative to the monarchical model of governance through their opposition to its Stuart variant. It also provided a humanist challenge to the authoritarian agenda of *Leviathan*.[1] Harrington's republicanism was the logical consequence of his most arresting insight, which was that the wider dispersion of landed property (which had accelerated with the wholesale confiscation of Church lands coincident with the English Reformation) had rendered the feudal system and the monarchy obsolete as methods of both social organisation and government.[2] This pleasing historical justification for the champions of the Commonwealth ensured a wide readership once the book had passed the censors after the direct intervention of Cromwell's daughter, Elizabeth Claypole.

To Harrington, the form of a country's governance should be matched to the patterns of ownership within it, although he concluded that such landed wealth be capped lest its reaggregation in the hands of a few magnates led to a return of a system of monarchical government which reflected the more concentrated holdings of the Middle Ages. He recommended that wealth over a certain threshold be distributed to its owner's children. But just as the wars had thrown up the New Model Army, so too must England have a new model government. The foundation of this was to be a senate and assembly sitting in permanent session and chosen (by rotation) in secret ballots by men of property. This concept of a new Elect chosen by reasons of wealth, probity and disinterestedness (Harrington was highly critical of the subversive influence of patronage) rather than just religious integrity also appealed to the more ecumenical and secular-minded among the Commonwealthsmen. Less radically, he also urged that the state should be defended by a militia composed of citizens rather than by a professional standing army. But in its articulate defence of many existing assumptions, his thesis was more of a comfortable slap on the back for fellow civilian republicans than a call for action.

Although Harrington was able to attract a coterie of like-minded intellectuals, so that in time he was to form a political society known as the Rota, his impact on the immediate political debate is less easy to judge. In at least one sense (his attitude to monarchical authority), he was completely wide of the mark. The regime of the major-generals had been dealt a serious but not quite mortal blow by the vote against the Militia Bill and there formed a stronger consensus that only by offering the crown to Cromwell could a 'government according to the ancient constitution' be restored and the 'exorbitancies' of the military be curtailed. Although the narrative gives due weight to those parliamentarians and sceptics such as St John (now Chancellor of Cambridge University), and the legal experts Widdrington, Glyn and Whitelocke who pushed through the agenda, it was paradoxically given a hefty shove by members of the inner Protectorate establishment including Wolseley, Montagu, Broghill, Colonel Philip Jones and Nathaniel Fiennes.

By 23 February 1657 this caucus, into which Broghill marshalled a majority of the Irish and Scottish MPs, was sufficiently organised to enable its stalking horse Sir Christopher Packe, a city grandee and ex-Lord Mayor, to present a remonstrance to the House.[3] The impact on the professional soldiers of the imminence of a 'King Oliver' was immediate, and a delegation of London-based members of the Council of Officers anxiously demanded an interview with the lord protector. Four days after Packe's speech they were joined by Desborough, Lambert and Fleetwood in Cromwell's private chambers where took place one of the pivotal meetings of the republican era. In reaction to the soldiers' assumption that he was minded to take the ermine, Cromwell rallied himself and exploded. The crown was no more than a title, a 'feather in a hat', and anyway had not Lambert and others urged him to take it in the past? As he warmed to his theme, the army grandees were angrily denounced for serially mucking things up. They had insisted on the dissolution of the Rump, the farrago of the Nominated Assembly and more recently had completely messed up the elections. He was sick and tired of their endless whinging and moaning, and fed up too with being the army's 'drudge'.[4]

It was a bravura performance. There was no one else in that company with the same prestige and authority within the military and Lambert's experiment had arguably come to a dead-end. Neither the higher-ranking Desborough nor Fleetwood had the stature to challenge Cromwell's self-serving tirade, and may anyway have been inhibited by their familial ties to him. The winning side of the wars had tried every which-way to achieve a consensus around various constitutional models, but all had been presented on the point of a sword and each had floundered. As the Somerset MP John Ashe had argued, only adherence to the 'ancient constitution' could ensure stability within norms that had been successfully imposed upon Charles I, while by taking the crown Cromwell would cut the ground from beneath the Stuarts' feet.

If in their dressing-down the army's magnates had been metaphorically ordered back to barracks, Cromwell's eruption nonetheless contained an ambiguity with which he was personally to wrestle for the next few months as the 'kingship' caucus pursued its initiative. On the one hand, the proposals had much to commend them. To the remonstrance of Sir Christopher Packe was added further flesh in the form of the *Humble Petition and Advice*. Aside from a return to monarchy, the MPs also abandoned the form of a unicameral parliament with a proposal for a second chamber to be known as the 'Other House'. This was to consist of up to seventy notables, appointed by the protector and subject to the approval of the Commons, a stipulation that was later dropped. Here was a version of Harrington's senate which Cromwell was strongly minded to accept as a bulwark against the more intolerant impulses that had been revealed in parliament's treatment of James Nayler. For, as he had reminded the officers in their meeting of 27 February, the vindictiveness shown in the Quaker's case could just as easily be applied to the Nonconformists among the soldiers.

Here too was a plausible model of governance that crucially seemed to command the support of the civilians. The political objections of the high command could be discounted and were further whittled away as the *Humble Petition* was debated. Boteler led a rearguard action against the Bill for the major-generals and was supported with diminishing levels of enthusiasm by other senior officers who may each have come to see the constitutional point of the Other House, and may have contemplated their membership of it as a suitable reward for their past military contribution and civic efforts. The impressionable Fleetwood was seen to waver – perhaps the *Humble Petition* could be seen as part of God's providence too? Whalley also spoke up for the proposals in the House. The intermediate ranks had been purged of radicals at various intervals in the past; however, the sense that the 'Good Old Cause' was about to be betrayed was enough to galvanise a petition under Colonel Pride's name which also bore the signature of Desborough and 'Cromwell's Bishop', John Owen. The opposition of his protégé, vice chancellor of Oxford and architect of the Church settlement, was a particular disappointment to Cromwell, but the republican in Owen was likely motivated by a sense that the congregationalism which he championed would be placed in jeopardy by a restored monarchy's drive for conformity once the lord protector had passed away.

But on the issue of the title of king, as recorded by Thurloe, the lord protector was assailed by uncharacteristic paroxysms of doubt. The greatest impediment to his acceptance of the crown was most likely his own faith, which was reflected in a good many of his fellow officers. Had not God by his own providence decisively swept away the monarchical form? For a man whose political outlook was highly coloured by his knowledge of and reverence for the Bible, the meaning of the Book of Joshua seemed clear enough. To take on the title of king would invite the most awful punishment not only on himself but on the nation. He had been led by the Lord from his downcast existence in the Fens to be the most exalted in the land. How could he now assert his own will against that of his Maker? Notwithstanding this, the parliamentarians were determined and had made the protector's acceptance of the royal title and office a condition of the package as whole – he could accept all of it, or nothing. Wolseley had personally cajoled him – surely the people could call him what they liked, it was just a name? But he could not be forced to be king, even though the offer had been leavened with an inducement that he could appoint his own successor. For months the *Humble Petition* went back and forth but even at the eleventh hour, Thurloe was unable to predict the outcome.

As the moment of his personal decision drew near, the senior commanders about London once again urged him to abjure the title but all were conscious that their careers and religious sensibilities, and those of the men they commanded, rose or fell with Cromwell. But the protector also knew that such a fundamental change would be too divisive at a time when there was a pressing need for discipline and cohesion. The garrison in Jamaica had had to be serially reinforced as disease continued to carry away those who landed on the island. The Spanish had sent more troops to try to dislodge the invaders, but the Council considered that the island was too important a base from which to try to intercept the Spanish bullion fleets sailing through the Caribbean. It had to be held. Of greater significance, the commercial agreement with France had been hardened by a pact under which the Protectorate had agreed to provide troops to assist them in their operations against their Habsburg rivals in the Spanish Netherlands. For its part, Mazarin's government agreed to cede Dunkirk to the English once it had been captured, and to pay for the expeditionary force in the meantime. The strategic value of having a secure port on the other side of the Channel had been well established and the operation was approached with enthusiasm. Six thousand men were organised to take part, a large proportion of the home army's establishment.

The substantial force was placed under the command of Sir James

Reynolds, an experienced New Model soldier whose personal loyalty to Cromwell was unquestioned. His flirtation with radicalism as an army agitator and Leveller sympathiser had been brief and he played an important part in the suppression of the mutinies of 1649. He also led the advance party of Cromwell's campaign in Ireland and had taken part in the defeat of Ormonde at the battle of Rathmines. Reynolds proved himself to be as able a logistician as a fighting soldier, and was appointed as a senior commissary as well as being granted lands in Ireland at the campaign's end. Making use of the opportunities for speculative gain from the issue of debentures over titles to land that were issued to the victorious troops in lieu of pay, he managed to accumulate a substantial portfolio in the south-east of the country. His connection to the kinship group that surrounded the protector was cemented when his marriage made him a brother-in-law to Henry Cromwell and, as an elected MP for Waterford, he adhered to that part of the 'kingship' caucus organised by Broghill.

The position of commanders like Reynolds and Whalley, councillors like Jones, and the enigmatic agnosticism of others like Monck, show that the cheerleaders for the 'Good Old Cause' amongst the upper reaches of the professional army were not as powerful or as well supported as has sometimes been suggested. The attitude of the sailors was less easy to gauge and while Montagu's were reliable hands, they were fully engaged in the difficult task of getting supplies to the fleet as the financial position of the regime deteriorated. Blake, the Commonwealth's own titan, was still campaigning against the Spanish at sea. Over the winter months he had kept up his blockade of their fighting fleet in Cádiz while awaiting another opportunity to intercept a bullion-laden convoy from the New World. His ships and crew were showing the strains and the admiral was laid low by both the most excruciating kidney stones and the poorly healed injuries he had sustained against the Dutch. But in another spectacular engagement in April 1657, his fleet cornered an incoming convoy in the Canaries and completely destroyed it. The news came through as the protector was mulling over the *Humble Petition*. The victory, however, was a pyrrhic one: the Spanish commander managed to get most of the silver ashore before his galleons went up in flames, and the desperate and unpaid English sailors were left to argue amongst themselves over the scraps of their meagre 'prize'. A disappointed and exhausted Blake continued his patrols before returning with his clapped-out vessels in the summer: he died in the Channel within sight of land but his exploits had arguably brought a decisive end to Spanish naval power.

Whatever Cromwell's religious scruples, with the Republic militarily engaged it did not seem like the time to be taking risks with the establishment of a monarchy, and in early May the protector attempted to make it clear that whilst he would accept nearly all the particulars of the *Humble Petition*, he would not take the crown. As was becoming increasingly common with his civic pronouncements, his decision was clouded by obfuscation – he would, he said 'rather have any name from this Parliament than any other name without it'. For the 'kingship' caucus however, his decision was a humiliating reversal and arguably destroyed the one chance that Cromwell had to build a much larger political grouping among the elite that would have shortened the odds of the regime surviving beyond his death. His refusal of both the title and office of king condemned the state to a perpetuation of a republican military government that more and more of the establishment regarded as, at best, anomalous. The frustrated and disenchanted MPs reworked and debated the *Humble Petition* in ever diminishing numbers before presenting the new protectoral constitution to Cromwell on 25 May 1657, a settlement he accepted.

A month later, he was reinstalled in an elaborate ceremony at Westminster Hall that was a coronation in all respects save for the absence of a crown and the oil of divine anointment. The Chair of State on which had been enthroned every monarch since Edward II was dragged out of its corner in Westminster Abbey, complete with the Stone of Scone. The lord protector sat on it in a great purple cloak trimmed with ermine. Lambert's regime was now thoroughly compromised by the *Humble Petition* and in deference to the new constitution's origins, the Speaker took on the role of master of ceremonies. The Earl of Warwick was honoured to bear the Sword of State – the betrothal of his grandson to Cromwell's youngest daughter Frances reunited this distinguished public servant with the ruling regime and the lord protector may have hoped that his presence would act as a magnet to those well-affected members of the aristocracy whom he hoped to lure back to the Other House. Viscount Lisle, Montagu and Whitelocke also performed highly visible roles in a ceremony designed to emphasise the endorsement of parliament, a dynamic that had been noticeably lacking in the first investiture during the winter of 1653.

In the second week of July, as Cromwell's mind was diverted by the happier circumstances of the impending marriages of two of his daughters, Lambert came to his private chambers formally to tender his resignation. The two generals sat together uneasily reminiscing about old times, but really the character of the meeting was that between a headmaster whose attention to what was taking place in school was diminishing and a head-boy who had had enough. The personal relationship between the two men had become strained, and the younger may have felt thwarted by the elder's want of energy in cementing the original protectoral regime about which he had once seemed so enthusiastic. Lambert was likely alienated too by Cromwell's increasing reliance on a smaller inner circle of familial 'courtiers', from which he felt excluded. While united by their professionalism in war, they had been unable to make that shared experience work as successfully while the state struggled to find an enduring peace.

The *Humble Petition* had changed the fundamental principle of the *Instrument of Government* because the primacy of rule by a Council whose membership could not be directly challenged by parliament and in whose hands resided the power to appoint the protector, had now been replaced. Personal ambition may also have played a part in Lambert's démarche. His chance of succeeding Cromwell seemed to be waning, notwithstanding that the right of the protector to name his successor had not been given on the basis that the position was to be hereditary. The meeting of late February and the protector's protracted deliberations about the *Humble Petition* had revealed Cromwell's disenchantment with the constitutional arrangements of which he, Lambert, was the author. Although Thurloe had worried that Lambert would 'push the Army towards a distemper', the junior general had been negligent by not building a wider constituency of supporters for himself beyond his acolytes in the military and a small grouping of Yorkshire MPs in the House. Now, he was amongst the minority on the Council too. A proud and ambitious man with a streak of vanity, he signalled his disapproval by quixotically refusing to take the Oath of Allegiance that had been appended to the rubric of the *Humble Petition*. Cromwell was unimpressed by this haughtily paraded pang of conscience, but the two agreed that Lambert be spared the fate of Harrison and so was allowed to withdraw with dignity. His military commands were forfeited but he was granted a generous pension and retained his appointment as Commissioner to the new university at Durham. Once again, Lambert had cast himself into political exile and soon afterwards the Council of Officers pledged loyalty to their chief.

John Evelyn had returned from his own exile in 1652. His diary provides a vivid record of the rhythms of life under the shadow of the Republic as the aesthete sought out intellectual stimulation and the consolations of the sacraments. As a known royalist, he nonetheless seemed to enjoy considerable freedom of movement, and appeared untroubled by the vigilance of Thurloe's network of spies and the financial repression suffered by so many of his fellow sympathisers – indeed, he performed some minor public duties in London and his wealth held up sufficiently for him to support his relatives and to subscribe to the stock of the East India Company. By his own assertion, he passed on whatever useful titbits came his way through the royalist networks and he was certainly well connected, his circle of acquaintance including two senior members of the regime, Viscount Lisle and Sir Charles Wolseley.

As with many royalists, he seemed resigned to the likely permanency of the regime of 'usurpers' and 'rebels', but was hardly reconciled to it. He chafed, like so many others, at the impositions of an irregularly paid military establishment that continued to make use of free quarter and intrusive billeting arrangements; on May Day 1657, his home was overrun with soldiers on their way to fight in Flanders. But what really disturbed his sense of equilibrium and prompted almost feelings of dread was the climate of novelty, self-righteousness and ill-temper that had gripped the public debate about matters of faith. On a regional tour in 1656, he found the dilapidated remains of Colchester 'swarming in sectaries' and could not resist the thrill of viewing some hunger-striking Quakers imprisoned in Ipswich, 'a new fanatic sect of dangerous principles, they show no respect to any man, magistrate or other and seem a melancholy proud sort of people'.[5] Everywhere, 'blasphemous and ignorant mechanics' had usurped the pulpits and his own Church of England had been 'reduced to a chamber and conventicle, so sharp was the persecution'. On Christmas Day 1657, his peaceable celebration of the Saviour's birth was broken up by angry soldiers.

As the religious hysteria whipped up by the war against Spain had gathered strength, Evelyn was so concerned at being mistaken for a Roman Catholic that he reluctantly submitted himself to a service conducted by a Presbyterian, and was perhaps surprised to find that he was not further scandalised as the minister 'was as I understood duly ordained and preached sound doctrine after their way and besides was a humble, harmless and peaceable man'.[6] The diary is full of instances of Evelyn otherwise observing the Anglican rite wherever he could and he showed no awareness of conflict between his growing interest in scientific enquiry and his yearning for a well-presented sermon evoking man's condition founded on Scripture. In London, as elsewhere, many were determined that the old certainties provided by the Book of Common Prayer continued to survive if not flourish, even at the cost of arrest, fines and possible imprisonment.

Evelyn's witness perhaps shows the limits of toleration under the Protectorate. The claims that the regime mandated a genuine easing of repression of those outside the Protestant communion in England are often based on highly selective instances which are further extrapolated as signs of ecumenism. One of the most famous was the so-called 'readmission' of the Jews to England, centuries after their medieval expulsion by Edward I. On the same day that the rule of the major-generals was proclaimed, the chief rabbi of Amsterdam presented a petition on behalf of his co-religionists at Whitehall. Mennaseh Ben Israel was of Portuguese origin and had met and attracted Thurloe while the latter was taking part in St John's ill-fated mission to the United Provinces in 1651. The later interest shown in him by the protector's regime is attributed to his perceived value as a source of commercial intelligence because of his close association with the Dutch financial class. Ben Israel's motives seem to have been more chiliastic in their nature. In his overture to the Council, he praised the 'tender heart' of the people of the Republic and proclaimed his conviction that the time was plainly right for England to complete the diaspora foretold in the Book of Deuteronomy by readmitting the Jews.

His cause was taken up by Whalley and Hugh Peter and he was interviewed by Cromwell, who was charmed by his reverential demeanour (the rabbi apparently poked the protector to assure himself that he was in fact mortal) and persuaded by his great Scriptural learning. Given the scrupulous attention that the pious gave to the Old as much as to the New Testament, the reassimilation of a Jewish community would seem to have been long overdue; but as even Marvell speculated in his poem 'To his Coy Mistress', their conversion seemed impossibly remote, and Ben Israel was to die in 1657 with his hopes unfulfilled. The Council was less impressed by the petition's line of argument than had been the protector. Quite apart from the mercantile jealousy which the Jews attracted was their much more serious denial of the divinity of Christ. It was simply not politic to formally endorse such an antithetical belief system while the regime was busy quashing Quakers, Unitarians, Ranters and Fifth Monarchists. Ever alert to further deviation, the pen of Prynne was quickly deployed to drip unfriendly ink. Thus the 'readmission' was far from being a settled state policy and later came about almost by accident when a London merchant of Iberian descent called Antonio Robles was deprived of his property at the outbreak of war with Spain. Robles appealed and was vindicated, not because he was a Jew but rather because he proved he was not a Spaniard. On such slender threads, the Jews were eventually able to climb back to a licit place in British society.

In spite of his apparent sympathy towards Protestant Nonconformity, Cromwell never dismissed parliament on account of religious difference and as time went on, his disenchantment with the sects and anxiety about the threat that they presented to public peace became more pronounced. In Scotland, where the authorities were particularly sensitive to anything that might stir native unrest, the New Model officer Colonel Daniell wrote Monck a haughty letter that nonetheless revealed a growing exasperation that a number of the citizenry, and of his fellow officers, were being taken in by these heretical charlatans. 'But really my Lord I believe it may be said of this generation of stupid Scottish people as was said by the Apostle . . . that their [Quaker] words doth eat as a canker drawing men, especially where zeal and ignorance concur, to a contempt of authority and neglect of their duty and drawing the minds of many honest soldiers into such a careless frame . . .'[7]

Widespread enthusiasm such as that for the Quakers was subject to harassment and repression, and the Fifth Monarchy movement too was driven underground by the regime's successive purges of the army and gaoling of its civil and military leaders. A Fifth Monarchy plot organised by a London artisan called Thomas Venner had been easily foiled by the work of Thurloe's agents, and while Fox may have enchanted the protector, he still spent many months behind bars with large numbers of his confederates. Cromwell raged against the MPs' desires to 'pinch' other men's consciences but, once installed as protector, his interventions in individual cases, such as those of John Biddle, James Nayler and the Roman Catholic priest John Southworth, were both rare and curiously ineffectual. Unlike Henry Marten, whose defence of Nonconformity was based upon natural justice and even embraced the papists, Cromwell's more narrowly focused sense of toleration withered as the exigencies of office took hold. Independency was not, after all, to be the rubric at the core of the national Church.

A discordant religious climate and straitened economic circumstances did not make for a flourishing cultural scene. Notwithstanding the increasing evidence of a distinctly monarchical rhythm that was observed about his person at Whitehall and Hampton Court, the protector (who was now making more use of the distinctly royal plural in official papers) fell well short of the patronage that his predecessor had lavished on high culture, in particular the visual arts.[8] The development of music for the public sphere was arrested by both the closure of places of entertainment and by the trashing of those sanctuaries of the English aural tradition that had taken place during the wars. The cathedrals were in a very sorry state indeed. Attention was drawn to the 'music and frolic' attending the lighter domestic moments of the protectoral court, but the arrangements produced by David Mell and his little band of musicians inherited from the Stuart household had less to do with a conscious desire to encourage musical composition than with the insouciant sense that it hardly seemed worth booting them out onto the street.

More effort went into the architectural aesthetic, the sign of a desire on the part of those who had benefited from the recent and substantial changes in the ownership of land to leave a visible mark on their augmented property. In the Midlands survive some of the finest examples of the 'Commonwealth style', including Oliver St John's residence of Thorpe Hall on the outskirts of Peterborough that was designed and built by the talented artisan Peter Mills. Thurloe employed his skills for his rather less lovely restoration of Wisbech Castle, whose battered remains the Council secretary had acquired in the aftermath of the wars. Inigo Jones was considered to be of sufficiently Puritan sensibility for his legacy to be evolved by the likes of his pupil John Webb, who completed work for existing magnates of the winning side such as the Earls of Pembroke and

Northumberland. He redesigned too the magnificent Gunnersby House in Ealing for John Maynard, an astute Presbyterian lawyer and early critic of the king who had later defended George Cony and who was one of the leading lights of the 'kingship' caucus of the second Protectorate parliament. But the restoration and remodelling was eventually reduced to a trickle when the hard-up regime instituted a tax on new building work.

It was really the evolution and usage of the written word for which the period is most noted. The poets Cowley and Davenant experimented with the familiar metrics of their medium and the legacy bequeathed by John Donne, while Davenant is also credited with the *Siege of Rhodes*, the first English opera. Both men were royalists and endured exile at the end of the wars, but whereas Cowley favoured stoicism and the serene acceptance of his lot whether in Paris or on his return to England, the poet laureate was a man of action combined with a high sexual energy – his indiscriminate attentions had left him with a badly disfigured face, the consequence of a botched experimental treatment for venereal disease.[9] Davenant had accepted a commission from the new king to shore up the royalist cause in Maryland in the New World and had set sail with a crew of desperados from Jersey in early 1650. Captured at sea and instantly recognisable by his grotesque and nose-less countenance, he was put on trial for his life, but his roguish antics and obvious talent attracted the sympathetic attentions of Henry Marten, who argued for leniency.

He was to spend much time in custody but the enforced stasis allowed Davenant to complete *Gondibert*, an epic of love, struggle and heroism written for an epoch that could not seemingly get enough of such works, but which was bested in the canon of the period by Milton's later masterpieces, *Paradise Lost* and *Samson Agonistes*. The Republican poets were to suffer much opprobrium when the political and religious ground was later cut from under their feet, and the reputations of both Milton and John Dryden suffered from a perception that they had sacrificed their art in the service of an unnatural regime. The new laureate, Thomas Shadwell, was to spitefully lampoon his predecessor when he fell from grace by digging up Dryden's earlier collaboration:

> The next steps of advancement you began,
> Was being close to Noll's Lord Chamberlain,
> A Sequestor and a Committee man!
> There all your wholesome morals you suk't in
> And got your gentile gaiety and mien
> Your loyalty you learn'd at Cromwell's court
> Where first your muse did make her great effort.[10]

But in truth returning royalist poets were equally able to trim their sails to put food on the table and Cowley was as happy directing encomia to Cromwell as he was to Charles.

Milton's literary purpose remained firmly rooted in his faith, although he deprecated the narrow-minded intolerance of the sects as much as he had earlier deplored the dogmatism of the Calvinists. He saw that words were becoming 'agents of corruption' and in *Samson Agonistes* he urged the pious man simply to submit himself to the 'unsearchable' wisdom of God rather than assert his own interpretation of the Almighty's providences. In 1657 he handed over his duties as Latin secretary to the Council to Andrew Marvell. The poet from the Humber was more interested in worldly affairs than in generating a reputation as a wordsmith, but he astutely foresaw the fatigue that would set in with religion being used as the primary means of public discourse. His poetry was later noted for the ambiguity with which it treated the common themes of love, duty, piety and desire, a style that hinted at the time to come when categorical and public expression of matters of faith would be frowned upon as once they had been celebrated.

Yet perhaps the most significant change was the transmission of the written vernacular in the explosions of pamphlets, news-sheets and manifestos that proliferated during the period. This appears more remarkable still when considering the conditions of censorship that prevailed throughout the period. The connection of literature

with the demotic had been achieved with Tyndale's English translation of the Bible in the early sixteenth century, but it was really
the dynamic of the civil wars and their troubled aftermath that
drove the written word beyond the pens of the clerisy and of those
writers, proselytisers and dramatists whose more natural audiences
had been found among the well-to-do, the ministry and the court.
Barely a generation separated the publication of *The Faerie Queene*
from the pamphleteers of the mid-seventeenth century, but the
distance between the ornate high-Elizabethan of Spenser's paean to
human virtue and the articulate and easily assimilated outpourings
of the London presses known to Lilburne and his companions was
profound.

Able and articulate women were constrained by the scholastic
tradition if they were to be taken seriously as writers and Lucy
Hutchinson was celebrated for her translation of *De Rerum Natura*
by Lucretius. But her journal, along with the contemporary poems
of the 'matchless Orinda' and Aphra Behn, were written in a style,
and the verses with a clarity, that would arguably have had far wider
resonance with their contemporary citizens than that achieved by
the obscure and courtly language of many of their predecessors. A
skilled if acerbic diarist, Hutchinson also produced powerful verse in
her own right, and in her love poem to her deceased husband, 'To
the Garden at Owthorpe', she achieved one of the most haunting
and affecting pieces of the era:

> But could I call back hasty flying time
> The vanished glories that once decked my prime
> To one that resurrection would be vaine
> And like ungathered flowers would die again
> In vaine would doting time, which can no more
> Give such a lover, Loveliness restore.[11]

Away from Marvell's and Hutchinson's preoccupation with the
garden as a motif for their innermost thoughts, politically inspired
tracts achieved a level of sophistication and attention that was not

really exceeded until the latter years of the eighteenth century. In Tom Paine's *Rights of Man* can be found a powerful echo of both the style and content of his forebears. The same demotic energy and learning that he focused in defence of the liberties fought for in both the American and French revolutions can be experienced in an extraordinary pamphlet that appeared at about the time of the 'kingship' debates in the second Protectorate parliament. Entitled *Killing Noe Murder*, it was attributed to a radical called William Allen, although the former army agitator Sexby was also believed to have had a hand in its authorship. As with the arch and witty polemic that Paine aimed at his antagonist Edmund Burke in 1791, so too with *Killing Noe Murder* the writers' purpose was ultimately serious. Identifying the Protectorate as a tyranny, Allen appealed to the soldiery to return to that purpose for which they were originally raised. All tyrannies claimed divine sanction, for 'They pretend inspiration from Gods and responses from Oracles to authorise what they do, his Highness hath ever been an enthusiast. And as Hugh Capet in taking the crown pretended to be admonished to it in a dream by St Valery and St Richard, so I believe will his Highness do the same at the instigation of St Henry and St Richard his two sons.'

Drawing inspiration from Aristotle and the Roman Republic, the tract offered a *post facto* justification for the attempted assassination of Cromwell by Sindercombe; it quoted the Valerian law of Rome which had prescribed that 'who so ever took Magistracy upon him without the command of the people, it was lawful for any man to kill him'. Cromwell seemed to take the ornately argued incitement to end his life in his stride, but shortly afterwards Sexby was captured and thrown into the Tower. There, his last desperate energy was spent dashing out his brains against the damp and unyielding walls of his confinement as he took his own life.

The target of their denunciation now spent more time in the congenial atmosphere and surroundings of Hampton Court. Here, security of the protector's person was more easily achieved. The tone set within the household overseen by Sir Gilbert Pickering would attract much later mockery when the counter-culture of the

Restoration was at its height, but the court physician George Bate (by no means an uncritical observer) offered a fairer assessment of its dynamic when he wrote, 'Men's manners also at least outwardly seemed to be reformed to the better, whether by really subtracting the fuel of luxury, or through fear of ancient laws now revived and put in execution.' If this hinted at a job half-done, it also suggested a regime beset by intellectual exhaustion.[12]

The civilians behind the *Humble Petition* had moved the boundaries of governance more generally. Although the regime of the major-generals was nominally still in place, financial reality ensured that local government was dispersed once more into the hands of those unpaid men of 'quality' who had exercised it in the past. The ending of the Decimation Tax and official resurrection of the monarchical idea suggested too that the antagonism towards constitutional royalists abate. The regime was still badly in arrears and the financial settlement scoped by the *Humble Petition* was, after consideration of inflation, insufficient. Notwithstanding the active engagement of the army in Jamaica and Flanders, the garrison commitments in Scotland and Ireland and the need to re-equip the fleet, the MPs were determined to whittle the professional standing army back to a size originally agreed in the *Instrument of Government*. After a lengthy haggle, the annual supply for the civil and military establishments was set at £1,600,000.

The wrangle over the *Humble Petition* had been concluded in a compromise that pleased few. Once Cromwell was reinstalled, parliament was adjourned and the MPs returned in an atmosphere of anticlimax to their constituencies. Rumours that the protector would convert his title to a monarchical one continued to circulate, but Cromwell seemed to lose interest in constitutional arrangements and his attendance at Council dropped as well; his attention was more focused on events overseas, particularly Flanders. There, Reynolds's regiments had been placed under the overall command of Turenne and rather than concentrate on the reduction of the Spanish garrison at Dunkirk, the French commander had used the

New Model soldiers as reinforcements for general operations across the breadth of the Spanish Netherlands. Only by the promise of further troops was Turenne refocused on the objective that Cromwell thought he had agreed with Mazarin, but it was a frustrating affair and the expeditionary force of the English was whittled away as Turenne concentrated on the reduction of secondary positions close to Dunkirk itself.

With autumn turning to winter, the protector at last turned his mind to the composition of the Other House. Here was an opportunity to cement the professional military caste at the heart of the constitution, and Monck, Goffe, Hewson, Berry and Barkstead were among the seventeen serving soldiers chosen to sit alongside Desborough, Whalley and Fleetwood – even Pride was offered a place, despite the disobedience of his earlier petition. But the papers of both Thurloe and Montagu reveal the doubts and difficulties that were encountered in the drawing-up of the list for the seventy permitted places, and Cromwell's attempts to tie in 'well-affected' and senior members of the English aristocracy who were not part of the regime foundered. The list of invitees included Viscount Saye and Sele and the Earls of Manchester and Warwick, but all declined to sit with the exception of Lord Eure, an unremarkable old gentleman of godly demeanour who had graced Barebones, and Lord Fauconberg, who had very recently married Mary Cromwell.

The imputation that the nobles' refusal was motivated solely by a snobbish disdain to be seen sitting with those soldiers of humbler origin is, however, unpersuasive. The last formal political connection of the aristocracy to the men who overthrew the military power of the Stuarts had already been severed at Pride's Purge and there had been only one blue-blooded signatory to the king's death warrant. As a class, the nobility had been further alienated by the rule of the major-generals. Above all, there was profound opposition to the idea of a body whose membership would be determined by the whim of the protector and his chosen successor, rather than by the hereditary principle. The main constitutional point of the new House was that it would have jurisdiction over all cases referred to it by lower courts and only the device of impeachment was reserved to the Commons alone. But it was emphatically not the old House of Lords and its order of precedence in the passage of primary legislation was ambiguous.

Cromwell also saw the Other House as a way of placating known Presbyterian sceptics of the regime. From Scotland he invited Lord Wariston and the Earl of Cassilis, who had so sternly negotiated with Charles Stuart at Breda. Bulstrode Whitelocke received the summons and was further enticed with an offer of a hereditary peerage, but this he politely declined as an 'inconvenience'. The trawl for credible candidates continued. Henry Vane was far too outside the protector's zone of comprehension to merit inclusion but Cromwell somewhat naïvely extended his hand to Sir Arthur Hesilrige. The 'Bishop of Durham' was not so worldly as to compromise his own vision of the Commonwealth, and he disdainfully declined even to make a reply. But perhaps the most notable feature of the list was the omission of the name of Sir Thomas Fairfax.

Over the summer months, as the troops were fighting the Stuarts' Spanish ally, one of the most senior members of the royalist community had joined the former lord general's family. In mid-September 1657 at Bolton Percy Church, the Duke of Buckingham was married to Mary, the Fairfaxes' only child. The aristocrat's 'prematurely dissipated' nature concealed a more calculating mind and while Mary seemed genuinely to have fallen in love with him (she had in fact been betrothed to someone else), Buckingham more obviously regarded the match as a way back to ownership of his family estates, a good proportion of which were now under the stewardship of Fairfax.[13] His tantrum with the young king before Worcester had not deterred him from trying (unsuccessfully) to woo Charles's widowed and beautiful eldest sister as a way of climbing back into a position of influence. His weight at court had further diminished and he decided to return home. The Council took a somewhat dimmer view and, seeing him as a security risk, ordered his detention once it was clear he had broken the terms of his parole. Buckingham's formidable new mother-in-law travelled to London to demand his release and he was granted house arrest. But the incident caused great indignation in the Fairfax household, which was heightened when Buckingham was rearrested the following year.

When parliament reassembled in the following January, only thirty-seven of the sixty-three on Cromwell's invitation list attended the first sitting of the Other House. Although some, such as Monck and Sir William Lockhart (the Protectorate's ambassador to France), were detained by their duties elsewhere, it made for a less than comprehensive array of notables, even though it included members of the Council. By contrast, the Commons had been swollen by the return of the vast majority of those MPs who had been excluded by the pen of the Council and barred entry by the soldiers in the autumn of 1656. The *Humble Petition* had reasserted the authority of the Commons alone to censure and disbar its own members, and the opposition that had been pent up since the major-generals' botched election now found collective voice.[14] The noisy MP for Norwich, John Hobart, who had won his seat despite the bitter efforts of the local 'bashaw' Hezekiah Haynes, scathingly attacked the new constitutional arrangements 'For this Petition and Advice, if Pope Alexander VI, Cesare Borgia and Machiavelli should all come together they would not lay a foundation for a more absolute tyranny.'[15]

On the other hand, those behind the offer of the crown to Cromwell had been dispersed – its leading lights, including Broghill, Wolseley, Jones and Montagu, were now members of the Other House, with their residual supporters becoming a minority in a Commons swollen by the return of men who had had no part in drafting the new constitution.

The reconvening of the second Protectorate parliament on 20 January 1658 was thus rendered inauspicious from the start. A physically debilitated lord protector left the burden of the opening speech to Nathaniel Fiennes, who delivered a pompous address that was long on congratulations for the 'new' regime but far shorter on reporting the progress and costs of the war with Spain. In an attempt to set the right tone, the first act of the Other House was to call for a day of fasting and prayer throughout the Republic. This wholly uncontroversial display of public piety was however taken as a sign of presumption by the opposition in the Commons, and soon both Hesilrige and Scot were marshalling a caucus that disputed the powers, credentials and even the existence of their fellow legislators. In contrast to Fiennes's father Viscount Saye and Sele, who had deprecated the ersatz nature of the new chamber, the Commonwealthsmen thought that the Other House looked far too like the old House of Lords that had been swept away with the monarchy.

The taking of the new protectoral oath by the members proved to be no bar to determined criticism of the arrangements of the *Humble Petition*. Faced with such a querulous body, a dismayed Cromwell decided to deliver one of his trademark pep talks. As through the previous year, his attention was more fully engaged by foreign policy, where his undying dreams of a European Protestant union had received a setback with the aggression shown by Charles X towards Sweden's southerly neighbour, Denmark. There were serious economic issues at stake here too, for any conflict which had the effect of closing the Baltic would have deprived Britain of its critical access to timber and metal ore. The priority was to ensure that war was avoided at all costs. Faced with so many difficulties, on 25 January Cromwell nevertheless declined to take the members into his confidence and instead fell back upon the stock device of the threat presented by European popery in order to rally them. He leavened his exhortation with an appeal for more money, as the administration of the forces had left a 'poor unpaid army, the soldiers going barefoot'.

Hesilrige, Scot and the Commonwealthsmen, with tacit support from Ashley Cooper, were having none of it. The regime's priorities were ignored as debate in the Commons focused on dissatisfaction with the Other House and the presence of the Irish and Scottish MPs who were perceived to be mere stooges of the regime. There was too a great deal of resentment and suspicion amongst the English MPs that neither the Irish nor the Scots were pulling their weight in the funding of the Republic. Where support for the concept of a second chamber could be found, it was couched in an appeal to the Harringtonian concept that only men of property should sit in a 'senate', to which Major-General Boteler replied with asperity that land was not the only nor even the most important qualification for government by the godly. With stalemate in parliament, the regime's opponents now overplayed their hand. A petition was drawn up which challenged the legitimacy of the Protectorate in its present incarnation and thousands of copies were printed, many circulated among the London regiments. Reminding readers of the reasons for which the civil wars had been fought, the authors asserted the supreme authority of the House of Commons – only it could appoint the protector and whomsoever besides. But, as the support of the soldiery was seen to be crucial, it was added that servicemen could only be dismissed by a court-martial and not at the direction of civilians.

With the organisation of reinforcements for Flanders well under way, the blatant attempt to suborn the professional army and to diminish his own authority was altogether too much for Cromwell. Learning that the petition was to be read in the Commons on 4 February he determined to dismiss parliament on the very same day, brushing aside the feeble demurrals of Fleetwood, whom he angrily dismissed as a milksop. In freezing weather which had turned the Thames to ice, the protector stomped into the Chamber and treated the MPs to another tirade in which he accused them of bad faith and of putting the state in danger when it was still threatened by Stuart invasion. Given the vice-like grip of the navy on the Channel, this seemed an exaggeration. The members' attention began to wander and so, with a portentous final flourish, the first Citizen demanded of the MPs that they 'Let God judge between you and me.' It was an embarrassing moment – Cromwell's authority within his entourage and Council were unassailable, but it had palpably begun to evaporate in the House. His peroration was greeted by much eye-rolling and shouts of 'Amen'. The civilians had had enough.

The professional army was a different matter. Sensing that his son-in-law might be losing his grip on the men under his direct command, in early March Cromwell personally convened a meeting of 200 officers. In a somewhat more affable mood and with declarations of loyalty from Monck's regiments in Scotland in his pocket, the protector took refreshment with his subordinates and in the convivial atmosphere most loudly pledged to maintain a steadfast allegiance. Not all were convinced, however. William Packer, who had taken command of Cromwell's old regiment of Ironsides voiced his scruples, and for refusing to take the oath to the regime was cashiered, along with five other regimental officers. Packer's disobedience was significant: he had deputised for Fleetwood in East Anglia and was the Anabaptist whom Cromwell had so vigorously defended for his faith against the objections of the army's Scottish allies. The knowledge too that the Fifth Monarchists were attempting to make common cause with the more zealous Baptists brought a reminder of Henry Cromwell's bitter suspicion of them in Ireland. Attempting to regain the respect of his father-in-law, Fleetwood organised a further address from the officer corps, with all once more affirming their loyalty to the regime of the *Humble Petition*. The city authorities too pledged support and the London militia was reorganised, with those of dubious loyalty ejected.

The regime had already entered a twilight phase of deeper paranoia. In the Advent season the previous year, Reynolds had been recalled to England to answer the charge that he had consorted with the enemy outside Dunkirk, specifically that he had met with the Duke of York. His boat had sunk in the Channel before he could clear his name or otherwise, and the army lost one of its more able and loyal commanders. The slender odds of a successful royalist invasion from Europe had been rendered more vestigial still by the dispersal and destruction by the navy of a fleet of transports in the waters off Ostend that had been sold by the Dutch to the Spanish. Notwithstanding this, all Catholics and royalists were ordered to leave London and some former officers of the king's army were arrested. Sir Henry Slingsby, a Yorkshire gentleman who had conducted himself steadfastly on behalf of his sovereign both in the Long

Parliament and in the field, had consistently refused to swear loyalty to the regime, thus removing any chance of recovering his property. Now, he was incarcerated, together with an Anglican divine called Dr John Hewitt, on very slender and circumstantial evidence linking him with a royalist plot.

Thurloe's spies drew in more alleged conspirators, including John Mordaunt, son of the Earl of Peterborough. A determined intriguer and royalist renegade, he had spurned the timorous machinations of the Sealed Knot, and preferred direct and violent action. Now, the High Court was reconvened to try the principals for treason, but once again the judicial establishment demurred: all the regular justices declined to sit and only fifty of the 140 commissioners summoned to appear did so. Nonetheless, the men received what looked like summary justice although, in an ironic twist, the more obviously guilty Mordaunt escaped the gallows by the casting vote of the court's president. Both Slingsby and Hewitt were spared the grim ritual of hanging and disembowelling, and were instead beheaded. But, later in the spring, another conspiracy was uncovered and six men were sent to be hanged, drawn and quartered. Yet, in a dramatic denouement that managed to combine both vindictiveness and muddle, three were reprieved at the point of having the noose placed around their necks.

With Thurloe recovering fitfully from a serious illness and his spies chasing more shadows than actual insurrectionists at home, in Flanders arguably the last pitched battle of the British civil wars took place. Reinforced with seven British regiments now under the command of Sir William Lockhart, Turenne turned his attention to reducing the Spanish fortress at Dunkirk. The field commander in the Spanish Netherlands, Don Juan, had a similarly sized force at his disposal which included a regiment of English soldiers, one of Scots and three of Irish, together with the Duke of York's Life Guard. These he now marched to try to lure Turenne away from his siege of the strategically important port and to outflank him in the undulating sandbanks of the coastline. On 4 June 1658 the two armies met at the so-called battle of the Dunes. The Spanish had taken their stand a short way north of Dunkirk with their right flank on the beach and their centre composed of heavily armed infantry supported by artillery. Below them the New Model regiments were drawn up in their trademark scarlet and buff uniforms.

Their number had been depleted by the seemingly interminable marches around the Low Countries and the reinforcements had barely had time to acclimatise in theatre. Nonetheless, Lockhart proved to be as enthusiastic a commander as he had been a diplomat for Cromwell at the French court and the British troops attacked the central bastion of the Spanish lines with gusto, after labouring uphill in the ankle-deep and sliding sand. Once again, the oaths and yells of the British Isles were mingled as men grappled with one another on the shifting surface. Meanwhile, a naval squadron under Montagu bombarded the Spanish from the sea. However, the iron balls were uselessly gobbled up by the sand and the French commander soon realised that he would need something more than his soldiers if he was to dislodge the veteran Spaniards and their mercenaries. While the determined New Model troops took further casualties as they wrestled with Don Juan's elite soldiers, Turenne got the break he needed. Nature took its turn and as the tide began to go out the French were able to deploy their cavalry to attack on the harder surface of the shoreline.

Outflanked, the opposing force began to disintegrate and was soon in full retreat, leaving over 4,000 prisoners to be taken. Dunkirk was completely isolated, notwithstanding that in a last act of desperation the garrison broke the dykes around the town, flooding the ground over which the besiegers had to cross. But there was now no hope of relief and a week after the fierce battle by the seaside, the fortress surrendered. The very next day the nineteen-year-old French king, Louis XIV, together with a large retinue, entered the town respectfully to inspect the bloodied but victorious British professionals while his first minister dined aboard Montagu's flagship, *Naseby*. For the first time since Mary Tudor had lost Calais in 1558, the British had territory on either side of the Channel. Charles Stuart, who had been prevented from joining the action by his Spanish allies and hosts was perhaps by now inured to disappointment. Without a collapse of the Republic from within, his dream of recovering his birthright seemed truly to be at an end.

19

'Whatever whimsey breezes in the brains of the officers'

London

Does not your peace depend upon his Highness's life, and upon his peculiar skills and faculty and personal interest in the army as now modelled and commanded?

Henry Cromwell

Never was there a pack of men seen more deserted of God and emptied of wit, sense, reason, common honesty and moral trustiness nor the General Council of their officers.

Lord Wariston

In the last days of August 1658 a prolonged heat wave across England and Scotland was ended by a dramatic break in the weather. In the ensuing gales, people were thrown down in the streets, trees uprooted and carriages overturned. It seemed to be a portent. The lord protector was by now prostrate in his bed at Whitehall, stricken by a strain of malaria that he was thought to have contracted on the campaign in Ireland and whose rigours had revisited him on occasion since. But now his body was in its sixth decade and Cromwell was less able to fight the infections. He was almost bald, had lost weight and the skin on his back was marked by boils, and a painful and suppurating abscess. His spirit had been greatly lowered by the death of his daughter, Elizabeth Claypole, after her lengthy struggle with cancer. In what turned out to be the last fortnight of his life, he rallied sufficiently to conduct desultory discussions with his entourage and to hold a tense interview with his erstwhile commander, Fairfax, who had come to remonstrate about the further incarceration of his son-in-law, who was suspected of involvement in the most recent episode of cavalier disobedience. The former general (who had his own infirmities) had other reasons for his restrained anger as his household had by then also suffered the indignity of having a private entertainment broken up by the local Yorkshire justices on the grounds that it was an act of theatre, which was forbidden. Fox also came again to importune the protector, as he had earlier done at Hampton Court, but the Quaker evangelist was turned away by the nervous Life Guard.

Cromwell had returned to his sweat-stained sheets. Ludlow spitefully suggested that the attempts to keep him alive were an imposition on the Almighty, while Fleetwood simply could not bring himself to believe in the imminent demise of his patron and chief. Various divines from amongst the capital's independent congregations sent in notes that the protector was at the centre of their most earnest prayers. Other senior members of his Council crowded about his bed in an effort to learn who was to be his successor – the rumour that Cromwell was to take the crown persisted right up to the last week of his life and the institutional memory of these men probably inclined them to believe that the mantle would, and probably should, fall on the protector's eldest surviving son. In his extremity, he seemed to give his assent to the assumption. It was his last act of state and on the anniversary of his great victories over the Scots at Dunbar and Worcester, Cromwell died, his face a mask of inscrutable impassivity.

In contrast to his sturdy younger sibling Henry, portraits of Richard Cromwell show him to be a rather weedy-looking ingénu. However, whether by accident or design, he was an inspired choice as a successor. Born in the autumn of 1626, his character could not have been more different from that of his intimidating, authoritarian and reactionary parent. Even detractors of the Protectorate such as Lucy Hutchinson acknowledged the sweetness of his disposition, and his nature seemed to promise a more indulgent and less doctrinaire version of the regime after the hectoring earnestness and stasis of his father. Here was not a constable but a man of a less rigid sensibility and temperament. His early career seemed to have been a case of benign neglect. His father had expressed grumpy concern at his apparent lack of curiosity, somewhat idle ways and (far more seriously), his propensity for building up personal debt; yet he had made little attempt to bring Richard on by giving him meaningful responsibility. That mantle had fallen on the far more dutiful Henry, who so closely resembled his father both in looks and in parts of his character. But Richard was no fool and, unlike his brother and the head of the family, made up in charm what he lacked in intellect.

By one account he had a wicked sense of humour. He referred to his brother-in-law, the aristocratic Robert Rich, as 'Mrs Cromwell', but is likely to have been genuinely remorseful when the sickly husband perished so quickly after his extravagant marriage to Richard's youngest sister, Frances. In religious matters, his views seemed to be unexceptional, although his nature inclined him away from anything that smacked of fanaticism. Whilst Henry had been sent to Ireland, Richard seemed to be more content with a life of domesticity and his wife went on to produce nine children, a prodigious number in view of the fact that they were in each other's company as a married couple for a mere eleven years. He was elected to both the first and second Protectorate parliaments and was thus able to witness first hand his father's almost complete inability to work sustainably with the Republic's civilian representatives.

In the second half of 1657, however, the pace of his hitherto unspectacular political advance was accelerated. The terms of the *Humble Petition* gave the protector no reason to scruple at nepotism and Richard was promoted to the Protectorate Council and installed as Chancellor of Oxford University over the head of John Owen, who had so displeased his patron and resigned his post. Cromwell also appointed him to the Other House along with Henry, who nonetheless remained fully engaged in Ireland and thus remote from the centre of power and influence in London. More controversially, and despite an almost total lack of military experience, Richard was given command of Goffe's regiment, thus bringing him within the cadre of senior members of the Council of Officers. The support of the professional army would be crucial, but on balance his position seemed favourable: the withdrawal from national public life of Lambert and Harrison had removed that sliver of officers who could possibly claim a portion of the authority enjoyed by his father, while the retirement of Fairfax had left nobody who rivalled him for prestige.

Richard also received the enthusiastic support of most of his fellow councillors and established a rapport with Thurloe, who overcame his grief at his master's passing and appeared happy to transfer his loyalties to the son without demur. He could count too on the steady loyalty of his more experienced brother, who seemed to harbour no greater ambition than to hold the ring for Richard in Ireland. The senior soldiers Fleetwood and Desborough seemed a little more grudging and patronising in their support of the *faux* soldier, but, for the time being, were at least reconciled to him by those family ties that the former protector's behaviour had shown to be important. More widely, there seemed to be a strong desire that the succession should pass without any upheaval. Thus, when Richard was proclaimed lord protector in London, Edinburgh and Dublin in the days after his father's death the Republic was calm; indeed, petitions of loyal support flooded in from many counties and the city, while Monck sent him an avuncular note of support and advice which also cautioned him to be on the look-out for troublemakers. Apart from a small disturbance at Oxford, where some students pelted a group of the detested soldiery with rotting vegetables, there was an atmosphere of hopeful expectation and the many petitions from the provinces expressed the desire that the son would deal with those many local and domestic issues neglected by the father.

Preparations for Oliver Cromwell's funeral proceeded. Within the protectoral court, the shock and sadness at his death seemed sincere. The prodigious sum of £28,000[1] was set aside for the ceremonies, which indicates not only the importance attached to the event by the Council but also the devaluation of money since the extravagant arrangements made for the Earl of Essex exactly twelve years earlier. However, the initial procedure of embalming had proved to be a challenge and, as his corrupt body was moved around, Cromwell's decayed spleen exploded in front of the surgeons attending to him. His corpse was quietly interred in Westminster Abbey where his daughter Elizabeth Claypole had already been laid to rest. Instead, a grotesque wax effigy with its cheeks rouged and complete with purple cloak, black doublet and 'imperial' crown was installed at Somerset House in a suite of rooms covered from floor to ceiling in black velvet heavily trimmed with gold thread. Security was tight – the risk of another berserk assault on so profane an object had to be minimised and the spectators were strictly controlled. On 23 November 1658, the lifelike model was conveyed in solemn procession to the abbey for the 'official' burial. The whole rigmarole took over seven hours, and Evelyn noted the slack discipline and almost brazen indifference of the soldiers lining the route. By the time the dummy was re-erected in the darkened precincts of the church, the bored crowds had already drifted home. But at last a crown had been forced on the protector's lifeless and waxen head.

The demeanour of the soldiers taking part in the funeral was indicative of wider unrest and low morale amongst the professional army. Their remuneration was seriously in arrears, with the army alone owed nearly £900,000 in back pay, and there had been a brief mutiny at Dunkirk. Now the town was in British hands, the French saw no reason to pay the same subsidy as before (nor even offer a loan) and the regimental pay-masters were left empty-handed.[2] The Republic was in profound financial difficulty: expenditure exceeded income by nearly half a million pounds a year and when a parliamentary committee under Vane eventually looked into the matter in early 1659 the state was found to be in hock for £2,222,000. The corrosive effect of inflation was also being felt – the army in Scotland had been reduced by a quarter but the 10,000 men under arms there as the new year dawned cost the same as the larger force had done three years before.

Richard Cromwell thus faced a difficult legacy and problems that his more exalted father had been unable to surmount. With some sagacity and mindful of their interventions in the past, he saw that his most immediate task was to deal with the condition of the army while maintaining control over it. In his letter to the new protector, Monck had urged that it be 'remodelled' and further purged of Quakers, Baptists and other unruly elements as had been done in Scotland. The seat left by his father was, however, barely cold when a petition was produced detailing the soldiers' grievances and urging that the 'concernments of the godly' be treated as a priority. Although Cromwell could count on firmness in the support of officers such as Montagu, Whalley, Monck and Goffe, his brother-in-law Charles Fleetwood was far more susceptible to pious agitation by the soldiers, which tended to sway his judgement.

Nonetheless, Richard began sprightly enough and asserted his authority over the senior commanders. Fleetwood was formally appointed as lieutenant general in England, but the protector insisted he personally remain commander-in-chief, with the power to appoint officers, in accordance with the provisions of the *Humble Petition*. He assured the soldiers that this would not be exercised arbitrarily and that commissions would only be rescinded by courts martial. The ambiguity of Fleetwood's role in Ireland was removed with Henry's formal appointment as lord deputy with command of the forces there. He made it clear, in as genial a way as possible, that he would not tolerate military indiscipline occasioned by religious scruple. With crossed fingers, the protector also promised to increase the rate of pay for the troops, although as the Council was in the process of welching on the expenses for his father's funeral, it was not at all clear from where the money would come.

The financial realities could not be ignored. The only solution was to recall a parliament, which the Council ordered on 3 December

1658. The loss of its veto over elected members made it clear that as large a representative base as possible needed to be summoned and it was determined that the franchise and constituencies would revert to those which had been in place for the Long Parliament. It was hoped that the influence of the Commonwealthsmen and crypto-royalists would thereby be diluted while sealing the loyalty of the Presbyterians, who had not forgotten the Stuarts' alliance with the popish Spaniards. Cromwell also determined that the elections were to be a manifestly civil event: the soldiers were kept out of sight, although he took the precaution of replacing a number of sheriffs who were deemed to be too unreliable to supervise the ballot effectively. Of the major-generals who stood, fewer than a handful were elected, including Thomas Kelsey (who had overseen the south-east) for the borough seat of Dover. Thomas Harrison and John Lambert were also returned.

In the third week of January, the third Protectorate parliament opened. The chamber was filled to bursting as many of the 569 Members entitled to attend crowded in, their numbers swollen by the presence of the Irish and Scottish MPs. Amongst the latter was the Marquis of Argyll, whom Monck sourly noted was unlikely 'to do his Highness's interest any good'. Approximately two-thirds of them were newcomers, including a pleased-looking Andrew Marvell, who had been elected for Hull. But the polls also saw the return of experienced Commonwealthsmen such as Vane, Ludlow, John Bradshaw and Thomas Chaloner, who had withdrawn from prominence after the forced dissolution of the Rump and the subsequent exclusions. The biggest murmur of sensation arose when a rather melancholy figure, his jet hair and goatee beard streaked with grey above a prematurely lined faced, advanced with dignified but pained steps to claim a seat as one of the two county representatives for Yorkshire. It was his first appearance in the Chamber as an elected member. With a few cautious nods to those around him in the unfamiliar surroundings, Sir Thomas Fairfax sat down beside Sir Arthur Hesilrige.

After a sermon from the Independent divine Thomas Goodwin, Richard Cromwell stood to address the quizzical and hopeful-looking representatives. Many would have been aware of the savage lampooning that the thirty-two-year-old had already received in royalist pamphlets – one of the kinder opined that 'The vulture died and out of the ashes arose a titmouse.' In the event, on his first outing Richard Cromwell achieved a rhetorical impact that had seldom been achieved by his prolix and abstruse father. Exploiting his benign reputation, the protector gave a brief, conciliatory and thoughtful address of welcome, the effect of which was somewhat spoilt by a tedious recitation of the government's programme and implied desperation for money by Nathaniel Fiennes, who, as lord keeper, was a member of the controversial Other House. Nevertheless, for Cromwell himself, it was a well-received start.

One sign of the less oppressive atmosphere was the release of royalists who had been held without trial since 1655, and shortly afterwards the Fifth Monarchist conspirators Thomas Venner and Colonel Robert Overton also regained their liberty. The Commonwealthsmen, whose animosity was now more precisely focused on the position of the protector rather than the young man who occupied it, realised that they would have to act swiftly if the regime were not to enjoy a new surge of life to exercise those powers conferred by the *Humble Petition* with which they so fundamentally disagreed. As soon as the Bill of Recognition drafted by Thurloe was introduced, the argument about the constitution, which had been so rudely interrupted by Oliver Cromwell's peremptory dismissal of parliament the year before, was resumed. After a number of rumbustious debates, including one chaotic one in which a prankster got into the House to take part in a motion to suspend the over-excited Ludlow, the Commons voted to confirm Richard's title, subject to clarification of his role as 'Chief Magistrate'.

Many of the MPs, satisfied that things were on the right path, began to drift back to their constituencies to deal with more pressing personal and business matters. This gave the determined Commonwealthsmen a greater share of voice in the more sparsely attended chamber, with those like Hesilrige deploying their deep knowledge of parliament's arcane procedures to draw out the debates to an interminable length. However, the attempts by filibuster to induce agreement out of catatonic boredom had one dramatic effect as the new Speaker, Chaloner Chute (who had despaired that 'We are indeed in a wood, a wilderness, a labyrinth'), keeled over from exhaustion and died. His successor fell ill a short while later and had to be replaced in turn. But despite the opposition's efforts, those controversial aspects of the protectoral constitution such as the Other House and the presence of the Irish and Scottish members were endorsed by substantial majorities of those voting.

A larger body of the unpaid soldiery was now close to mutiny, with the junior officers agitating for redress in the absence of the politicking senior commanders. A petition was drafted by Colonel Ashfield (who had become a Quaker while on service in Scotland), demanding adherence to the 'Good Old Cause' and for the huge arrears to be settled. But the MPs were dilatory, even when in April Fairfax called for restitution for Yorkshire's large community of maimed soldiers and its 4,000 widows and orphans created by the wars. The fractiousness of the soldiers was enhanced too by the new parliament's determination to ensure orthodoxy, and when it issued a declaration censuring the magistracy for its inadequate efforts to stamp out heresy, the writing seemed to be on the wall for those sects and congregations to which many soldiers adhered. A majority of MPs were also in a mood of retribution for the more brazen injustices of the rule of the major-generals. The Lieutenant of the Tower had already been charged with embezzlement, and in the second week of April the Commons decided to impeach William Boteler. Even the republicans were unsettled by the wisdom of this move and to the Independents amongst them it smacked of a return to that judicial supremacy that had been exercised so vindictively during the Nayler case. It also further unnerved the military.

Unable to remove or even much dilute the Protectorate through parliament, the purists among the Commonwealthsmen instead decided to undermine it by making common cause with the very men who had previously urged their suppression with the expulsion of the Rump. In the uglier temper of the army about London they cynically perceived an opportunity and to their uncompromising republican zeal was now joined the political irresponsibility of the senior officers, Fleetwood, Desborough and Lambert, who had returned to public life as MP for Aldborough. Neither of Richard Cromwell's relatives-by-law were overburdened by great intelligence and both seemed piqued by the surprising sure-footedness of the new protector and the diminution of their authority. There had already been angry scenes in the Council, with Desborough throwing about his weight in jealousy of Thurloe and at the influence of Cromwellian courtiers like Fauconberg and Montagu.

Somewhat against his better judgement in light of the assurances he had already given, the protector had been persuaded to authorise a reconvening of the General Council of the Army. This acted as a magnet for the very troublemakers against whom Monck had cautioned and Fleetwood seemed disinclined to deal with the mounting insubordination. By now parliament had been fully acquainted with the mess into which the public finances had fallen but in the febrile atmosphere authorised a payment to the professional soldiers, at least to erase three months' worth of arrears. But the clamour at St James, where the Council had taken up residence, continued (below the apartments of the protector's mother), accompanied by loud and earnest prayer. Richard, alarmed at the signs of indiscipline, decided to assert his authority by ordering the officers and agitators back to their units, an instruction reinforced by a declaration to the same effect from the MPs.

Three days later, the Members determined to resolve the issue that had eluded them since parliament's military victory against Charles I by debating the incorporation of the professional army with the militia, controlled by it and the protector. Another pivotal moment had come and Desborough's frame of understanding was far too stuck in its Cromwellian mould to contemplate such a change. Although the cultural intrusions of the major-generals were much discredited, the security of the state seemed to be on a sounder footing. Critically, both Ireland and Scotland had reacted peaceably to the succession of Richard Cromwell, and the enlarged parliament had endorsed the protectoral regime in most of its particulars. The threat of a Spanish-supported invasion was very much diminished. As an insurance policy, there was a much stronger argument to be made for a renewed focus on the navy, where Montagu had just been despatched across the North Sea to deter Dutch interference in the renewed conflict between Sweden and Denmark and to protect unfettered British access to the Baltic. The most compelling reason for change was that the size of the present military establishment was simply beyond the state's means or its citizens' representatives' willingness to pay.

Fleetwood and Desborough, believing that the 'Good Old Cause' was imperilled, were reflexively determined to have another show-down rather than reach a reasonable compromise to settle arrears and reduce the ongoing burden of the military. On the night of 21 April, with Fleetwood ignoring the order to disband the General Council, Desborough furiously demanded that parliament be dissolved, and marshalled troops in the precincts of Whitehall. An attempt by Cromwell and Whalley to rally loyal troops collapsed and the collective nerve of the Council failed it, despite the pleadings of Broghill. The protector was unwilling to have blood spilt on his behalf and in the early hours of the following morning he gave his assent to a dissolution. Fleetwood composed a wholly disingenuous report to Monck that the army was acting at the behest of the protector and a red-faced Fiennes was sent to the House to deliver the news to the outraged MPs. These then spent the rest of the day angrily pontificating until they were turned out by the jeering troops, who proceeded to bolt the doors. It was a depressing moment in which the senior command of the New Model Army lost that shred of moral authority still attached to it.

Lambert, perhaps disenchanted that the Other House had failed to protect the army's interests against the Commons, had nevertheless missed the opportunity in the new situation to promote effectively his own position and show statesmanship by an unequivocal display of loyalty to Cromwell. The only soldier of recent experience who likely had the authority to face down the putsch, he instead elected to throw in his lot with the mutineers and their improbable alliance with the republican Commonwealthsmen. The coup was followed by a chaotic fortnight of manoeuvrings – the senior soldiers had evidently not thought through their peremptory action. There were outbreaks of indiscipline towards civilians suspected of being royalists or Catholics and even the diplomatic quarter was not immune to the soldiers' disorders: the Danish minister was hauled off in his nightshirt. Having expressed a desire to retain the Protectorate in some shape or form, Fleetwood's fragile integrity buckled in the face of the tumult from more junior officers, who demanded a return to power of their former sworn opponents, the members of the Rump. Protectoral defenders such as Fauconberg and the regicide Richard Ingoldsby were deprived of their commands and replaced by radicals including Colonels Allen, Rich and Overton; Hesilrige too received a commission. The loyalist Broghill fled back to Ireland. With censorship no longer properly functioning, the streets of London were treated to another burst of pamphlets, a number extolling the virtues of a new pantomime horse, the 'Good Old Cause' now joined with the 'Good Old Parliament'.

Another parliament was needed to authorise the badly needed funds and after meetings with the Commonwealthsmen, a Council of Officers in London accordingly permitted a return of the Rump. The civilians agreed with the soldiers that the pay of the army would be met, that they would be indemnified for past actions and that for his compliance with the coup, the debts of Richard Cromwell (still the nominal protector) would be paid off. Of the near eighty surviving MPs entitled to sit, forty-two marched arm-in-arm back to Westminster on 7 May 1659 as if, said one observer, they were going back into the Ark. A most reluctant William Lenthall was dragged out of retirement to be the Speaker. The members excluded by Pride's Purge and the more recently dismissed MPs were outraged. While some like Fairfax returned home in disgust, a number tried to regain admittance. William Prynne managed to get inside before being turned out and shortly after denounced 'The confederated Triumvirate of Republicans, Sectaries and Soldiers', and excoriated the Commonwealthsmen. It was strong stuff: 'When I had not only superficially viewed the outside but considerately penetrated into the true original seminal source and inhale of it, I discovered it to be in truth the Jesuits and old Gunpowder-Traytors most execrable plot and cause.'[3]

He had been joined by Sir George Booth, recently elected as a county member for Lancashire. A Presbyterian who had fought with some distinction for the parliamentary side in the civil war in England, he had sat in the Long Parliament and had been elected for each of the Protectorate ones. Yet by now he had suffered the indignity of having his mandate terminated on four consecutive occasions. Prynne further channelled his anger by writing another cross polemic entitled *The true Good Old Cause rightly stated*, but the appalled Booth had had enough.

The summer was marked by widespread unrest and outbreaks of disorder. Richard Cromwell formally resigned his office on 24 May and was followed by his brother in Ireland a few weeks later. The condition of the young protector was genuinely pitiable, and the pathos of his departure was well captured by a contemporary: 'Without any struggle he withdrew, and became a private man. And as he had done hurt to nobody, so nobody did ever study to hurt him, by a rare instance of the instability of human greatness, and the security of innocence.'[4]

Propelled into a position for which he had been most inadequately prepared, he had been abandoned by the very men whose elevation would have been inconceivable without the patronage of his father. With some confusion as to the distinction between his private debts and those attaching to his office, he had been forced to remain holed up in Whitehall and then Hampton Court to escape his creditors. His correspondence to his brother spoke eloquently of his betrayal. The financial settlement he was given evidently failed to square his personal balance sheet and he fled abroad. The Continent was now host to two prominent British exiles, the one a king the other a Republican head of state. But in a sign of the wind that was now gently blowing, 'Mr Clarke' hid away, fearful of assassination by vengeful royalists.

The zealots among the Commonwealthsmen used the divisions

in the army to seize the initiative. Having been restored by the soldiery, Hesilrige was determined to annul the acts of the Protectorate
(even the union with Scotland was to be rescinded) and to return
government to a civil magistracy with the armed forces firmly under
the control of parliament. In the first instance, a new Council of
State of thirty-one members was appointed in which the civilians
decisively outnumbered the swordsmen. Its composition appeared
as an attempt to represent a wide range of special interests: the wily
Ashley Cooper was there, having distinguished himself by resign-
ing from the protectoral regime he had once served. That this was
yet another shift in the subtle way he tended to give his loyalty was
seemingly overlooked. Major-General Berry was also included (as a
friend of the sects), and so too was Lord Johnston of Wariston – the
unbending and fervent Calvinist who had been described by Broghill
as a 'Fifth Monarchy Presbyterian' (a description which captured his
implacable zeal rather than his theology), took a turn as the group's
president.[5] But Wariston was soon lamenting the 'confusion and
universal discontent'. Hesilrige's aim was to keep the political agenda
firmly in the hands of the Commonwealth parliament, but the
atmosphere in the Council was one of uncertainty and mistrust. The
appointments seemed to cut little ice in public: Prynne wondered
why any gentleman would wish to 'hazard their estate with such a
crew' and the councillors were lampooned in the opposition press.[6]

As recorded by Wariston in his diary, wider governance was put
on hold while the shape of the revived Commonwealth was debated.
Lambert wanted a return of Senate populated by soldiers which would
have a veto over the transactions of the Commons. The pamphleteers
were unimpressed by this call for a military oligarchy masquerading
as a piece of Harringtonian good practice and in *A Negative Voice* the
proposal was prettily skewered 'as like the Other House as an Ape is
like a Monkey'. As an alternative, Vane favoured a government by a
propertied super-elite found in the pages of *Oceana* but his proposals
were obscured by pious qualifications and his mystical conception of
godliness. The more secular Hesilrige was motivated by his anxiety
about the military and he had been piqued by the refusal of the

senior soldiers to take the Oath to the Commonwealth – they had decided to affirm instead. So, in the first week of June, a parliamentary committee took charge of the commissioning of both naval and army officers, an initiative meekly accepted by Fleetwood on the understanding that the armed forces would remain commanded by the godly. But it was a development that would never have found favour under the older Cromwell. Although populated by a majority of men with military experience, the committee marked the return of the New Model Army to parliamentary control for the first time since the Self-Denying Ordinance.

With the judges and county officials waiting for their instructions, the purge of the military continued. Monck had managed to keep his men both paid and in a state of discipline, but now he feared a return of those radicals and chiliasts whom he had so assiduously weeded from his cadre of officers. Although he had assured the new regime of his loyalty, he sent a letter to the Commons asking that he retain the right to appoint those whom he regarded as reliable lest the peace and security of Scotland be compromised. However, this was refused and a number of his former officers were reinstated and others replaced. In a tightening grip, Thurloe's spy networks were restored to Thomas Scot, and Ludlow returned to Ireland to take command of the army.

The navy was made the responsibility of a different board of commissioners that included Vane, whose primary concern was the loyalty of the sailors and their present occupation. Accordingly, Algernon Sydney was sent in a fast frigate to the Sound of Elsinore to intercept and question Montagu who was on station there with his fleet. Having overcome his seasickness, the precocious commissar proceeded to take charge of the admiral's strategy, insisting he show more belligerence towards the Danes and their Dutch allies. Stung by Sydney's offensive needling, Montagu sent a message protesting his support of the new men in charge. But the later news of the rehabilitation of the Baptist Admiral John Lawson to command in the Channel and the transfer of Montagu's regiment (so recently bestowed by Richard Cromwell) to Colonel Alured, showed little sign of good faith. He too began to entertain warmer thoughts about the exiled king. When, contrary to orders, he sailed back to Britain in late August he resigned his posts and retired to Hinchingbroke.

In July, the religiously orthodox both north and south of the border showed signs of being gripped by a 'Quaker Terror'. In London, the pamphlet *An alarum to the City and Souldiery* warned of a Fifth Monarchy plot to overpower the New Model Army and set fire to the city. The death of Oliver Cromwell had re-energised the sects in their quest for religious freedom and the putsch was followed by the promotion to positions of authority of Fifth Monarchists and Baptists. By the summer, leading Quakers such as Edward Burrough were in discussion with the MPs about the ending of penalties and even advancement for themselves. James Nayler, remarkably still alive but virtually mute, was released. The public campaign against tithes was resumed and one petition was signed by over 7,000 Quaker women. However, in the country, the prospect of these religious radicals (who had only just recently graced the county jails) becoming Justices of the Peace or commissioners of the militia caused serious alarm after the oppressive novelty of the major-generals.[7] The satirists too continued their assault, even accusing the Quakers of bestiality:

> For if no respect of persons
> Be due amongst the sons of Adam,
> > In a large extent
> > Then may it be meant
> That a mare's as good as a Madam.
>
> No surely, quoth James Nailor,
> 'Twas but an insurrection
> > Of the carnall part,
> > For a Quaker in heart
> Can never lose perfection.[8]

More prosaically, Wariston too fretted about such men coming back into the army and about the resurgence of the debate about tithes, which the Scot considered to be sacrosanct. Henry Vane might be relaxed about heterodoxy and Hesilrige happy to co-opt the sects in support of the Commonwealth, but to the disenfranchised Presbyterian interest such a scenario was anathema.

In Flanders, the mood of the exiled court veered between confused excitement and despondency. The fall of the protector had seemed like an opportunity which then vanished with the alliance between the army and the Commonwealthsmen. Like a chained and starving dog staring at an out-of-reach bone, Charles and his advisers continued to dream of redemption while existing in a state of near penury, dividing their time between cramped lodgings in Brussels and Bruges. Candle wax was recycled, clothes were patched and other economies made, but the royal 'pension' was simply not enough to maintain much more than a skeleton household and there were endless disputes over bills. Nonetheless, Charles maintained a buoyant demeanour while fostering a charismatic mystique and, like his father, he was perfectly capable of showing *froideur* to preserve his royal dignity. In the threadbare circumstances, royal protocol was punctiliously observed – wherever he stayed, the king kept a small withdrawing chamber divided from his councillors by a velvet screen and took his meals privately on a pewter service whereas his entourage dined on what and from what they could.

As the days had lengthened, so Sir Edward Hyde had stoically enlarged his correspondence with agents back home in an effort to discover the weak links in the republican regime and ways in which they might be suborned. This was no time for sentimentality and he was heartened when, with breathtaking effrontery but with a view to the future, the New Model Colonel Richard Ingoldsby offered to switch to the royalist cause in expurgation of his sin of regicide. Discovering the disposition of the more senior members of the protectoral regime was trickier. Titles and other baubles were dangled as inducements to switch loyalties, but Montagu, Broghill and Monck were presently inscrutable, while a ham-fisted attempt to square Henry Cromwell so enraged him that he gave the agent sent to sound him out a pistol whipping – the son might be out of office, but he was not about to betray the legacy of his father. Yet whereas Hyde placed his patient faith in a collapse from within, the king remained alert to chances to give the regime as good a shake as possible from without.

Sidelining the faint-hearted and compromised duds of the Sealed Knot, Charles appointed Mordaunt (now ennobled as a viscount in his own right) to be his agitator-in-chief, and Massey was sent back to organise rebellion in his familiar stamping grounds of the lower Severn Valley. But the royalists had perhaps misunderstood the wider mood in the country – while there was apprehension at the goings-on in London, there was little appetite to compound it by supporting royalist unrest. Despite the planning of several risings, many were compromised by faulty security and poor co-ordination, while sympathetic notables found it hard to turn warm words into decisive action, just as had been the case in both 1651 and 1655. Fear of the New Model Army and of the efficient espionage capabilities of the regime remained too great for many. Where disturbances did occur, such as Byron's rally at Sherwood Forest, they were sufficiently small to be dealt with by the local militia. Only in the north-west did the insurrectionary activity present a more serious threat. Here the excluded MP and Cheshire magnate Sir George Booth raised a sizeable number of armed men and with help from the Earl of Derby (whose father had been defeated by Lambert on his march south to Worcester), the towns of Liverpool, Wrexham, Chester and Preston were occupied by groups of rebels.

Booth's decision to rise was motivated by outraged principle; he was no turncoat. His manifesto deplored the actions of the revived Rump but it was certainly not a call for a restoration of the monarchy. Lambert was ordered to snuff the insurrection out, but in a sign of the times it took well over a week for the general to get organised and it was felt necessary to put the army in Ireland and the Dunkirk garrison on notice to provide men should they be needed. Amidst outbreaks of indiscipline, a force only slightly larger than the one understood to be under Booth was marched north. The men were still owed money but their training and instincts were unimpaired, and just outside Northwich in Cheshire, after a desultory tussle with few casualties, Booth's men were scattered. Lambert seemed too embarrassed by the walk-over to follow up and most of the rebels were allowed to return to prepare for harvest without further ado. The ringleaders were arrested and Booth was consigned to the Tower after being caught in an inn near London, disguised as a woman.

Lambert's victory in the north-west was hardly of the scale of his earlier military achievements but it gave him renewed confidence. His ability to keep his dissatisfied troops together was of greater note than winning his scuffle with Booth and he used his momentum to press for the promises made by the Commonwealthsmen to be honoured. As his soldiers moved back south they stopped at Derby, from where Lambert authorised a petition which also sought to reverse parliament's control of the army. The demands included the permanent military appointment of the senior putschists, that no officer be cashiered except by court martial and that critics of the army be purged. Although Vane and Whitelocke were more inclined to humour the soldiers, Hesilrige and doctrinaire republicans like Scot were not; Lambert's initiative pointed to a return to government by military petition and an army unaccountable to civilians.

Over the following weeks, friction increased. As reported by Lucy Hutchinson, Lambert was 'exceedingly puffed up with his cheap victory' and certainly his report to parliament contained a strong overtone of Cromwellian bombast that was not perhaps justified by military events.[9] There was a good deal of satire expressed about the officers' oppressive interference with the civil state, and in *Several Resolves prepared by the Commanding Junto to pass the House*, military presumption was bitterly lampooned:

> Resolved: That the War with Spain be continued in regard it multiplies the number of Beggars in the Nation, and consequently we shall have good soldiers cheap to advance the Work of Reformation, being it is received as an

Orthodox tradition, that broken merchants make excellent Sword-Men.

Resolved: That whatever whimsey breezes in the Brains of the Officers, it be adjudged the sense of the private soldiery, though they never be consulted with in the business.

Resolved: That there be a restraint upon Presbytery as well as Popery and Prelacy because it somewhat resembles Christianity.[10]

Nonetheless, Hesilrige's demand that the general be thrown in the Tower for his politicking was vetoed in the House as being too provocative and there seemed a genuine desire on the part of the MPs to settle outstanding arrears to take the heat out of the soldiers' discontent. A new round of sequestrations was ordered. Sensing weakness and not to be outdone, Desborough issued his own petition and when the Council discovered that other officers were also about to issue demands, the pantomime horse cobbled together in the spring fell apart. Another *coup d'état* seemed imminent.

On 12 October, nine officers including Lambert, Desborough, Berry and Ashfield were relieved of their commands, and Fleetwood's role as commander-in-chief was subsumed within a seven-man committee (in which he was included) which was appointed to take charge of army matters. Monck, who had declined to sign the Derby petition and had sent word that he supported parliament was also co-opted, although the membership was dominated by Commonwealthsmen. The MPs declared that any attempts to raise money without their authority would be treasonable. For good measure, New Model troops were ordered to stand guard at Parliament. The following day was witness to tense scenes as Lambert marched his own soldiers into the precincts of Westminster and surrounded those drawn up by the civilians.

The stand-off continued for many hours while angry discussions were held back in the Council, with the soldiers accusing the

Commonwealthsmen of betraying the 'Good Old Cause'. The civilians argued back just as furiously and Bradshaw rallied himself from his sickbed to denounce Lambert to his face. As the day wore on the two sets of troops began to fraternise and share mutually felt grumbles as of old, and it became clearer that the loyalty of the soldiers under the orders of the Commonwealthsmen was drifting towards the rebel general, with whom they had collectively shared dangers and victories in the past. By nightfall and with bloodshed averted, the troops began to disperse. A faction of the army, on whose overall strength the power of the Rump ultimately depended, had won the day but its victory masked a more fundamental fragility even as it had driven a stake through the heart of the civilian republican cause.

20

'Everything is uncertain in this inconstant country'

Coldstream

The army in England has broken up the Parliament, out of a restless and ambitious humour to govern themselves and to hinder the settlement of the nation.

George Monck

We had now no government in the nation, all in confusion: no magistrate either owned or pretended, but the soldiers and they not agreed: God Almighty have mercy on us and settle us.

John Evelyn

Everything is uncertain in this inconstant country, which must amaze the world by the extraordinary things that are seen here daily.

Francesco Giavarina

The next six months were distinguished less by a strong royalist revival than the disintegration of the New Model Army as a coherent fighting force and its neutering as a political one. On paper, both Fleetwood and Lambert could count on the troops under command in England, and coup supporters such as Lilburne and Overton were sent to command the garrisons in the north. However, the support of those in Ireland and Scotland, which at over 22,000 strong outnumbered them, was far less certain. Henry Cromwell had successfully purged the army in Ireland of its more militant religious cadres, but once his brother fell, the object of its loyalty became highly uncertain. Leaving the professional soldiers in a posture of defence against 'Irish Papists and other common enemies', he gave up his office and retired to Cambridgeshire.

His replacement, Ludlow, had returned to Ireland in a fit of zeal: a brigade was despatched back to England to provide security against royalist disorders and the remainder of the officer corps was weeded of those suspected of residual loyalty to the Protectorate. The cull, and Ludlow's apparent insouciance about Irish security, alienated those veterans like Sir Hardress Waller and Sir Charles Coote, an Ulster Calvinist, who had prospered from the Cromwellian victory a decade earlier and spurred Broghill to reconsider where lay his best interests, for the Protestant landowners whom he represented were much dismayed by the lengthening instability in England. Unlike Scotland, and, in spite of the recent presence of the Irish MPs in the Westminster Parliament, the whole post-war settlement in Ireland was yet to be legitimised within the constitution – Ireland was still regarded merely as a colony rather than an integral part of the Republic. The turmoil caused by the conquest, the influx of new landowners and resultant demographic upheaval was still too fresh to allow a change of regime to be greeted with equanimity.

For the leaders of the October military coup in London, the army in Scotland was the more immediate problem given that Monck had already declared his loyalty to parliament and implicitly supported the subservience of the military to the civil power. Outside his personal loyalty to Cromwell, his relationship with the regime back in London had never been entirely happy and he had crossed metaphorical swords with the Council, and particularly with Lambert, about what he perceived to be the unequal treatment of soldiers stationed in Scotland vis-à-vis their English counterparts. Indeed, in late 1657 he had threatened to resign over the issue of arrears. He exploited the coup to reverse the changes in personnel that had been forced upon him by the Rump but also prevented officers sent from England by Fleetwood from taking up their appointments. Further, he conducted a deeper purge of those suspected of radical religious difference to ensure that his soldiers were commanded by men undistracted by anything other than personal loyalty. Those weeded out were corralled at the forbidding fortress of Tantallon Castle at the mouth of the Forth, before being sent back to England.

As the stand-off between the senior officers lengthened, their barely concealed internal propaganda war increased in volume. The affinity of the navy was critical as the first line of defence against an attack on Great Britain from either the Continent or Ireland. Monck had strong links with the sailors he had commanded against the Dutch and he sent a letter to the fleet urging them to support the civilians. Lawson inclined to the Commonwealthsmen, but his most pressing problem was the serious unrest amongst his unpaid crews and his vice-admiral had joined with Lambert and Fleetwood in condemning the split in the armed forces for which they themselves took no responsibility, preferring to heap the blame on their erstwhile colleague north of the border. Yet, while the latter had a smaller force, the soldiers under Monck had at least been paid – it was a distinction that was to prove crucial.

Back in London, government had been assumed by a Committee of Safety in which all the main groupings of those so recently in power enjoyed representation with the exception of the diehard Commonwealthsmen grouped around Hesilrige and Scot. Lambert and Fleetwood were joined by Desborough, Hewson, Lilburne and Berry as well as other less ambitious members of the former Cromwellian Council, including William Sydenham and the ever-calculating Whitelocke. But the veneer of solidarity was not enough to disguise its impotence and the splits in the army began to widen – on 1 November a lengthy polemic was sent to Fleetwood which ringingly asserted that 'The Parliament of England never raised or maintained soldiers to be law-makers, but to defend this nation against those who were law-breakers.' It was signed by Colonels Alured and Okey.[1] Yet Vane and Ludlow had also thrown in their lot with Fleetwood's clique, hoping perhaps to revive that coalition of Independents that they perceived as the only viable bulwark against both a rigid religious settlement and a restoration. For the chaotic impositions of the army and the government merry-go-round had at last revived the animal spirits of those sympathetic to the institution of monarchy while reigniting the hopes of the exiled court.

The king, disappointed with the outcome of the late summer risings and bored with all the futile hanging about in the confines of Bruges, had in the meantime decided to take himself off on a personal dip-lomatic fishing trip. He headed south to the Pyrenees to put in an appearance at the peace talks that were now taking place between the French and the Spanish. Although still nominally a guest of the Habsburgs, he perceived that Mazarin was perhaps beginning to regret the ceding of Dunkirk to the English and he had been encouraged too by the attitude of Turenne, who did not seem to bear a grudge at having his soldiers killed by British royalists at the battle of the Dunes. But between the French, who had other more imme-diate concerns and the Spanish, who presently didn't really seem to know what to do with him, Charles was unable to make much of an impression, so he travelled back towards his long-suffering advisers.

En route he stopped off to make peace with his estranged mother who, as politically unembarrassed as ever by her problematic reli-gion, had not till then forgiven Charles for taking charge of Prince Henry. Reunited with his surviving parent after a long upbringing by Protestant surrogates, the younger prince had chafed at his mother's attempts to turn him into a Roman Catholic and was anyway much keener to join his more exciting elder sibling. Charles had already astutely concluded that while an arrangement with a Catholic power could be justified by realpolitik (after all, Cromwell had done such a thing), to be seen embracing the popish faith as a matter of personal conviction would have irrevocably ended his monarchical hopes and those of his dynasty. Taking no chances yet unwilling to risk the wrath of the queen mother, who still provided some modest financial support from her French connections, Ormonde had instead been despatched on yet another complicated Stuart mission, this time to wrest Henry from her court. Henrietta Maria had stamped her tiny foot in frustration at the decline of her influence, yet had finally relented in the face of Ormonde's polite firmness. In the winter of 1659 she somewhat warily accepted reconciliation with her eldest son, a concordat eased by the charm and cheerfulness of the youngest of her children, Princess Henrietta Anne, now a sprightly teenager who was to form an intense rapport with the head of the family.

A happier Charles had returned to his own court, which seemed re-energised by hope. In retrospect, the removal from the scene of the competing Cromwellian dynasty in the late spring had not been enough to boost Stuart chances, but with the splits in the New Model Army, the other boot had dropped. The rapid and competing changes of regime had brought wider governance to a halt and the new government was assailed with messages that hinted at the confusion growing beyond London. Few seemed to know in whose name justice was to be done nor for whom the proceeds of the latest sequestrations were being raised. After a fortnight of devotions and fasting, John Evelyn published an explicitly treasonable tract entitled *An Apology for the Royal Party.* Its appearance on 7 November in London was of less note for its sentiments than for the fact that it attracted no retribution from the authorities. Gratified by the pamphlet's success (a second print run was ordered), the prim royalist was emboldened to make a direct attempt at suborning the governor of the Tower, who was an old school chum and thus expected to maintain *omertà*. Evelyn's luck held.

Lambert concluded that only a display of strength could resolve the impasse with Monck and on 3 November he left the environs of London with a large force determined to reunite the army or at the very least bring the errant general in Scotland to heel. Negotiations continued, but as Lambert inched northwards he would have become more aware of the growing isolation of his position. His surly troops were fed up and increasingly impervious to the pep talks of the godly amongst them. They were now marching back up the length of the country for the third time in as many months. Some began to desert. Unpaid, the others resorted once more to imposing themselves for free on the local population. As they passed through Nottinghamshire, they broke into Owthorpe demanding provisions but, as recorded by Lucy Hutchinson, were stoutly resisted by Sir John, who locked them in his dining room. The need for money was desperate, and back in the capital Lambert's colleagues tried to raise funds in the absence of parliament. A delegation that included Whitelocke and Fleetwood approached the city for a short-term loan but in the face of Desborough's bluster and threat to unshackle the sects, the appalled lord mayor and his fellow burghers refused point-blank.

As Lambert marched, Monck used the time to bolster his own political position. His representatives in London had already been approached by Hesilrige and Ashley Cooper with offers of preferment, but the wily Devonian was not yet ready to place his chips on a single dice-roll. Contact was made with Broghill in Ireland and an intermediary sent to sound out his old boss. Sir Thomas Fairfax thoroughly disapproved of the turn events had taken, the naked politicking of the senior officers and the actions of his former protégé, Lambert. He had ignored all the entreaties of the royalists but now offered Monck his support on the condition that the general act in the name of the elected parliament as a whole, not just a clique within it. Fairfax had had a long time to reflect upon the lesson of his part in the inadvertent establishment of the Rump eleven years earlier and now he too was an excluded Member. It was an important clarification as Monck considered his options.

By 7 December Lambert and his thinned ranks had reached Chillingham Castle in Northumberland. Behind him, the arsenal at Portsmouth had been seized by army officers sympathetic to the

Commonwealthsmen and from there Hesilrige issued a stern note to Fleetwood. Written in the manner of a sarcastic schoolteacher admonishing some naughty children it nonetheless declaimed that 'Neither do we think the Council of Officers competent persons to judge of governments, and to break parliaments, and to put new fancies of their own instead thereof as they please.'[2] London was gripped by disorders. The apprentices in the capital had presented a petition in defiance of a prohibition by the Committee of Safety and now they rioted. In the ensuing mayhem troops under Colonel Hewson opened fire, killing several, an event vividly recorded in the papers of an aspiring young civil servant and kinsman of Montagu called Samuel Pepys.

By contrast, Monck's rear appeared far more secure. He had summoned representatives from the Scottish boroughs and counties, and enjoined them to keep the peace. Although the royalist Glencairn was elected as their spokesman, the commissioners agreed: there was little appetite for troublemaking after such a hard-won period of stability, and for good measure the civilians undertook to continue to collect taxes punctiliously. Monck was also helped by his religious orientation. Although not a rigid Presbyterian he was certainly a stout one, and the actions of the revived Commonwealth and annulment of the Union with Scotland had roused all the Kirk's old fears of the English and their 'fanatic' army now under the command of Lambert. With his dispositions near completion, Monck moved the bulk of his forces to a holding area at Coldstream on the banks of the Tweed. Barely a day's march now separated him from his rival.

In the Advent season of 1659, the nerve of the leaders of the October coup back in London failed them. *Mercurius Politicus* kept up the pretence that all the disorder was the work of cavaliers and other malcontents but the cohesion of the military had fallen apart in its own way. With Monck and Lambert on the cusp of a fight in the northern borderlands, a near fatal blow landed from the navy. Lawson's Channel flotilla had been at anchor in the Downs, but now he came up the Thames with Thomas Scot on board. His agitated crewmen were short of pay, provisions were low and there was resentment at the chaos caused by the army. Lawson perceived that it was only by parliamentary authority that his matelots were going to get what was owed. He unequivocally declared for the Commonwealth and added a list of demands including the abolition of tithes and religious toleration. A group of naval commissioners led by Vane and Richard Salwey came aboard and tried to hold the attention of the sailors with their own ideas for the constitution. But a furious row developed amongst the civilians and Scot insisted that Vane be arrested. Exasperated by the irrelevant squabbling about such highfalutin ideas, the admiral instead ordered the indignant Vane to be dumped by the quayside.

To Fleetwood, the will of God had never seemed so unclear. He was assailed from all sides: the navy was blockading London from the east, Dublin Castle had been seized by Waller and he had received a petition from the hands of a contemptuous Ashley Cooper that amounted to a vote of no confidence from the excluded elite. Doubtful of the loyalty of both the militia and the New Model troops left in London he continued to prevaricate, but when urged by Whitelocke to either assert his authority or negotiate with the king, his residue of courage deserted him. After satisfying himself with anguished and lachrymose prayer, he resigned and on 26 December troopers now under the command of Colonels Okey and Alured restored those diehard members of the Rump whom the soldiers had so summarily ejected barely two months before.

In Northumberland, the over-extended force under Lambert was now caught between Monck on the Tweed and Fairfax in Yorkshire. The former lord general had evaded capture by troops sent to detain him, and near Otley in Wharfedale he had taken charge of that same brigade that had been sent over from Ireland by Ludlow. Left hanging about with neither a mission nor clear orders, the large body of troops had needed little persuasion to put themselves under such an august veteran and with his martial juices flowing once more, Fairfax led them off to secure York, which was surrendered by Lilburne without a fight. As Lambert turned south to meet this threat to his rear, Monck marched 6,000 men and their horses down to the freezing waters below Coldstream, and crossed into England unopposed on New Year's Day 1660. Trapped in a pincer and perhaps overawed by the news about Fairfax, Lambert's force finally disintegrated and by the time the Rump's order to disband reached him he had barely a squadron of cavalry at his command.

With the road clear of opposition, Monck's progress south through the snow took on the appearance of a triumphal march and once again government appeared to be back in the hands of a republican clique held up by the swords of the army. Yet, passing through York, he was reminded of his obligations by Fairfax, who emphasised the growing demand for a freely chosen and full parliament, a call that was echoed by the many petitions received by Monck's headquarters from principals of the city authorities and from the gentry in those counties through which his men travelled. By the time his leisurely advance reached St Albans however, the Rump was metaphorically digging in. Anyone associated with the October coup was either cashiered or banished, like Vane, to internal exile. Another ferocious purge of the army saw over a third of its officers dismissed and at Monck's insistence, regiments that had been held in reserve in the capital by Lambert and Fleetwood were led out of London by their new commanders.

Wider loyalty to the republicans was only skin deep and demands for the return of those members of the Long Parliament 'secluded' by Pride's Purge grew in intensity. The city authorities insisted that any loans would be conditional on the return of a full assembly and petitions flooded in from the county justices calling for an end to the lacuna in constitutional authority. The diary of Pepys records the scatological intensity of the hatred shown towards the clique at Westminster and citizens were treated to ribald pamphlets attacking both the politicians and the sects. At the Royal Exchange a gigantic pair of buttocks had been painted with a stool neatly dropping into the open jaws of Admiral Lawson, a graphic image to which a wag had added the words 'The Thanks of the House'. Elsewhere on the streets, the authority of the regime itself was publicly spurned: 'Boys do now cry "Kiss my Parliament" instead of "Kiss my arse", so great and general the contempt is the Rump come to among all men, good and bad.'³

But republicans like Scot were quick to perceive that the return of those unequivocal supporters of the Newport process of 1648 would lead to the unzipping of the entire Commonwealth settlement. A brief flurry of loyalty came by way of a counter-demonstration by the independent congregation of Praise-God Barebon, but the militantly devout were no longer as admired as once before and it attracted little support. In a sign of republican fear, those members who had failed to return or abjure Newport were formally expelled on the promise of speedy replacement, but when Hesilrige and Scot further proposed that the MPs present pronounce anathema on the Stuarts, they were narrowly defeated: clearly some of the residual Commonwealthsmen were beginning to entertain doubts.

In the first week of February, Monck and his men occupied Whitehall and its environs. Topped up from the Scottish war chest, their discipline was generally good although an incautious gathering of Quakers nearby was set upon and beaten up. Shortly after, the general delivered a respectful address at the invitation of the Commons in which he warned against both royalists and other 'fanatics', and advised the calling of fresh elections. However, Hesilrige knew that there were unhappy memories of generals who arrived in London with an army at their back, and did not fully trust the motives of the otherwise enigmatic soldier. He was determined to establish parliament's authority, most immediately by ending the stand-off with the mayor and his aldermen. He ordered Monck to enter the city precincts, arrest the most troublesome members of the city authorities and to destroy the barricades and defences that had been erected; the general unenthusiastically and grumpily complied. He had neither love for nor much confidence in the men who had so publicly and hypocritically humiliated him for his role in Ireland on the eve of the English invasion in 1649. At a conference with his subordinates and his wife that night, all his instincts were alerted to the unpopularity of his political masters and the chance of a clash between his troops and the London militia, a prospect which he dreaded.

Over the next fortnight the remaining props under the clique at Westminster melted away. Whether or not it was intended as an act of solidarity, Monck's decision to leave his men bivouacked and under tight discipline in the city precincts was taken as such by its citizens, and the news that his earlier advice had hardened into a demand for free elections according to the 1654 franchise was greeted with wild rejoicing. It was at this moment that the pejorative title of 'Rump' entered common usage and the hindquarters of many blameless animals were barbequed in the orgy of celebration that followed. As Hyde was dryly to observe, 'There can be no invention of fancy, wit, or ribaldry, that was not that night exercised to defame the Parliament and to magnify the general.'[4]

Even at this late hour, Hesilrige attempted to bring Monck to heel by insisting that he shared his military authority with the civilians, in direct contravention of the earlier promises that the general understood he had been given. In response he demanded a return of the secluded members and on 21 February 1660 many of the survivors re-entered the House under an archway of pikes formed by the soldiers and past the sullen stares of the republicans. In an immediate show of appreciation to the general, the newcomers confirmed Monck in his command of all land forces and proceeded to annul all those commissions made by their republican colleagues which had had the effect of placing 'the whole militia of the kingdom [sic] into the hands of sectaries, persons of no degree or quality, and notorious only for some new tenet in religion, and for some barbarity exercised upon the King's party'.[5]

The role of Monck in the restoration of the monarchy has undergone much revision and even the convenient shorthand that he acted as its willing midwife has been shown to be exaggerated. Certainly, the royalists felt less inhibited in drinking the king's health, but at this point his return was not a foregone conclusion. Hyde later depicted Monck's moves as part of an odyssey in which the general was seen to favour the model of the Dutch republic (with himself as a sort of British Stadtholder) and was only later reconciled to the idea of a Stuart restoration in the absence of any better ideas for his own employment.[6] This is perhaps unfair, although perfectly understandable in the context of Hyde's own endurance of exile in contrast to Monck's easier enjoyment of a change in the political wind. In truth, Monck was a soldier's soldier whose rudimentary political instincts were given a final polish by Fairfax as he travelled south. If he had harboured the ambition attributed to him by Hyde, then his meeting with Fairfax would certainly have disabused him. In backing the return of the secluded members, he issued his own manifesto in which he admitted the impossibility of the return of a king and placed his faith in the restored members to 'secure' the Commonwealth based upon a moderate Presbyterian settlement with a degree of toleration. If there was any emphasis in his agenda, it was that the soldiery be fairly treated and he issued a separate order-of-the-day to those under his command reassuring them of their pay and title to property.

By this stage of the drama, Monck's role was very nearly complete. A new Council of State was convened which was a kaleidoscope of those who had illuminated the political and constitutional process over the past twenty years. Holles and St John were given places, but so too were Cromwellians like Thurloe and Montagu, who was restored to command of the fleet, an appointment to which Lawson now happily agreed. There were no places for republican ideologues or champions of the sects, but a number of prominent Rumpers remained in positions of influence. Herbert Morley, the old political partner of Henry Marten and that governor of the Tower whom Evelyn had attempted to suborn, was appointed to the Council too. He was perhaps a good example of that type of Commonwealthsman whose outlook was more firmly conditioned by practicality than by ideology and to whom the purism of men like Scot, the impenetrability of Vane and the impulsive authoritarianism of Hesilrige were ultimately unattractive. Meanwhile, the affable but turncoat regicide Richard Ingoldsby was restored to his regiment, and in a sign of the times the sect-supporting Colonels Overton and Rich were eventually persuaded by the clink of long overdue coins to submit their soldiers to the new authority. For in a seal of approval, the city fathers had given a loan to tide over the regime: it was at twice the level for which they had originally been asked.

While a number of the returning MPs were merely content to enjoy the filip of fortune, William Prynne did not allow an excess of discretion to spoil his return to the national stage and soon this scourge of the republicans, sects, Jesuits, soldiery, et al, was loudly proclaiming in favour of a sovereign. Cromwell himself had wanted 'something of the monarchical' and the MPs were aware of the core intention of the *Humble Petition*, but as the diary of Pepys makes clear, Charles Stuart was only one of the names on people's lips and, in the Council, Oliver St John argued for the restoration of Richard Cromwell. Those with a more fleeting attention span thought the mantle would fall on that man-of-the-moment, Monck.

But the direction if not the actual speed of the wind seemed clear enough and in some despair John Milton rallied himself to another intellectual defence of the regime which still gave him employment. His *Ready and Easy Way to Establish a Free Commonwealth* was a principled effort in the face of events. To the poet, a republic had too much of an abundance of qualities to be discarded and he asked:

> What government comes neere to this precept of Christ, then a free Commonwealth; wherin they who are greatest, are perpetual servants and drudges to the publick at their own cost and charges, neglect thir own affairs; yet are not elevated above their brethren, live soberly in thir families, walk the streets as other men, may be spoken to freely, familiarly, friendly, without adoration. Wheras a king must be ador'd like a Demigod.[7]

He promoted the idea of a Harringtonian super-elite embodied in a 'Grand or General Counsel' that would sit in perpetuity. By contrast, a parliament could only ever be ephemeral. But as events rapidly unfolded, Milton struggled to keep up, and in successive editions he got into a muddle even as he strove for consistency. Like many intellectually brave and clever people under pressure, Milton was sometimes prey to naïvety.

Regarding the choice of person to be head of state, the survivors of the Long Parliament were enigmatic, but in one of their initial acts they decisively changed constitutional course in favour of a monarchy. The MPs reset the rubric of the rebellion against Charles I by authorising the republication of the Solemn League and Covenant and shortly afterwards the oath of fidelity to the Commonwealth was abolished. Religion was also something the returning MPs could enthusiastically get their teeth into, and there was a belated attempt to revive the Presbyterian model of Church governance approved by the Westminster Assembly. But the desire of the new majority in the Commons to do this perhaps showed how little progress had been made in the various efforts to institutionally embed it over the intervening years.

The rule of the major-generals had arguably marked the high point of the attempt to inculcate godliness through discipline and the period since had witnessed a gradual move in some quarters towards a more pastoral approach. As adopted by the Puritan divine Richard Baxter in his parish at Kidderminster, mentoring and catechising rather than fire-and-brimstone were instead being used to promote the message of Christianity to 'willing and tractable minds'.[8] For the more conventionally inclined like the Scottish divine Robert Baillie, there was much hand-wringing at the 'new and unsound doctrines' of Baxter and other reformist divines like John Goodwin.[9] Lucy Hutchinson too felt that the advancement of godliness in the republican period had been illusory: 'True religion was now almost lost, even among the religious party and hypocrisy became an epidemical disease.'[10]

In a sign of the times, maypoles were also making a reappearance, and despite the outraged and isolated efforts of some soldiers and magistrates to tear them down, there was little appetite to enforce the banning of libertarian acts that did not threaten public order. Notwithstanding that the Solemn League explicitly acknowledged the position of a monarch and national Church, and that Charles had himself signed an appendix to its antecedent, the writs for the new parliament were issued in the name of the Republic. It was an irony that was not lost on Thomas Scot, who used the closing hours of the parliament to make a brave, truculent and impassioned speech defending the decision to chop off the king's head and his pride at the part he had played in it all.

21

'*The ancient and fundamental laws of this kingdom*'

Blackheath

Though I know not where to hide my head at this time,
yet I dare not refuse to own that not only my hand but
my heart also, was in that action.

Thomas Scot

I can now say I am a King and not a Doge.

Charles II

The return of the secluded MPs had not been greeted with much joy
by the exiled court in Brussels. As far as Hyde was concerned, any
who sat who had been elected after war commenced in 1642 were
illegitimate. In particular, he was wary of the prospect of a rein-
troduction of those Presbyterian terms offered at Newport 'which
his late Majesty yielded unto with much less cheerfulness than he
walked to the scaffold'.[1] But the Stuarts had very few moves left
which they could make on the political chessboard and the first was
the decision to quit the Spanish Netherlands. Charles's continued
sojourn amongst hosts who were still at war with the Republic was,

in the changed circumstances, needlessly self-defeating. Packing up their meagre possessions (it didn't take too much time), the courtiers evacuated to Breda in the United Provinces, a home with which they were familiar. Too late, the Spanish realised that the king was of much greater strategic worth than could be inferred from his pawn-like circumstances. Their former ambassador, Cárdenas, who had subsequently been appointed as Habsburg emissary to the exiles, was furiously upbraided by his masters in Madrid for allowing Charles to escape. To his audience back home however, the king's move gave assurance that his own restoration, were it to come to pass, would not be achieved with foreign troops.

The mood music emanating from England was further improving for the royalists. Leading monarchists, like the 'Engager' Earl of Lauderdale, and those senior members of the Anglican hierarchy, such as the Bishop of Ely, who had been loitering in prison for many years were released. Even Sir George Booth recovered his liberty, although the memory of his recent insurrection was still fresh. Indeed, he was reinstated as a commissioner for the militia in his home county. But Lambert, who had vanquished him in Cheshire, was thrown into the Tower after he failed to raise the prodigious sum demanded for his bail. In Ireland, the Cromwellian putsch organised by Sir Hardress Waller had in turn given way to a counter-coup organised by Sir Charles Coote. Dublin Castle had again been seized and Waller was packed off to Athlone as a prisoner, together with five other regicides whom Coote hoped to use as collateral for his change of loyalty.

Although there was much mutual suspicion between the Calvinist and the more patrician Broghill, there was a coincidence of interest in protecting the Protestant ascendancy that had been embedded by the English invasion in 1649. An Irish Convention was summoned which met in the first week of March. Attended by over 160 Protestant landowners, of whom nearly a fifth were ex-soldiers who had settled, the representatives endorsed the plantation and the segregation of Connaught and adopted a thoroughly anti-Catholic tone.[2] Back in England, the new president of the Council was Sir Arthur

Annesley. He was another Anglo-Irish magnate of Presbyterian persuasion who had sat for a Welsh constituency before leaving the Long Parliament in the wake of the 1648 purge. He had sat too in Richard Cromwell's parliament as the Member for Dublin and became one of the unofficial members of the caucus that successfully agitated for a return of the members secluded by Colonel Pride. The readoption of the Solemn League effectively legitimised contact with the sovereign, and soon Annesley had commenced a cordial sequence of correspondence.

Hyde had previously sent Sir John Grenville, a kinsman of Monck's, to sound out the general and now his initiative bore fruit. In the early spring and for the first time, the army commander responded. Much romance has attached to Monck's 'conversion', contained in correspondence that was mostly delivered verbally. However, the events in the restored Long Parliament pointed logically towards a rehabilitation of monarchy, if not a recall of the Stuarts, and Monck anyway had his hands full in 'remodelling' the army and ensuring the settlement of the navy, where he had been appointed as joint general-at-sea with Montagu. The former officer in the royal army was still minded to disguise the direction which his loyalty was taking (he had already assured Hesilrige of his attachment to the Commonwealth), but he advised the exiled court that their recall would only be per-missible in circumstances where the professional army was properly looked after and that there was no attempt to annul all the changes of ownership of property consequent to the civil wars.

Meanwhile, the Long Parliament took a further step towards a restoration when a motion introduced by Thomas Scot and Henry Marten which would have prevented any who had fought for the former king from voting in the forthcoming elections, was defeated. But although the elections were to be 'free' it was not the intention that they be a free-for-all. Commoners or peers who had fought for the late king might vote, but they were not permitted to become members, and in London a proclamation was issued barring cava-liers and disbanded officers from the capital for the duration. In the tense atmosphere, an Anglican clergyman who published a nakedly royalist tract, *The Fear of God and the King*, was jailed for his pains. The subsequent electioneering and the poll were rumbustious but remarkably free of bloodshed, although Quakers and sectaries continued to be roughed up. Marchamont Nedham attempted an early prototype of 'fake' reportage by publishing *News from Brussels*, a piece of scaremongering allegedly written by a cavalier which promised all sorts of bloody revenge should the Stuarts be restored. But the editor's value in whipping up a claque for the Republic was way past its peak and the Council ordered that he be dismissed and that *Mercurius Politicus* be placed in more disinterested hands. In fact, it was Pepys who seemed more accurately to intuit the direction of public opinion when he observed 'that the Sectarys do talk high what they will do; but I believe all to no purpose . . . And it is now clear that either the Fanatiques must now be undone, or the Gentry and the citizens throughout England and clergy must fall, in spite of their Militia and army, which is not at all possible I think.'[3]

The most sensational news of the campaign was the escape from the Tower on 10 April by John Lambert, by the simple act of sliding down some knotted bed-linen to his accomplices on the riverbank below. With both the army and the militia in the midst of a reorganisation, he hoped to exploit residual resentment amongst the soldiery. But the money for arrears was by now getting through and troops were being gradually disbanded, their service complete. Further, on the day before Lambert's escape, Monck had pledged the army's oath to be bound by whatever constitution the forthcoming parliament should decide upon. The news about Lambert caused alarm nonetheless and was the event that crystallised Monck's change of loyalties – Grenville was speedily sought out and instructed to tell his master that in the event Lambert was to secure part of the army, Monck would stand against him in the name of the king. Even at this advanced stage, the Devonian's change of heart was still conditional. His antagonist made his way to the Midlands and quixotically chose Edgehill as a rallying point. As the scene of the first major encounter of the civil war in England it held a certain resonance but Lambert seemed to have forgotten that for the king's opponents, its outcome had been inconclusive at best, while others had considered it a narrow royalist victory. Richard Ingoldsby was sent north and, just outside Daventry, he ran the gang of desperados to ground. After a somewhat pathetic attempt to evade capture across newly ploughed fields that slowed his exhausted charger, Lambert was led back to the Tower in ignominy. En route, he was made to stand under the gallows at Tyburn, his public humiliation complete.

In Breda, the advisers around the king very quickly perceived that in the uncertain conditions back home, they were only ever likely to get one attempt at plighting the Stuart troth to the residual stewards of the Republic: there would be neither a rehearsal nor a rerun. It was now that the part of Charles's brain bequeathed by his maternal grandfather Henri IV took precedence over that which he had inherited from his father. Beyond the allure of the mystique of monarchy and its quasi-mythical association with the 'ancient constitution', Charles had virtually nothing to offer beyond his position as the next in line to the 'martyred' king. He had not yet even sired a legitimate heir to ensure continuity. But he and his close advisers were very aware of the chances that his father had squandered, at both Hampton Court and Newport, to place the onus for the successful delivery of an acceptable settlement on the king's antagonists. They were not going to repeat the blunder.

Accordingly, Charles and his counsellors worked up a manifesto that was shortly afterwards made public as the Declaration of Breda. With a masterly use of language suggesting that the tangibly powerless monarch-in-waiting had never truly been superseded, the king graciously outlined the most pressing issues confronting the state and his willingness to be led by parliament in solving them. His proposal to address the contentious issue of religion was lifted straight out of the Cromwellian manual, with liberty of conscience permitted so long as it did not clash with the requirement for public order. He was happy that this be left to the ultimate discretion of the MPs, as well as any rearrangement of the vast upheaval in the patterns of land ownership that had occurred as a consequence of civil wars. In its statesmanlike attention to an important matter that even Ireton had missed in his Heads of Proposals, the king exhorted the parliament to settle the arrears of the state's soldiers in full, the better to secure the peace. Additionally, pardon was offered to all former opponents who metaphorically came out with their hands up within a grace period of forty days from the official date of the Declaration. Naturally, there were certain (un-named) individuals who were beyond the pale of forgiveness, but again the king proposed to leave retribution in the hands of the MPs.

The Declaration was as important for what it left out, such as the powers that the king might expect to enjoy. It was also very much directed towards the parliament in England and neither Scotland nor Ireland was referenced. There was no need to complicate matters with digressions about two nations the Republic had already conquered and which would, anyway, be unrepresented in the forthcoming assembly. In the case of Ireland, the omission may be explained by the judgement that it was best not used as a royalist 'springboard', a dynamic that had contributed so decisively to the commencement of hostilities eighteen years before. Indeed, the king had already spurned a suggestion from the turncoat Sir Charles Coote that he go to Ireland to do such a thing. Charles was already king in Scotland, but his memories of it were entirely unhappy and neither he nor Hyde presently felt any residual duty to further conciliate the dominant interest group there which had caused the Stuarts so much grief. The Covenanted monarch had last been on Scottish soil in the first week of August 1651, and nearly two centuries were to pass before a British king set foot north of the Tweed once again.

But the biggest omission was any desire for revenge beyond justice for that small and, by implication, unrepresentative group which had had a hand in his father's execution. Indeed, the language of Breda suggested an intention that was almost entirely benign: 'Because the passion and uncharitableness of the times have produced several opinions in religion, by which men are engaged in parties and animosities against each other (which when they shall hereafter unite in a freedom of conversation, will be composed or better understood)

we do declare a liberty to tender consciences, and that no man shall
be disquieted . . . in matter of religion.'

An ignorant or impressionable reader of these sentiments might
be forgiven for thinking that the wars had arisen out of a regrettable
lapse of good manners rather than the passion of titanic and irreconcilable forces. Thus edited, the document was sealed and entrusted
to the critical care of Sir John Grenville, who was tasked with the
stage management of the Declaration's official appearance and, most
importantly, that it be promulgated by the new parliament. The
court could now do no more than hold its collective breath and wait.

In the interval, the alert senses of the ruling elite in the United
Provinces were quick to pick up the change in the weather and soon
Charles was being treated with much cordiality and, in his invitation
to the Hague, as a de facto head of state. The trickle of visitors and
letter-writers to the exiles at Breda grew into a tide of supplicants
and place-seekers, all keen to profess their new loyalty. Both Hyde
and Charles were sceptical of these fair-weather royalists (the king
was reported to be nauseated by the displays of self-interested syco-
phancy) but in the meantime many brought or sent money and
gold, and at last bills were paid and the long-suffering members of
the household staff were given both their wages and a bonus for
their loyalty. Lucy Hutchinson was caustically to note later, of the
scramble for preferment, that the king 'saw nothing but prostrates,
expressing all the love that could make a prince happy. Indeed it was
a wonder that day to see the mutability of some and the hypocrisy
of others and the servile flattery of all'.[4] But she perhaps missed the
important point that beyond his closest companions, advisers and
one or two key facilitators back in England, Charles was really very
little obliged to anybody.

The Convention Parliament opened on 25 April 1660. Monck's
advice that it be composed according to the franchise and seats of
the first Protectorate parliament had been ignored and the members of the Long Parliament had gone back to the rubric of their
own election in 1640. In the event, over half the members of the
Commons were newcomers and many were younger men who had

been children at the outbreak of hostilities with the king, and were accordingly far less impressed by, or even understanding of, the preoccupations and zeal of their parents and older kin. Despite the restrictions, over sixty unambiguous royalists were elected, including Massey for Gloucester, where the citizens had rioted in his favour. By contrast, Thurloe failed to secure a seat, despite the personal backing of Monck. A mere sixteen surviving members of the Rump were returned (Hesilrige had gone into hiding), but the victories of both Ludlow and Scot were contested and shortly afterwards they were ejected from their places. Their decision to maintain such a high profile was both principled and brave, but others were made of less stern stuff and soon the republican Luke Robinson, a close ally of Scot, was making tearful apologies to his fellow Members for his previous loyalty to the Republic.

The man chosen to be Speaker of the Commons was Sir Harbottle Grimston, a fifty-seven-year-old Puritan who had assisted Holles at the negotiations with Charles I at Newport. He had been a leading critic of the New Model Army and the way in which the profession-als had superseded the militia in the fight against the king. Briefly arrested at Pride's Purge, he had been one of those elected to the second Protectorate parliament, and again had been excluded. In the selection of Grimston, the Presbyterian members appeared to put down a marker that whatever settlement emerged, it would adhere to that outlined by the Westminster Assembly. In the meantime, these plans were overshadowed by the return of the old House of Lords, an event which made the return of a king likelier still.

On the day that parliament reassembled, led by the Earl of Manchester, those peers who had declined the invitation to sit in Cromwell's Other House and others who were Independents resumed their seats in the Lords. The following day, and after a polite kerfuffle, the soldiers on duty at Westminster allowed entry to the Earls of Middlesex, Dorset and Rivers. Having spurned Cromwell's Other House for its subversion of the hereditary principle, those like Manchester, Saye and Sele, and Pembroke could hardly object now to the return of their fellow aristocrats, many of whom had come of age during the previous two decades. Shortly after, the newly elected MP Heneage Finch proposed full admission of their lordships and thus filled an upper chamber that was determinedly royalist.

With a great sense of timing, the faithful Sir John Grenville sprang into action and, on May Day 1660 and with the leave of the Council of State, the Declaration of Breda was read out in both Houses of Parliament. The Lords declared that 'according to the ancient and fundamental laws of this kingdom, the Government is and ought to be, by Kings, Lords and Commons'. In a combination of bombast, wish fulfilment and lack of tact, the Lords had nonetheless seized the initiative and a few hours later in the Commons, their less socially august colleagues concurred. It was an extraordinary reversal of the dynamic of the last twenty years. Yet it was a full week before Charles was confirmed in his wider inheritance. The king's personal intentions might be benign, but who was to say what would follow in his wake? There were many in both Houses who had been happy to underwrite the rebellion against the Stuarts while favouring the institution of monarchy itself. Broghill had already written to Thurloe that he dreaded the temper of a cavalier parliament. More importantly for the court, a restoration would be difficult if not impossible if any of the armed forces resisted it.

At this stage, Montagu had a trickier job as his cadre of officers had not been so thoroughly purged as had been the New Model Army over the past tempestuous months. With the ending of Lambert's *coup de théâtre* in the Midlands, he and other holdouts like Okey and Axtell had gone into captivity. Residual units that were suspected of stirring for the 'Good Old Cause' were paid off and disbanded while the large London militia was now commanded by men unashamedly inclined to the king. Two principle officers of impeccable Cromwellian loyalty, the regicides Whalley and Goffe, fled across the Atlantic aboard the aptly named ship, the *Prudent Mary*. Accompanied by Pepys as his secretary, the admiral nervously read the royal manifesto to his senior officers on 3 May. He was helped by the compliance of Lawson but the more junior of his officers seemed, according to Pepys, rather grudging in their acceptance. After all, the navy was still chasing royalist privateers around the Channel and the Western Approaches. In the end, pay, the imminence of a prisoner exchange with the Spanish and a desire among the ratings to go home to see their families proved decisive: between the lower decks and the senior wardroom, the intermediate ranks were squeezed into submission. The admiral was both relieved and delighted, and later revealed to Pepys some of the correspondence, hitherto concealed, into which he had entered with Charles and his brother, the Duke of York. The diarist was impressed that 'my Lord should carry all things so wisely and prudently as he doth, and I was over-joyful to see him in so good condition; and he did not a little please himself to tell me how he had provided for himself so great a hold on the King'.[5] Evidently, Montagu had in his own way too been playing a long game.

Back on dry land and despite the hopes of the Presbyterian caucus (which had been inclined to see Monck as one of their own), Newport and the Solemn League were by now redundant. Charles had crossly rebuffed the divines who had travelled to Holland to try to persuade the king to abjure the Book of Common Prayer. The proclamation of the royal title had not been conditional and appeared to take the Declaration of Breda at its word. Indeed, a more forthright reaction against the Puritan settlement had already taken root and on 10 May Richard Baxter delivered a frightened-sounding sermon to the Lord Mayor and his aldermen in which he deplored the public hostility to the ministry and the number of assaults that were now taking place, many (so he claimed) at the instigation of sectaries. Anglicans on the other hand began to feel stronger stirrings of hope, in contrast to those former servants of the Republic who were by now in fear of their liberty if not their lives, and rushing to secure pardon. Among them was Herbert Morley, the Councillor of State who returned to John Evelyn for help having previously blanked him. The prickly royalist had been somewhat put out by what he now regarded as a lack of gumption by the former governor of the Tower and he passed him on to Mordaunt who had rapidly established himself as a gatekeeper for the newly penitent. Morley was able to buy his absolution for £1,000.

Others were not so fortunate. Although Charles had left the matter of retribution in the hands of parliament, it was well known that he expected the spilling of some blood in recompense for that of his father. Key regicides like Harrison, who had calmly and bravely awaited his fate at home, were taken into custody. On 9 May, Heneage Finch introduced a Bill of 'Pardon, Indemnity and Oblivion' to the Commons which was used to formalise the hunt for the regicides. Appointed Keeper of the Records, William Prynne was soon hard at work as the chief of evidence-gathering and tartly observed to the Speaker that 'I have been almost choked with the dust of neglected records, interred in their own rubbish of sundry years, in the White Tower'.[6] Of the fifty-nine men who had signed the king's death warrant, twenty had since died, including the president of the court that had tried him. John Bradshaw had emerged from an unremarkable career as a jurist to become one of the leading lights of the Republic and a determined critic of the serial interventions of the army in its affairs. His last act of service had been to confront Lambert for his ousting of the Rump the previous autumn, but he had died a sick man a few days later. However final, death – whether of natural causes or at the hands of the hangman – did not necessarily confer oblivion, and many of the MPs were inclined to harden the capital sanction with acts of attainder which would deprive the guilty not only of their lives but also their property, thus condemning their kin to destitution.

Perceiving that a vengeful mood might prove the route to royal approval, some outdid themselves. Sir John Lenthall, who had been knighted by Oliver Cromwell in one of his more royal flourishes, was the son of the former Speaker and had recently been elected for a seat in Oxfordshire. With the wisdom of inexperience, he proposed that not just the regicides but all who had drawn swords against Charles I were guilty. This effrontery was altogether too much for his older colleagues and he was booted out of the Commons, his tainted knighthood forfeited. Nonetheless, for the time being the floor of the House was treated to various instances of abasement and recantation. As well as the tears of Robinson, Ingoldsby staged

a convincingly lachrymose display in which he placed the blame for
his alleged calumny firmly in the lap of the former lord protector.
Despite the best efforts of his wife Lucy to paint him as a granite
pillar of rectitude, Colonel John Hutchinson too sent in a letter of
abject regret which was not, however, enough to prevent his expulsion as an MP. Amongst all the heightened emotion, it fell to Sir
Thomas Fairfax to provide a more dignified recollection when he
observed that 'If any man must be excepted [from pardon], I know
no man that deserves it more than myself, for I was General of the
Army at that time and had power sufficient to prevent the proceedings against the King; but I did not think fit to make use of it to that
end.'[7]

Another fortnight was to separate the proclamation of Charles as
king of England and his landfall in Kent. Both he and his advisers
were conscious that he was a presently impoverished sovereign taking on a penurious state and the urgent need for cash to grease His
Majesty's wheels coincided with a statesmanlike understanding that
the mystique of monarchy would best be preserved if the king was
not seen to be grabbing at his inheritance. Both the city and the MPs
had voted a loan of £100,000 and a £50,000 down payment respectively, but this was but small change in the context of the known
liabilities and was heavily discounted once the promises of cash were
converted into bills of exchange on the Amsterdam money market.
The Dutch had the means and the motivation to be more generous
on their own account. The British republican regime had been an
almost continuous antagonist of the United Provinces, despite the
coincidence of their religious outlook and the best efforts of Oliver
Cromwell. The restoration of the Stuarts seemed to promise a more
harmonious relationship and it was well known that Charles wished
to bring an end to the costly war with Spain, Holland's most important trading partner. Accordingly, the Dutch merchants and regents
between them promised to arrange a sum very nearly four times that
which Charles had been pledged by his compatriots.

But the actual money took time to gather, and in the meantime
the court moved to the Hague. Here, the king met parliament's

commissioners on 16 May 1660 in the august surroundings of the Mauritshuis. The delegation was composed of the principled and the self-serving and included six members of the House of Lords and Sir George Booth, whose revolt now seemed prescient. In the first instance however, the dilapidated appearance of both the sovereign and his retinue appalled his visitors: patches, worn-down heels, and frayed and dirty trim abounded and, as recorded by Pepys, it was wondered if the entire ensemble on display was worth more than forty shillings.[8] Amidst the expressions of cordiality and regret about the length of the interregnum, Charles held a private audience with Sir Thomas Fairfax and emerged looking pensive and somewhat subdued. His spirits were, however, raised when Grenville appeared with a small trunk full of gold coins (an advance from the city), and his composure momentarily deserted him as he gathered his family around to view the trove. As preparations continued for his return aboard Montagu's fleet, the new sovereign and his family were further honoured by their Dutch hosts. A ball was given in which the king danced with his elder sister Princess Mary. Charles was clothed entirely in black: it was the suit that he had worn in mourning of his father in 1649 and was the only elaborate costume he possessed which was not presently falling to pieces.

Sending his brothers ahead the night before, a better-dressed Charles boarded Montagu's flagship the *Naseby* on 23 May. A last-minute purge of any rating who might stage an assault upon His Majesty had taken place and the king was greeted by an enormous amount of cheering by the sailors and by the bystanders who had gathered on the shoreline at Scheveningen. His first act was to rename the fighting ship the *Royal Charles*, although the elaborate carving at the head of the prow was to remain for a good while longer – it showed an easily recognisable protector satisfactorily trampling upon wooden representations of all England's enemies of the past eleven years. Amidst the ceremony, everyone seemed impressed by the king's demeanour, which was both affable and thoughtful, but soon his higher spirits broke through as he treated his enlarged entourage with the story of his escape after Worcester. The hand of

God had clearly saved the monarch for this very moment and the events were recounted with great enthusiasm to the agape courtiers. However, the long years of danger, exile, penury and frustration had also produced a much wiser prince than could be said of his father at the time of his own accession, and there was genuine hope that Charles was a man who could suture if not completely heal the great divisions in his realm.

The king stepped ashore at Dover on the afternoon of 25 May and among the first to greet the royal party was Monck, whom Charles greeted somewhat effusively, or so it seemed, as 'father'. Yet whatever Monck had or had not done to facilitate the return of the king, his most decisive contribution was that he had not stopped it. Among the returning exiles, Ann, Lady Fanshawe, had been on hand to recall 'the joy and gallantry of that voyage' and certainly her head was turned by the enthusiasm and discipline of the Jack Tars and the spruce appearance of the ships. Her enthusiastic recollection has become a staple of all the accounts of the Restoration but amidst the colour and rejoicing, Charles had to give immediate thought to the shape of his new government. He could hardly be faulted for his lack of detailed knowledge of each individual now at his disposal but he instinctively understood the need to balance reward for his most steadfast loyalists (amongst whom Lady Ann's husband, Sir Richard, was prominent), with the bringing together of those associated with the former regime who had recent experience of government and those who could be the most politically useful. The early ceremonial of his homecoming was arguably the easiest bit – both Monck and Montagu were created Knights of the Garter, amongst the four who were so honoured. More practically, upon arrival at the dilapidated environs of Canterbury Cathedral, the king convened his first Privy Council.

The great offices of government were divided between the royalist exiles Hyde (who was confirmed as lord chancellor), Sir Edward Nicholas and the Earl of Southampton. Sir Edward was appointed as one of two secretaries of state, the other being William Morrice, a hitherto obscure functionary who was the secretary and adviser of

George Monck. The wily Devonian, himself now a privy councillor, knew that gratitude had a very short shelf life in the rough world of politics and he was determined to have a trusted worker bee at the top of government who could give advance warning if at any time the king was inclined to depart from his side of the implicit bargain he had made with the general. Lady Ann Fanshawe was less impressed by the promotion of this Cromwellian relic to the position that she had expected her husband to fill, and deprecated Morrice's humble background as that of 'a poor country gentleman of about £200 a year, a fierce Presbyterian and one that never saw the King's face'.[9] The disappointment of the royalists was to be an enduring theme of the Restoration.

On 29 May, his thirtieth birthday, the king rode with a now vast entourage towards London. At Blackheath, Monck had assembled one of the largest concentrations of troops seen since the wars in a display of menacing loyalty that stood between the monarch and his eagerly waiting citizens of the capital. It was a dry day with a brisk breeze catching the elaborate feathers that now adorned the courtiers' brand-new hats. The troops were drawn up at attention. In front of each rank stood a file of officers, some of them newcomers appointed for their political reliability. Behind them however stood many of the old sweats of the New Model Army. The religious radicals had since been weeded out and their less valued colleagues demobilised; here now were the veterans of Naseby and Dunbar, and some who had been on hand for the royal comeuppance at Worcester. Others had returned from the campaign in the Spanish Netherlands. They were all united by their fighting ability and shared comradeship, perhaps the first truly professional army of Europe.[10]

Charles II and his brothers rode forward and came to a halt a few yards in front of the massed formation. From beneath their helmets and from scarred and grizzled faces, many eyes met those of the sovereign. Only the heads of the horses stirred; apart from the wind, there were no other sounds beyond the snorts of the animals and the jingle of their bridles. After what seemed an interminable pause, the king removed his hat and was likewise slowly followed by Princes

James and Henry, and those of their entourage. There was a short shout of command, seemingly miles away, and the massed ranks stepped forward one pace and with an immense rattle of weaponry, laid their pikes and muskets on the ground. They then stood back at attention for some moments before another order had them pick up their weapons. The New Model Army had symbolically transferred its allegiance to the king. At the back of the press of horses around the sovereign and on his own bay charger sat a swarthy-looking and plainly dressed gentleman, his jet hair and goatee beard flecked with grey. If you had observed him closely, you might have caught just the faintest welling of tears in his dark eyes.

Epilogue

Chepstow Castle

We bring before your Lordships into judgement this day the murderers of a King. A man would think the laws of God and men had so fully secured these sacred persons that the sons of violence should never approach to hurt them. For, my Lord, the very thought of such an attempt hath ever been presented by all laws, in all ages, in all nations, as a most unpardonable treason.

Sir Heneage Finch

On the evening of 9 September 1680 a man in his late seventies sat picking at a meagre supper. He was heavily wrapped in a shawl and wore fingerless mittens as the cold air rising from the River Wye below insinuated itself into every nook and cranny of the fortress in which the man was incarcerated. Halfway through his meal, the prisoner began to choke violently on a piece of food that he could neither swallow nor regurgitate. He fell gasping to the floor and, unable to control his convulsions, he died. Yet apart from the discomfort of the cold and his dramatic end, it had not been a particularly onerous confinement by the standards of the age – the man had his own furniture, and books and papers, and had been able to take as much exercise as his elderly frame would allow. He even had the company of his mistress. The man had been held at Chepstow Castle and its environs for well over a decade, having been moved from gaol at Windsor Castle by order of a sovereign who simply could not bear to have him so close to the royal presence in London. Accordingly, the bleak fortress on the Welsh side of the border with England was chosen as a particularly apt place for the prisoner to reflect upon his misdeeds, for Wales had been strongly royalist in the late civil wars and the prisoner was the regicide Henry Marten.

At the Restoration, Marten would have considered himself fortunate had he known that he would live to a ripe old age. He was one of the few survivors of that vanguard of MPs in the Rump who had pressed for the end of the monarchy as well as taking part in the trial of the new king's father and signing the warrant for his death. He represented enduring political danger. Nonetheless, he defended himself with some brio at his own trial, at first by outrageously claiming that his arraignment was a case of mistaken identity. He was certainly not going to abase himself as other republicans had done and he scorned the 'royal party' which 'could contrive no one sacrifice so proper to appease the ghost of their often soiled cause, both in point of revenge and interest, as the persons who had the boldness to make an example of their Ring-leader'.[1]

Evidently, he had friends in high places who recalled the consideration that he had shown towards defeated royalists and who perhaps admired the almost brazen indifference that he displayed to being called a traitor. Certainly, his letters to his mistress, Mary Ward, while he awaited his fate in the Tower revealed both his stoicism but also his determination to outwit his vengeful opponents. To him, 'The skill is not in being weather wise, but weather proof.'[2]

Thirteen of his fellow regicides were not so lucky. The Convention Parliament made heavy weather of compiling the list of those whose blood was to be forfeited for that of the martyred king, but in the end thirty-two men (including the unidentified axe-man, who had merely been doing his job) were selected to be beyond the pale of mercy. Charles II signed the Indemnity Bill some four months after it had originally been introduced and, on 9 October 1660, twenty-eight of those 'excepted' from pardon went on trial for their lives. One of the first to be hauled before the bar, Thomas Harrison, bitterly noted the irony of being judged by men such as Denzil Holles, Monck and Viscount Saye and Sele, who had themselves rebelled against the late sovereign.[3] But this, and the argument that the regicides had been acting in accordance with the instructions of the parliament, was brushed aside by the prosecution team led by Sir Heneage Finch.

The result of the trial was a foregone conclusion, although in its scant regard for the Common Law it could be said to have resembled the judicial treatment meted out to Charles I, to which could be added the further injustice of legal novelty. The majority of the condemned, including Marten, were held in confinement awaiting the king's pleasure, but in the third week of October ten men were sent to the scaffold to suffer death by the excruciating torture of hanging, drawing and quartering. The first to die was Harrison, who was followed a day later by his fellow Fifth Monarchist, republican and regicide John Carew. The flamboyant general was an object of particular loathing for the royalists, not least because of the perceived inferiority of his social status but also because of the outrageous claims of his religious views, which had also upset many of his fellow republicans. Nonetheless, he bore his end with great fortitude. On 13 October he was hauled to Charing Cross on a low hurdle, his body bruised and splattered by the juddering journey across cobblestones and through the mud and filth. He was hanged from a huge triangular gibbet and, still conscious, was cut down and stripped of his clothing. The hangman ripped open his abdomen and was just about to cut away his genitals when Harrison rallied and managed to punch the enraged executioner in the face. It was his last act, as his entrails were torn out with pincers and thrown onto a nearby brazier.

Over the next six days the others followed in grisly ritual, including the idealist lawyer John Cook and the Republic's first spy-master, the fanatical Thomas Scot. But the crowds at Charing Cross soon got restive – the last dignified moments of the condemned began to attract sympathy, while the inhabitants of the area complained that all the gore and the frightful smell of burning guts was letting down the neighbourhood. The site of execution was swiftly moved back to Tyburn, where two officers (Colonels Axtell and Hacker), who had been shopped by their former colleagues and were judged to have been complicit in the king's end, were killed in their turn. Three other men who had been condemned to death *in absentia* thought that they had managed to escape to Europe. But the commercially minded Miles Corbet (who had been the last of the fifty-nine to put his name to the death warrant), Colonel Okey and the irascible former governor of the Tower, John Barkstead, were later betrayed by the turncoat republican George Downing, who had returned to the Dutch republic as a representative of the new regime.[4] For Okey, there was the added insult that Downing (who was rewarded for his perfidy with land next to Whitehall) had been a former subordinate in the New Model Army. Hauled back to England, all three were put to death in April 1662.

Although surviving regicides, such as Edmund Ludlow who had managed to flee abroad, were relentlessly pursued, the appetite for show trials and displays of vengeance in England petered out in the summer of 1662. There was, however, one final spasm. The earlier death of the leading lights of the rebellion against the monarchy had frustratingly denied the new elite a sacrifice of stature. In a loathsome spectacle, the bodies of Cromwell, Ireton and Bradshaw had been disinterred from their resting place in the Henry VII chapel in Westminster Abbey, and ritually 'executed'. Even the republican hero Blake was dragged out of his grave in an act of petty and demeaning spite. Among the survivors, and although not a regicide like Marten, Arthur Hesilrige too would have considered himself fortunate not to have been caught by the swell of retribution at the Restoration. Monck had stood by his word to plead on behalf of his former antagonist, but it still required a vote in parliament to stop the autocratic Commonwealthsman from being added to the list of those to be punished. But the strain of the preceding year had evidently broken him and he died, a prisoner in the Tower, in early 1661. Now, in June 1662, it was decided to proceed against General John Lambert and Henry Vane. As with Hesilrige, neither had been on the original list of those 'excepted' from the Act of Indemnity but, under pressure from a new assembly at Westminster (the so-called 'Cavalier Parliament') which was determined to show its own abhorrence of the execution of Charles I, his son was persuaded to renege on his implicit pledges of mercy. Lambert took a soldierly attitude, humbly accepted his responsibility and pleaded for his life, which was spared. But the intellectual in Vane simply could not resist a principled stand in the dock. What Marten had achieved through sheer chutzpah was denied the convoluted theorist. He was considered just too dangerous a talisman to leave alive and he was beheaded on Tower Hill, his last insistent words of self-exculpation drowned out by the drummers around the scaffold.

Scotland too was to experience bloodletting. Having carefully put his affairs in order, the Marquis of Argyll presented himself at court, but, instead of receiving an audience with the man whom he had crowned at Scone ten years before, he was promptly arrested and returned to Edinburgh for trial. The wily Covenanter had been sure-footed enough in the past to display his convictions orally rather than commit them to paper and at one point it looked as if his prosecution would fail. But at a crucial moment, Monck provided the documents which proved his collaboration and help in the suppression of Glencairn's rebellion. It was enough to condemn him, and the nobleman was beheaded by a rudimentary guillotine known as the 'Maiden' on 27 May 1661. An enfeebled Wariston was captured two years later. Years of enforced hiding and the apparent disloyalty of his Maker had so preyed on his mind that his nephew recorded that 'It was apparent that age, hardship and danger, had done their work effectually on his iron nerves, and the intrepid advocate of the Covenant exhibited the mental imbecility of an idiot.'[5]

But he was tried all the same and managed to recover his lucidity on the scaffold to deny his treason with some passion before the hangman kicked the ladder away from beneath his feet. For the king, the bloody denouement was perhaps his sweetest moment of revenge. His animus against the Scots for their original rebellion and for their overweening presumption in victory ran deep, a hatred that had been repeatedly stoked by Hyde. His adherence to the Covenant was declared null and void, and copies of the Solemn League were burnt by the public executioner. The Declaration of Breda had given no undertakings in respect of Scotland, and a ferocious clerical reaction developed in the wake of the Restoration. Episcopacy was reimposed and a brutal purge of the presbytery saw many ministers ejected from their livings. For objecting to the change, the Remonstrant leader James Guthrie was hanged and his adherents faced years of persecution.

Although the Restoration was neither bloodless nor free of vengeance, at least outside Scotland it was relatively restrained. The king was not by nature implacable, although he did allow many of the surviving regicides and leading republicans to fester in prison for want of the will to pardon them. His most immediate and signal service was to put his new subjects at their ease and to forestall any thoughts of wider physical retribution or of a return to a republic. According to Hyde, his affability and apparent sincerity so captured the two Houses of Parliament that the king could not but rebuke himself that he had been away so long. The chancellor was perhaps over-claiming that '. . . did the merciful hand of God in one month bind up all these wounds . . .' but Charles instinctively recognised the pressing requirement to restore the dynasty's prestige and to regild the mystique of his position.[6] Thus the monarchy as public theatre was swiftly revived as a unifying force. On 6 July, John Evelyn went to the Banqueting House to watch the sovereign 'Touch for the Evil' by which a royal caress was believed to banish any ailment from the person so honoured. Even the sceptical Evelyn seemed taken in by the hocus-pocus with its incantations and elaborate ritual.[7] The ceremony proved such a wild success that encore performances had strictly to be limited by ticket and were in no way diminished by the knowledge of the death from smallpox of Prince Henry and the king's eldest sister, Princess Mary, before the year was out.

Two days after passage of the Indemnity Act, a Bill had been introduced to wind up the New Model Army and to put the security of the state back into the hands of the part-time militia and navy alone. This time, there was to be no messing about with the payment of arrears, and the king stood by his earlier promise to Monck and Fairfax. The final process of disbandment was brought to its conclusion remarkably smoothly and John Evelyn noted without a trace of rancour that 'I paied the greate Tax of Pole-money, levied for the disbanding of the Army, 'til now kept up; I paid as Esquire 10 pounds and 1 s[hilling]: for every Servant in my house etc.'[8]

Shortly thereafter parliament voted the new sovereign an annual allowance of £1,200,000 which was far less than had been voted to Cromwell pursuant to the *Humble Petition and Advice*, but generous enough in the context of a very much reduced military establishment. Everyone in authority seemed eager to put the past behind them and to preserve that impulse of hope that had animated the earliest days of the Restoration.

On St George's Day 1661, and amid much colourful pageantry, that was a deliberate rebuke to the dour aesthetic of the Republic, Charles II was crowned in London. A goldsmith (Robert Vyner, who was promptly knighted on delivery) had been commissioned to replicate, for the sum of £30,000, the coronation regalia that had been turned into scrap during the Commonwealth.[9] Both Pepys and Evelyn were on hand to observe and record the celebrations from close quarters, although having been in the abbey since first light, Pepys missed some of the ceremony as he 'had so great a list to pisse' that he had to creep out. The following day, and while the younger diarist nursed an almighty hangover, the snooty aesthete was further honoured to read to the sovereign a panegyric which he had himself composed. Evelyn would doubtless have been put out to learn that His Majesty had whispered to an aide his hope that it would not go on for too long, but at least the royalist went to bed that night well satisfied. The Son of David had returned.

The Republic had lasted a little over eleven years. An enormous

amount of ink was spilled over the following centuries to explain
the meaning to be found in the bloodshed and turmoil and it would
be presumptuous now to try to trump all those who have been, and
are, far better qualified to offer an objective judgement. There are
perhaps some strands, among many, that can be pulled together. The
monarchical state that Charles II inherited was in most of its particulars the one to which his father had reluctantly acceded during
the constitutional crisis of 1640–2. The king then decided to make
a fight of it, and in spite of the unfavourable odds, by showing great
resilience and resourcefulness, he very nearly achieved an improbable
victory. His cause was broken in the field by the powerful Scottish
army and by the English Parliament's second iteration of its own
fighting force – the New Model Army. In the wake of Charles's
military defeat, there were three attempts at a settlement by the
different (but linked) constituencies that had fought against him:
the Covenanters at Newcastle, the New Model Army at Hampton
Court and the English parliamentarians at Newport. All foundered,
but the second Civil War galvanised the most radical of his opponents with the realisation that the only way out of the impasse would
be through Charles Stuart's removal.

But having negated the constitutional legitimacy conferred by a
monarchical sovereign, the Republic was unable to find it on its own
account. Pride's Purge had reduced the parliamentary coalition to
a small and unrepresentative caucus, but it was this grouping (the
Rump) which delivered a republic. It might have made a go of it had
it kept faith with the New Model Army, for the relationship between
the civilians and the swordsmen was arguably the defining feature
of the era, most particularly in England. The New Model Army's
involvement in the political process was evolutionary rather than revolutionary. Initially it was restricted by the Self-Denying Ordinance
(which was serially resurrected and which hindered the formation of
a coherent and consistent army 'voice' at Westminster) and by the
reluctance of its first commander to involve himself in matters that
he believed were the concern of his civilian masters. Much later it
was defined by the refusal of the high command (despite the more

ambiguous position of the intermediate ranks) to countenance the army becoming an agent of extra-parliamentary agitation by making common cause with the Levellers.

In between, the New Model Army made itself felt by taking charge of the person of the sovereign and by negotiating with him, ultimately unsuccessfully, at Hampton Court. The far more overt involvement of the army in the political process caused consternation among the civilians. But with Fairfax in charge, the fatal breach that occurred in late 1648 may have been avoided had the politicians addressed the one issue that to him was a matter of personal honour, namely the welfare of his troops. Because of all the mysteries of this story, one of the more salient is the serial inability of the politicians to fully attend to their obligations to the armed forces which had delivered their victory and which maintained them in power. The biggest material issues were pay and indemnity, of which the former provided one of the main catalysts for direct action. The reaction of the powerful Presbyterian caucus to the army's fair demands in 1647 was crass and precipitated an unnecessary crisis which was further inflamed by religious antipathy. Thereafter, the civilians tried, with varying degrees of sincerity and effectiveness, to pay what was owed. But the bar for future confrontation had been set and the civil state's attempts to deal with these obligations were handicapped by the size of the military establishment growing far beyond the tight and (it was hoped) temporary force for which there had been an appetite in early 1645.

To some extent, the expansion of the armed forces (particularly the navy) after the defeat of the king was as much an act of discretion as one of necessity and this suggests that the problem of arrears was not just driven by the poverty of the state or by the inefficiency of the mechanisms to collect revenue. The uncertain infancy of the Republic, its determination to assert its authority in Ireland and the decision to subdue Scotland argued for large armed forces. Military adventures further afield, whether against the Dutch, the French or the Spanish added to their longevity. Cromwell was central to these developments and his continuous association with serial military success, until the debacle of the 'Western Design', added immensely to his prestige and authority. His clearing of the Rump in 1653 left the military caste unambiguously in charge. If Cromwell was the *Leviathan* however, he was a remarkably poor one and there were three attempts to reframe his usurpation in order to make it acceptable in the eyes of the overwhelmingly civilian governing elite. But once the land forces became a tool of more overt domestic control under the regime of the major-generals, the always uneasy coalition of interest between the army and civil state snapped completely and resulted in the confusion and disorder of the final years of the Republic.

The attempt of the Republic to build legitimacy (beyond the offer of security) foundered in its conflation with a militarised state which was both expensive and, by degrees, oppressive and which seemed to have no end. The Levellers offered a rubric of popular sovereignty based upon natural rights to which those like Henry Marten were sympathetic. Levellers such as William Walwyn also articulated an attractive humanist agenda while John Lilburne argued for a respect for the rights of the citizen to live in peace with equality before the law. But the Levellers had minimal appeal to the Elect, and the movement was confounded by the army high command whose inclination was to defend the rights of property and the social hierarchy that the Levellers were perceived to threaten. The Levellers' attempts to infiltrate the main body of the troops ran into the ferocious application of military discipline as well as the spiritual orientation of those soldiers who saw themselves first and foremost as members of a godly army, rather than warriors for social justice. Their suppression in 1649 was one of those rare instances in the Republic when the attitudes of the civilian elite and the top ranks of the army were almost completely aligned.

Yet the efforts to reconcile the wider community of the godly to the new type of state by way of a national Church and by a common rubric of religious manners were also unsuccessful. The civil wars did not cause religious heterodoxy, but they arguably accelerated it. In the wake of all the destruction and the breakdown of justice and of law and order, it was much harder for the Elect to justify their elite status, and their claim to order the affairs of state and the gradations of society for everybody else. Yet the guardians of the Republic proved grudging in their extremely limited toleration of perceived religious deviation and immovable in the case of its social variant. The futility of the attempt to create a loyal citizenry and secular harmony by way of religious conformity was neatly captured by Hobbes in *Leviathan* – how could man be reliably and consistently loyal to his God, his conscience and to his state when their purposes diverged? Although they used different premises, the Fifth Monarchists and Quakers had posed the same question. As did many of the soldiers. In the end, and as Milton conceded, the questions just seemed too difficult to answer. Arguably it took the later architects of the American constitution to provide the solutions, but in the meantime the British state was returned to the familiar and much tested formula of rule by powerful and co-operative elites with a family dynasty at its centre. But it was not to be the house of Cromwell.

Bibliography

PRIMARY SOURCES

Perhaps the most arresting primary source of the period is comprised in the voluminous Thomason Collection held in the British Library. It consists of over 22,000 pamphlets, books, news-sheets and manuscripts collected between 1640 and 1663 by the London bookseller George Thomason. My thanks must go to the staff of the National Library of Scotland (NLS) for their help in navigating through this prodigious resource.

Some of the correspondence between Charles I and Henrietta Maria was found online in the Camden Society papers. A compilation of the speeches and letters of Oliver Cromwell produced by the Cromwell Association was accessed in the same way.

My thanks are also due to Lord Arthur Hazlerigg for arranging access to the archive notes of his eponymous ancestor.

Other primary sources used and referenced in the text are:

William Allen (attrib.) *Killing Noe Murder* (Early English Books Online)
Richard Baxter *Reliquiae Baxterianae*, part 1 (NLS)
Robert Baillie *Letters and Journals* vols II and III (NLS)
John Berkeley *Memoirs* (NLS)

Bishop Gilbert Burnet *Memoirs of the Lives and Actions of the Dukes of Hamilton* (NLS)

William Clarke *Puritanism and Liberty, being the Army Debates* part 1 (Online Library of Liberty)

Thomas Edwards *Gangraena* (NLS)

John Evelyn *Diary* (Everyman 2006)

Sir Thomas Fairfax *Short Memorials* (Early English Books Online)

Christopher Feake *Certain Queries Humbly presented in way of Petition* (Early English Books Online)

Anne, Lady Halkett and Ann, Lady Fanshawe *Memoirs* ed. John Loftis (Oxford Clarendon Press 1979)

Sir James Harrington *Noah's Dove* (Early English Books Online)

Thomas Hobbes *Behemoth* ed. Paul Seaward (Oxford University Press 2014)

Thomas Hobbes *Leviathan* (Penguin Books 2017)

Lucy Hutchinson *Memoirs of Colonel Hutchinson* ed. Revd Julius Hutchinson (London 1965)

Edward Hyde, Earl of Clarendon *The History of the Rebellion* (Oxford University Press 2007)

Alexander Jaffray *Diary* (NLS)

Edmund Ludlow *Memoirs* (Oxford Clarendon 1894)

Henry Marten *The Independency of England Endeavoured to be Maintained* (Early English Books Online)

John Milton *Complete Works* (Yale University Press 1962)

George Monck *Two letters from the Sea, touching the late fight* (Higgins/Leith NLS)

Samuel Pepys *The Diary* eds Robert Latham and William Matthews (Penguin Books 2003)

William Prynne *The Republicans and others spurious Good Old Cause briefly and truly anatomized* (NLS)

Cardinal Richelieu *The Political Testament* (University of Wisconsin Press 1961)

Scottish History Society Folio 31 *Scotland and the Protectorate* (NLS)

John Thurloe *State Papers* vols IV, V, VI and VII (Birch Edition NLS)

Clement Walker *Animadversions upon the Armies Remonstrance* (New Books in Politics)

William Walwyn *Just Defence* (Early English Books Online)
William Walwyn *A Whisper in the Ear of Mr Thomas Edwards* (Early English Books Online)

SECONDARY SOURCES

Adair J E *Puritans: Religion and Politics in Seventeenth-Century England and America* (Sutton 1998)
Adamson J *The Noble Revolt* (Weidenfeld and Nicolson 2007)

Barnard T C *The English Republic 1649–660* (Longman 1997)
Barber S *A Revolutionary Rogue: Henry Marten and the English Republic* (Sutton 2000)
Buchan, J *Oliver Cromwell* (The Reprint Society 1941)

Capp B S *England's Culture Wars: Puritan Reformation and Its Enemies in the Interregnum, 1649–1660* (Oxford University Press 2012)
Clarke A *Prelude to Restoration in Ireland: The End of the Commonwealth, 1659–1660* (Cambridge University Press 1999)
Cliffe J T *Puritans in Conflict: The Puritan Gentry during and After the Wars* (Routledge 1988)
Coward B *The Cromwellian Protectorate* (Manchester University Press 2002)

Dawson W H *Cromwell's Understudy: The Life and Times of General John Lambert* (London 1938)
Denton B *Cromwell's Soldiers: The Moulding of the New Model Army 1644–1645* (Denton Dare Publishing 2004)
De Krey G S *Restoration and Revolution in Britain: A Political History of the Era of Charles II and the Glorious Revolution* (Palgrave Macmillan 2007)
De Lisle L *White King* (Vintage 2018)
Dow F D *Cromwellian Scotland, 1651–1660* (John Donald 1979)
Duffy E *Reformation Divided: Catholics, Protestants and the Conversion of England* (Bloomsbury 2017)

Durston C *Cromwell's Major-Generals: Godly Government during the English Revolution* (Manchester University Press 2001)

Evans J *Emigrants: Why the English Sailed to the New World* (Weidenfeld and Nicolson 2018)

Farr D *Henry Ireton and the English Revolution* (Boydell 2006)

Ferguson N *The Ascent of Money: A Financial History of the World* (Allen Lane 2008)

FitzRoy C *Return of the King: The Restoration of Charles II* (Sutton Publishing 2007)

Fraser A *Cromwell: Our Chief of Men* (Panther Books 1975)

Fraser M *The Rivals: Montrose and Argyll and the Struggle for Scotland* (Birlinn Ltd 2015)

Gentles I J *The New Model Army in England, Ireland and Scotland, 1645–1653* (Oxford Blackwell 1992)

Gentles I J, Morrill J S, Woolrych A *Soldiers, Writers and Statesmen of the English Revolution* (Cambridge University Press 1998)

Gosse E *Seventeenth-Century Studies. A Contribution to the History of English Poetry* (London 1913)

Gribben C *Polemic and Apocalyptic in the Cromwellian Invasion of Scotland* (Queens University Belfast 2014)

Hainsworth D R and Churches C *The Anglo-Dutch Naval Wars, 1652–1674* (Sutton 1998)

Haswell J *The British Army: A Concise History* (Thames and Hudson 1975)

Hibbert C *Cavaliers and Roundheads: the English at War, 1642–1649* (HarperCollins 1993)

Hill C *God's Englishman* (Pelican Books 1975)

Hill C *The World Turned Upside Down: Radical Ideas during the English Revolution* (Penguin 1975)

Hill C *The Experience of Defeat: Milton and Some Contemporaries* (Verso 2016)

Hirst D *Authority and Conflict: England, 1603–1658* (Edward Arnold 1986)

Hopper A *'Black Tom': Sir Thomas Fairfax and the English Revolution* (Manchester University Press 2007)

Hopper A *Turncoats and Renegadoes* (Oxford University Press 2014)

Hughes A *Gangraena and the Struggle for the English Revolution* (Oxford University Press 2004)

Hutton R *The Restoration: A Political and Religious History of England and Wales, 1658–1667* (Oxford University Press 1993)

Jones C, Newitt M D, Roberts S, Roots I A *Politics and People in Revolutionary England: Essays in Honour of Ivan Roots* (Oxford Blackwell 1986)

Jordan D and Walsh M *The King's Revenge* (Abacus 2013)

Kishlansky M *A Monarchy Transformed: Britain, 1603–1714* (Penguin Books 1997)

Kishlansky M *The Rise of the New Model Army* (Cambridge University Press 1979)

Little P *Lord Broghill and the Cromwellian Union with Ireland and Scotland* (Boydell 2004)

Little P *Oliver Cromwell: New Perspectives* (Palgrave Macmillan 2009)

Little P (ed.) *The Cromwellian Protectorate* (Boydell 2007)

Little P and Smith D L (eds) *Parliaments and Politics during the Cromwellian Protectorate* (Cambridge University Press 2007)

MacCulloch D *A History of Christianity* (Allen Lane 2009)

Macinnes A *The British Confederate* (John Donald Publishing 2011)

Mallinson A *The Making of the British Army: From the English Civil War to the War on Terror* (Bantam Press 2009)

McDowell N *The English Radical Imagination: Culture, Religion and Revolution, 1630–1660* (Clarendon Press 2003)

Morrill J S *Oliver Cromwell and the English Revolution* (Longman 1990)

Impact of the English Civil War (Collins and Brown 1991)

Ogg D, Bell H E, Ollard R L *Historical Essays, 1600–1750. Presented to David Ogg* (London 1963)
Ollard R L *Cromwell's Earl: A Life of Edward Montagu, 1st Earl of Sandwich* (Harper Collins 1994)
O'Siochru M *God's Executioner: Oliver Cromwell and the Conquest of Ireland* (Faber 2008)

Parker M *The Sugar Barons: Family, Corruption, Empire and War* (Windmill Books 2012)
Pennington D and Thomas K (eds) *Puritans and Revolutionaries: Essays in Seventeenth-Century History Presented to Christopher Hill* (Oxford Clarendon 1978)
Pincus S C A *Protestantism and Patriotism: Ideologies and the Making of English Foreign Policy, 1650–1668* (Cambridge University Press 1996)
Porter S *The Blast of War: Destruction in the English Civil Wars* (History Press 2011)
Prebble J *The Lion in the North* (Penguin Books 1985)
Priestland D *Merchant Soldier Sage: A New History of Power* (Penguin Books 2013)
Purkiss D *The English Civil War: A People's History* (Harper Perennial 2007)

Readers Digest *Heritage of Britain* (Readers Digest Association 1975)
Roots I *Bicameralism in the 1650s* (Cromwell Association)
Roots I *'Into Another Mould': Aspects of the Interregnum* (University of Exeter Press 1998)
Rowse A L *The England of Elizabeth* (The Reprint Society 1953)
Royle T *Civil War: The Wars of the Three Kingdoms, 1638–1660* (Abacus 2005)

Schama S *A History of Britain: The British Wars, 1603–1776* (BBC Worldwide Limited 2001)

Sherwood R E *The Court of Oliver Cromwell* (Croom Helm 1977)

Southcombe G and Tapsell G *Restoration: Politics, Religion and Culture in Britain and Ireland, 1660–1714* (Palgrave Macmillan 2010)

Spencer C *Killers of the King* (Bloomsbury 2015)

Spiers E M, Crang J A, Strickland M J (eds) *A Military History of Scotland* (Edinburgh University Press 2012)

Spurlock R S *Cromwell and Scotland: Conquest and Religion, 1650–1660* (John Donald 2007)

Stevenson J and Davidson P *Early Modern Women Poets, 1520–1700: An Anthology* (Oxford University Press 2001)

Stubbs J *Reprobates: The Cavaliers of the English Civil War* (Penguin Books 2012)

Uglow J *A Gambling Man: Charles II and the Restoration* (Faber and Faber 2010)

Underdown D *Royalist Conspiracy in England, 1649–1660* (Newhaven, Connecticut 1960)

Warner O *The British Navy: A Concise History* (Thames and Hudson 1975)

Wedgwood C V *The Trial of Charles I* (Penguin Books 1983)

Wheeler J S *Cromwell in Ireland* (Gill and Macmillan 1999)

White M A *Henrietta Maria and the English Civil Wars* (Ashgate 2006)

Willes M *The Curious World of Samuel Pepys and John Evelyn* (Yale University Press 2017)

Wilson C *Profit and Power – A study of England and the Dutch Wars* (Springer 1978)

Woolrych A *Britain in Revolution: 1625–1660* (Oxford University Press 2002)

Woolrych A *Soldiers and Statesmen: The General Council of the Army and Its Debates, 1647–1648* (Oxford Clarendon 1987)

Worden B *The Rump Parliament, 1648–1653* (Cambridge University Press 1974)

Worden B *Roundhead Reputations: The English Civil Wars and the Passions of Posterity* (Allen Lane 2001)

Worden B *Literature and Politics in Cromwellian England: John Milton, Andrew Marvell, Marchamont Nedham* (Oxford University Press 2007)

Worden B *God's Instruments: Political Conduct in the England of Oliver Cromwell* (Oxford University Press 2013)

Wroughton J *An Unhappy Civil War: The Experiences of Ordinary People in Gloucestershire, Somerset and Wiltshire, 1642–1646* (Lansdown Press 1999)

Wroughton J *The Civil War in Bath and North Somerset* (Victor Morgan Books 1973)

Young J R *Celtic Dimensions of the British Civil Wars* (John Donald 1997)

Notes

Chapter 1: 'To fight against the King' – Naseby

1. Nicholas McDowell *The English Radical Imagination* p. 38
2. Edward Hyde, Earl of Clarendon *The History of the Rebellion* p. 235
3. The role of the nobility in the political and religious crises that preceded the wars is well described in John Adamson's *The Noble Revolt*.
4. Thomas Hobbes *Behemoth* Dialogue I 109
5. Austin Woolrych *Soldiers and Statesmen* p. 18
6. Edward Hyde, Earl of Clarendon op. cit. p. 238
7. Mark Kishlansky *The Rise of the New Model Army* p. 40
8. Manchester's defence of his war record is cited in Barry Denton's *Cromwell's Soldiers* pp. 7–12
9. Mark Kishlansky op. cit. p. 42
10. Ibid. p. 41
11. Barry Denton op. cit. pp. 36–7
12. Christopher Hill *God's Englishman* p. 64
13. Ibid.
14. Austin Woolrych op. cit. pp. 16–17
15. Barry Denton op. cit. p. 177
16. Diarmaid MacCulloch *A History of Christianity* p. 719

Chapter 2: 'There is no probability but of my ruin' – Selkirk

1.   Diarmaid MacCulloch op. cit. p. 649
2.   Murdo Fraser *The Rivals* pp. 25–7
3.   John Wroughton *The Civil War in Bath and North Somerset* p. 105
4.   Robert Baillie *Letters and Journals* II 146
5.   Richard Baxter *Reliquiae Baxterianae* I 50–3
6.   Initially, four Scottish commissioners were named. The Marquis of Argyll was one of two additional members appointed in July 1644, but he did not join the Committee until 1646.
7.   Christopher Hill *The Experience of Defeat* p. 82
8.   Allan Macinnes *The British Confederate* does much to rebalance the traditionally jaundiced view of Argyll.
9.   Edward Hyde, Earl of Clarendon op. cit. p. 234
10. Leanda de Lisle *White King* pp. 9–11
11. Cardinal Richelieu *The Political Testament* p. 111
12. Ibid. p. 76
13. Trevor Royle *Civil War* p. 14
14. MSS Letters of King Charles I
15. Brereton didn't hold back: 'This City [Edinburgh] is placed in a dainty, healthful pure air, and doubtless were a most healthful place to live in were not the inhabitants most sluttish, nasty and slothful people. I could never pass through the hall, but I was constrained to hold my nose . . .' Quoted John Prebble *The Lion in the North* p. 244
16. There is a lively account of the course of the siege and its aftermath in Christopher Hibbert's *Cavaliers and Roundheads* pp. 230–1

Chapter 3: 'We are here by the King's madness' – Newcastle

1.   Michelle White *Henrietta Maria and the English Civil Wars* p. 152
2.   MSS *Letters of Charles I and Henrietta Maria* Camden Society Vol. 63 pp. 22–3
3.   Ibid. p. 96

4.　Ibid. p. 96
5.　Michelle White op. cit. p. 184
6.　Thomas Edwards *Gangraena* p. 116
7.　William Walwyn *A Whisper in the Ear of Mr Thomas Edwards*
8.　Amongst his retinue was Hyde, who had started to write *The History of the Rebellion* while in the Scilly Isles.
9.　Robert Baillie op. cit. II 392
10.　Ibid. II 384
11.　Michelle White op. cit. p. 182
12.　Allan Mcinnes op. cit. p. 195
13.　Robert Baillie op. cit. II 412
14.　Donald Pennington and Keith Thomas (eds) *Puritans and Revolutionaries* pp. 124–6
15.　Edward Hyde, Earl of Clarendon op. cit. p. 89
16.　Blair Worden *Roundhead Reputations* p. 124
17.　Lucy Hutchinson *Memoirs of Colonel Hutchinson* p. 13
18.　David Farr *Henry Ireton and the English Revolution* p. 77
19.　Richard Baxter op. cit. I 53

Chapter 4: 'Against all arbitrary power, violence and oppression' – Holdenby House

1.　Christopher Hibbert op. cit. p. 252
2.　The scene was later described to Fairfax's secretary, John Rushworth. Trevor Royle op. cit. p. 400
3.　Christopher Hill *God's Englishman* p. 87
4.　Austin Woolrych op. cit. p. 30
5.　Christopher Hibbert op. cit. p. 257
6.　John Berkeley *Memoirs* II 365
7.　Edward Hyde, Earl of Clarendon op. cit. p. 294. Hyde speculated that the Leveller spirit had been conjured up by Cromwell's 'witchcraft', but acknowledged that the movement 'gave him real trouble at last'.
8.　Thomason E. 398 (28)
9.　Richard Baxter op. cit. I 61

10. Fairfax was far more exercised by military discipline than he was about the myriad religious orientations of his soldiers. He himself patronised godly ministers of many persuasions and his Life Guard was populated by men who were not just Baptists, but 'Particular Baptists'.

Chapter 5: 'For the common good of man' – Putney

1. Clarke Papers Record of 28 October
2. Ibid.
3. Thomason E. 412 (10)
4. Clarke Papers Record of 29 October.
5. Ibid.
6. Austin Woolrych op. cit. p. 251
7. Edward Hyde, Earl of Clarendon op. cit. p. 297
8. Austin Woolrych *Britain in Revolution, 1625–1660* p. 397
9. Thomason 669 fo. 11 (104)
10. Blair Worden *God's Instruments* p. 40
11. John Evelyn *Diary* p. 20

Chapter 6: 'To struggle with inevitable fate' – Preston

1. Richard Baxter op. cit. I 54
2. Austin Woolrych *Britain in Revolution, 1625–1660* p. 421
3. David Farr op. cit. p. 139
4. Letter, Fairfax to A. Hesilrige 19 June 1649. MSS in possession of Sir Arthur Hazlerigg Bt.
5. Trevor Royle op. cit. p. 481
6. Clement Walker *Animadversions upon the Armies Remonstrance*
7. Lucy Hutchinson op. cit. p. 263
8. Austin Woolrych *Britain in Revolution, 1625–1660* p. 427

Chapter 7: 'In the name of the people of England' – Westminster Hall

1. Lucy Hutchinson op. cit. p. 263

2. Antonia Fraser *Cromwell: Our Chief of Men* pp. 269–70
3. The emerging republican caucus grouped around Marten, Scot and Chaloner was already material and included Sir John Danvers, John Blakiston, Humphrey Edwards, Gilbert Millington, Sir Gregory Norton and John Carew. All regicides, most were to die before the Restoration in 1660. Blair Worden *The Rump Parliament* p. 37
4. Diane Purkiss *The English Civil War: A People's History* p. 473
5. Ann Hughes *Gangraena and the Struggle for the English Revolution* p. 52
6. Antonia Fraser op. cit. p. 277
7. C V Wedgwood *The Trial of Charles I* p. 138
8. Ibid. pp. 154–5
9. The testimony was recorded by Princess Elizabeth, a grave and serious-minded teenager who was to die two years later in custody on the Isle of Wight. The king's personal philosophy in the face of imminent death shines through: 'He wished me not to grieve and torment myself for him, for that would be a glorious death that he should die, it being for the laws and liberties of this land, and for maintaining the true Protestant Religion. He bid me read Bishop Andrews' *Sermons*, Hooker's *Ecclesiastical Polity* and Bishop Laud's book against Fisher, which would ground me against Popery . . . He bid me tell my mother that his thoughts had never strayed from her, and that his love should be the same to the last.' Ibid. p. 178
10. Blair Worden *The Rump Parliament* p. 25
11. Andrew Hopper *'Black Tom': Sir Thomas Fairfax and the English Revolution* p. 113

Chapter 8: 'The restitution of our shaking Freedom' – Salisbury

1. Blair Worden *The Rump Parliament* pp. 51–2
2. Letter, Mr Norwood to A. Hesilrige (undated). MSS in possession of Sir Arthur Hazlerigg Bt

3. *A Declaration by Colonel Scroope's and General Ireton's Regiments at Old Sarum* Thomason E. 555 (4)
4. A full account of the mutinies in Wiltshire is contained in *The New Model Army in England, Ireland and Scotland 1645–1653* by Ian Gentles pp. 331–48
5. Henry Marten *The Independency of England Endeavoured to be Maintained* p. 12
6. Christopher Hill *The Experience of Defeat* p. 52
7. Diane Purkiss op. cit. p. 48
8. Christopher Feake *Certain Queries Humbly presented in way of Petition*
9. Simon Schama *A History of Britain: The British Wars, 1603–1776* pp. 185–6
10. Blair Worden *Literature and Politics in Cromwellian England* p. 28
11. John Milton *Complete Works* vol. III p. 198
12. William Walwyn *Just Defence*
13. Christopher Hill *The World Turned Upside Down* p. 133
14. Ibid. p. 229

Chapter 9: 'The righteous judgement of God upon these barbarous wretches' – Drogheda

1. Andrew Hopper *Turncoats and Renegadoes* pp. 173–6
2. Ann, Lady Fanshawe *Memoirs* p. 123
3. The daughter of a farrier, she was to exercise considerable purchase on the thinking of her husband. Certainly, the overemphatic disdain of Edward Hyde hinted at a woman of influence rather than the opposite. Although Monck 'had no fumes of religion which turned his head, nor any credit with, or dependence upon, any who were swayed by those trances; only he was cursed, after a long familiarity, to marry a woman of the lowest extraction, the least wit, and less beauty, who, taking no care for any part of herself, had deposited her soul with some Presbyterian ministers, who disposed her to that interest.' Edward Hyde, Earl of Clarendon op. cit p. 403

4. Christopher Hill *God's Englishman* pp. 110–11
5. Ann, Lady Fanshawe op. cit. p. 125
6. Bishop Gilbert Burnet *Memoirs of the Lives and Actions of the Dukes of Hamilton* p. 112
7. Robert Baillie op. cit. III 66
8. Ibid. III 89
9. Ian Gentles op. cit. p. 361
10. John Evelyn op. cit. p. 250
11. Ann, Lady Fanshawe op. cit. p. 123
12. Christopher Hill *God's Englishman* p. 115

Chapter 10: 'Think it possible you may be mistaken?' – Dunbar

1. Alexander Jaffray *Diary* p. 56
2. Murdo Fraser op. cit. p. 215
3. Stephen Porter *The Blast of War: Destruction in the English Civil Wars* p. 64
4. Ibid. p. 118
5. John Wroughton *An Unhappy Civil War* p. 238
6. John Evelyn op. cit. p. 259
7. Lucy Hutchinson op. cit. p. 274
8. Crawford Gribben *Polemic and Apocalyptic in the Cromwellian Invasion of Scotland* pp. 4–5
9. Letter, O. Cromwell to A. Hesilrige. MSS in possession of Sir Arthur Hazlerigg Bt.
10. Anne, Lady Halkett *Memoirs* p. 55
11. Robert Baillie op. cit. III 465
12. John Evelyn op. cit. p. 262

Chapter 11: 'The pure light of God dwelling within you' – Worcester

1. Blair Worden *The Rump Parliament* p. 237
2. Sir James Harrington *Noah's Dove* p. 1

3.   Christopher Hill *The Experience of Defeat* pp. 153–4
4.   Ibid. p. 143
5.   Nicholas McDowell op. cit. p. 33
6.   Blair Worden *The Rump Parliament* p. 256
7.   Matthew Parker *The Sugar Barons* p. 70
8.   Stephen Pincus *Protestantism and Patriotism* p. 29
9.   Van Dyck's study of Charles astride a magnificent dun charger fetched £200, the highest price then reached for the work of the recently deceased artist.
10. Trevor Royle op. cit. p. 595
11. Edward Hyde, Earl of Clarendon op. cit. p. 348
12. The comprehensive round-up of the Scottish government caused much hilarity to Marchamont Nedham, who scoffed that 'the nobility of Scotland that are at liberty may all sit about a joint stool'. Ian Gentles op. cit. p. 411

Chapter 12: 'Winning all by fight' – Dover

1.   Edward Hyde, Earl of Clarendon op. cit. p. 299
2.   Ibid. p. 305
3.   *The Right Picture of King Oliure from Top to Toe* Thomason E 587
4.   Edmund Ludlow *Memoirs* II p. 133
5.   The silver fleets were laden with Spanish bullion used to pay the Dutch for the grain and timber that the United Provinces procured from their dominant trade in the Baltic.
6.   David Roger Hainsworth and Christine Churches *The Anglo-Dutch Naval Wars, 1652–1674* p. 52
7.   This was the genesis of the Royal Marines.
8.   Antonia Fraser op. cit. p. 399
9.   Blair Worden *The Rump Parliament* p. 117
10. Ibid. p. 112
11. David Roger Hainsworth and Christine Churches op. cit. pp. 61–6
12. Steven Pincus op. cit. p. 84

Chapter 13: 'I say you are no Parliament' – Westminster

1. Christopher Hill *The Experience of Defeat* p. 57
2. Trevor Royle op. cit. p. 632
3. Christopher Hill *God's Englishman* p. 131
4. Thomas Hobbes *Leviathan* p. 103
5. Ibid. p. 508
6. Ibid. p. 106
7. Ibid. p. 265
8. Ibid. pp. 275–6
9. Thomason E. 692 (6)
10. Austin Woolrych *Britain in Revolution, 1625–1660* p. 539–40
11. George Monck *Two letters from the Sea, touching the late fight*
12. Among the demands made by the Council of State was an insistence that the Dutch cede several of their ports to the English as a pledge of future good behaviour.
13. The Nominated Assembly was so named after one of its members, a liveryman and leader of his own London congregation, 'Praise God' Barbon.
14. Austin Woolrych *Britain in Revolution, 1625–1660* pp. 548–9
15. Ibid. p. 555
16. David Roger Hainsworth and Christine Churches op. cit. p. 51

Chapter 14: 'The inhabitants perishing daily from want' – Galway and Edinburgh

1. James Scott Wheeler *Cromwell in Ireland* p. 224
2. Austin Woolrych *Britain in Revolution, 1625–1660* p. 575
3. Ian Gentles op. cit. pp. 380–1
4. According to the contemporary survey conducted by William Petty, over 34,000 Irish soldiers accepted exile, the majority enlisting for service on the Continent.
5. James Scott Wheeler op. cit. p. 229
6. Gookin went on to become the Republic's commissioner in the commonwealths established on the eastern seaboard of North America. He was specifically charged with trying to persuade

their citizens to join the godly colonists in both Ireland and Jamaica. His audience was decidedly unenthusiastic.

7. Frances Dow *Cromwellian Scotland 1651–1660* p. 38
8. Ibid. p. 40
9. R S Spurlock *Cromwell and Scotland: Conquest and Religion 1650–1660* p. 70

Chapter 15: 'Oh ye tyrants, who shall be your lord protector?' – Whitehall

1. Evelyn watched the procession in the company of 'Mr Hobbs [sic] the famous Philosopher of Malmesbury'. The accuracy of Evelyn's on-the-spot observations over two pages of text strain credulity and it is likely he was given a programme. But he was clearly impressed. A fortnight later came the news of Worcester, to which the 'mortified' aesthete devoted a mere two lines. John Evelyn *Diary* op. cit. pp. 274–6
2. Christopher Hill *The Experience of Defeat* pp. 56–7
3. In 1650 Trapnel had joined the Baptist congregation of John Simpson at St Botolph's in Aldgate. She accompanied Vavasor Powell when he was questioned about his opposition to Cromwell at Whitehall, and it was this that prompted her 'seizure' and visions that went on for nearly a fortnight. She later went on a public preaching tour in Cornwall and is thought to have died in 1660.
4. Richard Baxter op. cit. I 70
5. John Wroughton *The Civil War in Bath and North Somerset* p. 120
6. Richard Baxter op. cit. I 72
7. Scottish History Society Folio 31/90
8. Scottish History Society Folio 31/100
9. Frances Dow op. cit. pp. 125–6
10. John Thurloe *State Papers* II 257
11. Notwithstanding the importation of bullion from the New World, the Spanish state was bankrupted by the Thirty Years War and defaulted on its debts in 1647. Their French antagonists followed a year later.
12. Matthew Parker op. cit. p. 94

Chapter 16: 'A man whom pride hath overcome' – Oundle

1. Christopher Hill *God's Englishman* p. 162
2. Antonia Fraser op. cit. p. 512
3. John Milton op. cit. IV p. 673
4. John Thurloe op. cit. IV p. 380
5. Ibid. IV p. 179
6. Jane Stevenson and Peter Davidson *Early Modern Women Poets 1520–1700* p. 327
7. John Thurloe op. cit. IV p. 133
8. Ibid. IV p. 40
9. Scottish History Society Folio 31/Intro p. 38
10. Patrick Little *Lord Broghill and the Cromwellian Union with Ireland and Scotland* p. 116
11. Christopher Hill *God's Englishman* p. 168.
12. John Thurloe op. cit. IV p. 380
13. Ibid. V p. 329
14. Ibid. V p. 341

Chapter 17: 'I feare little will be done for the future' – Bristol

1. Antonia Fraser op. cit. p. 444
2. John Thurloe op. cit. IV p. 79
3. Ibid. V p. 124
4. Christopher Hill *The Experience of Defeat* p. 139
5. Austin Woolrych *Britain in Revolution, 1625–1660* pp. 648–9
6. Christopher Durston *Cromwell's Major Generals* p. 211
7. John Thurloe op. cit. VI p. 38

Chapter 18: 'A feather in a hat' – Hampton Court

1. Nicholas McDowell op. cit. p. 186
2. Austin Woolrych *Britain in Revolution, 1625–1660* pp. 644–5
3. Patrick Little op. cit. pp. 147–8
4. Austin Woolrych *Britain in Revolution, 1625–1660* p. 653

5. John Evelyn op. cit. p. 338
6. Ibid. p. 341
7. Scottish History Society Folio 31/351
8. The rhythms and character of the protectoral court are well described in Antonia Fraser op. cit. pp. 457–66
9. John Stubbs *Reprobates* p. 112
10. Roy Sherwood *The Court of Oliver Cromwell* pp. 138–9
11. Jane Stevenson and Peter Davidson op. cit. p. 281. Colonel John was imprisoned as one of the regicides and died in the Tower in 1664. It was a poignant symmetry – his wife had been born there in the winter of 1620.
12. Roy Sherwood op. cit. p. 135
13. Simon Schama op. cit. p. 172
14. Austin Woolrych *Britain in Revolution, 1625–1660* p. 684
15. Patrick Little and David Smith (eds) *Parliaments and Politics during the Cromwellian Protectorate* p. 100

Chapter 19: 'Whatever whimsey breezes in the brains of the officers' – London

1. Antonia Fraser op. cit. p. 684
2. The French state was itself virtually bankrupt – it had defaulted on its debts in 1648 and was to do so again in 1661.
3. *The Republicans and others spurious Good Old Cause briefly and truly anatomized.* Thomason E. 983 (6)
4. Don Jordan and Michael Walsh *The King's Revenge* p. 117
5. John Thurloe op. cit. IV p. 557
6. Charles FitzRoy *Return of the King* pp. 54–5
7. Christopher Hill *The Experience of Defeat* p. 134.
8. Thomason 669 fo. 21 (33)
9. Lucy Hutchinson op. cit. p. 307
10. Thomason E. 986 (11)

Chapter 20: 'Everything is uncertain in this inconstant country' – Coldstream

1. John Thurloe op. cit. VII 771–4
2. Ibid. p. 795
3. Samuel Pepys *The Diary* 7 February 1660
4. Edward Hyde, Earl of Clarendon op. cit. p. 411
5. Ibid. p. 413
6. Ibid. p. 413
7. John Milton *Complete Works* V p. 360
8. Eamon Duffy *Reformation Divided* p. 339
9. Robert Baillie op. cit. III 391
10. Lucy Hutchinson op. cit. p 209

Chapter 21: 'The ancient and fundamental laws of this kingdom' – Blackheath

1. Edward Hyde, Earl of Clarendon op. cit. p. 416
2. Patrick Little *Lord Broghill and the Cromwellian Union with Ireland and Scotland* p. 175–6
3. Pepys op. cit. 18 April 1660
4. Lucy Hutchinson op. cit. p. 319
5. Pepys op. cit. 3 May 1660
6. Don Jordan and Michael Walsh op. cit. p. 172
7. FitzRoy op. cit. p. 189
8. Pepys op. cit. 16 May 1660
9. Ann, Lady Fanshawe op. cit. p. 140
10. Allan Mallinson *The Making of the British Army* pp. 27–8

Epilogue: Chepstow Castle

1. Charles Spencer *Killers of the King* p. 131
2. Donald Pennington and Keith Thomas (eds) op. cit. p. 127
3. Don Jordan and Michael Walsh op. cit. p. 222
4. Charles Spencer op. cit. p. 210. The site of Downing's reward is better known today as the home of the British prime minister.

5.   Don Jordan and Michael Walsh op. cit. p. 287
6.   Edward Hyde, Earl of Clarendon op. cit. p. 424
7.   John Evelyn op. cit. p. 372
8.   Ibid. p. 375
9.   Jenny Uglow *A Gambling Man* pp. 113–17

Acknowledgements

I am indebted to a number of individuals who offered much help and encouragement in the writing of this book. In particular, I would like to thank Professor Andrew Hopper FR Hist, FHEA of the University of Leicester, for so carefully reading through the text and for bringing my attention to a number of errors of fact and of emphasis. Thanks are also due to Professor Emeritus Sir Tom Devine Kt OBE DLitt HonMRIA FRSE FBA University of Edinburgh; Charles, Earl Spencer; Lord Arthur Hazlerigg and Professor Julian Goodare of the University of Edinburgh for reading the text and offering many useful suggestions. Finally, my thanks to Hugh Andrew of Birlinn Publishing for encouraging me to write the sort of book that people may enjoy reading.

Index

References to notes are indicated by n.